W9-CCR-217

THE
PEOPLE
TALK

American Voices
from the Great Depression

BENJAMIN APPEL

WITH AN INTRODUCTION BY
Nathan Glazer

A TOUCHSTONE BOOK
Published by Simon and Schuster
NEW YORK

First Touchstone Edition, 1982

Published by Simon and Schuster
A Division of Gulf & Western Corporation
Simon & Schuster Building
Rockefeller Center
1230 Avenue of the Americas
New York, New York 10020

TOUCHSTONE and colophon are trademarks of Simon & Schuster

Manufactured in the United States of America

1   2   3   4   5   6   7   8   9   10   Pbk.

Library of Congress Cataloging in Publication Data

Appel, Benjamin, date.
    The people talk.

(A Touchstone book)
    Originally published: New York: Dutton, 1940.
    1. United States—Social life and customs—1918-1945.
2. United States—Social conditions—1933-1945.
3. United States—Description and travel—1920-1940.
4. Oral history. I. Title
E169.A63 1982   973.91   81-18507
                              AACR2

ISBN 0-671-43809-3 Pbk.

By the People
and
For the People

Introduction

by NATHAN GLAZER

I read *The People Talk* for the first time in the late 1940s when I was working with David Riesman on the research that eventually became *The Lonely Crowd*. We were trying to describe the American character, and we were looking for a technique, an approach. We were impressed with the relatively new and rapidly expanding random-sample public-opinion poll as a way of finding out what people thought and what moved them, but we were disappointed, too, by its inevitable thinness. Summing up in a percentage how many people in a random sample said, for example, that their lives were getting better, and how many worse, told one something, but not much. We wanted a denser sense of people, but we wanted at the same time to get beyond the detailed immersion in the psychodynamics of single individuals which was then popular among social scientists.

The People Talk suggested an intermediate approach. Every person, of the hundreds in the book, is an individual about whom we very rapidly learn a good deal. The approach was "journalistic," undoubtedly, except that it was not hinged to newsworthy events. One might have called it "novelistic," except there is no hint of fiction, and Benjamin Appel, amazingly for this kind of book, written in the Depression, did not editorialize or ideologize. He was not trying to make any specific point, whether it was that America was various (which it certainly is), or that Americans were mobile, or uprooted, or optimistic, or pessimistic, or oppressed.

R. L. Duffus wrote in his review of *The People Talk* that Americans appeared worried and uncertain, but that was not Appel's

3

intention. He was an interviewer, reaching as many people as he could, and each had a story to tell as to where he or she had come from, what work each one did, how each one lived. His approach was surprisingly akin to the kinds of things we ourselves were trying out in the interviews, with all manner of people, that we eventually used for *Faces in the Crowd*. Unlike some of our fellow social scientists, we were willing to range very widely, in our questions, and in the people to whom we put them, willing to remain not very clear as to just what we were looking for, and willing to put down and try to make sense out of anything interesting that came out. We did have a theory, of course, which Appel did not, but the approach that Benjamin Appel pioneered intrigued us.

I looked around for other such books. The Depression had been a time when journalists and writers headed West by car, talking to people. James Rorty had preceded Benjamin Appel (with *Where Life is Better: An Unsentimental American Journey*), but he was writing a consciously Socialist account and critique of what he saw. Appel, in contrast, it seemed, had decided to erase himself almost totally. One gets no hint of the political attitude with which he approaches people: In New York City, where his book begins, he records the accounts of two Workers Alliance members (one white, one black) who had been beaten up at 104th Street and Columbus; and he describes an attack by passersby in Times Square on people selling copies of Father Coughlin's *Social Justice*. One cannot tell which side he is on, in either encounter. Is he indifferent to the need to demonstrate to us that the first victims are "Communists," the second "Fascists," their attackers a "mob"? That is just not what he is after. Corny as it sounds, he wants to "tell it like it is"—and he so fully effaces himself in the effort that we don't even know who should be given the credit for trying, and doing it.

And in the doing, a huge gallery of ordinary Americans, and a whole society, caught in 1939, comes to life. All of them have stories to tell—where they came from (almost always, very far away), what they work at (in an amazing variety of jobs, most of which have literally disappeared in the forty years since he wrote), how much they make, how much (rather, how little) they pay for their rooms and their meals. All done, it is true, unsystematically, but there is an incredible amount of authentic information on Depression America in this book—which makes it indeed more interesting today than when it was published. It now has the additional virtue of telling us about an America that seems to have disappeared in forty years. Not a single one of the businesses that he describes in the area of New York City in which he begins his travels is there now.

There was, of course, systematic public-opinion research in 1939. It was only three years after the disaster of the Literary Digest poll of 1936 which predicted a victory for Landon over Roosevelt. Gallup and others, having demonstrated how much more accurate a picture of how the American people intended to vote they could give than the unsystematic approach of the *Literary Digest,* were already asking a lot of interesting questions. But to get deeper, one really had to talk to the people, and Benjamin Appel had the energy and the enterprise to do so.

One would like to have learned more about Benjamin Appel himself. Why did he decide on this kind of book, how did he present himself, who was willing to speak to him, who not, how did he pick his subjects? These questions remain unanswered. The book is without introduction or conclusions. It begins abruptly: "At One-Hundred-and-Fifth Street and Riverside Drive." He starts talking to "a stout man of sixty in a blue suit . . .," watching workmen build Riverside Drive Park. Then to a grocery delivery boy, then to an Irish street cleaner pushing a garbage pail on wheels. And so it goes, westward through the Great Plains, back to the East through the South, ending with a transcript of a debate in the House of Representatives: "Mr. Speaker, I want to appeal to the membership of the House to do something to help us in Michigan with reference to our industries. . . ." On New York's West Side, the Irish workingman's bars have been replaced by chic sidewalk cafes serving quiches instead of boilermakers. I know we no longer have "street cleaners" pushing brooms and pails on wheels, but "sanitation men"—and now, women. Michigan is in the same situation (again), but in-between, there were three good decades.

We have had in recent years a spate of books in which "the people talk"—and talk, and talk. We now have many tape-recorded and edited records of the talk of workers, immigrants, women, children, Puerto Ricans. Indeed, it seems the easiest way to make a book these days is to open a tape recorder. I find that the pre-tape-recorder approach of Benjamin Appel has certain virtues. For one thing, when a reporter has to record in his own hand what people say, he is briefer—much briefer—and concentrates on the more interesting parts. Getting the gist is not quite so wearying and time-consuming for the reader as the book of tape-recorded talk. We do lose something, of course. The specific voice of each talker loses some of its distinctiveness (though much comes through in this form of reporter's recording, too). But in any case, that technology was simply not available at the time. And for a record of Americans as war was coming and the Depression was ending (people feared the first, had no hope of the second, we learn), Benjamin Appel's *The People Talk* is unique and valuable.

CONTENTS

THE CROWDED LAND

Big City Folk

NEW YORK CITY

"The district of which Hines was political overlord is composed of a mixed population living on varying social strata. Slums, poverty, racial problems and unemployment are prevalent. Within the same area there also dwell responsible householders and persons who are prominent in the business and social world."

From the text of Hines' probation report.

"James J. Hines, one of the most powerful Tammany politicians in New York City, dominated the upper West Side of Manhattan until his trial and conviction for illegally using his influence to further his material gain."

Facts about Hines.

AT ONE-HUNDRED-AND-FIFTH-STREET and Riverside Drive, the Hudson River like a railroad track of water separates residential Manhattan from Edgewater, New Jersey. On one side, the apartment houses and mansions of the wealthy. On the other side, the plants of Mazola, Jack Frost Sugar, Valvoline Oil and Henry Ford. Behind their smokestacks the nation rolls west to the Pacific, the United States of blast furnaces and steel, wheat and bread, cotton and cloth.

To the north, the George Washington Bridge hurls across the Hudson to New Jersey like the silver dollar once thrown across the Delaware by the mighty George. Under the river, the Lincoln and Holland auto tunnels weld the city to the continent, the seven million to the one hundred and thirty millions of people.

West, in the afternoon sun, lies the mainland. . .

The city's western shore is Riverside Drive Park with its green lawns and ballfields swarming with boys. The new filled-in stretches, not yet sweated into skating rinks, shine raw and coppery in the sun. Laborers are working here.

A stout man of sixty in a blue suit, brown shoes and brown hat is watching the wheel-barrow men. He looks as if he had just come downstairs from one of the apartment buildings. He stands solidly on his legs, his grayish-blue eyes narrowed against the sun. "It's a nice park they're building," he remarks to me. "And they're not boondoggling. You can say that for them." He grins cautiously.

I nod.

"P.W.A. is all right. But it all has to stop soon. Where's the money coming from? The Government's cutting a sewer uptown. Two and a half years and not finished yet! Money won't come out with all this spending. This country will be like Germany was twenty years ago. I was in Stuttgart some time back and one room in the hotel where I was stopping was called the billion-mark room. It was all plastered up with marks. . . The business men got to run this country! We can't depend on that gentleman! He better get out of the White House and give *carte blanche* to the business men. Or else make his peace with us. This P.W.A., W.P.A. can't go on forever! There are eleven million men on the Government projects or on W.P.A. We owe forty-one billions of dollars and it will soon be forty-five billion!" He wipes his brow. "That gentleman's impractical. He's no business man. His forebears, his father, his mother, left him his money. He has to surrender the reins to business! It's a business man's job. I'm connected with a bank over in Hoboken. We're afraid to let the money out!" He stops. He has shown me. There can be no better proof. The bank is afraid to let the money out.

"Were you always a banker?"

"I'm not a banker. I'm connected with a bank, a little bank. We have five million in deposits, two million in cash. But we can't let that money out!" His lips cleave open, the tip of his tongue malicious as it poises for a second between his teeth. "I wasn't always against him. I voted for him in 1932, even donated a little to his campaign. I thought the big evil was prohibition. I thought if we repealed that, things would straighten out in a year or two. I was in the liquor business myself but when prohibition came I couldn't do business any more. You can only deal with white men. And all the prohibition enforcement agents were Jews and Eyetalians. That was when I went into real estate. . . Business is afraid. That's why the money won't come out. Eleven million men depend on the Government! Even if they only get a dollar a day, that's eleven million dollars a day. Eleven million dollars a day for eleven million men. That's some pay envelope! There's only one solution. Private employment has to take care of the nation's pay envelope."

I count the windows of the five-story mansion on One-Hundred-and-Fifth Street and Riverside Drive. There are fifteen windows on the Drive, thirty windows on the side-street.

"Who lives here?" I ask a grocery delivery boy.

He stops his pushcart, scratches his head. "It's that baking-soda guy. He's got forty-three rooms and fifteen servants. He ain't the only big shot, neither. Faber, you know? He makes all the pencils. He lives at Three-Thirty-Five."

East of Riverside Drive is West End Avenue with two fifteen-story apartment houses to a street. An aging Irish street cleaner is working in the gutter. He wields a broom whose long handle has been cut down. He puts the broom inside his hand-wagon, an iron pail on two wheels, and rests a minute. Even now he concentrates on the pavement, his Popeye-the-Sailor face doleful. His white World's Fair jacket with its pylon-trylon symbol seems to have been borrowed from a younger, happier man.

"You keep West End clean all right," I say to him.

He spits into the hand-wagon. "It keeps you busy, m'boy." He speaks fast as if shoveling out his words. "It'd be cleaner but for them trucks! Contractor trucks with stuff to dump. And they dump onna streets. One of 'em got a summons from the cop. The judge fined him t'ree bucks. Them judges're tough 'round here," he says with satisfaction.

"How many pails do you fill a day?"

"Four cans a day it runs. I bring 'em down to Columbus Avenoo for the Sanitation trucks. Four cans're somethin'. Keeps you on the move all day. I got rheumatism and a bad heart, but I got to stay on. I just come on from two days sick. In another year I get my half pay. Eighty-nine bucks a month if I stick it out. . . M'boy, I'm lucky not to be down on Columbus. One block down there gives you ten cans a day. The summer comes and them kids just pile up the dirt all day long." He shakes his head. "I been almost twunny years on the job. And never found a penny. You wouldn't believe that. Some fellers only on five years find wallets. I never found not one penny." He spits again. "The boss comes 'round about two to see if you're onna job. One of the fellers—you couldn't find him for four hours. Off drunk. He got fine five days pay. Five days pay for four hours! I lay off sick two days, but how can you lay off? Rent, shoes cost money. Everything costs money."

Further up on West End, a brown bus, large as a Greyhound, is parked in front of the Lancaster Furnished Apartments. A lettered cloth covers the spare bus tires: CURT HAUCK'S CATALONIAN MUSIC. Seated at the windows, three or four of the Catalonians are reading newspapers as if the bus were already on the road. Two more Catalonians come out of the Lancaster. The blond has the build of a good tennis player, his handsome face spoiled by a red pimplish complexion. The short dark musician with him has the mild appearance of an old-fashioned bookkeeper.

"Where are you fellows bound for?" I pause, near them.

"Back to Los Angeles," Handsome answers, sizing me up. "It'll be hot going through Wyoming. But the Greyhounds do it in four and a half days. We'll do it in six."

"It'll be awful hot through Wyoming," the second musician agrees sadly. "Wyoming's all barren and rocky and they haven't any food, decent food, out there. There's nothing in Wyoming."

"How'd you get Minnesota plates on your bus?"

"Oh, just stopped there." Handsome looks at me carefully. "What are you going to ask next?"

"What band do you like?"

"Now Benny Goodman's good. But I like Artie Shaw better for swing. Artie can play sweet."

"But he doesn't want to," the second musician chimes in reverently.

"We played sweet over the Park Central, a little swing," Handsome condescends to explain. "I also like Crosbie's Dixieland music. It's lazier, it's slower."

"What do you play?" I turn to the musician who likes his comfort.

"I'm the pianist. I came from St. Louis. I studied in New York and Chicago. Only a topnotcher can hit the top. I went out to California a few years ago and joined the band. It's a California band."

Handsome smiles. "California's right. The mascot we had couldn't stand it here in New York. He was a bull terrier. We couldn't ever leave him alone. He'd tear up everything in sight and leak all over the place. He was from Los Angeles and he didn't like the cold. He died, the poor little thing." His voice goes soft-boiled for a second.

I walk off down One-Hundred-and-Fifth Street towards Broadway. New York, city of come and go. Come and go town.

The apartment house on the corner, the Elizabeth, was new fifty years ago. North and south, the traffic moves on Broadway. But inside the Elizabeth's lobby with its tiled floor and open ironwork elevator, an empty Maxwell House Coffee can tied to the ironwork for an ash tray, the ghost of the forgotten horse-drawn city lingers on.

The Superintendent is a gray-haired Czech. "How many apartments have you got?" I ask him.

"We have two eight-room apartments on a floor," he answers me. "They're furnished rooms. We got a hunerd-toity-five tenants, toity-two Home Reliefs. We got two three-room apartments on a floor. In them, storekeepers."

I press the elevator button. The building fills with the zoom of the elevator. A shabby old lady in a black coat and a black hat precedes me into the cage.

"Want an apartment?" The Superintendent calls.

"No."

The elevator operator shuts the door, spins the hand lever. The elevator climbs.

"Leslie, I met a man in the store," the old lady confides to the operator. "The worst kind of a man. . . Old as I am, I would take a job right this minute, but it isn't a question no more of wanting a job. It's who you know. If you know the right party and he takes you by the arm and says: 'Take this man here. Give him a hundred a week . . .'" The elevator stops at her floor. She scurries out.

Leslie smiles at me, a medium-sized man who wears his

green uniform like a soldier. His eyes are brown, his hair black and wavy. "That lady's on Relief."

"How do you like your job?"

"You'll be riding all day. Up and down. We're supposed to work eight hours a day, but because this is a Class C apartment house we work more than we're supposed to. We do porter work and clean the halls. One week I'm on from eight to six, and the next week I'm on nights six to one."

"You seem to have an English accent?"

"I was born in Rio, but I grew up in London and British Guiana. But my dad was of Portuguese and German parentage. . . I never thought I'd get into the up and down line. I used to be a foundry worker out in South Brooklyn, but it wasn't steady work. The new machinery did away with lots of people. Many plants moved out and we were thrown out of work. There was nothing steady and I had to have something steady."

A tenant buzzes for the elevator. In the box above the starter a white number five clicks up. We go up to the fifth floor, pick up the buzzer.

"Where were we?" He asks after the tenant hurries out. "Eighty-two a month is what this job pays. It isn't enough, but I had to get something to depend on. When I was single . . ." he shrugs his shoulders, "I'd go to sea. I shipped on all the lines. . . As I look ahead, the only half-decent future I can see for me is to go to school and fit myself for industry. I'd like to study about Diesel motors and air conditioning. But how can I go to school? One week, I work days. One week, I work nights. There's no school for me."

We pick up a tenant in the lobby and let him off at the fourth floor.

"The war broke out while I was at school in London. They took the big country boys, but they wouldn't have me. I was small and slight. But I won't try to volunteer this time if we have war. I'll defend this home, my habitation, but I won't enlist." He smiles the little helpless smile of the little man. "Now America's the great melting pot, but those particular groups keep things stirring. There's no peace any more. I can't see war! I tried to volunteer back in London, but when they wouldn't have me I went back to Brazil. The coffee and cocoa shipped out was shipped at your own risk.

After a few ships left Rio and were never heard from again, nobody would ship. The coffee and cocoa rotted in the warehouses, but that didn't stop the people from growing the stuff. That's how you get your de-pressions."

Broadway with its trollies and subways is the railroad track that divides the district into wealthy Riverside Drive and West End and poor Amsterdam and Columbus. Broadway's stores belong to middle-class folk. At night their neons flash a boundary of light between the apartment houses and the tenements.

Inside the huge Self-Serv Market on the corner of One-Hundred-and-Sixth Street with its motto: *Serv Yourself And Save The Difference,* a crowd of women, massed three deep, are waiting their turn to buy butter, eggs, cheese. The Self-Serv is a department food store. At the bread and cake counter, a small pink-faced woman yes-ma'ams the many sharp voices of her customers. In the center of the store, women pick up wire baskets and click past the turnstiles into a region of food in cans and boxes, jellies, sardines, olives, Red Heart Dog Rations, cornflakes. Each item is priced. The shoppers jam the aisles between the shelves. A stout lady drags a bewildered wire-haired terrier along the sawdust sprinkled floor. SERV YOURSELF AND SAVE THE DIFFERENCE.

Near the plateglass window, four or five butchers in white aprons are disemboweling chickens and displaying trays of rib lamb chops to the wary shoppers.

"I'll take a sirloin, about four pounds, but you must trim the fat off," a youngish woman dickers. She looks as if she's just stepped out of a beauty parlor.

"Can't do that ma'am," the butcher smiles. He has dull yellow hair and a liverwurst complexion.

"Where's the boss?" the dickerer demands.

"There's the boss." He points at a dark-haired young man cleaning a chicken with surgical deftness.

"I'll take a four-pound sirloin, but I want the waste trimmed off."

"Lady, the waste's already trimmed off," the boss replies.

"Are you the boss?"

"I'm in charge, but I'm not the boss."

"You won't trim the waste off?"

"I can't do that, lady."

She huffs back to the yellow-haired butcher, ignoring his wide grin.

"Where do your meats come from?" I ask the butcher in charge.

"All the meats, the chickens, even the balogneys are from Chicago." He speaks with the pleasing voice of a good salesman. "It comes down at One-Hunerd-and-Twenny-Fifth Street on the river. There's eastern meat, but we don't get it."

"So you're in charge?"

"Yep. I started apprentice eight years ago, eight dollars a week. Then I got a lucky break 'cause you got to know how to put your head into it." He nods sagely and dumps the dressed chicken into a brown paper bag.

"Got to know how to put your head into it," the yellow-haired butcher repeats as he dumps a four-pound steak on the scales.

Across Broadway, the Jewish owner of the Broadway Fruit Produce Market is standing in front of his store. Stocky, with a face cut like an Indian's, wide of cheekbone and hooked of nose, he seems ready to run out on the warpath.

"How's business?"

He grunts.

"No good?" I persist.

"How's business! How's business!"

"No good?"

"Do I live!" he retorts. "Here and there I shake around like a rag. I come here every day half-past eleven. Late at night I stop. Twelve o'clock, half past twelve o'clock. By the time I come home, it's half past two in Williamsburg. My wife complains I don't like her meals no more. A wife," he sneers. "All women got no use for you when there's no money. Call it a business? It's an existence. That's all. I leave too early to eat a heavy meal. I come back too late to eat a heavy meal. Excuse me." Shaking his head, his sleepy sleepless eyes switch to a customer.

"Yes, sir," he almost shouts.

"Ten cents bananas."

After the customer leaves he comes back to me. "I run out here, I run out there. I'm here fourteen years. Before that I work sixteen years in a shop. So now I'm in the vegetable business. Why, I don't know. It just happened that way. That's all. It's no good, the whole existence." He waves his hand towards Riverside Drive and West End. "Over there on the Drive, they think themself fancy, but it's a struggle for them like it is for me. For a few guys, the racketeer guys, it's good for them. Me, I got one son. He's the oldest. Four daughters I got. One's married, the others are looking for jobs. One daughter's a teacher from Hunter College. But in Nineteen-fifty, they'll give the teacher exams. Bookkeeping she knows, county clerk she knows, but no job until she got one for nine a week. Typing work. Now she gets fifteen, a li'l better." He nods reflectively, his anger softening. "Like a rag a man shakes up and down his whole life and what's going to be? Look what they want to do with the immigrant! Myself, I'm a citizen, thank God. But I got friends thirty years here in America but not citizens. The damn fools! They let it slip. So with them, they want to fingerprint them, send them out —Excuse me."

He returns. "That lady only wanted good California fruit. I have California fruit but it's not good enough for that lady." He grins, suddenly amused at the whims of his customers. "Good California fruit!"

"Where does your stuff come from?"

"All over. Spinach from Georgia. Carrots, peas, vegetables from California, Texas. Apples from New York State, Oregon State. It's a good idea to work the ground, but no existence. I got it hard, but them fellows who work the ground they got it harder."

The freight trains have been dumped into the windows of the Broadway stores. The fruits, the meats, the finished manufactured goods of the nation, are on display. Every block is an exhibition, a shelf crammed with simple products and complex skills. Between One-Hundred-and-Fourth and One-Hundred-and-Fifth Streets on Broadway, there is the Claremont Market, the A & P, the glittering Automat in its new bank-like building, the Newport Ladies' Accessories, and also the inter-state Postal Telegraph and the Hollywood movie.

I walk east down One-Hundred-and-Third Street towards Amsterdam Avenue, entering the city beyond Broadway's tracks. The owner of the gutter pushcart drowses on his feet. The mongrel black and tan dog sitting in front of the saloon lacks both collar and license. Little businesses, the Dakota Purity Laundry, My Valet Cleaner, Dan's Bootblack Parlor, cluster together behind narrow plateglass windows. In the middle of the block five tenements are boarded-up.

I ask Dan about them. He is a stout middle-aged Italian in a black coat sweater. His big hands, stained from shoe polish, hang on both sides of his paunch. "Fire in them las' winter," Dan answers. "Shine?"

I get up into one of the shoe-shine chairs. "Anybody burned?"

Dan rubs black polish into my shoes. "Four people burn up an' a li'l baby not born yet."

"Who were the people?"

"Two old lady. Man an' wife an' li'l baby not born yet. Happen early morning, three o'clock."

I pay for my shine. Dan elaborately minds his own business. He has nothing more to say. I might be a maker of trouble.

Next door at My Valet Cleaner, the man at the sewing machine glances up at me from the jacket he is repairing. "Hello."

"I hear there was a tenement fire down the block?"

"What can I say about a fire? People burned. I'm not a story teller. I don't know? People got burned. What can I say?"

Outside, the roofs of the five boarded-up tenements edge the warm sky. Seated on one of the stoops, a lanky man scribbles notes into an official-looking notebook.

"I hear some people got burned here?"

He scribbles industriously, his long mottled face intent. "Yeah. The lazy bums. Not too lazy to carry their Christmas trees in. Pay all kinds of money for Christmas trees. . ." All the time his fountain pen is busy. "But too lazy to carry the trees out. Leave 'em in the halls. After the fire the people begun to move out and the cats moved in. So the A.S.P.C.A. had to come down here with catnip and nets. They trapped every cat."

I leave the tenement inspector.

On the corner of One-Hundred-and-Third Street and Amsterdam, in front of warehouse-like Hotel Clendening, a Negro in old cracked shoes is busy flattening out cardboard boxes. One by one he smashes their three dimensions, loading the rectangles onto his pushcart. Already the two-wheeled cart is piled higher than its owner with cardboard.

He smiles politely when I ask the price of cardboard.

"I get twenny cents a hundred these days."

"Doesn't seem much."

"I can't get no job. Got a kid. They gimme my pink slip April 15th." His roughened hands cram another cardboard onto the load. "Work all day to get somethin' to eat. Somethin' bad to eat. Buy no clothes. Nothin' like that! Make a dollar, a dollar and a half a day. Have to get me five hundred pounds of cardboard. Sell the load over One-Hundred-and-Twenty-fifth Street and Third Avenue. What for they use it? I dunno. Maybe for somethin' in war?"

"You in this business long?"

"Never thought I'd be pickin' up cardboard. I come from Arkansas, fifty mile out o' Li'l Rock, Arkansas. My father rented before me. His father was a slave, but my father got a piece land. We had cotton, beans, sweet potaters. Back in twenny-two, my wife and me travel to Kentucky, to Chicago and South Bend. Sorry I ever come up north. Sorry I leave the farm. I read it's better down there now than up here. They got moving pitchers down there and regular toilets. They got electric lights from that big dam over Tennessee way."

He crosses Amsterdam Avenue. A bus honks at him. Motorists swerve their cars around the one-man-powered cart. He pushes by the red brick institution on the opposite corner. Over its doorway are carved letters: AN ASSOCIATION FOR THE RELIEF OF RESPECTABLE AGED INDIGENT FEMALES OF THE CITY OF NEW YORK.

I pause in front of the window of J. Eckes' store. Inside the window among the holy images, the statue of Jesus Christ is pointing to his blood-red heart. Near the statue a sign is

propped up: *Irish Horn Rosaries Made in Dublin.* Eckes'
news-stand displays *Amazing Stories, Operator 5, Strange
Stories, The Catholic News, The New York Sun, The Daily
News,* the Spanish *La Prensa,* the Jewish *Der Tag,* Father
Coughlin's *Social Justice. . .*

Far down the street the cardboard man is pushing his
loaded pushcart.

Social Justice. . .

The little stationery store owner is a thin Jew of about
sixty with a storekeeper's pale complexion. We become
friendly after a few days.

"Father Coughlin—"

He interrupts me. "I know nothing about Coughlin."
But his eyes contradict his words. His eyes become fixed in
his face like a man before a mob. Terror, like a third person,
stands between us. Quickly, he shrugs his shoulders, smiles.
"This country needs a man like Theodore Roosevelt. A good
man, but strict."

"Do you remember Theodore Roosevelt?"

"First, Theodore Roosevelt was Police Commissioner.
Then he went away with the Rough Riders. He come back
from Santiago Cuba with the cavalry. They wear blue waists
like sweaters, khaki pants and holsters and knives. Their faces
so burned from sun! Some without a hand. They paraded in
Brooklyn and I didn't go to work that day. Theodore Roosevelt," he speaks proudly, dignified by his recollections. "He
hold the reins of the horse. Like all the soldiers he looks
with glasses on and gloves on. Like the Brooklyn boys. I
watched all day. It was summer. A lovely day. . . There was
a cloakmaker strike when he was still Police Commissioner.
He come around to see the police don't break it up. He made
a speech to us in *Deutsch,* telling us to be peaceful so police
don't touch us. A good man, but strict. Strict."

He shakes his head. "I was not always working in this
business. I used to make forty-five dollars a week. I was a
cutter. I started later to be a contractor by ladies' waists. I
had twelve operators. I was contracting about two years.

Then I buy a stationery store. Then I buy a house in St.
Mark's not far from the Botanical Garden. Then the crash
come. For people like me the crash . . . Only the big people,
the millionaires, they don't lose their money. A small man
tries to make a living and then he loses everything. . . All
my life I think to own a little farm. I come from the farm
in the old country. I'm here." His hands sink towards the
floor as if to say: I'm here in this store until I die. He hurries
to the rear, returns with a cigar box crammed with old letters
and documents. "Here, read. You see."

I take one of the glossy circulars and read:

> Teddy Roosevelt once wisely said: "Every person who in-
> vests in well selected real estate in a growing section of a pros-
> perous community adopts the shortest and safest method of
> becoming independent, for real estate is the basis of wealth."
> Own Your Own Lots At Forked River, New Jersey.
> Only 6 miles from Barnegat—7 miles from Toms River.
> And ½ mile from Beautiful Barnegat Bay.
> Just Think Of It.   You can own your own lots for only
> $57.35.

"You read about Theodore Roosevelt?" He nods ex-
citedly. "A fine man. I vote for him." He hands me another
circular:

> "OPPORTUNITY KNOCKS BUT ONCE IN A LIFE-
> TIME—the opportunity to own your own lots, to cash in on
> future profits, to insure yourself in years to come.   FORE-
> SIGHT MEANS FORTUNE.
> Our development is located in the very heart of the beautiful
> pine-scented section of New Jersey.   Within a radius of
> 9 miles from Forked River are the homes of 25 million peo-
> ple.   New York City and Philadelphia, two of the largest
> cities in the United States. . .

"They bluffed and they made money." He smiles philosophically without bitterness, without admiration.

A customer enters, newspaper in one hand, nickel in the
other, leaves a half minute later with his newspaper and two
cents change.

"I still have two lots, forty by hundred-and-forty, a big
lot on River Avenue in Ocean County. I have it twenty years.
First, taxes is four dollars a year. Then taxes go lower and

lower. At a dollar-sixty, I get no notices for tax bills so then I write in to the town clerk. I used to think if I become a rich man, I build four bungalows for each child of mine, a bungalow on each corner. I like the land. . . I used to read all about nature. I pay my missus where I have a room, fifty cents extra for gas, and lay in bed and read about nature. All day I work by shirts. All night I read about nature."

Between Columbus and Amsterdam Avenues, the six-room flats alternate with furnished rooming houses whose shingles carry gaudy names: The Dahlia. The Royal Arms. Unemployed young men in their late teens and twenties play stickball in the gutter.

"You stink anyhow so what the hell're you talkin' about?" the pitcher yells at the batter. The stickball players come together in a debating cursing group.

I climb the stoop of a furnished rooming house near Amsterdam, ring the Superintendent's bell. A medium-sized man of fifty in blue work shirt and old pants opens the door. His broken nose slants to one side.

"Where do you come from?" I ask.

"Nanneycook. Say, who are you."

"How do you spell that?"

"You spell it n, a, n, t, i, c, o, k, e. Nanneycook. That's in Pennsylvania. Say, who are you?"

"I'm just talking to people."

"Oh!" He scratches his head, puzzled.

"Is Nanneycook a mining town?"

"I was in the mines when I was eleven. I picked slate in a breaker right in the dust."

"What did you make?"

"Forty cents a day for a ten hour day. That was in 1901. I worked in the breaker until I got seventy-one cents a day, the top pay. When I went down in the mines, I got eighty-eight cents for nine hours. You want to come in?"

We go into his ground-floor room. It is his living-room, bedroom and kitchen, a gas range near the wall. He reaches under the dresser and picks up a chunk of coal the size of a hat. He sets the chunk on the table between us. "The blue in it's the gas, the yaller's the watery dripping through. I got drivin' a single mule in the mines pullin' coal out. Then I drive a two-mule team for dollar sixty-nine cents. Later I get drivin' a three-mule team for dollar eighty-one cents. That's as far as I went. When we started shov'lin', my buddy would be six feet away, and we'd not see each other for the dust. You know what black damp is? Black damp's somethin' like fumes from a gas stove. It'll kill you. Black damp'll choke the light. The way they tested it was to take a canary in. In fifteen minutes, he's dead. He'll show you whether it's in there. . . A lot of people going to be dead soon," he concludes abruptly.

His wife comes in, a square woman taller than the ex-miner, a stack of bed sheets under her arm. She listens to her husband for a second.

"Why do you think people will be dead soon?" I ask him.

"My father was born in Poland. He come to Chicago, to Buffalo. Then he land down there. He used to be tellin' me as fur as I remember: 'A li'l nation in the east's going to win the new war.' " He rubs his chin and then his head. "I don't know what nation he means? But soon a lot of people going to be dead."

His wife puts the sheets in a closet, leaves.

"I'm through minin'. The strikes are not for me. . . Clubbin' the strikers, the State Troopers out every mornin'. . . They're gettin' seven hours now and no cut in wages. But I had to stop. You get wet, the water droppin' from the roof. It's warm down there in winter, but when you got out, your pants legs froze like stovepipes from the wet and cold. I got pneumonia. Then four years later I got it. And five years later. Here I get my room and light and gas free. And fifty a month."

I notice a young girl in the open doorway. She seems to have stood there a long time, a tall healthy-looking girl with plain features.

"You want to pay me for your room?" The Superintendent asks her.

"If I had three bucks I wouldn't be here."

"That's Ginger Smith." The Superintendent frowns. "She don't pay her rent and the landlord's after me."

"I'm going over Central Park for some sun," she says to me. "I'll tell you some stories. You're from the Government?"

"No." We walk together down the street.

"Anyway, I got no job. That dumb Polack gives me a pain. The whole neighborhood's full of Polacks. The girls work in the Automat."

"Where are you from?"

"I'm from Fall River, Massachusetts." Her smile is almost pretty. "There's five on Home Relief in that house. That's next for me, too, maybe. But never mind. There's a girl, she wants to be a model. There's a German guy married to an Eyetalian what's drunk all the time. There's a Jew. There's Irish, Spanish. There's a Chink that works in a restaurant. There's a trucker; he's Hungarian. There's a Swede and his wife. It's the League of Nations."

We cross under the roaring Elevated at Columbus Avenue.

"I'm sixteen," she says quickly. "Do I look it? Never mind. My father quit the mills in Fall River when my mother left him with another guy. He's a waiter downtown. He gives me money when he's got it. I'm telling you all this for a reason. But never mind that now. I've been a waitress myself. Take me. I got nothing. I got two dresses. This one and the one up in my room. See these shoes?" She raises one foot. "They're all the shoes I got. I got one coat. That's me, Ginger Smith. Where do I go from here? Back to Fall River? It's worse there. I'm going to show you a letter . . . It's personal, see. But I need some advice, see. That's the only reason I'm showing it to you." She opens her pocketbook, shuts it. "I change my mind. It's too personal." A blush softens her cheeks. "This guy writes me that he loves me. . . Love's everything. . . That's what he writes anyway." She looks at me. "He lives in the house. Listen. You think I ought to go with this guy? You're from the Government. He's got a good job as a dishwasher. Listen. You think it's all right to go with a Filipino?"

"From the boys the mothers should demand not to go to war. That's one thing. That's a promise. And the boys should think of their mothers. They should think of their mothers all the time. But if they don't think, there should always be a Mother's Day as a reminder. I don't really care for it although my boys give me flowers and candy. But mothers appreciate anything. I'm sick. I don't want to depend on my married boys. Times are so bad. But to make it short, sometimes I dream of things that will never be. . . I think to go to see my grandchild.

One of my boys has a son. He's very beautiful, very smart, and when I look at him I think of my boys when they were children. All of my children are good. And of course it takes me back to when I was a very young mother, and how I was young. . . At times I think it's only a dream, but it is not, because I love the children. Only times are so bad."

An Amsterdam Avenue mother on Mother's Day.

The avenues of the district are also main streets, Riverside Drive, the main street for the wealthy and the sun-seekers, Broadway for the shoppers and middle-class, Columbus for the people of the tenements and furnished rooms.

One-Hundred-and-Fourth and Columbus. The racing sheets at the corner news-stand include: TOP MONEY PIX THIS YEAR, THE DAILY GREEN SHEET, WILLIAM ARMSTRONG, JOCKEYS, SCRATCHES. Butcher stores and groceries compete for the dollars of careful women. North and south under the Elevated, the saloons and gin-mills cater to the men.

I enter the nearest saloon. "One light beer."

Down at the end of the bar two young men are killing time over half-finished beers. Near the door a barfly mopes over his empty glass. His collar is frayed. His blue tie looks about ten years old, stained and spotted from a hundred unsteady drinks. The bartender smiles, but doesn't get into talk with me. I'm a stranger and he makes me feel it.

The barfly rotates his empty glass, his watery eyes peeking at me hopefully.

"Want a beer?"

The barfly nods.

He drinks half the glass in one smooth gulp. "Thanks, buddy," he mumbles. "Turn and turn about. I wasn't bummin' drinks coupla years ago. Heard of me I betcha." His

breath stinks, a real barfly, always pickled, but never completely drunk. "Everybody heard of me. Lightweight con-
tender, that's me." He straightens his neck. And then his head
drops down again. His useless body has one function left,
that of an alcohol receptacle. "Heard of me? Betcha you did."

I nod.

"Sure you did, buddy. I fought with the best, with Benny
Leonard, Lew Tendler. In that ring I was out to get the guy,
no matter who the guy was, mick, wop or Jewboy. Fought
for the dough and spent my dough. A good feller. Anybody
tell you I was a good feller." A second gulp empties his glass.

"Two more."

"You're not sticking no clothespin on your wallet, buddy.
Way to be. Turn and turn about." He picks up his glass,
takes *one* sip.

I suddenly understand. He has guessed two beers are my
limit so he's going slow this time.

"Look at me, a bum," he declaims. "Don't spare my feel-
ings. 'S all I am, a bum hanging around. Fought with the
best."

"Fought the bottle, that's what you did," the bartender
says.

"I'm a sportsman," the barfly retorts. "I fought 'em man
to man. More'n you can say for the guys around here. Picking on two guys."

The bartender glances at me. I can see myself in the mirror opposite. I certainly look curious. "They beat up a coupla
reds," he explains.

"What kind of reds?" I ask.

"Workers' Alliance reds." He glances at me a second time.

The barfly yawns. "You don't need a coupla hundred
guys to wipe up two guys. I got no use for the Jewboys. They
come in and take the jobs. They're getting a living any way
they can. But you don't need a coupla hundred guys to wipe
up two reds, one of 'em a boogy. . ." As I move towards the
door, he waves good-bye. "So long, buddy."

I search for the Workers' Alliance office.

"One flight up at eight-eighty-four," a cab driver directs
me.

On one side of the entrance, a dozen photographs of newly
married couples, grooms in tuxedos and tails, brides in white,

smile foolishly out of a glass case. Under the silk hats and bridal veils, the faces of young working men and women. . . I climb up the flight of stairs.

Down the hall, the Workers' Alliance occupies two large bare rooms. In the first room, three wooden benches, a desk, two chairs, an elderly Irish woman consulting with a young girl. At the desk in the second room a gaunt man in a windbreaker is writing, the light pouring through the loft window upon his bony face. He has a broad forehead, the forehead of a bigger, heavier man.

"What happened here? Who attacked you?"

His eyes gaze through the window down to the side-street. "I'll tell you. I'll tell anybody. We were having a social meeting, as you'd call it. Eight of us, the committee and our wives, we was cleaning up. Then, they come in. They got kind of nasty." He gropes for words. "The wardheeler 'round here's got all the kids outa jobs. It's the wardheeler! The Whale, as he's called, a great big fat guy. It could've been all prevented. . . They smack us around, bust up things. Then they go downstairs. We clean up. Then I went down with five of the women to go home at last." His eyes shine, burning as memory fires them. "You never saw such a mob! Maybe five hundred. Right down there in the street. They filled the whole street up. The bunch that'd smacked us around, they was waiting. They had windbreakers on like mine. But it was like uniforms, the windbreakers. They had cue sticks." He lights a cigarette. "It must've been two in the morning. There they were waiting! They hit me with their cue sticks. Right here." His hand leaps to his temple. "I fell and my wife fell on me and they hit her. If she wouldn't have fallen on me, they would've killed me. There wasn't a cab around and all the time, any hour, there's cabs on the corners by the El station. They arranged it so perfect. There's always a cop around, but this night there was no cop."

I look down into the side-street.

"I was bleeding like a pig and some man—I don't know who he was, he give me his handkerchief to stop the blood. My wife says I should be taken up to St. Luke's over near Columbia College, but we couldn't find a cab. Then she and one of the other women, they help me to the Reconstruction Hospital. It was more like dragging me along. At Hundred-

and-Third Street there was a cop, but he didn't bother with us. They arranged it so perfect. One-Hundred-and-Second Street there was another cop, but he rushed away when my wife told him what'd happened. He was rushing away to Central Park. I took off my coat in the Reconstruction. All the change fell over the floor when I took my coat off. The attendant first thought I was in a robbery. Don't believe what I tell him. But when he sees the change all over, the interne believes me it was a social meeting. He told me to go to the house—the police station. I never was hit before. . . Two years ago I had a nervous breakdown when I lost my job." He beckons to a young colored man in a blue suit who has just entered the room. "Come here. Tell him about that night."

The young man pulls a chair over to the desk. His tired face breaks into a smile. "I was in on it, too," he says as if he were talking about a ball game. "I went downstairs after him. Soon as I get to the door, an iron bar sails through. It got me on the left side of my scalp. I felt blank for awhile and then one of the fellers helped me back upstairs. When the police come at last, around half past four, police ask: 'What was the trouble?' There was four cops. I said we was peaceful which we had a right to do. The cop punched me: 'You wanna fight, I'll give you a fight!' If I would've raise my hand he would've killed me. The police arrested us and we was the ones attacked."

"You never saw such a mob! They passed the word by the grapevine through all the bars on Columbus. Lots of 'em belonged to the Neighborhood Club where Hines's captains supervise 'em."

"When I come back upstairs after the iron bar gets me, I hollered: 'Police!' through the windows. And from the crowd, they shout up: 'Shut up you, nigger bastard! You wanna get killed?' " He smiles again. " 'You nigger bastard! You wanna get killed?' My wife went out and they didn't touch her. They was layin' for us men. My wife, she said they were standing around in hallways, two and three in each. Waiting, with iron bars and pipes."

"They want to break down the membership. We got two hundred and fifty dues-paying members, Irish, Jewish, Spanish, Greeks, Negroes, Polish. Going to the relief station in-

dividually you have li'l chance what with the W.P.A. cut and
dumping people on Relief. The relief clients here are under
influence of Tammany Hall. Tammany Hall will send us all
their hangers-on for members. They don't mind until we use
progressive methods. They don't want us to educate 'em.
When we do there's trouble. This neighborhood. . ."

The man in the blue suit walks into the next room.

"It's in a whirl for the people here on Relief," the man in
the windbreaker says. "They're in a stage of misery. They
come out of the saloons ready to kill. Many attacks on Negroes, but the Negroes fight back. The Jews don't know
whether they're coming or going with this Christian Front
business. I go in to buy a bulb at the German hardware store.
He says right out in the open: 'Them kikes. They don't get
out we'll push 'em out.' Last election they whitewash a swas-
tika on the sidewalk in front of the Jewish stores and write:
Jews not wanted in this neighborhood. It's all in the open.
They sell Coughlin's *Social Justice* on the street corners and
in the saloons. The bums and hangers-on sell 'em." He speaks
simply. "Over on Riverside Drive, the rich Jewish people,
they ought to know what's happening to the poor Jewish
storekeepers down here in this misery neighborhood."

A few days later I pick up a throwaway smudged by many
heels:

"CALL TO WEST SIDE CONFERENCE FOR RACIAL
AND RELIGIOUS TOLERANCE

At Grace Methodist Church

131 West 104th Street

Recently the West Side area of Manhattan was the scene
of an attempt to arouse un-American prejudices. A pamphlet
seeking to stir up religious hatred was distributed on the
West Side. A number of local storekeepers and business men
were listed in the pamphlet as supporters of this activity.
Investigation into the facts shows that many of the names
listed were obtained by fraud and others were those of non-
existent stores. Many of the storekeepers are very confused

as a result of the representations made to them by obtaining their signatures and a number are openly anti-semitic. This is not an isolated event, it is part of a growing, sinister movement in our city which has already resulted in personal assaults and the destruction of property and if it continues unchecked, will undermine the very foundation of our American democracy."

The night of the meeting, One-Hundred-and-Fourth Street crowds with people. I follow them into the brown brick church:

> *You are a Stranger Here*
> *But Once*
> *Welcome to your Father's House*

I loiter in the lobby. A poem hangs on the wall:

> *O Lord, and Master of us all,*
> *Whate'er our name or sign,*
> *We own Thy sway, we hear Thy call,*
> *We test our lives by Thine.*

It is half past nine. The speakers occupy the chairs on the platform. The audience, mostly neatly dressed middle-class people, sit in their seats as if all their lives had been spent in schools and churches. There are a half dozen Negroes with faces so solemn they seem like young boys. Standing in the rear, nine or ten working men, Irishmen with lean faces cut sharp as gun barrels, seem a little self-conscious in this Protestant church. The cross of Christ rises in front of the pulpit.

When the seats are all gone, a man hurries to the piano and plays *My Country, 'tis of Thee.*

The crowd rises, sings. The crowd sits down, whisperless.

The chairman, Samuel Blinken, steps forward. His voice is nervous. "What are the facts that have brought us together? They are ominous facts. These indexes are being distributed throughout the United States. We have copies of this Christian Index which states: 'Think Christian. Act Christian. Buy Christian.' We have sent what we know to District Attorney Dewey and to the F.B.I. But these attacks will not disappear until we combine in organizations to fight this menace!" He pounds his fist at the specter. His voice booms, but all the time he seems overwhelmed by foreboding as if he alone can see fascism's black ghost, not only hovering over the church, but over the land. . .

The next speaker, Arthur W. Hilley, stout, gray-haired with stooped shoulders has the ingratiating voice of a man in politics. "What does the word *tolerance* mean? The word *tolerance* means we must bear up with one another. I am not here tonight as the successor to James J. Hines, as leader of the Eleventh Assembly District. I stand before you as an American and a Catholic. I stand before you as one who came up from the sidewalks of New York City, born of Irish parents. Because I was born an American, I was able to achieve the exalted position of Corporation Counsel for the City of New York." He smiles persuasively as if to say: Here I am, a Success. His hands swing out in priestly gestures. "It was taught to me at my mother's knee to love my God. And the second commandment was to love your neighbor as yourself. Think it over, how you love yourself, neigh-borr!" The crowd laughs. "I am here not as leader of the Eleventh Assembly District, but as an American Catholic to denounce the temerity that we should buy Christian. Ere this ugly pest has time to raise its head we must crush it out, and prove there is in this community true and undying Americanism!"

The next speaker, Emmett May, is a Negro. His voice has a softness as pleasing to the ear as the softness of his skin to the eye. "In sixteen-nineteen when the first cargo of slaves was brought here, oppression for the Negro began. When we preach brotherhood let's look around the corner to see if we're practising brotherhood for our Negro neighbor."

Arthur W. Hilley rises from his seat, shakes hands right and left, and leaves down the side.

Emmett May takes no notice. "In sixteen-nineteen, a Captain Sitter, a coordinator of slave ships and a German, the Nazi of his day, brought the first slave ship to these shores." History rolls from his tongue. He is not a Negro. He is a voice, recalling history. "Now we can talk from now until 1960 on anti-Semitism and anti-Catholicism, but there's only one way to stop it. New York City is one of the most cosmopolitan centers in the world, but if we Negroes wanted to move to the West Side the landlord would say: 'I can't rent to you.' Two hundred and ninety-three thousand Negroes are squeezed in two miles of Harlem. There should be written in the law that any landlord that refuses to rent, to lease or to sell to anybody would be committing a crime. Such a law would be the biggest weapon to knock out the prop from anti-Semitism. For it's the Negro on Monday, the Jew on Tuesday, the Catholic on Wednesday. The time must come so that in Washington, D. C., the conductor won't tell the Negro: 'Go on to the back coach.' The Stars and Stripes must wave for my freedom as well as for any other minority!"

The audience claps hard.

The new speaker moves forward with the levered grace of a man who uses his body. Like Arthur W. Hilley, Barnaby O'Leary has the easy poise of so many Irishmen. "Feller Amurricans," he says in a salty brogue, "T'night I think we can say democracy prevails. We all sweat by the same pores whether we like it or not, whether we wear white collars or push a broom, whether we are lawyers or doctors or anything else. I know what I am. I know what they are behind the Christian Index. We call 'em rats in the trade union movement. I'm not the leader of the Eleventh Assembly District. I'm not the leader of the Tenth Assembly District. But I belong to the Transport Workers Union. I belong to the Catholic religion. My nationality is my own and I guess I can't hide it behind my Amurrican accent." As the laughter subsides he states: "We have reactionaries in the Republican Party. We have reactionaries in the Democratic Party. We have reactionaries in the Socialist Party. We have reactionaries in the Labor Party. But we have progressives in all parties! When we come to the union hall in the Transport Workers Union, we leave religion and race at the door and march in united as workers. But even in the labor movement we hear the Jew should not work in that union, the Negro don't belong with the Transport Workers, we foreign-born should not work with the native born, the Irishman shouldn't work with the Eye-talian, the black man with the white man. But if a black man and a white man are dead and if you didn't call the embalmer in a few days, you wouldn't know who was black and who was white. In the picture of the Last Supper I see twelve Jews in that picture. I don't see no Irishman in that picture!"

The audience stares. A white-haired lady gasps.

"So I say to you what the railroad workers say: 'Stop! Look! Listen!' So if there's a depression on Columbus Avenoo they say the Jews are the cause of it. I ride down to Hester

Street in the East Side and see the same conditions among the poor Jews as among the poor Irishmen. I ride to Harlem and I see the same condition among the poor Negroes as among the poor Irishmen. We must unite more than ever!"

STRIKE.

COAL SHORTAGE.

The headlines shriek the news: The big city needs the nation. Tenements, furnished rooming houses, apartment houses, subways in which the millions ride, all need coal.

Coal companies, meat packers, wholesale butter-and-egg firms line Twelfth Avenue, the river-edge avenue north of Riverside Drive Park. High above on the upland of apartment houses, the thousand windows glitter in the sun.

Down below on Twelfth Avenue the steel derrick of Weber and McLoughlin Coal is lowering a bucket into the hold of the *Sadie M. Weber.* The coal barge lies at anchor, its wooden side pressed against the land. White puffs of steam flower against the sky and again, the bucket sinks down, down, down, from the top of the bunker, into the hold of the barge.

In the office off the yards, a long-nosed man wearing a vest and no jacket, the sleeves of his shirt rolled up on his arms, is busy writing at a desk. He replies to my questions in an impatient voice. "This is the receiving and distributing point. We charter those barges. The captain, he lives on board boat and goes to the coal ports over in New Jersey. The coal comes in on rails to Perth Amboy, South Amboy, Edgewater, Weehawken. The freight cars dump the coal right into the barges and that's all there is to it."

I get the idea that he is a busy man.

The trucks of retail butcher stores stand in a row in front of the Armour and Company building at One-Hundred-and-Thirtieth Street. Armour's employees, in white blood-stained slipover aprons, are smoking cigarettes in the tail end of their lunch hour.

"Where does the meat come from?" I ask them.

"Chicago."

"You see the manager, Mr. Cornell. He knows better than we," a second worker suggests. "Go up one flight to the second floor."

I find the manager busy on the phone. He motions me to sit down, a vigorous man of sixty with straight light brown hair. He, too, wears a butcher's apron, white and stainless. His strong jaw, the alert eyes behind their glasses are those of an executive in an advertisement. Dozens of wall ledgers cover the wall. A display ad:

THE HAM WHAT AM
Tender
ARMOUR STAR HAM

is tacked over a counter of canned products. He concludes his telephone talk, listens to me and then leans back in his swivel chair. "Let's see how the damn thing looks. . . All of the large wholesale packers purchase their livestock, cattle, sheep, lambs and hogs in various stockyards in the Middle West and North West. The farmers and livestock raisers ship the live animals to these stockyards to commission merchants who sell to the buyers representing the packers. These animals are slaughtered almost immediately, put in coolers after being dressed, and when properly refrigerated are loaded in refrigerated cars that are properly iced to assure even temperature until they reach their destination." His repetition of the word *properly* spotlights his own exact abilities. "On reaching their destinations, they are unloaded into branch house sales coolers where they are put on display and sold to the retail meat dealers in the vicinity of the branch."

The phone rings. One of his salesmen. "I don't keep dry sausage prices at my finger tips. Now you hold on." He swivels around, flicks through one of the wall ledgers. "A Greek would want Italian sausage. I'll talk to Pappas myself." The operator connects him. "Anything I can do for you, Mr. Pappas? You tell me what you want." He is silent, attentive. "We have Star Genoa and Savona Genoa at thirty-seven and a half. I'd rather see you take Savona because I know your customers will be pleased. Which is wrapped in silver paper? I don't know. I'll have my dry sausage salesman tell you. He has it on his finger tips."

I glance at another wall display:

BRINGING HOME THE BACON
Better Management. Better Profits.
Better Management Outline for May 1939

The manager connects Mr. Pappas with the dry sausage salesman and then phones his credit man. "Will you okay forty dollars dry sausage for Pappas?"

"You work at high speed," I remark when the transaction has been completed.

"Yes." He is pleased. "I never worked by the clock in all my life. Let me see? It is necessary to estimate three to six weeks in advance and to make the necessary preparations. You know the population and you know what meats and meat products they'll consume. . . I've been with Armour for forty years. I came from an Iowa farm," he speaks modestly, but with self-awareness of his climb in life. "I started in Chicago in May, 1892. I've done practically everything in the packing house. I've been a meat cutter and salesman in all departments, manager and assistant manager since 1902. I've been in this building twenty years as manager and general sales manager and general supervisor. There's something new coming up every day. Different methods of servicing the trade." He stands up, bundles into an old overcoat. "I'll show you the place."

We enter the candling room. He picks up an egg, holds it against the eye of light in the candling machine. The light x-rays the egg's contents. "There should be no spots, no shrinkage in a good egg."

He swings open the door into the sales cooler. Quarters of beef, hooked through their fifth ribs, hang in long red rows. "The buyers come here and select what they want."

We walk downstairs. "I was back in Iowa a short time ago. I think they have more insight into city requirements than in the past. Farmers want a fair return for their labor and they're not getting it. And they won't get it until we get a balanced economy. There is only one way for a period of sane prosperity. And that is when business expands and labor gets a fair livable wage so they can consume the output of our farms and factories. Roosevelt has accumulated a forty-five billion dollar debt, five hundred dollars for each man, woman and child, citizen and non-citizen. We must change the present administration!" He lingers on the sidewalk, the sun on his healthy face. Confidently, he applies his lifetime's experience in the meat business to the business of a nation. "We must open up our foreign markets and get on friendly relations with all the European countries. And I mean all. We should keep our noses out of their internal affairs. No man living can tell me that war has settled any question." He nods, returns to his office, to his fortieth year with Armour's.

I wander along Twelfth Avenue. Ahead, an old rotting pier juts into the river. A peanut man, basket of peanuts at his feet, sits in the blow of the wind. I buy a bag. "Do you eat peanuts?"

The peanut man smiles. "Sometime. Yes, eat." His American has been learned in monosyllables. He still clings to a thick foreign-looking mustache. "Sit. Sell peanuts. Sometime, no sell. Sunday best. Winter time, sell hot chestnuts." His wrinkled face shows a big smile as if he were about to tell me a joke. "Peanuts, chestnuts."

-'Where are you from? The city?"

"No. Me Greek." He misunderstands my question for a second. Suddenly he nods. "Peetsbog. You know?"

"Pittsburgh?"

"Yes, yes," he responds eagerly. "There on cheemny. Work long time. Ten year. Lose job cheemny. Wife die. Boy go 'way. Come here. Live on Amsterdam. Peanuts. Yes." He picks up three or four extra peanuts to put in my bag. He is so glad to talk to somebody, to anybody.

I walk down to the end of the pier.

The river smells of the sea. Here are the fishermen, at least thirty of them, baiting hooks with segments of sandworms, whirling their weighted linen lines around their heads like lassos. Negroes. Mothers tending lines and baby carriages. The choppy waves merge into one blue-gray water extending beyond the George Washington Bridge, beyond the stone pier of the last Palisade. To the south, Grant's Tomb on Riverside Drive seems more fort than tomb.

A woman with a pink bandanna tied around her hair pulls up on her line. The unemployed spectators, young

men, old men, drift over. Her bait is gone. She rebaits, tosses
her line out into the river and then glances into the baby
carriage near her. Her child sleeps.

"They eat these fish," an old man says to me. His blue
eyes behind their gold-rimmed glasses flicker unsteadily as if
they were behind a sheet of water. "Some people would eat
anything. They keep the tommies, but throw the small eels
away. Those fish come off the bottoms and there's sewage on
the bottom. Sixty years ago, before the sewers, there was
weakfish and codfish, but now there's only crap."

"Do you remember sixty years back?"

"I was born here seventy years ago. October 23rd, 1896,
I caught a striped bass that weighed eight pounds right there
by Grant's Tomb. I grab my line and pull it in. That bass was
about that size." His aged yellowish hands spread far apart.
For a second, he holds onto that ancient vanished fish. "It was
hard to land him! 'He'll get away! The hook'll break!' I said.
But my friend, he went down to the rocks and scooped it up
with his hands. Ten minutes later he struck the female. She
weighed four pounds. They go around together, they do. But
in *The World*, they said: 'Henry St. Louis caught a striped
bass and his friend jumped overboard.' " His long white hair
is uncut, his shirt frayed at the collar. But his glasses are
gold-rimmed. "It's a good place here to knock the day around.
I seen One-Hundred-and-Twenty-Fifth Street lit up with
oil lamps. Like a regular village it was. . . All dead. I used to
know them all. . . All dead. Three score and ten, hey!" He
grimaces, wanting me to give him a rabbit-foot word of luck.

"You look strong and healthy."

He nods, satisfied. "I heard of a man one hundred and two
years old. When you can't navigate there's no use in living.
I was an engraver years ago. Cut the letters on steel to stamp.
I worked for a man who worked for Faber, the pencil man.
You heared of him? He lives here. There were forty or fifty
girls like in a school, at the presses. Stamp the letters right on.
They're all dead, hey? Think there'll be a war? Or is it paper
talk?" His voice is suddenly anxious. "Paper talk to draft my
money. Now supposing a person has two or three thousand,
hey? Suppose they'd draft that for a war?"

"I wouldn't worry about it."

"You think so, hey?"

A kid gallops down the pier, reins himself in. "Hi-o, Silver!"

The old engraver comments. "They don't teach them to play music now. Only these yells. I played the piano and violin but just for amusement."

A fisherman pulls up an eel. Tearing it from his hook, he smacks it down hard against the pier. The eel wriggles sea-green on the gray planks. The fisherman tosses it to the swooping gulls.

"See them gulls," the old engraver says. "They don't have to work hard, feeding on fish killed for them all day long."

On Memorial Day, Grant's Tomb becomes a solemn theater for the living. A stocky World War veteran in an overseas cap sells poppies near the entrance with its carven prayer:

LET US HAVE PEACE.

A little parade marches towards the Tomb. Two Boy Scouts carry the flags of the Republic, of *Lafayette Camp No. 14 Sons of Union Veterans of the Civil War*. Old men and middle-aged men follow the flag-bearers up the stone steps.

Inside the Tomb, the sons of the veterans, their wives and children crowd the circular balcony. Below, under the eyes of the living, the coffins of General Grant and his wife lie side by side covered with many wreaths. Young men in shirt sleeves, veterans of no wars, stare like school children. A venerable Negro stands next to a bald old man with a *Sons of Union Veterans of the Civil War* pin in his lapel. A grandmother, swollen with the fat of extreme age shifts her weight from one flat-bottomed shoe to another.

"In the name of God, we thank Thee that another year has been added to our lives. . ." The minister bows his white head. Next to him a girl of eight holds a big wreath against her chest.

One of the young men moves his tattooed forearms, the

red and blue mermaids gleaming like a simple fairy tale. The girl with the wreath slides her fingers across the silk ribbon. The old stand quiet.

"Help us keep alive the flame of American chivalry. God bless our native land, Long may she ever stand. . ." The minister's voice rises. He intones: "Hallowed be Thy Name, Thy kingdom come. . ."

The men and women follow him in chorus: ". . . give us this day our daily bread. . ."

"Amen," the minister says at last.

"Amen."

The minister begins to sing: "Praise Father, Son and Holy Ghost. . ."; the voices of the old women rising, quavery and shrill, their lost youth entombed in their singing voices.

"Who's the minister?" I ask the grandmother.

"The Reverend? That's the Reverend Doctor Seagle. The little girl with the wreath is his granddaughter. He's a Southerner, Dr. Seagle. From North Carolina, but he's been in the same church forty years."

Now, the little girl with the wreath, accompanied by an old man dressed in the blue uniform of a Union soldier, the gold letters G.M.A. on his bivouac cap, descend into the Tomb. Slowly she climbs the ladder against the side of General Grant's coffin. Her face is tense as if seeing a ghost. She deposits the new wreath and climbs down the ladder.

The Reverend Mr. Seagle pronounces the benediction. "Give us peace, faith, hope and courage both now and forevermore. . ."

A Boy Scout plays taps and old women fling flowers down onto the coffins.

I walk over to the ancient in the bivouac cap. He has a wan white face, a small white mustache and a blotchy veined nose. He glances at me without curiosity, without emotion.

"I'd like to know who you are?" I ask him.

"I'm Captain George Burnside. I'm here forty-eight years. I'm the nephew of General Burnside. You know who he was? He was Commander of the whole army until General McClellan became General." The old war, the Civil War beats its forgotten drums—John Brown, Abraham Lincoln, General Lee on his white horse. . . "I sealed General Grant and his wife up in their caskets in 1897."

Out in the sun, I buy a poppy from the World War veteran. "Were you over there?"

"Five months. I was at Argonne. I slept on these poppies. They smelled nice." He has a craggy face of a trucker or long-shoreman. "I lost my hearing in my right ear. Concussion of a shell. I'm living on a pension." He holds the artificial poppies against his dark blue shirt. "The war was a failure. If they attack us, I'll let my kids go to war. But that war was a failure. That King has an awful nerve to come over here when those English owe us three and a half billion dollars. The nerve of that King!"

I read the print on the little yellow slip attached to my poppy:

Made By Disabled Veterans
U. S. Veterans Hospital
Northport, N. Y.

Subway Service Cut 25% by Mayor on Account of Coal Shortage

Black as coal, the Saturday headlines attract the passers-by on Broadway. They clique around each corner news-stand. A shoeshine boy buzzes at them. "Shine, mister? Shine, mister? Please, mister. Lemme shine your shoes. A good shine, mister. Five cents. A good shine, mister."

He daubs polish on my shoes. "How old are you?"

"Nine, mister." There is no sentimentality in his answer. He is talking facts like any other business man.

"How's business?"

"Business is bad, mister. I oney made twenty-five cents. But I haven't got it because I had to eat. Even a li'l feller has to eat."

After I get my shine I descend into the subway. The platform is full of waiting people. Service *has* been cut. At last a train pulls up. The subway roars downtown. . . Seven million people in a subway car, seven million people in a city that needs coal.

Through the windows, white lights flash by, bright arrows lightning along the tracks. The stations thunder into sight, waxworks of tile and electric blaze, populated with clothing dummies. The subway stops. Dummies change into passengers. It seems as if the whole neighborhood's bound for downtown.

I hang onto my strap. Seated in a long row in front of me, eleven people sit. Two sleep, five read the newspapers, four stare in front of them with subway eyes as if they have left their minds at home. Above the subway faces, advertising placards shine splendidly: Wrigley's Spearmint. Kolynos Toothpaste. Del Monte's Fruit Cocktail. Beechnut Bacon. Angelus Lipstick. White Rose Tea. Planters Peanuts. Above the pouchy face of the girl in the flat red hat and the long-jawed face of her Saturday night boy friend: Bumblebee Salmon. Above the old man with the jerking lips: Immac (takes the odor out of perspiration).

To the right of the automatic door, the map of Manhattan with the subways in red, shows the rectangular island with its blunt pencil point jabbing into the Atlantic, its famous streets and avenues in neat letters, Broadway, Fifth Avenue, Wall Street.

At Times Square half of the passengers get off. They trudge up the flights to the glitter of the Big Stem. The cardboard girl in the Dr. Lyons Tooth Powder ad flashes a welcoming smile from her bright spot inside the Liggett's plate-glass window. The subway folk shuffle by, stenographers, factory girls, high school students, white collar clerks and their girls, the men and women of the furnished rooms, the out-of-towners in to see the World's Fair.

The crosstown trolleys clang down Forty-Second Street past the New York Times Building. Inexorably, the news, the electric-yellow news, circles around and around the stone page of the New York Times Building.

People gape up at the moving headlines: M A Y O R R O S S I   O F   S A N   F R A N C I S C O   V I S I T S W O R L D S   F A I R.   F I N A L   B A S E B A L L.   N A - T I O N A L   N E W   Y O R K   2   P H I L A D E L P H I A 1.   H I T L E R   W I L L   N O T . . .

People take a peek at *The News,* and in their minds re-arrange the international score.

The shuffling crowds come to a halt in a listening semi-circle right in front of Liggett's and the cardboard Miss America in Dr. Lyons' ad.

Something is happening here *now*.

"Buy your *Social Justice* and read the truth!" The sales-man for Father Coughlin's magazine stands near the curb, his back to the crosstown trolleys. Tall, lank, hatless, his dark hair falls down over his forehead. His mouth shoots open. His fingers clutch on the *Social Justice* he waves at the crowd. "Read *Social Justice* for the truth."

Two feet away from him, a second salesman retails *The American Nationalist*. "Read all about the Jewish war mon-gers!" His lips parrot the headline on his stack of papers: JEWISH WAR MONGERS. He glances over towards the drugstore on the corner where three cops are on the ready.

A third salesman stands to the right of *The American Na-tionalist*. "Buy!" he shouts. That's all he says about his armful of German language *Der Deutsche Beobachter und Weck-ruffs*. "Buy!" Perhaps he doesn't know much English?

The three voices bellow a mixed broadcast of: "Buy! Jewish War Mongers! Read All About! Buy! Read *Social Justice*!"

Nobody buys. People stare, amazed. "Hollering about the Jews on Times Square?" a man whispers. "That's something brand new for this country."

An old Jewish lady grabs her husband's arm. "Max! Come home. The Communists, the Nazis are all alike. Come home. Why do you want to look?" The pogrom fear stiffens her fin-gers on her husband's sleeve.

"Here in the city. . . In New York City," he says, choked.

They hurry away. Newcomers, men, boys, young couples, keep on padding the crowd.

"What're they peddling?" a high school kid asks, his eyes darting over to three giggling girls.

"It's the Protocols of Zion, that faking business!" a stout man explains. His face is white. Angry, frantic, he seems de-termined to educate, to be logical. "Coughlin prints all lies about the Jews. Coupla months ago he prints some stuff that an Abraham Cohn is nobody but General Ma, the big-shot General behind the Chinese fighting the Japs. Everywhere it is the Jews. I'm a Jew, too. Maybe I own Wall Street, too?

Maybe I'm Morgan and Rockefeller and all them big-shots, too?"

Above the United Cigar Store across the street, the neon sign of Admiration Cigars, one story high, shines red, blue and yellow information: EVEN THE LAST INCH IS MILD AND MELLOW.

The crowd grows. A drunk bronx-cheers everybody, salesmen and spectators, Father Coughlin and the Jews, everybody. He staggers over to the Liggett's, examines the Ingersoll Yankee watch at $1.50, the Mickey Mouse wrist watch at $3.25. He leans heavily against the blue and gold World's Fair draperies that cover up the grimy stone between the plate-glass windows.

"The young thugs! The young thugs should not be allowed! That is how they carried on in Berlin. In exactly this fashion." The man in the gray Homburg doesn't sound like a New Yorker. His words flow clearly as if he had been phrasing and rephrasing them a long time before opening his mouth.

"It's a free country, ain't it?" a voice shouts. "They got as much right as the reds to speak."

A stocky man cuts through the crowd to the *Social Justice* salesman. "You Catholic?" he demands. "Why don't Coughlin do somethin' about Hitler jumping on the Catholics in Germany?"

"He does." the Coughlinite retorts. He lifts his sales copy higher. "Buy your *Social Justice* and read the truth."

"He does not! He didn't write one thing about how the Cardinal got stoned in his palace!" the stocky man thunders.

"Where'd you read that stuff? In *The Daily Worker*?" *The American Nationalist* salesman shouts. "Read about the Jewish War Mongers!"

The man in the gray Homburg cleaves his way up front. "Pardon me! Pardon me," he says. He might be a doctor, or a lawyer. It is easy to see that street arguments are brand new for him. "I am not a Jew," he declares to *The American Nationalist* salesman. "But you, you . . . You're a young thug inciting against a helpless minority."

"That's tellin' them Nazis!"

"Yeah!"

"Give it to him!"

"Stickin' up for the Jews, he must be a Jew!"

"Shut up!"

Suddenly the inching pressure of the crowd accelerates. Hundreds surge forward a foot, a yard. The three cops as if waiting for this moment, football into action, ramming elbows into the mass. "Keep movin' everybody!" The cops order. "Keep movin'!"

In a second it is all over. Ripped *Social Justices* litter the street. *The American Nationalist* salesman cringes next to a cop. A second cop escorts the salesmen to the corner. Up on The New York Times Building the news circles around and around.

"Look! Over there!" a little man exclaims to his friend. Both of them have the starched fronts of white-collars who have worn out their ambitions and pants seats for some corporation.

They cross Broadway. To the north, a mass of neons blaze: FOUR ROSES A TRULY GREAT WHISKEY. CHEVROLET gleams in yellow. PLANTERS PEANUTS flashes red, white, red, white, red. The dome of the Capitol Theatre, an imitation of the Capitol in Washington, is outlined in neon. The Big Stem is a spendthrift blaze. More than ever it seems to be burning up the city itself, burning up the great silo of the city, high as a skyscraper and full to bursting with the mines, factories and farms of the nation. . .

The two white-collars stand tiptoe at the edge of the crowd on the southwest corner. Inside the Nedick's, the hot-dog eaters also stare. There's a free show on Times Square tonight. On the other side of Forty-Second Street, The Republic French Follies, The Apollo 2 Big Features Continuous, compete with neon promises: *Here it is! Whatever you want! Whatever you hope! But it'll cost you so much and so much! No more. No less!*

A pretty Irish girl brandishes *Social Justice*, the eyes of the crowd on her, the eyes of all the single men who live in furnished rooms. "Read the only uncontrolled paper!" she cries. A young boy of eight or nine, holding on to his mother's hand, gapes at the neon movie of Chesterfield cigarettes. Further uptown, the red and yellow tropical fishes of Wrigley's Spearmint breathe out rising white air bubbles. The little boy is fascinated by advertising's fairyland.

"The only uncontrolled paper!" Behind the pretty girl, a heavy-jawed woman with a wart on her chin waves an American flag.

"Only uncontrolled paper! Only uncontrolled paper!"

"Only controlled by Wall Street." A big smiling man calls to the girl. "Young lady, you ought to be at a dance Sat'day night 'stead of selling Coughlin."

Sudden rumbling laughter.

The heavy-jawed woman with the American flag whispers advice to the girl. A man with a brief case scoots around the corner on his way home or to an appointment. "Some day, we'll kill these Jews!"

"Beat it, you skunk!"

"Nuts to you!"

The crowd wads up to a few hundred. A young man parades around and through the crowd like a toy with a definite route, declaiming in a monotone that also seems wound up inside him. "Oughta call this Moscow Square and not Times Square."

Voices in the crowd detonate: "Gwan back to Moscow!"

"Gwan back to Hitler!"

"Quit your pushin'!"

"Who the hell—"

Again the cops pop out of the sidewalk cracks. "Down the subways! Going home! Down the subways!" they command.

Down the subways. The free show's over. I drop my nickel into the turnstile, wait for the train.

It comes in a head-on roar. I get on. The one page edition of *The Subway Sun*, free for the eyes of all passengers, headlines: SEE NEW YORK FIRST. A cartoon conductor bawls out a neatly lettered invitation: 'All Aboard the Main Line To The World's Fair.'

Not three feet away from me on the platform, the flesh and blood conductor sways to the rhythm of the lurching express. He is a frail man of fifty, his complexion prison-white.

"What do your duties consist of?" I ask.

He smiles, his teeth gold-capped. "We don't only open the doors and let the people in and out. See that lamp?" A kerosene lamp hangs on a hook. "That's the law in case there's a wreck. It's awful dark down here. There might be a wreck although I ain't been in a wreck and I'm here nine years. Just got a raise through the union. It's five-fifty a day now. But it ain't healthy down here." He talks just to me with the poise of any city man in a crowd, indifferent to anybody else listening in. "Mike Quill, he's president of our union, and pretty good he is. Some say he's a radical like Tom Mooney." He hops up onto two iron shelves between the cars. The express pulls to a stop. He levers the doors open. Many people get off. The train pulls out and he rejoins me. "New York people don't have time to talk. It's only business with 'em here."

"What about Mooney?"

"The labor movement won't stand a prison bug like Tom Mooney. He was a radical although I'm glad he got his freedom. It was circumstantial evidence on Tom Mooney."

"I just came from Times Square. They were selling *Social Justice*."

His voice lowers although there are few people on the platform now. "Father Coughlin's got the dope, let me tell you. He's right about Wall Street and that ain't the only thing he's right about, let me tell you. He's got the dope all right. There's all kinds here in New York, all races and religions. . . The Jews got all the business sewed up! It's all one network, Wall Street and the Jews."

The next station, One Hundred-and-Third Street, is mine. As I get off, the conductor pats my shoulder. "New Yorkers don't talk to me like that," he says in farewell.

The express pulls north.

'ALL ABOARD THE MAIN LINE TO THE WORLD'S FAIR.'

Under Manhattan, under the East River, the subway roars, climbing into the sun on reaching Queens. Far on the horizon, Manhattan's skyline seems as fragile as the clouds, the sky the palest of blues. The endless rows of two-family houses stretch in stolid summer. Queens, borough of baby carriages, borough of clerks, storekeepers and little business men, is also the borough of the World's Fair.

Perisphere and trylon, the ball and the shaft, jut into sight. The subway passengers stare through the windows at the vast Coney Island built on the flatland. White buildings. Yellow buildings.

The subway stops. The men grab the arms of their women, call to their kids. The families, the couples, the cliques of boys file through the turnstiles. The thousands stride into the hot endless afternoon. Endless the holiday afternoon seems, the sun hung like a blazing Christmas bubble in the sky.

In two parallel rows, the flags of the forty-eight states wave a hundred colors as exciting as drums and bugles. There is the flag of the green pine tree and the blue snake and the motto: 'Don't tread on me.' Taller than the young trees, the statue of George Washington, like a titan grandfather looks upon his descendants, the American people.

The wind whirls the yellow dust up from the grassless plots. A little boy hops up and down on one foot to shake the speck out of his inflamed eye. His father, a man in a straw hat, measures the height of George Washington with the eye of a carpenter. He reads the tablet set in the base of the statue: "The Preservation of the Sacred Fire of Liberty, and the Destiny of the Republican Model of Government, are Justly considered as staked on the Experiment Intrusted to the Hands of the American People. . ."

"Papa, who's that?" The little boy has gotten rid of the speck in his eye. One eye clear brown, the other teary, he looks very solemn.

"That's George Washington," his papa replies. "He was the First President and the best. Didn't you see him before in school?"

"He looks different, Papa."

"Is your eye all right?" His wife fusses around her son.

"Yeah." The boy takes his father's hand. The family wander into Borden's Exhibit: THE DAIRY WORLD OF TO-MORROW.

Cows stand on a moving merry-go-round, mechanical milkers attached to their udders. Milk jets up through the rubber tubing into the modernized milk pails, shining glass tanks above the cows.

"I can see milk any time," the man in the straw hat comments. "Come on."

They stroll past the Belgian Pavilion with its hospital-like glass front.

"Who's the lady with the water, Papa?" his son asks.

"That's Italy." He peers up at the huge spearwoman, at

the cascades pouring from the edge of her skirts. "That's Italy." He squints up at the Soviet worker on top of the Soviet Pavilion. "That stainless steel makes it look bigger than it is." The sun flashes on the chromium steel body, on the hand holding the red star, on the second hand, its fingers separated and seeming to rest on a cloud.

A World's Fair three-car train tootles its warning, East-Side-West-Side-All-Around-The-Town signal.

At the Perisphere, double escalators like those in a department store carry the crowd up into a bluish light, the light of new horizons. Men and women are silent on the escalators as if on trains en route to an unknown destination. Silently, on top of the Perisphere the people take their places on the revolving platforms. It is night dark. Above, is a sky and stars. Silence . . . Now, out of the darkness the sudden pealing light of singing voices: "From the east and the west, from the south and the north . . ."

The platforms move, the chains of people move. Below, a City, ships in its harbors, bridges across its waters!

The singing voices rise: "City of man in the world of tomorrow . . ."

Day breaks on the City. The sky lightens. Blue, the sky. Green, the fields. Everywhere, green, the green of the people, the green of the future. Day twilights into night. A voice speaks in the vast tongueless silence. "Each man seeks home the good life . . . a brave new world. . ."

It is over.

The people exit into the world of today, down the stairless helicline that corkscrews to street level, to the exhibits of Chrysler, Firestone, Ford.

WORK THE RIGHT OF EVERY AMERICAN.

The letters are huge. The letters are in the W.P.A. Exhibit, the title of the huge photographic mural on the wall. Here are the workers of America at their thousand jobs. Here are the faces of the American people: The man with the sledge hammer. The riveter. The laborer with the wheelbarrow. The woman at the Singer sewing machine. The scientist at his microscope. The architect at his blueprints. The musician with his instrument. The strong, patient faces are intent on their tasks. They say nothing. But the mighty letters become their common voice. WORK THE RIGHT OF EVERY AMERICAN.

THE FOUNDATION UPON WHICH THIS NATION STANDS IS THE
DIGNITY OF MAN AS AN INDIVIDUAL . . . WORK NOT CHARITY.
WORK IS AMERICA'S ANSWER TO THE NEED OF IDLE MILLIONS.

Outside, the giant cash register of the National Cash Register Company, like a moving chimney, rotates slowly on top
of its building. ATTENDANCE TODAY 192,648.

It seems as if half the attendance are waiting on line at
the General Motors Building with its keyword in two vertical
columns:

H   H
I   O
G   R
H   I
W   Z
A   O
Y   N
S   S

"Only three more miles to the homestretch." The girl in
the yellow dress smiles at her classmates ahead of her on line,
smiles at her teacher.

"I'll get a hundred if you put your answers on, Miss Johnson," the girl in the blue dress giggles.

Miss Johnson is too tired to do anything but smile. She is
standing between the two school girls.

"Oh, Miss Johnson," Yellow Dress squeals with delight.
"We're moving."

The line enters the General Motors Building. Outlined in
violet, the map of the United States sweeps into sight out of
the darkness.

A Voice speaks warningly of the traffic jam in 1960. Like
a magician, his verbal prophecy becomes a green spider web
of roads on the map. The green roads vanish. The faces of
the people tint red. Motorways in red appear on the map.
Clean straight drives. "The moving chairs below the map will
transport you to 1960!" the Voice says.

The crowds descend, sit down, two to a chair, chairs like
flying carpets, the Voice trapped like a magic gnome's in the
ear-level sound boxes. Confidently, the Voice speaks as the
chairs move along the future, the future in miniature, the future behind glass: "Sunshine, trees, farms, a world of beauty
. . . 1959 . . . farm roads into motor ways . . . Fifty, sev-

enty-five, one hundred miles an hour . . . 1960's motorists
speed along in safety and security . . . Highways set the pace
for advancing civilization . . ."

I relax in my plush chair, listening to the prophetic Voice.
I gape at the next generation racing along in cars shaped like
teardrops. The chairs keep pace with the cars. Tomorrow
roars into sight. ". . . night falls on the countryside . . ."
And tomorrow's night. An amusement park. A steel town
with glowing Bessemer. The winged chairs never stop, keeping level with the cars speeding now through dawn-lit canyons. ". . . who can say what horizons lie before us . . . See
America first takes on new importance . . ." The seven-
lane motorways whiz along canals with flood-control locks.
". . . on top of the world, fifteen thousand feet high . . .
the mountains of America . . ." The cars climb up among
the peaks, curve down into the flatlands. ". . . a vast towering city forty miles away. Directly ahead another city . . .
new techniques . . . the great metropolis of 1960 . . .
Residential, commercial, industrial, re-planned around a
traffic city . . . each skyscraper separate unlike 1939 . . .
abundant sunshine . . ." The magnificent separate structures, their glass gleaming, shine with the luster of the future
itself.

"1939 is twenty years ago . . ." the Voice concludes.

The chairs stop.

The people hurry out into the sunlight. With each step,
the intense hallucinated expressions fade from their faces.
With each step they return to 1939, to the United States of
their living lives.

U. S. Route Number 1

The handy-andy store, north of New Rochelle, north of
New York City, is covered with signs to hit the eye: ALL RE-
PAIRS. In the shadowed interior, the proprietor looks like a
gnome of all work. In his big cap and smudged apron, he
smells of leather. "Business is terrible," he says, without
seeming to take any interest in his own observations. His
long-fingered strong hands stir at his sides as if to say: After

all, what can be mended with the mouth? "It's terrible. It's not 1/85th of what it used to be, it's so terrible. And I repair everything, jewelry even."

"You figure it as exactly 1/85th?"

He nods. "It's not 1/85th of what it used to be."

Out of New Rochelle, the fine homes of Westchester County with their shade trees and blue jays appear to belong inside some unnamed serene park, a park without boundaries or fences, including the art exhibition in Greenwich, Connecticut, the antique stores on the highway, the cat hospitals, the dog kennels, the inns, even the license plates on the Maine cars—the motto: VACATION LAND above each number.

A road sign welcomes:

WELCOME TO BRIDGEPORT
THE INDUSTRIAL CAPITAL OF CONNECTICUT

West Haven, Connecticut.

Black hills of coal range Long Island Sound, the barges on the water.

Fall River, Massachusetts. The looms of the Pepperell Fabrics Corporation clatter, clatter.

New Bedford, Massachusetts.

On the old rivers, the textile mills weave together the Puritan's waterwheels and the new smokestacks. Memorial Day wreaths commemorate the concrete highway, named for the Grand Army. Roadside merchants sell cherry cider and fuzzy-wuzzy toy dogs to the tourists.

The air cools. The new-mown hay smells sweet. The blue Union regiments march again in the fragrance . . . the New England of many wars, the New England of history, marching over all boundaries of time . . .

Beyond the yellow dunes, the blue of Cape Cod Bay shines into the evening not come yet.

Sandwich, Massachusetts.

Provincetown, Massachusetts.

People of the Vacation Shore

PROVINCETOWN

"Another World of Tomorrow, Open House Vermont!"
"Maine, the Land of Remembered Vacations!"
"New Hampshire Skyscrapers, Nine Times Higher Than the
Trylon at the World's Fair!"
"Vacation in Massachusetts, Every Minute a Joyful Memory."
From the advertisements.

"Already Provincetown is thoroughly awakened to its annual
excitement of the coming season. Gone is the long hopelessness
of its winter. Forgotten is the dearth of business and scarcity
of money, during, by far, the major part of the year.
Now comes the little period we have been waiting for, now
comes the revenue which must sustain our town and our
people when autumn opens the drear doors of winter. Already
the cash registers are beginning to ring their pleasant music."
Editorial in the Provincetown Advocate.

LIKE ALMOST EVERY OTHER HOME IN Provincetown, Mrs.
Medeiros' white frame house on Conway Street has a ROOMS
sign stuck into the lawn. Inside the living-room, the linoleum
reflects the sun, the proverbial kind of floor one could eat off.
And warily, Mrs. Medeiros keeps an eye on her niece's daughter, little Avis Joseph. Two-year-old Avis, her brown eyes
spying out on the world through tumbling curly hair, is as
hard to mind as a bear cub. Again, Mrs. Medeiros picks the
child up, carries her into the adjoining kitchen, this time
placing a chair across the doorway like a bolt across a cage.

"She'll stay in there now!" Mrs. Medeiros declares. A big
graying woman of two hundred pounds, her face has the stern
magisterial features that sometimes go with size. Behind their
glasses, her eyes have an unaltering fixed calm as if all her
anger has been forgotten. "I wanted to show you the picture
of my husband when that little Avis—He's a fireman down
the wharf. See if I can find him?" She examines the picture

54

of the military band on the wall, the big drum lettered: *Regimental Band 301 Engineers.* Her finger stops at a thin soldier with a cornet. "That's him. He only gets off Memorial Day to play the cornet in the Provincetown band. Rest of the year he works from Sunday to Sunday."

I glance from the thin soldier to the picture of her two sons on the wall.

She smiles proudly. "Richard is ten. Kenneth is eight. They had the whoopin' cough a while back. All the children go by coughin' and coughin'! It fooled the doctors. It was whoopin' cough . . . Kenneth has to go to Communion Sunday, but he won't study."

Over the desk, there is a third picture. Two young girls kneel at prayer among red curtains and flowers. "Your husband ever work on one of the fishing boats?"

"Fishin'!" She grimaces. "No! The fishermen were better off in the old days. There was whalin' and the Grand Banks. My father was a fisherman. He came from Portugal. In the old days they used to make money. My father was a sea captain. Go to the Grand Banks for two, three weeks and then to Boston. The Italians would sell him a whole bunch of bananas for a quarter. We had bananas, apples, oranges and mixed cookies in our house. Oh, well," she sighs for the days of plenty. "My husband was out of work four months last winter. Nothing to do. Couldn't get any work in his trade. He's a carpenter. But we manage, rentin' rooms in the summer. When we took this place it had no wallpaper. I had to wash all those ceilings and wallpaper the whole house. It took over a month. I had a stiff neck for weeks. It isn't the paint that costs. It's the labor. What a stiff neck I had!" She shows me the kitchen wallpaper with its ship design, and the bedroom wallpaper with its drums and American flag motif. "You and your wife got the boys' room. Did you know that? Pretty?"

I nod. Mrs. Medeiros smiles happily.

Later, the boys come home. Richard, the older, immediately picks up the funny sheets on the couch, reading them as if he'd never seen a funny before. His face is as round and soft as a cake, a real plump cake boy. Kenneth, thinner, angular, first glances at the books on the desk: *Andersen's Fairy Tales. The Three Hundredth and First Engineers, A History*

1917-1919. Webster's Dictionary. 20,000 Leagues Under The Sea. He raises his innocent eyes towards his mother.

Mrs. Medeiros nods. "Kenneth, why don't you study?"

Resigned, he picks up the small prayer book.

I go into my room, reach for the gray celluloid Mayflower attached to the end of the electric light string. I pull on the historic boat for light to read by.

Beach Highway loops out of Provincetown among the stunted evergreens. Like a sea of sand, the dunes wave towards blue Cape Cod Bay. . .

Richard lies flat on his belly in four inches of water, examining the dime-sized colored stones. Like a jeweler, he carefully arranges his selections on a piece of driftwood.

"What're you doing?" I ask him.

"I'm bringing stones from Africa. See those yellow ones?" The eroded stones gleam on his palm. "They're gold nuggets."

Everywhere, the sea beats against the mile curving sands with their broken shells and boulders worn down to pebbles. Everywhere, the vacation-land people sun themselves on the brilliant funeral floor of the beach.

When we get back from swimming, Mrs. Medeiros smiles a welcome from the flower bed near the house. No flowers are growing. But a stick has been shoved into the sandy soil. An empty seed envelope, *Salpiglossis Exquisite Mixed Colors* caps the stick. "Richard planted them. Just plant them and say grow," Mrs. Medeiros laughs quietly. "The summertime's the time for flowers. I don't like the winters. It's a trance, don't you know. It's all gone on Labor Day. We had a nice time last summer. There was a couple from New Jersey. And the barber in the room next to yours. He had asthma. But in the winter—I do a lot of sewin'. I used to make quilts. I made a rug last winter from old rags. Oh, well. There's nothing here any more and it's getting worse. Down here, down at the end of the world. . . Some day things will be different when I'm a little old lady with a cane going around." She walks to the screen door. "All in's in. All out's out."

"We took great store of codfish, for which we altered the name
to Cape Cod."

From Captain Gosnold's account in 1602.

The white clapboard houses, the white picket fences, the
hollyhock gardens on Bradford Street, or Back Street as the
natives say, belong to the whaling days and the years before
electricity. Down Bradford, past the Shell gasoline station,
two Portuguese kids run shouting: "Hi-O Silver! Giddyap!"

One block east, Commercial or Front Street, borders the
blue harbor and the anchored fishing boats. One block east,
the honky-tonk eating places and souvenir stores cater to the
tourists. But everywhere between Commercial and Bradford,
between Front and Back, the side-streets seem more like horse
and buggy lanes than motor driveways.

I call on Captain E. W. Smith on narrow Law Street. I
sit in the parlor with him, the Captain in one of the four
rockers. His head is almost completely bald except for a thin
white down like a bird's. He is like an old bird himself, with
his blue eyes staring out between eyelids wrinkled with age,
his cheeks mottled with brown spots like a mottled sea shell's.
"I'm the oldest man in town. They gave me the *Boston Post*
cane for being the oldest man in town. I will be eighty-eight
the twenty-second of this month." In his parlor on Law
Street, he seems like the oldest man in the world. Two red
vases and two yellowish-white whale teeth adorn the mantel.
"I've been into different kinds of business, fishin', whalin',
West Indian business. There's been lots of changes the last
sixty, seventy years . . . There were forty-four houses over
on Long Point when I was a little boy."

How extraordinary to think of this sea captain as a little
boy!

"The people went fishin'. Handy to go fishin' . . . My
grandfather, Eldridge Smith, built the first house on Long
Point. He was taken by the English in the War of 1812. He
was taken to Dartmoor Prison in England. He, being a Mason,
they let him out before the others." He rocks gently, his big
hands clasped. "He lived then on Long Island, New York.
After he'd been home a while, he thought he'd come to Provincetown. He came here in a small sloop and built a house

down on Long Point by the Fort. The Fort was built by West Indian Negroes in 1861. The whalemen used to bring in these colored people as their crews. They'd sing chanteys they used to sing on the vessels, as they built the Fort." Slowly he reconstructs the vanished legend of his life. "I guess I was seven year old when my folks moved to town. They had an epidemic of cholera at the Point and my grandfather, his wife, his daughter and her son died. Four of them dead within a week. That was in 1848 before I was born. After I grew up, I went fishin'. The first vessel I commanded, I was seventeen years old. The *Ada A. Lewis*. That was her name, a schooner. As I grew older I had charge of larger vessels. I married Captain Law's daughter and sailed with him to different parts of the West Indies. The Island I used to run to principally, Grand Cayman, was one hundred miles south of Cuba. I picked up what coconuts I could and bring it to Boston. Once, I sailed out of the harbor and came back in forty-eight days. That was the quickest trip to do what I done."

He smiles, but he isn't really smiling, too old to smile. "I drove her. I was young. I was anxious to get back before it was too cold. Seventy-five miles southwest of Cape Hatteras the gale struck. The vessel was leaking all the time. I saw more water on that deck than in all my goin' to sea. But we weathered it." He blinks, pride in his old accomplishment a flicker, already forgotten. "There used to be a hundred and seventy-five fishin' and whalin' vessels at one time, bigger than they have now. Anywhere from one hundred to one hundred and fifty-five tons. Part of 'em went whalin' and part of 'em to the Grand Banks. There were only three or four Portuguese then. My mind isn't so clear as it used to be. The Portuguese . . ." He pauses as if trying to remember their faces. "They hang onto their religion. But the Protestant people don't attend church as they used to." He starts off on a new slant. "This house belongs to my oldest daughter. She works for the Foster Travel Service in Philadelphia. Keeps her busy. The other daughter . . ." He points to one of the pictures on the wall, "lives out in Peoria, Illinois. She has a boy and a girl."

"Where did you get those whale teeth on the mantel?"

"They're from a sperm whale." Again, he laboriously remembers. "I used to go after whales in different vessels. I helped beach fifteen whales off Race Point, off Sandwich way. They landed fifty-six whales that spring. I don't know the date. Might've been in the 1880's? That was the most ever landed. . . I'm purty well played out now. I am purty well gone."

"Where did you get those red vases on the mantel?"

"My wife saved 'em. We used to sell them in the West Indies. It isn't what it used to be. It's a different mode of fishin' nowadays and it's growing worse. This beam trawling is a detriment to fishin' and makes the fish more scarce every year." Now, a flicker of wrath fans his speech. His hands build a beam in space. "Used to have a beam and drag it over the bottom. On each end of the beam there was a shoe made of iron. That was the first beam trawl. My brother and another man made the first one and kept it a secret. I took it up. That's how it started." The pioneers speak with his voice, the pioneers of the American frontiers, the pioneers challenging the frontier of the sea with its teeming fish. "Now, the bigger the boat, the bigger the shoe. A line runs from each shoe to the center. A net drags behind. They go draggin' 'em over the bottom and everything goes into the bag. They dump out thousands of fish too small to sell. Bail 'em overboard. They catch the mother fish with the spawn in 'em! Not to be wondered that the fish are scarce. Years ago, get four hundred, five hundred pounds of haddock in no time. Now they depend on whiting and mackerel. The whales are gone. . . And the whalefish, the black fish. . . They were twenty-two, twenty-three feet long. We used to drive 'em ashore on the Truro shore. Take the blubber off 'em and boil 'em for the oil. In the head there was the melon, the choicest oil in the world for watches and things. Twenty-five cents for a bottle that size." He measures off three quarters of his forefinger. "One time we beached seventeen hundred and eighty whalefish up in the head of the Bay. . ."

Around the corner from Captain Smith's house, Dopey, the Dwarf, candle in hand, decorates a *Rooms and Bath* sign. On Commercial Street, tourists on bicycles ride among the cars. A young girl in a roadster stares at two Portuguese fishermen in caps and blue dungarees. On a bike, a third fisherman pedals home to lunch, several mackerel and the tail half of a whiting in his wire basket. An elderly man in white flannels enters the Cape Cod Tea Garden, its windows red-lettered in Chinese. And in the center of town, Manuel N. Lopes Square, is a country fair of people.

The Town Wharf, and Sklaroff's Wharf with the excursion boat from Boston, *The Steel Pier,* docked alongside, finger out into the Bay. A wharf vendor sells seashells to the Bostonians. His shells are painted red and blue, the ugly colors completely concealing the natural sea tints.

The breeze changes. The smell of fish from the Atlantic Fisheries freezers floats into the nostrils of the tourists.

I walk out on Sklaroff's Wharf. "Stewart Joseph!" I call. "Where are you?"

A young man steps out of the Sklaroff packing shed on the end of the wharf. Dressed in blue stocking cap and blue sweater, square of jaw and thick of brow, Avis' father seems the son of all the men who follow the sea.

"Hello. What about this fishing business, Stewart?"

"How's Avis?"

"Fine."

"The original idea was curin' the fish in a solution of vinegar and sugar. Cure the herring, mackerel, whiting, according to the fish that ran in the different seasons. But now it's all filets. Out of the parchment paper into the pan. We pack fish on ice and ship 'em out fresh to the Boston, New York and Philadelphia markets. In June, July and August we employ seventy men by the hour. We own six traps of our own." He nods at one of the weir traps out in the Bay. "We also pack fish for the Atlantic. They operate about sixty traps." He points towards the harbor, to Commercial Street fronting on the water. Like a feudal watchtower, the Pilgrim Memorial rises above the clapboard houses, above the three Atlantic freezers. "Atlantic bought up the independents. That last freezer furthest out . . . That's where they make fox food and dog food out of the refuse from the fish. One time they froze everything." He shifts his weight. His work shoes are covered with fish scales. "But now it's all filet. The demand for fish has caused the methods of fishing to change. Big companies like the General Sea Foods operate these beam or auto trawls out of Boston. These great big steamers come up here into local waters and fish two and three weeks at a time. They sweep up the bottoms and they're killing the fishing."

"Mrs. Medeiros told me you studied engineering?"

"That's right." He smiles. Whenever he smiles, he looks more like his English mother than his Portuguese father. "But I couldn't get anything. I'm the timekeeper here. I take charge of the telephone and do all the business with Mr. Frank Rowe over at Atlantic when we pack for him. Now, you see those little boats out there? The ones with the houses aft? They go after the ground fish, cod, halibut. Two men to a crew. They throw out a hook every foot and a half and then haul 'em back. Those little trawlers are not killing the fishing. In five or ten years you won't smell a fish. It's getting worse and worse every year."

"I'll go back now."

Down near the shore end of the wharf, kids are swimming in the green water. A lanky boy holds onto an anchored dory, kicking up white foam with his feet. Overlooking the swimmers, a belated fisherman, a short thin Portuguese with a jutting gull-like beak, his hip-high boots coated with fish scales, is cleaning a pail of fish. He stalks over to one of the sheds on the wharf, where the independent fishermen store their tackle. He comes out, returns to his pail.

"What kind of fish is that?" I ask him.

"Sea robin." He guts it, begins on another.

"What's that?"

"Flounder."

"What's that?"

"Porgie." He seizes a second sea robin.

"I didn't know people ate sea robins?"

"Good to eat." He grunts. His knife flashes.

"Fish scarce?"

He turns sharp and quick, the sun on his tanned cheek-bones. "Scarce all the time! We go to poor house when the fish get scarce!" He washes his knife, splashes water from the pail upon his boots. "Pay for box! Pay for ice! Fisherman catch the fish, but make nothing! Company makes the dollar! My brother owns the trawler. I work with him. We set line, haul line, clean our fish, but Company makes the dollar! Can't ship our fish to better markets. Cost too much! The freezers buy our fish! When we have a lot of fish, the price is low. No money! When it's no fish like now, good price. But who got fish to sell!" He picks up the pail with his family's dinner in it and walks townward. I follow more slowly on my way to the freezer.

Atlantic Freezer No. 1 is a big frame building opposite the Provincetown Historical Museum. ATLANTIC COAST FISHERIES CORPORATION OF NEW YORK, PROVINCETOWN DIVISION the painted letters read. I go inside and meet the manager. Mr. Frank Rowe's office is streamlined. The paneled-wood walls, the modern electric fixtures set into the ceiling like skylights could be imports from a New York skyscraper. But the man behind the handsome desk is a Bostonian, small and spare, with a thin bony nose. "The fishing industry is coming ahead," he says. "The trouble with Provincetown is that there are bills in Legislature that would close the Bay to dragging. Now we operate thirty-nine traps here in local waters . . ." The telephone rings. He picks up the receiver. "Boston fish are poor," he answers, reaching for a yellow slip of paper. "Three and one-half kegs of large. Eleven kegs of small."

When he hangs up, he swats at a fly. "Those flies are driving me foolish! I'll be here from four in the morning until ten at night, sometimes. The boats'll phone me from a Coast Guard Station if they've got something large. Nine boats, one after the other . . . When you have your total of fish, you have to dispose of them. Different markets take different kinds of fish. Foreigners eat the small fish." He smiles. "We've just installed some machines that we've been perfecting for years. People knock the machines for putting men out of work. But these machines clean the fish perfectly . . . There'll be more hiring of men at the packing end of it instead."

I drive out to New Beach in the gray twilight. The cloudy sky meets the grayer ocean at the horizon. Gulls and terns wheel and soar from dark flight, diving down to sea edge to pick up the tiny silver herring stranded by the incoming tide. The gulls are in the hundreds, whiter, larger, blunter of beak than the terns. The birds feed on the living thousands, the sand lice hop out of the dead. Among the driftwood, untouched by gull or tern, a three-foot dogfish lies on the beach, its broken head bloodied by the beam trawler's oar, its white skin stone-smooth. Up ahead a sea robin, the head and tail left, the body stripped clean, lies in a tracking of gulls' feet. Beyond, is a second sea robin, a big one, also stripped clean, a third, a fourth, a fifth, a sixth, a seventh, an eighth, skeleton after skeleton.

> "Jerry Farnsworth, well-known artist of North Truro, received word today that his painting, *The Yellow Bird*, has received the first prize of $300 known as the President's Prize."
>
> *News item.*

In the rear of her big corner house on Pearl and Bradford Streets, Mrs. Julia Martin is taking down her sheets from the lines. "The season is slow starting, but we're all getting ready." She laughs, her chin sinking into the soft roll of flesh below it, her hazel eyes shining like a girl's. "I depend on tourists to keep up this property, to pay the taxes. Most of the population feel the same. The rooms just help a little. I don't even get the price of a pair of shoes. I have six rooms to rent and it's a two-month business. The way Maine and New Hampshire are situated they have the fall tourists. I know! You see, I was brought up in Provincetown, but I've lived in Boston twenty odd years. In Maine they have the hunting season. We have the art colony, but there's nothing after Labor Day. The real natives tried to stop shorts and halters."

We go inside her kitchen, sit down. "But we're real friendly here even if the Town Crier is dressed up like a Dutchman more than a quaint Cape Codder. But without the art colony, Provincetown wouldn't have one-half the tourists. The reason Hawthorne came here as a young man was the air. The sunlight was the nearest thing to Europe. There isn't another spot in the whole country that has the light effects. I've had artists in my home and they say the same. It's the light they're interested in." She seems to be reading from a Chamber of Commerce brochure. Suddenly, she laughs. "It doesn't require brains to be an art student.

The average student takes up art because he has failed to make the grade elsewhere. But there are some bright ones. Of course art today is a luxury. . . We used to have a few alert students from the middle classes. But, it's the children of the well-to-do taking up art now. And the tourists come here from all over the country, even from Honolulu, and Provincetown's changing all the time. In 1900 it was Nova Scotian and Irish, but now the town's mainly Portuguese. The old New England stock are reserved, but the Portuguese are real generous."

Her voice lowers. "I'll tell you something. The Ku Klux Klan came in about ten years ago." With each word she appears older. "Years ago, the American stock had *that* feeling, but they found the Portuguese were clean and thrifty and they began to intermarry. But with the Klan. . . It's wicked! It's broken up the town. A Protestant neighbor was telling me about this feeling between Protestants and Catholics and he said: 'I wonder who brought it in?' He, himself, married a beautiful girl, part Portuguese. The other side feel superior, but the Portuguese children are smart, and up and coming. It's been such a sacrifice for the Portuguese parents to see their children through school, but they've made good." She hesitates. "I'll tell you something. Most people through New England think the Portuguese are colored. They're not so! They're mixed like any other nationality, but they're not colored. We are a Latin race!"

The shack Sydney King shares with her room-mate, Priscilla French, has the here-today, gone-tomorrow atmosphere of a Greenwich Village studio. Rough-hewn beams support the ceiling. The exposed wiring carries power to the box radio on the table and the unshaded electric bulb overhead. The flat trough-like sink is painted blue, the towels hanging on a rack nailed to the door of the combination living-room and kitchen.

Five of us sit around, watching Polly, the part-collie, part-terrier moping in the center of the room, her long tail drooping.

The painter, Charley Heinz, hardly talks, his right hand handcuffed around the wrist of his left. A middle-aged man in old white pants, blue shirt and yellow tie, he has a spare, reticent face.

Sydney lights the gas range. She opens up a can of Campbell's chicken soup, pouring the cold stuff into a pot to heat. Her body moves with the solid grace of an experienced artists' model. In her green tweed coat and yellow fishnet turban, she looks as if about to blow out on a date. Instead she glances anxiously at Polly.

The moment arrives. Sydney offers a plate of hot soup to the dog. Polly sniffs, tastes the soup as if out of politeness. Tail drooping lower, she tastes the soup a second time.

"I guess Polly had too much to eat somewhere." Sydney's dark brown eyes are like those of a disappointed mother's.

"Dogs turn down soup while models starve." Nineteen-year-old Jean Shay, blond hair fluffing into a bang over her light blue eyes, stretches her bare legs. "Me and my scurvy! That's what I get for living in Provincetown. Living on fish doesn't help any." She laughs the high laughter of the very young and then bites on her lower lip. "Have you a cigarette, babe?" she asks Charley.

Charley gives her one. She lights it, smokes with the picture-making skill of a model who has learned a few things from painters.

The door pushes open. A brunette, taller than Sydney, swaggers into the room. "I'm Priscilla French," she announces, her voice sing-songing unsteadily. "I met several very nice people . . ."

"Polly is Prissy's dog," Sydney says to me.

"I also met *our* friend with whom I have an engagement tomorrow night. Also, met a half a dozen others. Also met *our* mutual friend . . ."

"To you dear. Not to me," Jean interrupts.

Nobody bothers with Polly anymore. The dog slumps to the floor.

Jean chews on her nails. "Charley, I haven't had anything but coffee all day today. I'm starved." She rises, tall and slender in her blue dress, almost beautiful. "Prissy, you remind me of a French poodle."

"Maybe I am in disguise!" Priscilla retorts.

Out on the dark street, Jean takes the wheel of Charley's 1929 Ford. "I'll bat your teeth in, Charley!" she cries out nervously. The car jerks forward down Bradford Street. She swerves around two pedestrians. "Look at them on the road! The dopes! I'll bat their teeth in! I'll bat their teeth in!" Drunk with speed, she chants, "I'm starved, I'm starved!"

The car slows down by itself, stops. Jean jams her foot down on the starter.

"No gas," Charley says.

We pile out. "Charley!" Jean threatens. "I'm going over to Taylor's for dinner. You get some gas and meet me there."

We walk east to crooked Commercial Street, empty of people now, its wooden houses under a shoal of stars.

"Swordfish!" Jean orders at Taylor's. "I always order swordfish in this damn place." Her face is very pale.

Both models have an identical sunless look. Sydney's yellow fishnet turban is too vivid for her. "You know I didn't come up here to pose . . . I came up to get a job as a waitress or secretary. I can make more money in a straight job. The artists, nine tenths of them, have no money. They take the Portuguese kids and pay them a quarter for three hours. They sit the kids on the beach, the water as background, and put a straw hat on them, looking very picturesque." When the swordfish comes Sydney murmurs: "I'll have to try that sometimes."

Jean doesn't answer.

Sydney watches the swordfish go. "Out here a model doesn't get the rates she gets in the city. She may be the Mona Lisa or Venus and she still gets fifty cents an hour."

"Oh, my teeth," Jean groans, pressing her palms against her jaws. "I should drink orange juice or eat an onion every day for my scurvy."

"Why don't you?" Sydney asks.

"I can't afford the orange juice and I hate onions."

"How did you get into modeling, Sydney?" I ask her.

"Through a fluke. I had been doing secretarial work in New York. One bright day I walked out on my job and I was among the unemployed. I had nothing to do and a friend of mine told me of a place on Fifty-Seventh Street where you could have tea and look at pictures, The Art Students' League. I had tea and was shocked at the nudes. Yes, I was shocked.

Now I look at nudes and all I see are color and light. Well, a little blond girl came over and asked me for a cigarette. She told me she was a model posing for cigarette money. Then an artist came over and asked her whether she'd pose that night. She said yes. Then he said to me: 'You're a model, too?' I thought, what have I to lose? I said 'Yes.' " She smiles with the memory of how she began, with the glow of *I*, of *me* and no one else. "Last year Jerry Farnsworth did this large canvas, a costume picture, a Victorian picture. . . He perched a yellow canary on my thumb. It was a stuffed bird. These mounted birds have little wires through their claws. . . This painting *The Yellow Bird* was exhibited at the Carnegie International at Pittsburgh. It's been at the Corcoran Gallery in Washington. The *Cape Cod Times* said it was typical of the pure tradition in American art."

Charley sits down at the table.

Jean pushes back her empty plate. "My first summer here, I worked in a night club, The White Whale. I was too young to serve liquor." Not hungry now, her blond face is more relaxed. "In the fall I went to New York. I couldn't find any job modeling clothes. I was a taxi-dancer at the Orpheum. The Yale, Harvard and Princeton boys used to come up to dance." She laughs derisively. "I worked there four months. Then I worked at the Village Barn doing the Big Apple with Arthur Murray's Big Applers. I lost fifteen pounds so I had to quit that. My family was paying my rent and giving me five a week for carfare. I spent all my money on cosmetics and liquor. That was the winter I got scurvy." She laughs defiantly, a chip on her shoulder. "My family dragged me back to the Cape. I lived out on the sand dunes without a God damn soul in sight. The scurvy didn't bother me until the middle of the summer. This'll kill you," she says, smiling, but smiling as she laughs, defiantly. "I didn't have any money. I bought a half dozen eggs and a loaf of bread. For a whole week I lived on an egg a day. Then some lady invited me to lunch and gave me egg salad sandwiches."

Sydney laughs, her face sympathetic as when she was heating the canned soup for Polly.

"The next day I got a job at the Aquarium Restaurant from eleven at night until three in the morning. One week, I had a contest with a garbage man. . . Who could stay up longest? I stayed up one whole week and got fired from the Aquarium for getting drunk on my night off. What are you giggling for, Charley?" she snaps at him. "He went to art school with my mother so he thinks he can giggle at me like that." Her mouth saddens. She is quiet, no longer getting any fun out of her experiences. "All I think of is being a fashion designer and then marrying a wealthy husband. I've been married, you know. I was married at sixteen. I met my husband at a costume ball. 'If you're not in at eleven-thirty,' my daddy said, 'You'll go back to New York.' It was past eleven-thirty so I married this local boy. We signed a license in a barber shop. I was wearing faded slacks. Give me a cigarette, Charley. . . He was a habitual drunkard. His family's filthy with money. His grandfather owned the cold storage plants before Atlantic bought them out. His grandparents spoiled him."

Every morning, Mrs. Medeiros turns on the radio for the Boston Fish Pier broadcast. The announcer calls out the figures in a hard exact voice: "Two schooners at Boston Fish Pier. *Cape Ann*, 22,000 haddock, 20,000 scrod, 2,000 cod, 5,000 mixed fish. *The Imperata*, 32,000 haddock, 13,000 scrod, 38,000 cod, 12,000 mixed fish. Market cod, 2.10. Haddock, 2.75 to 3.00. Black bass, 2 cents. Pollock, 1.85. Lemon sole, 3 cents. Yellows, 1.75. Codfish, 2.10. Nineteen small boats docked this morning at Boston Fish Pier with 231,000 pounds of mixed fish. One mackerel boat, the *St. Providenza*, with 800 pounds of mackerel . . ."

"You see those Italian draggers from Boston?" Mrs. Medeiros remarks. "I used to like to listen to them sing. Play on a banjo and eat spaghetti and drink wine until it's a wonder they didn't burst." She picks up a pair of torn pants. "They're Richard's. Boys get into the dirt more than girls." She listens to the announcer, smiles. "Maybe fish have gone to Europe or to the World's Fair? Down here they're catching some whitin'. That's a nice fish though they call it silver perch in the restaurants. Oh, those fishermen! It's a hard life.

No fish and they're like clams. Won't talk. My father used to go out in a motor dory with his brother, the one they called Mocha, and get one thousand weight haddock. Now that's all gone."

"Mocha?"

"His nickname. They call my husband, Speed. Others they call, Squidface. . . When my mother moved down from Gloucester, they called her Cape Annie. Cape Annie," she repeats.

Outside, Richard, red baseball cap on head, is practising how to hold a bat. He stands in the shade of the maple tree near the fence. The sun flashes down the white pickets.

"Don't hold your bat crossways. You'll break your wrist in a Big League game," Richard's adviser, a boy of twelve, says critically. The adviser walks towards his pupil on legs twisted from infantile paralysis. He speaks with authority. "And choke your bat! Here, I'll show you how you choke your bat."

"Watch me hit a home run!" Richard pulls away. He jumps up and down, banging his bat against the lawn. He swings on air, swats one over the bleachers. . .

Kenneth bangs out of the screen door, watches Richard.

"See that home run!" Richard cries.

"Home run?"

The crippled boy shuffles over to the two brothers. "You fellers going to pick blueberries this summer? Taylor's pays ten cents a pint."

"I sell them for five cents a quart," Richard states.

Kenneth glances at his older brother pityingly like a smart business man at a foolish one. "It's ten cents a pint. Twenty-five cents a quart!"

"Why twenty-five cents for a quart?" I ask. "There are two pints to a quart and if you sell them at ten cents a pint, a quart ought to be only twenty cents."

Richard thinks, smiles with the corners of his mouth. "It's twenty-five cents a quart because it's a quarter. It ought to be only a penny a pint!"

The other boys ignore him. "A quart holds more than two separate pints," the baseball authority says. "That's why it's twenty-five cents. We make a lot of money with blueberries."

At twilight, the flounder draggers from Boston at anchor off Town Wharf look like the souvenir photographs for sale in the stores. The fish-shaped boats, empty of their crews, take on cargoes of shadow, the gulls wheeling above the red-lit waters.

Docked alongside Town Wharf itself, the mackerel seiner, the *Frankie and Rose,* much too long for its narrow width, seems like a boat modeled by a kid. The orange-painted deck has long faded into a seasick hue. From the two masts tattered red and green flags are flying.

A member of the crew springs from deck to wharf.

"Hello," I call to him. My wife smiles.

"Pardon?" His eyes are blue between lids that seem stretched apart as if from staring at distant objects. His blond hair waves back from his red-burned forehead.

"You're from Boston, aren't you?"

"We're from Gloucester. Those flounder draggers come from Boston," he smiles. "We seine for mackerel, south to Virginia, north to Nova Scotia."

"Much money in it?"

"We got sixteen in the crew. The boat gets six shares and the crew gets sixteen shares. Twenty-two shares in all. We go seining and get ten thousand pounds mackerel. . . That just pays for oil and ice and grub. There's grub for us all the time, but gray hairs for your family, if you got a family. Sometimes we fish a month and get nothin' for it," he smiles again, yarning. "I've been in it since I was eight. My father was a fisherman in the old country, in Italy. He still goes draggin' and he's sixty-two. He broke me in. He took me trawlin' and then seinin'. I'd like to break away from fishin', but I don't know no other line. We got some fellers on the boat, they went to high school and then they come back fishin'. So what's the use of going to high school?"

"How long do you go out at a time?"

"We go away two, three weeks. We just come in from Nova Scotia with 45,000 pounds to the Boston Fish Wharf. We sell it at auction. They buy 35,000 pounds at 4 cents a pound. Then they want us to sell the other 10,000 pounds, cheaper. Them buyers is all together. We said: 'It's all good fish.' They had some fish in the freezer and they expected more boats to come in. That's how it goes. It's a tough racket. The fisherman, he never is sure. We had to go back home and sell for 2 cents in Gloucester."

Two members of the crew come up the wharf, escorting four laughing Portuguese girls.

"Maybe you want to see the boat, too?" His politeness expresses itself in voice and manner, a formal old world politeness. He jumps from wharf to deck.

We climb down into the forecastle, rows of bunks on both sides. Five or six of the mackerel seiners, all young boys in their twenties, are reading newspapers. "Hello Flash," they greet our guide.

"They call me Flash. I don't know why," he smiles in explanation. "This is our kitchen." On a shelf six freshly baked Italian breads are cooling off. Two pictures, a movie actress's, a head of Christ are pinned to the wall.

"We can eat!" Flash says with simple pleasure. "Sometimes I eat six eggs at a time. The cook—he ain't here now, he's a li'l fellow, spry for his age, he's fifty-six . . . he buys us sixteen steaks and they weigh thirty-four pounds. We call this seinin' a lazy man's existence. When the fish ain't runnin' we go to port and do nothin'."

He tours us through the pilot house, where the four town girls are taking their ease like debs on a yacht, and then sailor-climbs down the iron ladder to the engine room.

"The engineer, he sleeps here." Flash points to a bunk separated by a six-inch aisleway from the throbbing engines.

"Isn't it hot?" I ask the engineer.

"No," he says, gruff and smiling. He is as young as the rest of the crew, but not tanned like them. His face, pouched under the eyes, is pudgy white. "The cool breeze comes right down from the port hole." He folds his tattooed arms across his chest. "That's a hundred horse power engine."

On the deck again, Flash waves his hand at the seining boat on the larboard side of the seiner. In the darkness, the mackerel net appears larger than its true size, filling up half the boat. A string of unlit electric bulbs supported on iron pipes is also part of the equipment. "When the fish run, we go for them day and night. Sometimes, the birds show us where the school of fish is. But the look-out up in the mast there by the boom, he can see them in the day. At night you can see them unless the moon's out and it's too bright to see."

Salt sea night, black and starry, tents over the *Frankie and Rose*. "I hear them talk about the romance out on the sea. I never find no romance, but there's somethin'. I couldn't be ashore. It makes you restless." Flash looks at the boat, at the wharf. "All my brothers are fishermen. My oldest brother, he been savin' for three years to get married—to save five hundred dollars. He ain't got it yet. The fisherman, he can't save his money. He got his family to help. If he smokes, he got to buy cigarettes, oilskins. I go seinin' from May to late in the fall. Then I go dragging or trawlin'. I make fifteen hundred, maybe, over the whole year and I got nothin' left. The union man from the A.F.L., he come down to Gloucester and say: 'Join up with us. The Portygee fleet's in it. The Americans are in it. We vant the Italian fleet in it.' If we all in, we get a standard price for mackerel. Maybe get five cents a pound? Now we come in with a low stock, we get nothin' for it for ourself. We sell the fish and first we pay for grub and oil."

The engineer joins us on deck. His go-to-town sport shirt is yellow. The color comes clear through the darkness.

"There's no factories much in Gloucester so we got to take it as it comes," Flash adds. "But there's nothin' in it. The big beam trawlers go way deep out for a month at a time. Their fish ain't fresh either when they come back. They're out so long, they spoil it."

The engineer snorts. "It's the big steamers!"

Flash shakes his head. "Get a 10,000 stock and you just break even. I'm twenty, but I feel older. I been fishin' since I was eight."

"I been out to sea since I was ten," the engineer says. "I never went to school. I pick it up little by little. Sometimes they pick me up crawlin' drunk, put me into the engine room. I start her up."

"How about a drink now?" I suggest.

"Okay, I'm in the mood," Flash smiles.

We walk down the wharf to the Atlantic House. The bar and the dancing room behind the bar are crowded, the big wooden floor packed with couples. I recognize Sydney King.

In red velvet evening pyjamas she dances smoothly. Artists' models, waitresses from the restaurants and their beaus, all jitter to the hotcha music box. We sit down at a table near the wall and order beers. Flash and the engineer spot the scattered seiners from the *Frankie and Rose*.

"Skipper likes a young crew." Flash nods at Skipper, a dark stocky man of about twenty-eight, dancing with a blond tourist. "His brother got killed in an auto accident so the father bought the *Frankie and Rose*. She used to be a sub chaser in the war. Skipper, he gets the six shares. He worryin' all the time about the notes. He couldn't pay for her all at once."

The engineer's eyes roam to the women, the tourist girls. the Portuguese waitresses, the artists' models. He displays his arms with their tattoos, a head of Christ, a hula hula dancer called Rosita, a cupid called Carol. "Got drunk so they put them on me. Carol's my kid." He takes her picture out of his wallet, glances at the little three-year-old blond. "She lives with my mother. I come home, I give some dough, they want some dough," he says roughly as if there's no sentiment in him. "I don't care." He hands me the picture.

"Where's the mother?" my wife asks.

"Aw, she was a rummy. I give her the air. I go off to sea, she run around with other guys."

"Who was she?" Flash asks.

"One of the Finn sisters with the blond hair." Terse, hard-boiled, he tosses his life out of the window. "I don't like this port. Cape May, Norfolk, you can have a good time."

"I don't blame you." Flash turns to my wife, asks her for a dance. They go out on the floor.

"Spend all my money." Melancholy, the engineer boasts. "What do I care! Them dames take it right off you." He studies the shapes of the dancing girls.

The music box uses up the last of its nickels. A tourist in a sweater strolls over to the piano, plays blue jazz. Flash and my wife return. "Think this crew be off tomorrow?" Flash asks the engineer.

"Sure."

"I hope so. *The Dorothy,* that flounder dragger, they say they see mackerel off Chatham. I'm tired hanging around." He lifts his hand, the old scars healed white. "That's from the dogfish. They come in, eat the mackerel and net. They cut me las' year. I go to medicine chest and nothin' there but some iodine and bandage."

The engineer circles his empty beer glass around and around. "Lost a nail this year. That's all. We hit striped bass once. . . That was luck. Them're expensive."

"That's something!" Flash agrees. "But it don't happen often. Look at Skipper."

Tirelessly Skipper whirls the blond tourist up and down the floor.

From the tables, different members of the crew bellow encouragement. "Hey, Angelo!"

"Angelo, you stay in port!"

Skipper only smiles for answer.

"Good friend you call Angelo. Skipper's name is Joe." Flash lights another cigarette. "He don't care about the fish now." His voice deepens. "Fish day and night. And dream to fill the hold with all the mackerel she can hold! 75,000 pound! A good stock! With the dip net dumping the fish down the hatches. . ." He laughs away his serious mood. "It's a lazy man's life. Get a few minutes, you read them cowboy stories."

"Flash, what's your name?" I ask him.

"Peter Testaverde. He's Chet Stone."

The engineer nods. "Ask anybody in Gloucester. They all know me."

"We have to go," I tell them. "So long."

My wife and I walk home to Mrs. Medeiros' on Conway Street. The night is as full of stars as the sea was once full of fish.

Massachusetts State Route Number 3

On the road to Boston, the strawberry sellers sell their wares, their baskets bright June red.

FOR SALE PULLETS AND SMALL CHIX.

Plymouth, Massachusetts.

WELCOME TO HISTORIC QUINCY 313 YEARS OLD. The big sign sells the piled-up years to the tourists.

YOU ARE NOW IN HISTORIC BOSTON. At the end of the vast blue sky, the city's tallest buildings rise like stone columns as if no men lived in them. Up South Street, the smell of leather sour and dense coils out of the commercial buildings.

Cambridge, Massachusetts.

Northwest, are the green summer trees and Phillips Academy at Andover with its collegiately dressed preppers.

And the textile city of Lawrence, Massachusetts.

Mr. No Name Whatsoever

LAWRENCE, MASSACHUSETTS

"In New England are wildernesses with mountains, lakes, singing streams and virgin forests; trails and shelters; miles of
sandy beaches. These you will find not too far from historic
New England towns and cities. Throughout New England
there is a gracious atmosphere of peace and quiet, mellowed
by more than three centuries of living."
    *From an advertisement of the New England Conference
    of State Federations of Women's Clubs.*

ESSEX STREET WITH ITS 35c *Dinner* eating places is one of
those business thoroughfares built before the slick store-
front era. Solid, substantial, it seems tight with its dollars.

In front of the side-street entrance of the Essex House,
two old men idle, hands in their pockets, their watery eyes
rheumily speculative. Inside, the marble stairs, gray-faced as
the two old men, lead up to a floor of beauty parlors and
dentists.

The office of the Essex House is on the next floor, the
third, its door wide open on an interior of plush chairs.

"Hello." The landlady gets up.

"I want a room for my wife and myself."

"I have twenty-five rooms and all single young men." She
smiles bawdily. "You want to leave the lady here?" Her brown
eyes shine in her wrinkled sagging face.

"The men work in the mills?"

"All work in textile mill. I show you your room you stay."
She shuffles out along the linoleum, not joking any more.
Unlocking the door numbered 4, she asks: "You like?"

"I'll take it."

She shuffles back to her office.

Number 4 is a large room, wallpapered with blue and
yellow flowers. Tacked on the closet door, the calendar ad-

76

vertises: FOR HEADACHES AND MUSCULAR PAINS USE DR. MILLS
ANTI-PAIN PILLS. A framed motto completes the decorations:

> *Most any poor*
> *old fish can*
> *float. And*
> *drift along and*
> *dream; But it*
> *takes a regular*
> *live one to swim*
> *against the stream.*

The textile worker who lives on my floor in the Essex
House, the one I've nicknamed 'The Silent,' myself, and a
middle-aged worker I've met for the first time walk over to
Al's for 35c dinner. We sit in one of the side-wall booths,
The Silent and myself opposite the middle-aged man, who,
tall and slim, wears his last summer's straw hat with sartorial
elegance. He digs into his potatoes, smiling.

"I didn't get your name," I ask him.

He nods at The Silent. "He didn't tell you and neither
will I. You can call me Mr. No Name Whatsoever."

The Silent grins, cuts up his meat, eats hungrily.

"This is no place to talk," Mr. No Name Whatsoever
remarks after we drink our coffee. "Unless we talk about
baseball."

"I have to go back at eleven," The Silent says. "I'm
on the night shift now."

"It's four hours before eleven. Let's go over to your place."
His face is thin, netted with fine lines. Unsmiling, it is an old
man's face.

We leave Al's, cross over to the Essex House, climb the
flights to The Silent's room with its windows on Essex Street,
on the Community Savings and Broadway Savings banks
across the way.

Mr. No Name Whatsoever smokes his cigarette half down.
"I see you're looking at our banks," he says to me. "Behind
them's Pacific Mill Number 10." Block square, the mill is

like a fort in the ending light. "See those stacks behind Number 10? Those mills're out of business and so are we tex-tile workers. Your friend here has no dependents so he's better off in this place." He shrugs. "When I came over here in 1912—"

"From where?"

"Just from nowhere." He smiles and again The Silent grins. "I speak no word of English at the age of fourteen, alone. Without no family, relatives, in a strange country, alone. I went right into the mills in Taunton. Cotton mill, of course. To start with, six dollars per week. Mind you, that was in 1912. The dust in that perticular mill was so thick, compel me to quit, to get a job weaving. And up to now I remain in the weave room. We go on at six-fifteen in the morning, three-quarter hour for lunch at noon and quit at three in the afternoon. Go home in such a physical condition that I must lie down for an hour to recover vigor enough to go for a walk. Ain't that so?"

The Silent nods his head.

Mr. No Name Whatsoever leans forward. "There is the looms, the workers talking before the speed starts up. . . Start up the motors! Start up the looms! And from that time on we're too busy to talk to one another, piecing up broken threads, filling the batteries, tending the looms, weaving the cloth. Too busy to think! I don't know how to describe it? It's a sweatshop. Take that Number 10 out there. It's the hottest! It's the worst working conditions! Company union runs it and you can't unionize it. Too many stool pigeons! They don't fire you at Number 10. But they make it so hot you quit for your health. You ask him."

The Silent doesn't move. He seems not to hear.

"The mills have no improvement for the worker!" Mr. No Name Whatsoever declares angrily. "Whatever improvement in machinery, the workers don't share in it. Twenty years ago, we used to run one and two hand-fed looms per weaver. Now since they invented automatic looms, the weaver runs six looms and making about the same pro-potion in pay as in two looms. It was fifteen, sixteen dollars for two looms twenty years ago, and now it's thirty-odd dollars for six." His hands with their blackened fingernails swoop down on his knees. "When they made the machine automatic, it should've been an improvement for the worker, but instead they tripled the load of looms!" He stares out of the window. "This town got a great working class tradition. Sacco Vanzetti were killed by the law in this State." He speaks the names of the two dead men as one, as if they were *one* man. "It was a raw deal for the working class as much as for Sacco Vanzetti. They thought, those mill owners in their nice houses out to Andover—Nice houses! We got the slums! They thought to set back the working class, but Sacco Vanzetti draw attention to the injustice per-petated to workers to hold them down." His anger blazes out of him. Hopelessly he mutters, "Now many workers turn their coats inside out. Others believe in the old idea, but remain quiet. It's some life, my friend. To remain quiet, to come home to rest, to drink a glass of beer, to go to the movie show, and to go to bed. Maybe the C.I.O. may bring to the town the re-awakin' and the willingness to organize as a means to stop the speed-up and stretch-out."

He shrugs apathetically, but still stirred by a desperate rebellion. "I'm a knocker! I see something wrong, I squawk. The mills've robbed my life away. I got no more money than when I started. It's a perpetual bankrupt condition. Save a hundred, and next year go a hundred in the hole! Forty years ago, a worker with plenty ambition and a few breaks got promotion. Lamont at American Woolen, he grow with company to position he holds today. Today, promotions come other way around. It's their sons who get choicey positions. Land of opportunity—No such animal! By God!" He flames as if he had been asleep, as if now again, some alarm clock has exploded in his brain. "We workers, we American, English, Italian, French, tex-tile workers, we haven't much time to talk in the weave room. The noises are so terrific. We have to speak loud in a worker's ear to understand what we're talkin' about! But we talk! What's going to be! There was the I.W.W. here! There was the Amalgamated! The National Textile Workers in 1928 to 1931. Now the C.I.O.!" His fingers squeeze together. "This is the truth. There was a movement, many movements showing the mills as exploiters. . ."

No one says anything.

The Silent stirs: "Father Milanese, he come into the union

hall while the workers holdin' a meeting and call to the workers: 'Come out from here. They're red.' The men almost spit on him. Sure, when the workers not working, out on strike, how can they give money to build Father Milanese's church?"

Mr. No Name Whatsoever's smile is acid. "I do not remember whether it was 1919 or 1912. . . The workers have a parade over here. And in the parade there is a big sign: NO GOD NO COUNTRY. The stool pigeons plant the sign and march with it. They making believe workers no believe in God and country. After this a priest by the name of Riley have another parade for God and country. Since that time the most priests here, especially Father McDonald, is against the workers. Father McDonald led the Citizens' Committee against the strikers in 1931. The best way to get a job in Pacific Mills is a letter of introduction from a Catholic priest, especially from St. Ann's Church. I got a chip on my shoulder against those babies! The priests should be for the poor workers. . . I begin to think, I get a lump in my throat. Spit it out or swallow it!"

Pacific Mill Number 10's hundreds of windows become gold-plated. The electricity is on, the juice is on in the pyramid.

"What time now?" The Silent asks.

"It's a long way off," Mr. No Name Whatsoever yawns. "No night shifts for me. A friend of mine, his wife works in the mills. It's the weight now. It's how much wool you put out. You don't put it out, other girls get the job."

"What time?" The Silent repeats.

"Almost nine."

The two textile workers glance out at Number 10 ticking into the night like a huge never-stop alarm clock.

The next morning Essex Street looms grayer, more commercial in the steady drizzle. At last I duck inside the building I want, climb a flight of stairs to a frosted-glass door:

T.W.O.C.
of the
C.I.O.

The offices are crowded with workers waiting to see somebody. Patiently they sit on the pull-up chairs, their faces rigid with the infinite patience of the poor.

Joe Salerno, director of the Massachusetts T.W.O.C. (Textile Workers Organizing Committee) smilingly greets me in his office. Dark-haired, handsome, in his early forties, he seems to have modeled himself after the President whose suave smiling picture is on the wall: FRANKLIN D. ROOSEVELT, A GALLANT LEADER.

"What about textile in Lawrence?" I ask him.

"At one time there were fifty thousand tex-tile workers here. Now there's thirty thousand. Some mills have moved into the South and some mills have died natural deaths." He strides up and down the narrow room, his white sport shoes twinkling past the desk of his busy typing secretary. "But on account of the largest tex-tile mills being located here, every labor union has made an attempt to organize the industry. The I.W.W. came here in 1912 with Bill Haywood, Arturo Giovanitti. The Amalgamated came here in 1919 and roused the people. Street cars were tipped over. Workers were shot and wounded. Machines were broken. Cloth was damaged. Violence was the thing of the day. But never did they succeed to get collective bargaining. All those unions stopped at the doors of the factory with clenched fist looking up, the management with hands in pocket looking down. . . The strike of 1922 was the result of a twenty-two and one-half per cent cut in wages. The strike was won. But three months later there weren't thirty members left. The stool pigeons—"

He shrugs. "The sum total of twenty-five years of history in Lawrence was no organization. In 1937, not even twenty union members in the whole city of Lawrence. Here came a man—his brother design the airship for Lindbergh—August Bellanca, Vice-President of the Amalgamated Clothing Workers of America, who laid the basis for organization. I took his place a month before the 1937 election. Two days before election, the Civic League distributed 25,000 pamphlets written by an ex-Lawrence tex-tile leader, Fred Beals, an ex-Communist. They used him as a stool pigeon. The churches and the Mayor spoke against the C.I.O.: 'Vote Against the C.I.O. and John L. Lewis, Communists.' "

The typewriter clicks steadily.

"At the end of 1937 a severe depression set in. The speed-up has increased to such an extent that one-half of the workers in woolens and worsteds can do all the necessary work in less than six months. Fear reigns strong in the Pacific and Arlington Mills. Yet we have increased the membership from a few hundred to several thousand dues-paying members. We find that the radio has been best to educate the crowd. We broadcast every Sunday between one and one-thirty. The leading politicians, foremans and bosses are the best listeners." He smiles. "They nicknamed me the Father Coughlin of labor. I don't agree with Father Coughlin, but I'm supposed to be a strong mover of crowds. . . Persons in the labor movement who can usually stir crowds are usually not practical labor negotiators. Being a Latin, I'm sentimental and romantic, but I still hold my head on my shoulders."

"Father Coughlin?"

"I don't like the nickname, but the style, pronunciation of words—"

I return to the Essex House. The door of The Silent's room is open. I go inside. The cracked shades are pulled down. Stretched out on the bed, The Silent sleeps, his eyelids sunken, his mouth clenched tight as if holding onto the deepest blackest sleep of all.

I nudge his shoulder.

Instantly, his eyes open as if he hadn't been sleeping.

"I'm leaving now. Don't get up. I just wanted to say so long." I hesitate. "I keep thinking about what Mr. No Name said—"

"He's all right. A man struggles, gets older. . . The workers, they'll win some day."

"Well, so long."

"So long," The Silent says.

We shake hands. He turns over on his side, falls asleep.

The alarm clock ticks on the dresser.

Massachusetts State Route Number 110

"What do they catch on those lakes between Lawrence and here?" I ask the waiter at McArdles Restaurant in Lowell.

"Most likely bass. I don't know. I don't get out to fish." A boy of twenty-six or seven, he wears his white service cap far back on his blond head.

"The mills working here in Lowell?"

"Stopped right now. The New Deal stopped too before it got here. New Deal?" he scoffs. "They forgot to cut the deck. That's what we say around here."

The long chain of industrial towns, Lowell, Fitchburg, Greenfield, rivet the mills tight into the inland forests.

The Mohawk Trail dips, curves up to Ye Trail Inn perched on the next hilltop, its wooden observation tower like a staring eye. The elderly lady proprietor shows me the view, *her* view. Neatly dressed in Sunday best, she waves her hand into the sky. "They come from all over to see this. There's Vermont. New Hampshire's straight ahead. And Massachusetts, of course, is down below where those tobacco farms are. A prettier view is hard to find anywhere. You see those dark gray buildings down there? They cut the tobacco and hang it up on racks in those drying sheds. The sides are open to let the wind blow through. Then they ship it to the factories. There are two, three, four farms right there. See that chimney on the mountain? The Connecticut Valley's on the other side and all through the Valley they have tobacco farms. Twenty-seven of those sheds were blown down in the hurricane! We never heard of a hurricane this far up north! It was the first time in history. It had rained four days. And there was a six-months-old baby with us and a twelve-year-old boy. We older women had to keep calm. The boy thought it was a Wild West show. He placed kettles to catch the leaks. He put his raincoat over the radio as the signs blew off the place. He ran around shouting while Miss Mansfield and I were saying our prayers upstairs."

West of Ye Trail Inn, west of Williamstown, Massachusetts, upstate New York rolls into the horizon, a road of corn into the continent. . .

Cosy Vale Clean Cabins.

I rent one of the oversized (no running water and no toilet) chicken coops and follow the proprietor to the main house. "There's a mighty fine livin' for some people here. I'm getting too old. I'm sixty-one. Hale and hearty, I am, but—" He pauses, lifts up one of his legs. "Waricose veins. Yes, sir. Waricose veins. I can't be gettin' around like I used to. I'll be taking thirty-five hundred for this place. It's worth more. In the season, in the swift months, we put out the lights and they come rapping and knocking and saying: 'Have you just one cabin for tonight?'" His round face screws up piteously. "'Have you just one cabin for tonight?' A young man could be building a gas station, but I'm too old. A young man could make a fine living here, but the young men have no money to—"

Another car pulls up. The proprietor hurries forward. The car pulls out, whizzing up the road. "There he goes," the old man complains. "Scairt. It'll cost him more for a room now. You have to watch 'em like a spider a fly. Where are you bound for, Albany?"

"No, Ithaca."

The Graduates

CORNELL UNIVERSITY

ON TOP OF THE STEEP HILL, the Cornell campus, like other campuses, looks like a feudal stronghold. At the foot of the hill, the dingy frame homes, the smokestacks. On top of the hill, Sage Hall with its tower slit-windowed as if designed for bowmen, Goldwin Smith Hall on its broad ducal lawn that a lord might walk across.

Off-campus, our room has a window on a backyard garden, red and pink roses glowing on their trellises. The walls of our room are a picture gallery, the illustrated philosophy of predepression college generations. One picture has to do with Home and Family, the Dignity of Motherhood and Fatherhood: A beautiful long-haired mother, dressed in white, lies abed with her new baby; modestly, the husband whispers to her from behind his hand. A second picture deals with Purity and Hope: A blond baby with upraised hands is floating around in heaven.

But on the dresser, two photographs have forever recorded two real commencements in man's life. In the first, a boy of five or six stands on a huge regal chair. He wears a fluffy lace collar and is scowling at the formality, the convention of posing. In the second picture, the same boy has grown up to be a soldier in uniform. He isn't scowling now, patriotic and heroic, believing in the War to Save Democracy.

For the last time the seniors stroll the campus with their proud dads and teary mothers. Tomorrow, in twenty-four hours, the Class of '39 will be speeched and sung out of the green womb of college, out of freshman hazing, sophomore football Saturdays, junior study, senior dignity, out, out, out. . .

Black-gowned and black-capped, the boys and girls about to graduate throng towards Goldwin Smith Hall for "The Last Sing." On the broad lawn, parents, friends, alumni gather in a standing audience. The fading light sheathes the statue of Andrew Dickson White. In long metal gown the FRIEND AND COUNSELOR OF EZRA CORNELL towers above the spectators. Up front, the black gowns have arranged themselves as if for a farewell photograph, their maroon banner lettered 1939 like a flag above their heads. The first black gown steps up to the loudspeaker. He says a few words and a brown dog bursts into hoarse warning barks.

The crowd laughs, but the brown dog keeps on doing its duty as a watchdog.

Black Gown retorts. "Anyone else who'd like to leave at this point?"

The dads in their summer gabardines and flannels laugh approvingly as if in chorus: Ready tongue has never harmed a young man!

Black Gown speaks fervently, concludes fervently. "We who are about to face the world are grateful for our four years at Cornell."

The second black gown, cap in hand, sings a college song, sings for his class and for all their twilight thoughts and hopes, sings for the class of 1939 on all the country's campuses, for the college grads and the high school grads and the public school grads, for all the youth upon the land. . .

And from the library tower, the chimes bong, bong, bong. . . The metal lips call the hour, this especial hour, this last eight o'clock before commencement.

The next black gown, Austin Kiplinger, is introduced. "This is not an oration. I'm trying to say aloud what you are thinking silently. This should be a period of careful scrutiny." Austin's young voice peals out as if already the best part of him is looking backward on his college years. "Education is one of those things like democracy. An ideal rather than a fact. There is one thing we should learn from our college training. That we are not educated. The four years or five years or six years we spend in formal education is a springboard into further education. There is an aura of fallacy around the phrase that we are about to *step* forward into the world, as if we are about to face entirely new circumstances."

The setting sun oranges through the clouds over Lake Cayuga. The birds sing their evening songs. "There is a confusion in the world of which we are a part. . . The world is questioning the way we produce basic goods, the way we govern ourselves. We belong to an age of transition. But that is no more true than it has been for centuries. Civilization runs in slow and sweeping curves. . . We have been happy for four years and that is its own excuse. Cornell for better or worse is a permanent part of our lives."

The brown dog begins to bark again. The dog speaks too: Watch out! Watch out!

The captain of the football team follows Austin at the loudspeaker, a long pipe in his square hand. "This morning I had to clean the old tobacco out of the bowl," he begins. "It seems that in 1878, the graduating class had an idea they'd like to pass down something to the class of '79. They didn't have much money so they bought a pipe. That pipe was to represent the traditions of Cornell. The Junior class accepts the pipe to carry on the Cornell tradition." He lights a match, puffs. "Therefore—" The pipe goes out. He lights a second match. Tobacco smoke curls up. "It is with great pleasure that I light this pipe again. I call on the class of 1940 to receive this pipe."

The representative of the Junior Class steps forward, accepts both the proffered square hand and the pipe of Tradition.

Still, the brown dog barks. Now as "The Last Sing" nears its end, as the dusk moves like a tank across the campus, the seniors remove their black caps, and their dads their panamas, and all the voices rise in "The Evening Song:

> *"When the sun fades far away*
> *In the crimson of the west,*
> *And the voices of the day*
> *Murmur low and sink to rest. . ."*

Melancholy, nostalgic, the song floats in the dusk, song of the class of 1939, song of the classes before. . .

"Music with the twilight falls
O'er the dreaming lake and dell;
'Tis an echo from the walls
Of our own, our fair Cornell."

Silence.

"That's the works!" somebody says.

The black gowns rejoin their parents. A tall boy in glasses kisses his mother, shakes hands with his dad. "I was so bored listening to those boys shoot their line," the tall boy comments.

A middle-aged alumnus in a maroon blazer hugs his wife, coltish here on the campus.

A black gown arranges his family, smiling dad, smiling mother, smiling brothers, for a candid camera shot. A picture peddler with a tripod camera hunts for customers. Voices mumble, laugh, mutter, quicken in how-do-you-do of introductions. A pretty little senior holds last court on the campus. She smiles and smiles at two under-class boys. "I'll write," she promises. "I'll write. You'll see." She seems conscious of space, vast space between herself and the two undergraduates staying on at school.

New York Route Number 13

Across the hilly fields, the farmers follow their horse-drawn plows, men, tools, beasts, one-machined against the earth.

Near Bolivar, tanks and pumps mushroom up from the cornless fields. No hay grows here. No barley. The woods have been hacked down.

A gray frame house, the color of old rags, looks like a forgotten box on the edge of the highway. I walk to the door. A pregnant woman of thirty-five watches me. A blond boy peers out and a young unsmiling girl of sixteen, holding a baby in her arms, stares from the bedroom window.

"Hello. What are those tanks for?"

"Crude oil's what they're pumpin'," the pregnant woman answers. The missing teeth in her mouth have never been replaced. In her old broken shoes she looks as gray as her house. "They don't take all the oil the land gives. Sinclair buys so many barrels from a lease."

"Lease?"

"The leases own the land all through here. They get two dollars a barrel. They sell to the refiners like Sinclair. It used to be a dollar thirty-five." The blond boy in the kitchen, the young girl in the bedroom haven't moved once. "When you buy farm land here you don't buy the oil rights. The leases have the rights."

I drive into Bolivar and buy a copy of *The Bolivar Breeze*. "I never knew there was oil in New York State," I remark to the storekeeper.

"It's sixty years old," he says grudgingly, paying out his words one by one. "Monday was the anniversary of the coming in of the Allegheny field. Back in 1879, Taylor proved there was oil in this country. His well's still pumping, the old Triangle. . . Taylor had a notion all right and he stuck to it. I'd like to have had the notion."

Frame houses cluster together in Bolivar. In front of one of them, an oil worker has converted a hot water boiler into a big flower pot, his roses growing out of gray metal. Drizzle seeps down.

Again, the forests with their deer crossing signs, the oil wells in clearings axed out among the trees.

Bradford, Pennsylvania. HI GRADE OIL METROPOLIS OF THE WORLD. HOME OF KENDALL AND BRADFORD OIL REFINERIES.

An evangelist has come to the woods with nails and hammer: JESUS IS COMING SOON.

There are frame houses in Sargent with its giant Sargent Wire Glass Company building.

In Johnsonburg, they make paper, not glass. I brake to a stop alongside a man in a leather windbreaker hurrying to work. "How many men work in that building?" I ask him.

"They employ over a thousand men here. *The Saturday Evening Post,* the paper you read, it all comes from here."

"What do you papermakers get?"

"Forty-six cents an hour."

There are more frame houses in Du Bois, and railroad yards of glistening steel tracks, freight trains, dozens of iron locomotives.

Another of the evangelist's signs is tacked to a tree: JESUS IS COMING SOON.

The land climbs two thousand feet above sea level. The drizzle thickens. Gray fog like fill-in dirt completely plugs up the valley alongside the steep descending road. Below in the valley Johnstown, Pennsylvania.

Mr. Cop

JOHNSTOWN, PA.

"CONGRESSMAN ROSE BUILT this house. Then he died and sold it to the K. of C., and then I came here." The landlady sighs, a tall lady of sixty-five with genteel eyeglasses. "The Flood took everything I had and the bank wouldn't do anything. And since the bank wouldn't, the Red Cross wouldn't either. I had to do something." Congressman Rose's house has golden-brown walls and marble washbasins in the bathrooms. "The dam broke in 1889 and Conemaugh Lake covered the City. The Flood took everything I had."

The sidewalks of Johnstown bear the initials of their makers. At night the initials fill the darkness: *W.P.A. 1936.* Street after street repeats: *W.P.A. 1936.*

On Front Street the freight trains are rolling into huge buildings as if into a series of endless railroad stations. Freight after freight is swallowed up, the buildings stomaching them all.

In mid-street, a cop directs the traffic. The bright electric flashes of the headlights glare at him. He is bow-legged. Not young. Long of face. Hard of face.

"What's going on across the street?" I ask him.

He comes to the sidewalk. His sloping shoulders still hold iron in their aging curve. "That's the Cambria Plant. That's Bethlehem Steel or part of it. See that smoke down there? That's a blast furnace. This is one of the biggest plants in the country. Eight miles long. See that?" He points to one of the huge buildings, its roof slanted like a barn's. "They roll the steel in there." He points to the freights. "That's the B. & O., the Baltimore and Ohio. This is one of the best payin' sections the B. & O. got just because of the mills." His long welt of a mouth slits into a grin. "Two years ago you couldn't stand on this corner like you can now."

"Why not?"

"The mills were out on strike. That's why. The strikers brought the Mexicans up from Aliquippa. On our end of it—" His voice deepens. "We broke that strike!" He brags with the gusto of an aging man telling his exploits. "But the Sheriff didn't have any backbone. He had to call in the State Troopers. See this scar in front of my ear?" he asks like a hunter who shows a friend a bear scratch. His finger taps the exact spot.

"Yes."

"That's from the nails they threw into our faces. But I couldn't take that. I give it to 'em!" His hand curls around the handle of his club. "There were four of us and four thousand of them. We held 'em off awhile, but then we had to call for help. The lieutenant come in with the tear gas and stuff. They started to throw bricks. One of the boys shot one of the Mexicans twice. He killed that Mexican. They had a picket line around the whole plant, day in and day out. We put the tear gas into 'em! The strike begun Saturday. We broke it Monday, but the Sheriff had to call in the State Troopers."

Above the Cambria Plant, above the dark streets and the narrow valley, the hills are like a giant thumb and forefinger formed in a circle.

A car honks at the corner for information.

"Excuse me," the cop says.

"You're busy. I don't want to take any more of your time."

"You wait for me. We like to do this."

Bowlegged, he swaggers to the car, directs the driver. "Do you want to see a coal mine?" he asks on returning. "I'll show you one on my beat." We walk off together down a lit-up street. "That's the drygoods section of town." He spits between his teeth, nods at an acquaintance. "Our beats are getting bigger and bigger. They ain't appointin' no more men when you get killed or die. Only got sixty-five cops left. When one dies they don't appoint no more. . . This is a fast town when the mills're goin', but since that strike things ain't the same. The mills ain't come back yet," he mourns. "I've seen this town with the mills goin'! I've been on the force since 1909." How important the mills are to him, as if he were manufactured in a mill himself, complete with long face, badge, gun. THE MILLS. That's what counted. The mills

going, the town fast, the mills going, going, going! THE
MILLS. That's what counted.

"There's coal under all those hills," he says. "There's coal
under the sidewalks, under the river."

I stare down at the pavement. "Under here?"

"Under all over. This is the biggest soft coal district in
the country," he boasts, full of pride in *the biggest.*" He
marches up to a shaft opening in the side of a dark street,
flashes his light into the solid black square. Solidity is hurled
back into shadow, the shaftway sloping down into the coaled
earth, wooden beams supporting roof and walls, steel tracks
gleaming down the tunnel. "The men walk four miles in
every day to where the coal is. And four miles out. My
brother-in-law gets a kick out of it when I show him around.
This mine goes under that hill."

Back we go through a street of dilapidated houses, men
and women sitting on the door-steps. "Anybody ask you if
you've been in a tough neighborhood, you can tell 'em:
'Yes.' All the toughies and the niggers live here. We keep 'em
well in hand."

The streets widen out with respectability. He nods at
the adjoining offices of the United Mine Workers and the
Steel Workers Organizing Committee and spits. "Used to be
a crowd in front of here so thick you couldn't get by. Now
there's no one here." Still the streets seem to expand under
the multiplying neons. Mr. Cop glances at two miners in
front of Sears Roebuck's windows. In their blue work shirts,
they have the appearance of not belonging to the town, as out
of place as farmers in to shop on Saturday night. "This is
Main Street. The druggists are here for their convention.
When things're going, it's a fast town." He scrutinizes my
face as if I were a miner and then brandishes his club in
farewell.

He has looked into my face. I have looked into his.

Mr. Owner

PITTSBURGH

"83—Graceful Guy
91—Keno
984—The Ace
20—Tom Mix"
*From the numbers and names of various horses owned by
the Pittsburgh Traffic Police . . . Tom Mix was given
to the city by the owners of the leading department store.*

RAILROADS AND RIVERS, those fingers across the land, knot
into a giant fist, black as coal, the city of Pittsburgh.

On the tracks, the freight trains are pulling in tons of the
big-chunked bituminous. On the Monongahela and Allegheny Rivers, joining together at the Point into the Ohio, the
paddle-wheel river boats are pushing the coal scows. Pull,
push. Pull, push. Pull, push. Coal for the mills.

Extending up and down the river valley, the mills are like
a row of separate iron towns, yellow smoke and black smoke
and white steam rising from their smokestacks into the sky,
up, up above the brick-dot wood-dot homes on the surrounding hills, up, up, yellow smoke, black smoke, white steam,
yellowblackwhite, the flag of the city.

"Pittsburgh is the home of Stephen Foster, who wrote 'Old
Folks at Home.'" In her blue cotton dress and turban towel
wrapped around her head for housecleaning, the little musician looks milder than milk. She sits down on the edge of the
couch as if ready to start dusting again at a second's notice.
"Years ago we had a symphony under Victor Herbert. But
Pittsburgh isn't known as a musical center." Her lips pucker

up in the gentlest of smiles. "My family were all musicians. My mother played the 'cello, my father played piano. They did lecture work, but after I came—" she says discreetly as if she were still the young girl of a generation ago. "Mother stopped for me to go to school. I went to the Pittsburgh Conservatory. . ." Her hand flips downward at the wrist. "Pittsburgh's going backward terribly in music. Years ago I played night and day. I made seventy dollars a week. I had a nice pipe-organ job in the Methodist Church here for eleven years. But it's always been the millionaire class who supported music. They make a poor mouth of it now."

Photographs of quartets and symphonies hang on the walls like pictures of graduating classes. The stack of magazines on the radiator include *Musical America, National Geographic, The Saturday Evening Post.*

She sits on the very edge of the couch. "Now Andrew Carnegie was a great promoter of music. He'd put a pipe-organ in a place if they'd raise half the price. His organs and libraries, too, are all over the country. He was interested in all the churches getting pipe-organs. But Andy Mellon wouldn't give a nickel for music. It's just a pastime for the millionaire class here. We have a friend who teaches at Shady Side Academy. It's very exclusive, very selective. . . When the boys graduate they're ready for college. What they want mostly in music is banjo and guitar."

"Do you teach?"

"I teach four instruments myself. In the last fifteen years, I had four students who turned out very good. But there's no music in Pittsburgh except roadhouses," she laments, her voice resigned. "At anything good, you can almost see the same faces. Many of them can't tell one note from another. They go just as they get a new ermine wrap. . . The people who appreciate music are up in the second balcony. It seems unfair. Paderewski was here two weeks ago. I heard him thirty-eight years ago. He was wonderful then. . . But now he comes out and takes such little wee steps. Even the men took their handkerchiefs out and wiped their eyes."

She imitates Paderewski, stooping her thin shoulders. "It was pitiful how he has slowed down. That's the end, I thought when he played his last number." She nods slowly to herself. "We know fine musicians who are driving a taxicab. I know a musician, he hasn't one nickel to rub against another. A woman here has a class of six and she charges them ten cents a piece for a half hour lesson. It's terrible." She picks up her duster. "It just rains and rains here, too. It rained so much we had a big flood in 1936. You could ride past Kaufman's Department Store in a boat. The water was up to the balconies in the theaters. . . I remember the Johnstown Flood . . . the houses floating down with people on them. It was a terrible sight." She digs her duster into the couch. "It just rains all the time. Pittsburgh's only good for people in the coal and steel business."

Downtown Pittsburgh. The Carnegie Building. The Frick Building. The Koppers Building. The Buildings and the Banks. And the men with brief cases who belong to them, hurrying between The Buildings and The Banks.

Seven big lighting fixtures in shape like upside-down skyscrapers, widest at their ceiling-attached bases, fill the cool marble lobby of the Koppers Building with cool marble light. On the Directory, the names of The Building's tenants are listed alphabetically:

AMERICAN CYANMID AND CHEMICAL CORPORATION   2401
AMERICAN TAR PRODUCTS CORPORATION   1201
CARBONDALE MACHINE CORPORATION   1945
CYCLOPS STEEL COMPANY   2420
DULUTH, SOUTH SHORE AND ATLANTIC RAILROAD
        COMPANY   1901
EAVENSON, ALFORD AND AUCHMUTY   2050

The elevator races up to the twentieth floor, to the height of a smokestack, stops. I get off.

Corridor and doors. Numbered doors. 2050. EAVENSON, ALFORD AND AUCHMUTY.

The bookcase inside 2050 is full of books on coal. There is 'Coal Analyses' listing the states it covers on its binding:
        Alabama, Arkansas, Illinois, Indiana. Iowa, Kansas,
        Kentucky, Missouri, Montana, Ohio, Oklahoma,
        Pennsylvania.

The pictures of three presidents, George Washington, Abraham Lincoln and Theodore Roosevelt are on the walls of Mr. Eavenson's private office. Seated at his desk, jacketless, vestless, with dark red stone links in his cuffs, Mr. Eavenson looks exactly what he is, a man of authority on a summer afternoon. He listens to me and then says. "I went to Swarthmore College and the first job offered me was in the Virginia coal fields. I went there and I've been in the coal business ever since. That's forty-seven years. . . I'm pessimistic about coal. I don't think it has much future. Perhaps after oil and gas are exhausted? Coal is being sold lower today than thirty years ago, considering the wages. Not one company out of ten is making any money." He pulls down the shade behind his desk, Pittsburgh's streets two hundred feet below 2050's windows. "I don't expect to be here fifteen or twenty years from now after oil and gas are exhausted. I'm talking about *me* at the moment. Some day, perhaps, coal'll come back if the fellows who have it can hold it that long. The Pittsburgh Terminal Mine has gone into receivership. The Pittsburgh Coal Company is losing their shirt. I don't think there's a big coal company in western Pennsylvania that has made any money in the past ten years. It's probably nearer thirteen years. There isn't one coal company out of ten throughout the country that's making money or breaking even."

The red stones in his cuffs gleam as he shifts forward on his chair. "Conditions in western Pennsylvania are a bit worse than throughout the rest of the country. The Government's been readjusting the industry during the past four years, but things are worse. Hoover worked on it for a while when he was President. . . There's just too much coal in this country! If the Government would buy coal as they buy silver at two or three times what it's worth, that'd help." A frown liquidates his smile. "We're working out the best coal and giving it away. Most of the steel mills mine their own. Carnegie-Illinois, Weirton, Republic, Bethlehem, they all have their captive mines. We operators sell our coal to the small mills and manufacturing plants and to the railroads. Coal! It's about the worst business of any. It's the only business I know of with so many troubles. Trouble with the deposits. Trouble with labor. Trouble with markets. Trouble with finances. In gold mining, the only trouble is to get it out. The market is fixed. The output is fixed. There's a steady price. All you have to do is dump it in the mint. In copper mining, you know the price you'll get when you do sell it. But in coal, you have to chase your markets and chase your banks. Your wage situation is one hundred per cent union with the Government back of the union. I think we ought to have a union to stabilize wages, but the Government shouldn't back a union. Everybody knows that. But a new administration wouldn't change the picture a damn bit. The Coal Bill is a John Lewis policy. He got it through so he can get the wages for the miners that he wants. The cost of labor is about sixty per cent of your total cost, and that is pretty nearly inflexible. You can't change it and that doesn't leave very much to work on. I don't know what old age and social security benefits come to, but it's three cents or four cents a ton. And that's a lot of money when you're not making any money."

He snatches at his fountain pen and starts to skim through the sheaf of letters awaiting his signature. He signs his name with steady bold stroke. His hair is steel gray, but his hand is firm. "That boom in 1920 was the worst thing that could have happened. The new fellows took as high as twenty dollars a ton. Now the average price is about a dollar seventy to a dollar eighty at the pit mouth. But it costs two eighteen to produce! That's the average in this district. It's a vanishing industry. Those new fellows won't have a damn thing left when their coal goes! They're not paying taxes, and every once in a while they go blooey and can't meet their payroll. That's happened more than once in the last eight or ten years. They give their property away and when they're through they have nothing left but experience!" He grins ironically at the plight of the newer operators. "You've got to meet your charges, the depletion charge to cover the value of the land, and the depreciation charge to cover the value of the plant."

He signs his name three or four more times. "The gas and oil fellows ship by pipe-line. They can give it away if they want to. We ship by freight rates which come to about fifty per cent of the delivery price. No coal company can borrow money from a bank because his security's no good. I don't blame the banks a darn bit. But if you do borrow, you have to borrow at a high rate of interest. We've been in this spot since 1926. We didn't have good business in 1928, 1929, when everybody else did. We weren't prosperous then. . . A war would open new mines of course. That was what happened in the last war. A lot of new mines open up and then those new fellows try to live. It keeps going 'round and 'round in a circle. It doesn't make sense! Now, I've got to get these letters off. . . The coal business was over-developed even before the World War. Those new fellows, when they can't pay the taxes on the mines, they surrender the land to the counties. The operator who goes blooey scraps his material and just walks off and leaves it. Like anything else that's worked out."

Green hills. Then a coal patch, rows of miners' houses, mountains of slack in vast burial mounds, and the mine, a complicated man-made leech on the land.

Bethlehem Steel owns the captive mine at Ellsworth, the company-owned store, the company-owned hospital. Each company-owned miner's house has its own out-house. Private.

Fires burn on the slack mountains, burning slack into the road material called red dog. The tires of the car ahead wheel up clouds of red dust.

The brick coke ovens are not working at Cokeburg Junction. The miners come out of the pit mouth in their blue miners' hats. Their faces are blackened. Their hands are blackened. Piles of logs, props for the tunnels below, lie near the shaft. Slowly, the miners walk to their wooden homes on the red dog roads, to their families, to their gardens, to their chickens.

At the abandoned mine, the shaft is ruined. But the freight trains still wait as if for the day when coal again will fill the depleted veins in the earth. The birds sing in flute and pipe. If you shut your eyes, you hear the summer, the birds, the cluck-clucking hens, the shouts of kids.

Open your eyes.

The company-owned houses have long ago peeled off their last flecks of paint, the wood the color of wood on a beach. The coal is gone, but the coal miners have stayed on. An ex-miner comes out of his house.

"When did the mine close down?" I call to him.

"Mine close down in 1931. Pittsburgh Terminal own the houses. Pay ten dollar rent for four room. It's falling to pieces by now. But pretty nearly all the coal miners stay here."

"Why'd they leave the freight trains?"

"Them's old cars down there. They collect rent every two weeks. Some one don't pay they lose ten dollar, so now they come every two weeks and collect five dollar. We got no water at all. Get drinking water way up on hill."

The ex-miner's two daughters come out on the porch to stare. The younger girl, a kid of eight or nine, is as dirty as the old plank on the road. But the girl of fifteen is as pretty as the little flower garden in front of the gray house. Spotless, in her cotton dress and high-heeled shoes, she seems to have stepped from a glass box onto the porch.

"All big ones for eating, but no one to helpin'." The ex-miner glances away from his daughters. The younger one still belongs to him. Not the older one. She doesn't belong any more to these gray houses, to the creek full of rusted tin cans. When will she run away to the city? Already, she belongs to the city, to waiting on table in a city restaurant, to smiling at the customers in a city whore house.

High up on the hillside, a farmer has put a fence between his land and Pittsburgh Terminal's. A lone fat goat feeds on the farmer's side of the fence.

"Brickyard here, too," the ex-miner mumbles. "That stop." His voice is the voice of a man whose guts have been mined out.

Workers With Names

McKEESPORT, PA.

"Th' feller who's satisfied is rich, no matter how much money he's got or how many people he owes. Fate is about the only thing we have left that money can't fix."

From the sayings of Abe Martin, cartoon philosopher appearing in the pages of the McKeesport Daily News.

PITTSBURGH.

Homestead.

Duquesne.

McKeesport.

Steel mills. Smokestacks.

Smoke over Pittsburgh. Smoke over Homestead, Duquesne, McKeesport.

Blast furnaces and their complicated entrail-like mass of pipes.

Mountains of red iron ore, shades lighter in color than the Pennsylvania Railroad freights.

And from the mills, a mighty sound, the whirring sound of steel-making, a sound, a note unlike any written by Stephen Foster, a sound, a note, a song like thunder.

McKeesport. . .

Trollies clang on Fifth Avenue past the movies and the department stores, Ruben's, and Helmstadter's: THE BEST STORE FOR VALUES. In clean white evening shirts, in sports shirts, the steel workers and their wives study the prices of the furniture, radios, auto accessories and clothing behind the plate-glass windows.

A passenger train highballs its signal. It is coming, coming, steel wheels on steel rails, coming, coming. The train slants across Fifth Avenue at Locust Street. For a few seconds, the passengers at the bright electric windows gape out at the strange men and women on the sidewalks of a strange town. The train chugs past. The steel workers turn away from the locomotive plunging east, to the store windows.

I climb up steep Sinclair Street on my way home. Halfway up the hill, a summer crowd loiters on the sidewalks as if waiting for an ambulance, a lingering curious crowd. In the glare of the lamp-post, the adolescent faces of the youngsters are sharp as those of shoeshine boys.

A stout woman trudges up from Fifth Avenue. Her breath comes short. Her eyes flash questions and then her voice. "What—what's the matter?"

A woman with black hair parted in the middle answers. "They're settin' her out."

The stout woman shakes her head. Nearby, five young girls in their teens kill time, humming jazz in chorus as if at a dance hall. The cowiest girl of all places two plump hands on the shoulders of the girl in front of her and sways her big body to the jazz rhythm. They hum quietly in deference to whatever has happened.

A blond man wearing thick-lensed glasses and a narrow-brimmed black hat mutters. "Set her out all right."

Across the street, in front of a shoe repair store with a big shoe drawn on the window, a home has been pulled out from the shelter of four walls and a roof and piled on the sidewalk, a policeman on guard.

"That's Councilman Beckman," the blond man whispers.

Standing near the policeman, a tall man in a linen suit and straw hat seems on the point of making a speech. Few men in the crowd are wearing their jackets. The Councilman and the policeman both appear uniformed.

"They set her out this morning," the blond man says. "I wouldn't live there. I looked at it. There's two rooms. She kept her furniture in the front room and lived by herself in the other room. The partition between the rooms and the shoe store don't go all the way up. Try to sleep, huh, if the shoemaker's hammering? It ain't worth twelve dollars a month."

"She must've owned a big house once," somebody behind me remarks.

A red-haired woman smiles enviously. "She has two rolls of linoleum."

The blond man is silent, thinking. "Whoever set her out was mean." He is silent for another second. "There ought to be a law against setting out anybody. But if I was to own a house and the party didn't pay the rent, I'd have to set them out." He pauses. "But I won't ever own a house."

"The Sheriff set her out in the morning," the red-haired woman says. "All she owed was fourteen dollars. She been settin' there all morning. 'You got to move me with my furniture,' she said."

The owner of the home on the sidewalk now sits down on a kitchen chair near the policeman.

People sigh, whisper, mutter as they stare, quiet with the horrible quiet of long remembering, at . . . themselves, their homeless selves.

A car climbs up the hill, brakes to a stop between the policeman and the crowd. A thin man hurries out of the car, the Salvation Army representative. He talks to the owner of the home. She remains seated. He talks some more. She rises. Escorted by the Salvation Army she enters the car.

"Look," the red-haired woman says. "They couldn't make her move all day until now."

"Maybe the Salvation Army will find her a job?" somebody hopes.

The red-haired woman nods at the car speeding away. "Poor old soul. Two rolls of linoleum."

"They'll find something for her to do? Sewing?" the hoper against hope persists.

"Lucky it didn't rain on her furniture," the red-haired woman says. "There's the truck."

A Department of Sanitation truck pulls uphill in reverse gear. "They'll move her stuff into the city garage," the blond man comments.

The truckers shift the home from sidewalk to truck, loading the furniture and the years of living and using the furniture onto four wheels. The cow-like girl hums a tune. The grown-ups gaze apathetic and depressed. Overhead, an airplane bound for the Pittsburgh County Air Port roars, roars.

World in the sky, world of men and women perhaps staring down now on the steel towns, on the golden flying ropes of glow tied to earth, to the bessemers. . .

Across the new George H. Lysle Boulevard, named after the Mayor, the new building of the *McKeesport Daily News* gleams like the twentieth century itself, the twentieth century of the architects. White stone alternates with black stone, white stone and black stone and glass.

I find the Editor and President on the third floor. Mr. Mansfield is a vigorous middle-aged man with white hair that somehow adds a modernistic touch to his appearance. "What do you want to see me about?" he asks swiftly, smiling swiftly.

"Steel."

He shakes his head in a *no*, the smile remaining on his lips.

"How did you become Editor, Mr. Mansfield?"

"It's all luck. That's all I have to say."

"Luck?"

His smile broadens. "It's all luck."

Saturday night in McKeesport. The store neons on Fifth Avenue seem brighter, the men in their best sport shirts neater. The big blond girls and the little dark girls march along in twos, threes, fours.

"I never missed a Bank night yet until last Thursday," one of the girls gossips. "Was I nervous! Suppose they would-'ve called me?"

Suppose! Saturday night in McKeesport.

Cars fill up all the free parking spaces at the open-air gambling concession. Electric bulbs on wires light up the booths. The operators spin their wheels to lure the crowd. People place their dimes on the lettered numbers that divide the counter into compartments of luck. The wheel revolves. One number wins.

The bird-cage operator upsets the bird cage. The dice

tumble. Six wins. Five wins. Two wins. The winners bet again from their winnings. The losers dig up still another bet.

The cautious and those who can't afford to risk dimes pitch away their pennies at the penny game. Hundreds of numbers, each enclosed in its own square, form a checkerboard of chance. The central number is $1. The pennies flick out from many hands. One smiling winner collects 4 cents. A rule of the game reads: *Checks Must Not Cross Any Line.* The winner's penny has beaten the rule to the tune of 4 cents.

A woman, her cloth bag of pennies suspended from her shoulder, makes change, paying out five pennies (checks) for a nickel. A penny man with the wise guy, contemptuous manner of the small-time gambler rakes in the many pennies that cross the lines.

"That one good!" a heavy man exclaims after each pitch.

"Cross the line," the penny man announces, raking the penny off the checkerboard.

"That one good!"

"Cross the line."

The penny woman pays a winner 8 cents. The heavy man glares. Why, he hasn't won in ten throws! In ten throws!

At the next booth, the poor are busy with bingo.

I walk back to town along the new George H. Lysle Boulevard. Old shacks border the concrete, a buffer state of stockingless women and dirty kids between the Boulevard and the National Tube Works. The Works are mountains in the night, the smokestacks pinnacles.

A drunk staggers out of one of the shacks, his straw hat tilted far back on his head. He stops in front of me. He has a round face with a flat nose tilting upwards. "See them fellers? They go make information." His breath is sour with Saturday night's booze.

"What fellers?"

"They go make information! Say I insult 'em. I flag a police car. . . Call me hunky! We all American? That right? I no want to talk about ole country so they call me hunky. I show you." He digs into his pants pockets. "I got paper. *Hidden Empire* paper. I show you. Aw, I lose it! Everybody American, but not the lousy Jew. Kick the lousy Jew out!"

"*Hidden Empire*? Is that the name of the paper?"

"You read it sometime? No pay for it. It good paper."

I leave him and cut over to Fifth Avenue, the Tube City beer neons gleaming red. Young girls enter the little store that offers: BIGGER AND BETTER 12-INCH HOT DOGS.

I climb up the public flight of stairs on my way home to Union Street. Sixty feet or so above the business section, a terrace overlooks Fifth Avenue and the National Tube Works beyond it. Young men hang around the stone terrace wall as if on a corner.

The hills across the river parallel the rolling mills, the blast furnaces, the open hearths. Sparks like golden brilliant confetti whirl up from the Bessemer where the air blasts are being shot on the cast iron. The sparks whirl higher as the young men on the terrace gossip.

The daytime sun seems to have fallen into the bessemer; a sunrise glows and yellows, brightening the night.

Six or seven little boys and girls patter out of the darkness like mice. Jeering, they charge the young men, tossing pebbles and chunks of earth at them. Their dirty faces are ecstatic, contorted with the game.

"Boo!" one of the young men cries at the kids. "Boo! What's the matter with you?"

"You're yeller! Yeller!" a little girl hoots.

"Yeller! Yeller!" her companions chorus.

"Boo!"

Suddenly, the kids vanish.

"What was eating them?" one of the young men asks.

"They go nuts sometimes," a third says.

"What're you doing in the fall?" the boo-er yawns.

"Don't know? I know a fellow over in Glassport. . . He was telling me that he was thinking of getting into the F.B.I."

"That sounds good. But I'd like to go to college if I can. Who's going to the picnic?" The boo-er tosses his cigarette over the terrace wall.

All their voices quicken to answer.

"I am."

"I'd want a frying pan about this size." The speaker measures a pan about three feet long with his hands.

"That'd hold a couple chickens. Boy, I'd like to go to a nice beer picnic!"

"I'll have to wait until I get a li'l money."

"Small matter, money."

"Give me some of it."

"How much you want?"

"About a million."

"Take it in pennies?"

"I'll take it in any form."

"Money's a small matter."

"I got seventy cents."

"What! With the banks full of money!"

An older man joins the terrace club. "Hello."

"You fellers getting vacations?" the boo-er asks him.

The newcomer snorts. "The Tube Works are getting vacations the week of July 4th and with checks."

"With checks!"

"With checks. Smith over at Tin Plate wants to give us a vacation. You know when? In December!"

The unemployed burst into laughter.

The steel worker grins. "We ain't through. The whole grievance committee'll see Smith. That Tin Plate's a great one for saving money. They started getting rich thirty years ago when they located in Port Vue to save taxes. But Smith's worried."

"About vacations?"

"About that Irvin works. A six-man crew produced four hundred and sixty-six tons of plate in *one* eight-hour shift!" Somebody whistles. "You take the Tin Plate. . . Nine men in a mill, twenty-four mills working, that's two hundred and sixteen men. And they can't produce that in a week!"

"You'll be looking for a job soon yourself."

"Not so soon. The new works hasn't made the steel porous enough so far. It's too glossy. Down in Baltimore, they use a sand blast on the last set of rolls and that roughens it up so the tin wears. It's not far away though for the Irvin Works. I can see it. It generally takes ten years when something new comes out to make steel as well as under the old methods. If Smith doesn't remodel the mills he'll die."

I walk away from the terrace, ascend the sidewalks to Union Street, a hill street above the hill streets below. On the porch of my house, a shadow is sitting on the swinging couch.

I sit down next to my landlady. "Hello!" I shout, my lips close to her ear. My landlady is almost stone deaf. In the darkness, her broad face seems more resolute than ever. In the daytime, her eyes are blue and her hair blond. "Where's my wife?"

"Wife? Upstairs. Where were you?"

"Downtown!"

"Around?"

"Downtown! Why don't you learn lip reading?"

She hears me now, pushing at my arm with bearish playfulness. "No time." She reaches for the bottle of Coca Cola on the side of the couch. "I don't like anything else. I had something else once. It was ter-rible. My throat swole up! From the cheap sugar in it maybe. I won't drink it again. Did you see my daughter's new feller? He's a nice boy. I don't mind where she goes so long as I know where." She shakes her head. "My daughter, she ain't strong. She's awful nervous. She can't take it like me. You know how it is? She's twenty and she can't get a job. My brother can't get a job. He's out of high school four years. He's twenty-one. You can't buy a job. It's ter-rible." She takes another drink of Coca Cola.

"You're the only one working?" I shout in her ear.

"I'm sewing for the Project. People are just out for themself in this town. And my mother, she argues with my daughter all the time. My mother thinks she can get a job."

Her mother is an old Slovak woman who works all day long in the rear garden, a tall woman with the leathery cheeks of a peasant. My landlady's daughter is fragile and blond, the second generation to be born in America.

Dolefully, my landlady yawns. "In some towns they help you out, so you can pay the taxes. My sister over in Donora, they see to it her boy gets some work in the mills. But my brother can't get a job. He'll do anything. He was promised but it's been four years now. He's a high school graduate. He's a nice boy. He'll do laboring. Anything!"

Cars bug downhill towards town and the movies. Far away, the trains whistle into the night.

"What about your father?" My lips almost touch her ear.

She faces me. "My father, he was an awful fine man . . ." Her voice trembles. "He was a swell man. He worked with a brewery concern, but then this thing come along. . . The thing that stop the beer and whiskey?"

"Prohibition?"

"Yes, prohibition. He lost his job and then he got a job

down the mill. But they sent him home when he got old so they wouldn't have to pay him his pension. It disgusted him. It was ter-rible. He was too old to find something else though he tried. He tried," she says as if answering some inner question. "He painted some and that paid the taxes, but he was disgusted. They kept promising him a job, but then he died all of a sudden . . ." She controls herself. "You have to be able to take it! My husband, he was no good. He wouldn't work. So I left him when my daughter was two years old. I make enough to keep her and me in clothes." She reaches for the Coca Cola bottle. "I had the flu twice. That spoil my hearing. I thought a specialist charge twenty-five dollars, but they only charge three or four dollars. It was too late when I saw one. You have to be able to take it? Ain't that right?" She suppresses a belch. "I guess it's all luck."

Sunday.
There are seventy churches in McKeesport.
There is the First Baptist.
The Hungarian Baptist.
St. Stephen's.
Swedish Full Gospel Assembly.
First Pilgrim.
St. Mary's Russian.
St. Sava's Serbian.
St. John's Lutheran.
Christy Park Free Methodist.
Holy Family Polish.
Saints Peter and Paul Czecho-Slovak.
First Presbyterian.
Free Magyar Reformed.
Holy Trinity Slovak.
Sacred Heart Croatian.
St. Mary's German.
St. Perpetua's Italian. . .
Bong bong of church bells.
Bong bong.

The advertisement in the *McKeesport Daily News* is sponsored by the National Bank and other business institutions:

"A SUBSTITUTE—
FOR STEEL? NOT YET—

A strong framework—not arms—not wealth—made our land the great nation it is today.
The builders—men whom religious persecution had filled with a love of liberty and a hatred for intolerance—the builders used steel.
Religion was the steel they utilized.
General apathy towards religion is the rust that is eating away the framework of our much vaunted civilization. . . The church and the synagogue provide the sole logical answer to a thousand problems. Support religion. Above all else——"

The McKeesport Labor Temple is on Fifth Avenue. The Ladies' Auxiliary of the S.W.O.C. is holding a meeting in the long rectangular hall. Many of the women have brought their peeking kids along.

Down at the end of the hall, three women are sitting at a table. The chairlady stands up, a thin woman in eyeglasses with the poise of an executive. Seated on either side of her are two big blond women with the looks of spear carriers in an opera, the one in pink chewing on a wad of gum as she steadily writes in a notebook.

"We want a committee for the mill picnic," the chairlady says. "It's quite a job. I'm sure the tin mill will have a wonderful picnic. All the beer and all that goes with it. I want volunteers from the women that can give one hour of their time. The men feel they can trust us with the tickets." She smiles. "Mrs. Schmidt, how about you?"

"I'm not sure."

"Say yes," Mrs. Schmidt's daughter nags. "Go on, ma."

On the wall near Mrs. Schmidt and her daughter, somebody has tacked up a sign:

Wine and Dine at Eddie's the Only 100% Union Bar in McKeesport. Where Your Money Buys More.

The chairlady gets her volunteers, sits down at the table between the two blond women. "The second point on new business is a committee for Labor Day—"

"We haven't had Fourth of July yet and here's it's Labor Day!" a woman wisecracks. Her apple-shaped chin drops into her jowl.

The chairlady laughs with the women. "The men had a meeting the other night with the A.F.L." The men, she implies; *the men,* and we'll keep up with the men! "It takes time in preparation. We want one of the largest Labor Days. We want volunteers."

"Maybe I'll be sick after the picnic," the wisecracker cries out.

Another woman speaks across the laughter. "If we're goin' to march in a parade we should have a real nice banner."

Everybody nods approvingly.

"There are enough women here to make tammies and to sew," says the woman who wants the real nice banner.

"Stick around and you'll get a pension," the wisecracker comments.

As the meeting continues, casual remarks tag names to the different personalities. The chairlady is Mary Baron. The two big blond women are Judith Widen, Recording Secretary, and Millie Miller, Financial Secretary.

At last the meeting is over. With the same efficiency with which she handled the chairman's job, Mary Baron now spreads neat feminine paper napkins on the table. "We'll have some refreshments," she says. "Some lemonade."

The women crowd forward.

"Is it good to eat Mary?"

"I should've brought my cake."

"You won't need it!" Mary Baron retorts.

The Financial Secretary ladles lemonade into the cups. Lemonade, cups, plates of cookies, cake, all seem to have appeared out of some magic kitchen. The laughing voices of the women pour sunlight into the dingy hall.

"This cake's good."

"You should taste my mother's cake."

"Did you go to that new movie? It's a good one and not so full of bunk . . ."

"More lemonade. Don't be so stingy either."

"Stingy? What's that, your tenth cup?"

"Mary, are you Slovene?"

The chairlady smiles. "No. I'm Croatian." She glances at the lemonade drinkers. "How many nationalities have we here tonight? There's Greek, Russian, Scotch. Millie Miller's German . . ." The Financial Secretary nods, munching on a cookie . . . "Judith Widen's Swedish. There's Italian. Polish." She smiles suddenly. "That reminds me of a story. I needed help one day to wash my clothes. Joe wouldn't help me so I told him: 'Joe, today you're *Hrvath*, so you *Hrvath* clothes.' "

"*Hrvath* means black crow," one of the women says.

"Who said so?" Mary Baron flares up. "*Hrvath* means Croatian. Anyway, we're all Americans. We've all been born here."

"Don't remind me of my birthday." Judith Widen groans.

The woman with the apple-shaped chin walks to the doorway and stops for a farewell wisecrack. She tootles noise through her fist. "Here's how you play the bugle for Labor Day."

"Don't remind me of birthdays," Judith Widen repeats to the chatting women at the table.

"My birthdays are over. I don't count them any more," Mary Baron says. "Remember that paper the men put out a few years ago with the charges against Mayor Lysle?"

"What charges?"

"The whiskey ring scandals. Voting machine frauds . . ." Mary Baron laughs. "The paper was called T.N.T. Truth Not Tripe."

Millie Miller smiles. "Mayor Lysle won't allow you to take pictures, especially of the steel works. You need a permit from the father of the city. Remember when we called him King George, when the English King George was alive?"

"He's still Mayor and National Tube has six thousand steel workers," another woman calculates. "McKeesport Tin Plate has three thousand. Firth Sterling and the Chrystie Park Works have two thousand between 'em. Then there's the unemployed steel workers. There must be close to forty thousand people who are steel workers and their families. And he's still Mayor."

"King George'll get licked," Millie Miller says. "Wait and see."

". . . that's for a chocolate cake without eggs," a woman concludes in the recipe-swapping group.

"I have a recipe: Flour and sugar and baking powder. And raisins. It has no butter, no shortening, no eggs. It's a depression cake. I got the recipe from an Ohio woman. I call it a poor man's cake."

"Don't talk cake," Judith Widen again vents her humorous groan.

The women laugh, enjoying themselves as if at a church picnic.

"How do you spell your name?" I sit back in the little living-room on Walnut Street.

"His name is Esau. E, s, a, u," the wife answers, hugging the thin dark-haired girl on her lap. "He comes from an old old country. From Syria."

Esau smiles at me from his rocker at the window, eyes brown, somber. "I landed on the United States shores in 1909 with no family. I was all alone."

Mrs. Esau hugs her daughter. "At the tender age of fourteen." A second little girl of perhaps twelve enters the room. "She's La Vera. She was named after the truth."

"I came to Pittsburgh," Esau says. "I started to work for the American Sheet and Tin Plate Company. I was a ketcher's helper. Then I came up here to McKeesport. It's hot in the mill. The rolls have about 550 degree heat. It must be about 120 degrees where you work."

"Mill workers float around the country although all my kids were born here except one." Momentarily, Mrs. Esau's humorous voice becomes just voice. "We just don't manage. You can't keep the kids properly clothed the way they should be. We struggle to keep 'em in shoes during school. In the summer time we don't care. This year all eight were going to school. Two graduated from high school. They got their applications in the 5-and-10-cent stores, but they can't seem to get in."

La Vera tosses her dark curls back from her forehead. "What're you looking at me for when you talk about shoes?"

"I don't know whether I'm a good working man?" Esau shrugs his shoulders. In his clean white shirt, he looks like a small storekeeper. "But in all these years, somehow, I was never discharged. We work three different shifts. One shift start seven in the morning to three in the afternoon. Other shift start from three to eleven in night. Other shift, eleven in night to seven in morning. We change these turns every other week. We work on tonnage. As much as we put out, we get paid. The roller make a report. The roller responsible for eight-man crew and himself. We turn out from five to five and half to six tons of steel a day. We get the steel in bars, and we cut them into different sizes. After we heat them we start to roll it. Out of two bars we make eight sheets. We stretch them to the required length. We heat 'em, roll 'em. Then they take 'em to other departments. They cut to sizes they want. They go to the black picklers where they clean 'em up with acid. They go to the annealing furnace. To the cold rolls. Then they put 'em back in the annealing furnace. After they come out, they go to the white picklers. Then to the tin house where they keep it in water so won't get rusty. Then they dip it into tin coating. The girls sort 'em, all the different sizes. Then they sell to Heinz, to Borden's, to American Tobacco . . ."

Mrs. Esau interrupts. "It's hard to lay aside money for the future. You're behind in the rent a month and they're right after you with a Sheriff."

"We're glad to be in America," Esau declares.

"The land of the free and the home of the brave," Mrs. Esau recites.

"What that makes us?" Esau asks.

"I was born in Austria-Hungary. I'm Austrian-Jewish." Mrs. Esau pats her little daughter's head. "My father came here to work for Westinghouse. I was too young to remember. He didn't know anything about electricity. He was killed the first week he worked here. It was told to me. I was three, four at that time." The child's breathing stops for a second at the often-heard legend of the grandfather who came to America, the strange grandfather who didn't know about electricity.

Another daughter comes into the living-room. Seventeen, slender in her red dress, she combs her black hair.

"That's Charlotte," Mrs. Esau says proudly. The child on her lap and La Vera stare with little girl admiration at their big sister. "My daughters call the garret the dormitory. Four girls sleep up there. My children had an opportunity for education here, but they're worse off than their parents." She sighs. "Years ago, the uneducated immigrant could make a living."

"I've tried all the department stores," Charlotte says. "We have to pester them. But there are thousands of girls ahead of me. There were eight hundred and forty-four high school graduates in June."

"They do housework," Mrs. Esau says. "If they can get it."

Esau lives on Walnut, William Henry on steep Jenny Lind Street. Esau is a white man, William Henry is a Negro. Both men live in frame houses. Both men rest in their living-rooms before shift starts.

"Catch a feller off-handed," William Henry grumbles as I come in. Tall and lanky, he is wearing pants and an undershirt, his brown arms muscled like a prize fighter's. But his manner is solemn as if he were faithfully following the framed sentiment on the wall:

Rest in the Lord and Wait Patiently for Him.

"How are things in the mill, Henry?"

"Working conditions is the main grievance. We find discrimination 'gainst the cullid. Cullid can only work in a few places in a mill. A Negro's never replaced by a Negro. . . I came up here in 1916. Den I was twenty-three. I'd just grown up on my dad's farm in Arkansas. That time farmin' wasn't so awful bad as it's got since. . . I'm a pickler, dippin' the tin into the acid. But not many Negroes in mill. The whites go to the new Irvin Works, but there ain't a Negro in the new works. There, they press a button and do the work for two, three hundred men. That's too easy for the Negro. When you press a button, the Negro gets pushed out. It's like the farmer with the horse. He don't need the horse, he shoots 'm. Along in the time of manual labor, in the time of John Henry, the biggest Negro that ever lived, they needed Negro. But now they put in machinery and that machinery too easy work for Negro. The average Negro says: 'What can we do 'bout it?' I say: 'We can organize or soon the Negro people'll get pushed out like the Jews in Germany.' During the election time the Negro say: 'All's crooked. Let the best man win.' I say: 'Who is the best man? The best man for you and the poor-class people needs helpin' out or the best man don't win.' "

He straightens his long legs. "I remember I come here to the re-ality company for a house. They give me two addresses. The doors were broken down. People usin' those houses for rest room. They said: 'All we got to offer for cullid.' I was makin' three hundred a month then. I was fully able to rent a decent place, but I had to rent a basement room and *that* was better what the re-ality company offered me. My wife had to stay there all day and that was the indirect cause of her death. I hold the white population indirectly responsible for the early death of my wife. There's plenty of houses on the hill, but slum good enough for cullid. . . I got her glasses. I changed the lenses and wear 'em for readin'."

A conch shell keeps the front door of the Lakenan home open to the summer breeze. Inside, old Mrs. Lakenan comes out of the kitchen as I enter. Her husband fills up one of the leather-trimmed rocking chairs, a solid old man wearing canvas-colored suspenders. His son, Frank, is over on the couch. Frank's black hair is thinning fast. In ten years he will have the baldish round dome of his father.

"What kind of name is Lakenan anyway?" I sit down. "I've meant to ask."

"We're English-Scotch and German." Mrs. Lakenan stands near the player piano. "Lakenan is a Scotch name."

"That's grandpa Lakenan." Young Frank nods at the portrait of a whiskered man in a gilt frame.

Old Joe glances at the portrait. "I'm seventy-four come October. I've put thirty-seven years in the steel works. I was bottom maker for vessels for twenty-four years and eight months. We had no protection in those days."

"It took years for steel workers to realize the fact they needed a union," young Frank says. "You take in 1933. . . We had no protection such as the Wagner Bill. There was hardly a lodge meeting without stooges. I'll never forget one of them. He's still living. He sold the boys out in 1933. That was when the coal miners marched into Clairton with Martin against the wish of the United Miners Association. They came to the conclusion Martin was a stooge, too. I remember that very well." His monotone never rises, as if he were relating a story told to him by his father.

"We was on a strike in 1901," Joe Lakenan recalls. "Shafer was president of the Tin Workers at that time. He sent us telegrams from Alabama for each man to go back to the job. Shafer lived in a big red brick house."

Frank Lakenan continues. "Take the Cossacks in 1919. . . I was in the seventh grade in school. We'd look at their black horses, the black straps under the chins of those State Troopers. We'd congregate and watch them. They'd see five or six of us kids and say: 'Break it up! Gwan home!' There was no free speech or assemblage," he adds casually as if he had said: There was no rain that year.

"Too bad each and every working man doesn't understand what to do for his benefit," Joe Lakenan booms out. "If they did there'd be a solid vote for the right man. Too many scabs, too many black sheep! In 1901, the Super'd read you the minutes of the meeting ten minutes after the meeting. Tommy Edwards, he was my Superintendent, he'd tell me: 'Joe Lakenan, I can read you the minutes ten minutes after the meeting.' I said: 'Tommy, if you can start the mill, start it. But you won't start it with me.' I never was an agitator but I wanted things straight."

Frank frowns. "You take in 1933, it was February 1933. We all decided we was going to Pittsburgh to see Mike Tighe about the union and then we was going to Washington. I didn't have a chance to shave. With my own car and two others, fourteen all told, we went to interview Mike Tighe. He didn't receive us very well. He was sitting with his feet on the desk. . . The papers were giving us unfavorable publicity because we were fighting the Amalgamated Association of

Iron and Tin Workers. We was after vertical or industrial unionism. . . The papers said we were Communists. . . I said to Mike: 'Is the N.R.A. a law?' He said: 'I don't know.' I said: 'You're a damn poor union leader not to be down in Washington fighting for its passage.' He said: 'I'll throw you out.' I said: 'You don't have to. We're ready to go now.' "

"Business men got to realize labor must be recognized," Joe Lakenan states.

"Mayor George Lysle refuses to let us pass out union literature," Frank says. "They passed a waste-paper ordinance. They can pass out what they want. But we can't go down to the mill gates with our stuff."

Mrs. Lakenan smiles at her son. "Frank talks more rolled than anyone in the family."

"Lysle's been Mayor for twenty-four years," Joe Lakenan says. "National Tube favors him. Another black sheep." He glances toward his wife. "Frank talks rolled. But I was the one born in Virginia." He gets up and returns with a letter. "My father wrote it from Mexico in the war of 1848."

I take the letter and read:

> "Camp at Buena Vista
> Jan. 31, 1848

Dear Mother:

　　Your esteemed and welcome letter written on the 31st day of July last, was received by me in Salitillo, in due time, and read with a great deal of gratification.　I have met out here with a great many Virginians that I am acquainted with, some of them old friends from Fauquiers.　We have lots of deer, bears, wolves around us here.　Our boys now and then knock over a deer.　Mexico I find to be a curious country, and the people in it are as curious as the country.　They are very dark in their complexion.　From the general drift of the news lately received here, we begin to have strong hopes of a treaty of peace between the two different countries before long.

　　How does Jack come on with Miss Catherine?　Are they married yet?　Tell him that as long as I am absent, and not able to have a fair shake, he must, if not yet married, do a little courting for me while his hand is in.

> 　　Your affectionate son ever,
>
> 　　　　*Abner J. Lakenan.*"

I return the letter to Joe Lakenan.

Frank nods at me. "After we saw Mike Tighe, we drove to Washington. We couldn't see Hugh Johnson. Hugh Johnson run out on us. We had it in our minds who was for us and who was against us. We left Washington and blazed a trail on the way back. There was a blizzard from Cumberland to Uniontown. We hit forty-five miles an hour." He smiles proudly, remembering the blizzard and his skill in driving. "Time drifted along. There must've been a stooge among the fourteen. . ."

Joe Lakenan puts the letter away. "My grandmother drew a pension from the war of 1812."

"But this committee of fourteen was the beginning of the steel workers' union. When the opportunity presented itself, Lewis took up the fight. My boss asked me: 'Frank, what do you think about outside organization?' I said: 'I think it's all right.' He said: 'What do you think of inside organization?' I said: 'I think it's rotten.' 'Why?' 'Because it's drawn up by the corporation.' 'But what's wrong with inside organization?' he asked me then. I said: 'There are too many wrongs to make it right.' "

Old Lakenan smiles. "They tried to force Frank out of the union. He's president of the National Tube Works Local. Yes, my father said that every tub must stand on its own bottom."

Pittsburgh.

Homestead.

Duquesne.

McKeesport.

Steel mills. Smokestacks.

Smoke over Pittsburgh. Smoke over Homestead, Duquesne, McKeesport.

And from the mills a mighty sound.

And in the hearts of the steel workers still another sound, still another note, still another song as thunderous.

Labor Mayor

CLAIRTON, PA.

"That was the town where they said before the C.I.O.: 'If Jesus
Christ came to Duquesne, He wouldn't hold a meeting.' "
From the folk sayings of the steel workers.

BOATS HAUL COAL UP RIVER, under the bridges, past the
Clairton Steel Works. Behind the works with its cooling in-
gots, freight trains, open hearth furnaces, red mounds of iron
ore and smokestacks, the company-owned houses cover the
hill.

On Main Street, the red brick Municipal Building balances the elegant Union Trust Company of Clairton across
the way.

Mayor Mullen's home on Mitchell Avenue is on top of
the hill. His wife, a blonde in her early thirties, wearing an
apron over her dress, glances at me, her eyes blue behind her
glasses. "John isn't in now. You might find him downtown."

"How does it feel to be a labor Mayor's wife, Mrs.
Mullen?"

She laughs, embarrassed, motions me inside. "It has its
good points. But some of the various groups in town don't
cater much to labor men's wives. I've been asked to join the
Senior Woman's Club, but I haven't joined because I know
they're not in sympathy with labor. The wives of the mill
superintendents and merchants, and the school teachers belong. My father was a coal miner of Bohemian origin. All my
relatives were coal miners. But the mines, they're finished
around here. There's an H. C. Frick mine, but it isn't
working."

A blonde girl of ten comes into the living-room, stares at me.

"I have four children," Mrs. Mullen says. "That's Mary Louise."

"Mary Louise," I ask. "How does it feel to be the Mayor's daughter?"

She frowns, innocent and smiling. "At school they all tell me I act smart and that makes me mad." Her smile widens. "I have lots of boy friends though."

"Do you let them carry your books?"

"I'm not that serious. But I have one that I'm very serious about." She pauses, exclaims breathlessly. "I want to be a musician and play the pipe organ."

A second younger girl and a boy of six enter the living room.

Mrs. Mullen smiles. "Some of the neighbors wouldn't speak to us when John was a C.I.O. organizer. He was chairman of the Employees' Representative Group, that was the company union. Even when he was no longer employed, the men elected him to bargain with the company. But when he took this job with the C.I.O. there was a coolness in the neighborhood. One Sunday, he made a speech at a picnic in favor of labor and the next day we were ordered to vacate in ten days. We lived in one of the company houses. We came here to live on Mitchell Avenue. This is the street of Mayors. . . John ran for Council when he was still a mill man. He lost by a hundred votes. Two years later he ran for Mayor. There were the usual tales about the C.I.O.! There've been so many. They said if he was elected Mayor there'd always be pickets, and the company threatened to move the plant if John was elected. He's thirty-four, the youngest Mayor in the State."

"I think a lot of him. I hope Daddy's elected for Mayor again some time," Mary Louise's sister says earnestly.

"That's Jacqueline," Mrs. Mullen introduces us. "And that's Johnny. One day Johnny got mad at me and he said: 'Pack my lunch, I'm going down to the steel works and get a job.'"

Mayor Mullen and I sit together in the meeting room at S.W.O.C. headquarters. The Mayor carries his office in his shirt pocket, two fountain pens, pencils. His face is thin, his dark hair graying. "I'm the first Mayor who's one of the boys. The other mayors were Superintendents. The chief clerk of the steel corporation was Mayor for two terms."

Just outside the door, the rain pours down on the street. The Mayor glances through the plate-glass window, moves one of his thin slender hands. "They have civil liberties here now to meet for any purpose so long as the meetings are orderly. The average policeman has a policeman's complex: To keep the other guy in line. I see that the police are liberal. As Mayor, I made every policeman go to school in Pittsburgh to learn police work." He speaks tiredly, as if he has read and signed letters all day long. "As a labor mayor I'm used as a speaker in all the mill towns in the tri-state area. But I'm not an orator. I talk the workingman's language." He lights a cigarette. "We have three Democrats and two Republicans in our Council, but one of the Democrats, Jackson, is a Virginian and an admirer of Carter Glass. . . The W.P.A. now. . . We had quite a turbulent W.P.A. history since I've been Mayor. Jackson, of course, has been sabotaging W.P.A. One night in Council Meeting I told him that, and he called me a damn liar. I told Council that Jackson wasn't sending our plans to Pittsburgh, that there were no plans there from Clairton. And at the same time, the W.P.A. workers were being told that I wasn't interested in them. The Republicans and Jackson were saying I was holding things up. Even now, with matters straightened out, Pittsburgh can't give us the go signal. I don't know why! They're eating regular meals in Pittsburgh."

The rain slices across the window, blurring the street outside.

"The politics here . . ." Mayor Mullen smiles. "We have a swimming pool that was built in 1929. The Service Clubs, the Rotary, the Chamber of Commerce, pushed it with the cooperation of the mill. For ten years the mill succeeded in keeping colored people out of the pool. But now the colored Republican people are forcing the issue. . . To explain that, I have to tell you about the Allegheny Housing Authority of which I'm vice-president. I tried to get a housing project, but

Jackson opposed it violently. He owns a lot of shacks around here. . . The Republicans said we were going to build housing for the colored people at the expense of the white people. As a result of all this propaganda, the housing project was licked by a three to two vote in Council. Now, after these reactionaries get the whites sore on this Housing Project, they arouse the colored people on the swimming pool by telling them we're going to keep them out. But when they were building the pool, as a means of raising funds, they asked each resident for five dollars which would give them a book of swims. They asked the Negroes as well as the whites. In fact, the mill coerced everybody to buy swim books. And all the time they knew that they'd never let the Negroes use the pool. And all these years that the mill ran the city, the Negroes didn't use the pool and the Negro Republican leaders said nothing. But now these Republicans are sitting back figuring they had me in the doghouse. So, in order to put the baby back on the doorstep where it belongs, I appointed a committee of leaders of all the Service Clubs to meet with the executive committee of the Negro Civic and Protective League. I appointed the General Superintendent of the mills as a chairman. They're all Republicans. They created the condition. Let them straighten it out. They're always gunning for me anyway." He whistles a short snatch like a boy surrounded by a gang.

"I'm the first labor Mayor in this city," he states defiantly. "Did they work hard to beat me! When I ran for Council in 1935, the mills gave me orders not to run. I was a heater then, in the heating division of the oven department. But I ran anyway." The smile on his tired face flashes, youthful and energetic as his daughter's. "That was the biggest day of my life! Bigger than being elected Mayor! To tell those babies where to get off! I called a special meeting of the company union . . . they had company unions then. At that meeting we adopted a resolution condemning the company for coercing employees along political lines and demanded that they issue a statement that the employees were free to register and vote as they pleased. The next day they sent for me and told me not to run. I asked them if it was a command or a request. The General Superintendent, Andy Whigam, said they would beat me, I didn't have a chance. I told them that if I didn't run, I'd spend the rest of my life wondering whether I did have a chance. They asked me what would we do if they refused to issue such a statement. I told them we would post our resolution through the mills and publish it in the daily papers. After a lot of bickering they agreed to issue it. This Whigam's father was vice-president of Carnegie Steel and he'd been brought up to regard the working man as an implement. That was the biggest day of my life! To make them issue that statement!"

On the wall opposite us, there is a large placard lettered: UNION IS STRENGH. Two hands are clasped in hand-shake above silhouetted steel mills.

Under those clasped giant hands, the steel mills are small.

U. S. Route Number 30

Glassport. A barefoot boy sitting on the doorstep of his house, pets his dog, a yellow-colored mill-town dog. A fat old woman brooms the sidewalk. She wears no stockings on her swollen legs, the toes of her feet bulging out through holes in her broken men's shoes.

At the railroad station, idle men yawn the afternoon away, the steel tracks carrying the sun west with glinting speed.

Shirt sleeves rolled up on his biceps, the man with the twisted nose says: "The train was moving at fifteen miles an hour and steppin' off, I cut my foot on a stake between two main tracks, tripping me and throwing me to the ground. The step of the engine hit me on the head and three hours after I was in the hospital. That was my only accident."

The squat man with the brown eyes sneers to himself as if he has made up his mind in advance not to believe anybody.

"One accident in how many years?"

"In 1921 I came from West Virginia to Glassport. That's a long time ago." The man with the twisted nose nods his bony head. He looks as if a raccoon skin hat would fit him well. "I started in as a brakeman for the P. and L. E. That was my only accident."

"They call you at any time of the day," the squat man complains, forgetting his sarcasm. "Get your instructions from the yardmaster about movements of cars."

"You get them orders up to quittin' time," the West Virginian adds. "But it's not so bad. Only work eight hours, and time and a half over eight hours."

"You railroad guys!" a third man says, laughing. "What you carryin' now?"

"Goin' in we have iron ore, steel, coke, coal." The squat man wipes his nose. "Going out we have the finished product, wire, copper rods, truck frames, the stuff for shipment to all parts of the United States. And bums like you! You must be a bum not to know what we haul."

"If you ain't a bum now, you'll be one tomorrow," the laughing man declaims philosophically. His little blue eyes roll skyward in mock piety. "How much of a run you got? Maybe I'll take a haul out myself one of these days."

"The run is one hundred and twenty-one miles," the squat man answers. "That won't take you to Detroit or Chicago. You could hop one of the symbol trains. They're still hauling steel for Detroit. We could get the yardmaster to get you a private car!"

"Thanks. Tip me off about the signals."

"We have practically twenty different signal whistles for different things," the West Virginian explains. "We have a grade-crossing signal. We have a signal while approaching a station. We have an air test signal . . ."

The squat railroader interrupts. "He don't need to know that. When you want to haul out for Detroit we'll give you a ride in the caboose with the flagman and conductor."

"Thanks."

"I know what you meant before when you said 'railroad guys,' " the West Virginian grins. "But times are changing. A railroad man's banquet used to be only the conductors would come, or the trainmen. Years ago, the engineer thought he was better than the fireman. The brakeman thought he was better than the track walker. But now, they're all together. The majority of the junior men'd combine into one organization instead of the twenty-one different unions. And the men'd like to have Government ownership. Railroad men aren't asleep at the switch."

"That's right," the squat railroader agrees.

"As time rolls by, the older men'll be pensioned off," the West Virginian says. "The younger men and the older men, too, feel there should be one organization among all classes of workers, steelworkers, miners, whoever they be. The C.I.O., the A.F.L. and the Railroad Brotherhoods should be one organization."

"Only no bums allowed." The squat railroader says. "Glassport used to be a regular railroad town. They used to weigh the coal here, but now the mines, they're all mined out. The railroads had to shut the scales down. The railroaders had to go to some other point to work. The old times are gone."

"Brother, now you're talking," says the man interested in a haul. "And the bums didn't make Glassport go down neither."

Pennsylvania. Ohio. A hay wagon, pulled by a brown horse and a white horse, wheels up the road, the sun on its high sweet mound; the haycocks in the fields the brown color of home and family, the color of man and his horse.

Salem, Ohio.

The gasoline-propelled cars speed across the rivers named after the forgotten Indians.

The Huron.

The Maumee.

To the west, Toledo's skyscrapers seem immense on the flat land.

Miles of freight trains, freight after freight spelling out in white letters: PERE MARQUETTE PERE MARQUETTE PERE MARQUETTE.

Flatness.

Flatness.

The smokestacks of the Detroit Steel Corporation.

Detroit. . .

It is dark now, the never-to-be-seen-again darkness that always covers a strange city for the first time.

The Tin Medicine Men

DETROIT

"Henry Ford drove a truck, worked in shipyards, machine plants and finally landed a job for $25 a week as an engineer at the Edison plant. He was 40 years of age before he began his great climb, but the years that had gone on before were not wasted. He was disciplining himself for the things that Destiny held for him 'around the corner.'"

From the DETROIT FREE PRESS.

THE CITY DRIVES OUT TO ITS PARKS on the hot July nights; to Belle Isle in the Detroit River, past the United States Rubber Company's stench. Once on the Belle Isle bridge, a cool breeze as if hired to function here, slips inside the lowered car windows.

On Belle Isle, the thousands spread their blankets on the grass near the river's edge. Opposite, the black shore of Canada is dotted with the gleams of the evenly spaced highway lights. On the blacker river, freighters move in black silence.

Three young couples explode the night with their horseplay.

"We'll wrap her up!" One of the boys grabs a blanket and begins to fold it and himself around the nearest girl. All their voices rise in squeal and shout. The boy with the blanket trips the girl up. She falls. He flops down on top of her.

"Let her up!" a second girl yells, pulling the blanket free.

Families sit together quietly, like well-ordered tribes, drinking lemonade out of Dixie cups. Fishermen toss their handlines out into the river. And on the low Canadian shore, four huge electric letters name the owner of the plant camouflaged by night: FORD.

I walk over to the nearest fisherman, a tall Negro with a long narrow head. His line is attached to a bell signal. He stands patiently, waiting for a fish to strike, for the bell to tinkle. The waves of a freighter's passing lap up close to our feet.

"What're you fishing for?"

The fisherman laughs, his white teeth shining. "I been fishing three weeks for them sheepheads." He flashes his electric light into a pail near the bell signal. The bottom is covered with two-inch crayfish. He puts the light back in his pocket, pulls in his line. He examines the lead sinker and the two hooks with their impaled crayfish bait. He straightens up, seizes the line four feet above the sinker, circles it around and around his head like a lasso, lets go. The line writhes up and off the ground. The sinker splashes. He fixes the end of the line to the bell signal and then folds both arms across his chest, kingly in the night.

"Understand me," he says. "For three weeks I been trying to get a sheephead. The sheephead's coarse. Back home. . . I come from Kentucky. I used to catch fish. We had goggle-eye bass, green bass and big mouth bass down there. My old grandma, she used to fish in the ponds down there. She put assifinity on her hook. The fish smell it and bite."

"Why did you leave Kentucky?"

"The number business." He laughs, quickly turns his head to look at me. "My cousin was in the number business up here in Detroit. He come down there with five hundred dollars at a time. And that's money down South! I was getting eighteen a week working in a garage. I had three kids, you understand, and that eighteen was as far as a colored man could get down South. I always had guts so I thought if my cousin could make that much money up in Detroit so could I. I been up here twelve years." He takes out a pack of cigarettes, lights one for himself. "Want one?"

"Thanks."

"I started up here with twelve a week, writing numbers, getting business. Understand me? If you write ten dollars worth of business a day, you get twenty-five per cent for your share. That's two and a half dollars a day. That's money for colored. Thousands of colored are writing."

"Thousands?"

"Yes, thousands," he declares. "It ain't hard to write ten dollars business. How many places can a colored man get two-fifty a day? Besides, if a number hits, you get ten per cent of the hit. The Mayor and the Governor and all them big shots, they know all about it. Let me be frank. The colored people would be starving if not for numbers. Numbers is a straight racket here in Detroit. A Jew and a couple others runs it, but Joe Louis's manager, Roxbury, he's supposed to be in it. He ain't really in it. But people hear his name and they know they'll get paid off if they win because they think he's in it. Anyway, it's understood that Negroes have jobs in the racket." On his lips the word *racket* sounds as ordinary as if he'd said 'business.' "Maybe it's wrong, but the Government don't care as long they get their income tax. That's all they want. They don't care how much you pay out for overhead," he complains like any other business man. "We have to pay social security and unemployment insurance. Have to pay the collectors good, too, or they'll steal. There's the overhead. It's a big expense and you have to have money to take care of the days when you're hit. That's two, three times a month. We pay out five dollars for a penny on every number that hits. What we need is simple numbers. That's what most people play, simple numbers like 123 or 456. Some box it by playing 123 six ways. Understand? We make money because most people play simple numbers. Some of the writers in the number business, they show off, go to cabaret show. You know what I mean. Not for me. I don't waste my money. I want to be independent."

He stoops to finger his line. "They never going to bite on my crawfish . . . I'd like to be Chief of Police. That'd be fine," he says, laughing. "I wouldn't be the Sergeant. The Sergeant can harm you, but he can't do you no good. To make real money you got to be on top. I make forty, fifty a week. I can write you a number," he boasts with a good salesman's pride. "If I come around tomorrow and tell you there's three hundred and sixty-five days in a year and if you play a penny a day . . . You can't lose, can you? You got to win sometime? Ain't I right?"

"Sounds right."

He smiles, satisfied. "Forty a week. That's money for colored. You understand. Colored can't get job all over. I'm a good mixer and they took me in!" He stretches his long arms. "You can sell anything to people in this town. It's just a big country town full of dumb people. They all come here to Cadillac, to Ford to get work. They don't give the Negro much. They get the heavy work and that's all when they get it. They come from the South, from all over to get work, the white and the colored. When auto's slack, the workers play heavy. When they're working they don't play. But things always gonna be a little slack for everybody. So everybody play numbers." He laughs. "You win five dollars for a penny!" He laughs louder, contemptuous of the number players. "Say, do they dream here, the colored and the white, too. They eat a big meal so they can dream at night. They wake up in the morning and look in the Gypsy Dream Book or the Three Star Dream Book and play the number 'longside the dream. Most any dream you can dream's in the book with the number. You come 'round and you hear them say: 'Did I dream! So here's a dollar on the number.' And it gets around. Everybody hears so-and-so's playing big and so they want some of that number themself. Dream, dream all the time. Just a big country town, but what do I care."

On the hot Sunday mornings, the picnickers tumble out of their parked cars, mothers with babies, fathers with bags of lunch, little boys with balls.

The green lawns of Palmer Park are homestaked for the afternoon, the concrete wading pool taken over by little kids, big kids, pale kids, sunburned kids, laughing kids, crying kids.

Beyond the pool, *The Pioneer Women* are holding an all-day picnic in the shade of two willow trees. Sunlight dapples through the leaves onto the red and white checkered cloths of the long tables loaded with piled-up paper dishes of hot baked fish, cold *gefillte* fish, pickled silvery herring, hamburgers, boiled potatoes, radishes, pumpernickel. Fathers, mothers, children sit on benches as long as the tables and eat. Two picnic committee members, a gray-haired woman with high cheekbones, and a rouged woman with gold teeth, race from the kitchen with more paper dishes of food. The kitchen is a big iron stove crowded with pots and kettles and tended by a Negro boy hired by the picnic committee. He tosses charcoal into the stove, his sweating face absolutely immobile as if he cannot understand the clear midwestern American of the younger generation or the juicy Yiddish of the older people.

"Why are you called *The Pioneer Women?*" I ask the gray-haired picnic committee member.

"We help the *Chalutzim*, the pioneers, in Palestine. This is for a picnic for the orphans there. Excuse me." She rushes to the table with a plate of cold slaw.

A dark little girl of twelve exclaims, "Gee, just what I want."

Next to her, a stout man drinks tea out of a glass, pushing his lower lip forward as a support for the rim. He looks at the cold slaw. "No room," he mutters. His tea shines golden yellow in his glass. The samovars gleam like miniature temples.

Those who have eaten lounge on the grass. I sit down near a youngish matron with brown hair parted in the middle. Her cheeks are round and full. There is no make-up on her face. She gossips with dignity. "That woman you talked to before has two daughters. One is married and lives in Oklahoma. Her husband has an accessory store. What has he got to do all day? She is busy in the Jewish societies. She got the milk. She got the cream. They got butter. They made six hundred *blintzes*. She has two boys. One boy goes to school. One boy loafs around. What has she got to do all day? She has six rooms and once a week takes in a girl. She does a lot of work for charity. But what has she got to do? Last year in March I had an operation. Five years ago I had an operation. For two weeks I couldn't turn around. I come home in bed for six weeks and then I must work. Always some must work. She comes from Poland. We got *Litvakas* here, too." She sighs. "I remember a fat priest used to walk by where I live in the old country in Lithuania. He weighed four hundred pounds. I don't believe it myself, but you do get older."

At one of the tables, a little bald man declaims furiously. "In Palestine, even the plumbers are poets!"

"Also a *Mensch*." The matron nods at the little man. "What have the Jews in Palestine? They make believe they have a country, but London's boss. He had a brother, he had to take his life." She sniffs at the smell of boiling coffee. "Lately, I drink tea. I can't have no coffee. I have an acid stomach. Look, there's my man. He's in the middle like a cockroach. He likes everybody. Everybody likes him." She points to a tall thin man in a white linen cap talking at one of the tables. "I'm a good listener since I was a girl. I'll listen to him again if I hear it a hundred times. My man used to be a laundry driver. He wanted to see a friend, he say: 'Come in the wagon. The dishes can wait.' Yes, you don't lose nothing. Dishes are dishes. . . He take me to the barber, a friend of his, and they talk. That's the way the Jewish people are. They like to talk. They like to know. The poorest devils, they'll go in a torn dress and shoes and let the children go to school. As long as the head is good, they let the children go. A boy I know, a nice boy, a smart boy, a *Goy* . . . his mother has a big store. Her boy went for a lawyer, but he couldn't get anything. Now he's away. I say to her: 'Send him some money.' 'I should say not!' she says: 'He had it good here. Now he's on his own.' " She shakes her head in pity. "What difference should that make when a child needs help?"

The volunteer cooks at the kitchen are taking chocolate cakes out of cardboard boxes. A big-beamed woman wipes and dries tea glasses.

"That one there—" The matron nods at the glass wiper. "Her husband, he goes to a movie and likes to see it twice. She likes to go to meetings. They are two different people. She is a leader. He is a follower. Only a few are the leaders, the runners. . . That one there, that's the one whose husband take his life. Before they happen to have a few thousand dollars and they got broke. He left a few notes: 'No one should cry after him.' He was in the linen business. They are all little business people. Grocers, butchers, hardware stores. Some make a nice living and some get along."

Somebody has set up a portable radio on the table. Ten or twelve men and boys are listening to the baseball broadcast.

The matron smiles, her calm brown eyes almost like a girl's. "Since they got Hank Greenberg with the Tigers even the old Jews listen to baseball like a disease. Is Hank Greenberg *der Messiach* to save the Jews? Baseball players are baseball players. When *der Messiach* comes he won't be Hank Greenberg."

Detroiters with a few dollars to burn drive beyond the city's limits on the hot Sunday afternoons, parking at the cube steak and chicken inns that line Woodward Avenue, Detroit's most important traffic artery.

Road signs compete for the motorists:

COME OUT TO DANCE AND EAT CHICKEN.
THE BLOOD OF JESUS CHRIST CLEANSES US FROM ALL SIN.
ZOO.

At Royal Park, the advertisement shows a huge snake roped around a wooden post, its evil head and tongue, a sign-post darting in the zoo's direction.

Many motorists stop at Royal Park. But the Shrine of the Little Flower attracts more folk than the zoo. Husbands and wives stare up at the world's largest crucifix on the Shrine's grounds. Above the head of the stone Christ, the chiselled letters are in Hebrew. Below the stone feet, nailed onto stone, the letters are in English:

FATHER FORGIVE THEM FOR
THEY KNOW NOT WHAT THEY DO.

The Shrine is crowded with the curious, the religious. Father Coughlin himself is invisible, his corporal body closeted in a sound-proof room as he broadcasts his Sunday message ". . . endeavoring to set up a form of Government contrary to our own. . ."

Bull's-eye of gleaming white, the altar is in the center of the octagon-shaped Shrine. It is like a stage in a modernistic theater that can be seen from all angles.

"Let me warn you in the most solemn manner . . ." The Voice deepens.

The unseen Father magnetizes the middle-class America in the seats surrounding the altar. A white-haired man's head lifts up as if searching for the flesh behind The Voice.

"In the Constitution of the United States nothing is said that is favorable to the existence of political parties. . ."

Daylight filters through the upper tier of violet-stained windows. The hanging lamps hold yellow light.

"So-called partyism or democracy. . ."

The Shrine has been constructed for both the ear-minded and the eye-minded, for the man who likes his radio and the woman who likes her picture magazine. Inset into the octagon walls are a series of altars, pictures in bright color and pretty stone. The click click of high heels, the shuffling scrape of men's shoes add a backstage sound effect to The Voice's oratory.

". . . that if there are disorders in the country, and if the disorders. . ." The Voice sinks as if lost behind mountains. "George Washington says the time will come when partyism will degenerate into dictatorship. . . Washington had an answer for that." The Voice rises, solemn, ecclesiastical, as if canonizing George Washington, the Protestant and Free Mason, as if enrolling the First President into a Society of which The Voice is president.

In the audience, an aging man, with gray hairs growing on his ear lobes, nods. A woman scowls. Two young boys wear respectful Sunday School faces. And unhearing, the gapers do the circuit of altars. They see a statue of the Virgin Mary, classical and Grecian as Minerva.

"It's pretty, isn't it?" one woman remarks to another in an awed museum voice.

They see the marble statue of St. Sebastian, heroic, unconquerable, marble shafts jutting out of his powerful gladiator's torso. St. Sebastian stands between two panels full of movie action, between runners and horse-men speeding on errands. In one panel, a football player in jersey and moleskins kneels in prayer; in the second a student: MARTYR ATHLETE, SOLDIER PRAY FOR US. A second motto reads: FOR GOD AND COUNTRY.

They see a workingman Christ between two icon-like red and blue panels, a Christ with tools. Above the panel lettered WORKER, a slogan like a newspaper headline proclaims: CAPITAL CANNOT DO WITHOUT LABOR. The panel is divided into four parts, one above the other like the storys in a house:

AGRICULTURE
TRADE
FINANCE
MINING

Yellow grain sifts down from AGRICULTURE through TRADE, through FINANCE to MINING where the grain becomes gold.

The second panel links:

SERVICE
COMMERCE
MECHANICS
INDUSTRY

It is lettered KING and headlined: LABOR CANNOT DO WITHOUT CAPITAL.

CAPITAL CANNOT DO WITHOUT LABOR.

LABOR CANNOT DO WITHOUT CAPITAL.

"That's good common sense," somebody whispers.

"That C.I.O. ought to get wise."

A small tired boy nags at his mother. "What do they do in there?"

"Sh! Sh! That's an altar."

"What do they do in there?"

"They pray. It's their religion. The Catholic religion."

The contrast between see-ers and the listeners is the contrast of a dream. Holding the dream together is The Voice, a medicine man's voice black-magicking church into Shrine, Shrine into museum, museum into movie lobby, movie lobby into newspaper, newspaper into political arena, political arena into street corners covered with blood.

"God bless you." The Voice concludes. The organ plays sweetly.

People wait in line to sign their names in the registry. Catholics drop coins in the *Offering* boxes and light the holy candles in the red glasses. Souvenir books are for sale at one dollar; pamphlets, "Helps To Purity," "Why Not a Mixed Marriage," at lesser prices. Another room seems modeled after Detroit's Hudson's Department Store. Relics and postals are turned over for cash by smiling efficient salesgirls. Momentarily hypnotized, two elderly ladies stand in front of the picture of St. Veronica's Handkerchief with its Christ's head and printed advice: If You Watch The Eyes Closely They Will Suddenly Open.

SUDDENLY the Shrine's interior and all within it become The Voice's unseen face.

Outside, a youth peddles *Social Justice*. The walls of the Shrine hold stones named after the States.

MAINE
MONTANA
TEXAS
WISCONSIN

Across the street from the Shrine of The Little Flower, the Shrine Inn sells refreshments to the thirsty. The license plates on the parked cars, Massachusetts, New York, Ohio, Michigan, California, match the forty-eight States masoned into the Shrine's walls.

The Shrine's roster of the nation, each State held fast, forever and unchanging SUDDENLY becomes the dream behind the Radio Priest's voice.

> "There are more evangelists here than almost any other city. Right now we got the Cowboy Evangelist, the Indian Evangelist, he's out in a big tent, and the Great Youth Evangelist from Houston, Texas, and dozens of others. I don't know why they all come to Detroit but they do. Governor Dickinson—You've heard of his private pipe line to God? He doesn't do anything without praying to God first. When God tells him what to do, he does it. That's what he said at a prayer meeting at Belle Isle."
>
> *Point of information offered by a gasoline station attendant.*

Wide Woodward Avenue, Detroit's chief traffic spine, is an ACCRETION of many main streets, a grabbag of enterprises. Our Lady of the Rosary Church stands next door to P. L. GRISSOM AUTHORIZED CHEVROLET DEALER. Stromburg Carburetors, the Toodle House, and the Detroit Institute of Arts are all neighbors. The Arcadia Book Shop and the Trianon Dance Hall share the same building. National Cash Register, housed in a modern structure, is next door to an old red-gabled mansion now a furnished rooming house: SLEEPING $2 AND $3. Churches, billboards, used car lots, hotels, archery ranges, drug stores, a sidewalk recruiting office: WEST POINT OF THE AIR, follow one another as if on a conveyor belt.

Up in the Hoffman Building, the pale secretary of the

Civil Liberties Union introduces State Senator Stanley Nowak to me. The State Senator has dark brown hair, blue eyes. Freckles dot his almost medieval face, a face like the faces in an old tapestry. "I know the Italian, the Irish, the Lithuanian groups besides my own group," he says. "The Poles are ninety-five per cent Catholic. This is what I see among the Catholics, the largest proportion of people here. When Coughlin came out first there was quite a pro-Coughlin feeling. Among the Poles that was strengthened by a Polish priest, Father Justin of Buffalo; also the local bishop here, Bishop Woznicki, who isn't exactly a Coughlinite but is pretty reactionary and pretty close to a Coughlinite. In my own district Coughlin sent out letters urging people to vote against me. I'm on the West Side, the sixteenth Congressional District." His red lower lip accentuates the depth of his smile. "I ran for the Democratic ticket and they underestimated me in the primary but when I won the nomination, the Hungarian clergyman opposed me. Coughlin sent out letters against me and then the Ford Motor Company sent out a picture of me, an ugly picture and a leaflet. The leaflet was distributed by the Service Department of the Ford Company. No signature was on it. We caught some of the young boys distributing it, and they pointed out private cars with Ford Service men in them, whom we recognized. In my district, two wards, the Eighteenth and the Twentieth, are in Detroit. The rest of the district are the towns of Ecorse, River Rouge, Wyanndotte, and the City of Dearborn. Altogether, about 100,000 votes. I received 44,000 to their 34,000. The Ford leaflet was a boomerang. It was so vicious: I was a red, an alien and anti-religious despite my entire Catholic background."

"I heard this story the other day. Ford was driving out in the country and came to a farm. They didn't know who he was. He sat down in the grass and began to talk of one thing and another. The farm woman told him about her sick son. Ford didn't say anything and drove away. But later a car came to the farm and they took that boy to his hospital in Dearborn."
Ford story.

"A school teacher has the right to be interested in Ford," Mr. School Teacher says hesitantly as we walk up Woodward Avenue. His head moves sideways as if a machine inside of him limits all his movements. "Out in Dearborn, the place is divided into three School districts, and I think the parts of two others. Ford supports Fordson and part of another district. There seems to be that overwhelming lord here!" He doesn't speak with a full voice, his words compressed. He doesn't gesture. "Has the city a right to use public funds to celebrate the birthday of Ford? I think the majority would say yes. But here we talk of spending city money illegally! The city gave him a gift, a representation of the *Free Press*, the front page in bronze. . . Everything circulates around the auto industry. Everything is done to make purchasing autos possible in Detroit. You take the parking situation. There is no attempt whatsoever to enforce one hour parking. They only enforce it in spots of special danger. That's not a drop in the bucket. And yet I think there is a lot of independence." His brow furrows. He half grins as if to say: I am a teacher. I walk on a tight-rope. "And yet this materialism. . . How can I explain it? The folks come from all over to get what they can and get out. And so many of the folk come from rural areas. We are sort of gullible, too, as well as this materialism. Consider the sale of homes out here. The method is to build on F.H.A. approved lots and then you look around to buy what you want. The folks do that rather than go to an architect. Last night I went around with a builder. He showed me all kinds of faults. Things are slapped together. This has been a real estate man's town. The city is in debt as far as it can go. A large amount of it was spent to put in sewers and sidewalks in the northwest part of town. Out on Seven Mile Road, big stretches are uninhabited. The sewers are all in where there isn't a single soul."

We walk another block.

"It's no further from the center of town to Highland Park where Ford used to be than it is to Dearborn and his new plant. Detroit has voted for incorporation but Dearborn never has and never will. Incorporation requires a majority vote of both areas." He clears his throat. "This materialism. . . River Rouge Park is on the outskirts of the city; there's Belle Isle, and Palmer Park out in the wilderness, and so on. The point I make is that the parks are too far away from where the people live. You can't get anywhere without an auto. There's the state-wide tax on food. On voting, involving direct expenditure of money, only the property owners who have property assessed for taxation can vote. That's undemocratic. And yet the big utility here, the Detroit Edison Company, is not part of any holding company. Its rates are no higher than other comparable utilities. They'll take out burned-out fuses without cost. They would rather do it themselves than you. The Hudson Department Store is the biggest in the world or next to it. But the prices are not high and they have immense good will because they have been so careful to make errors right. There *is* independence here," he reassures himself.

We walk another block. "Perhaps . . . I think . . . it's advisable that you don't use my name, I think."

In the hot still afternoon I drive out of Detroit. Near the city limits, a small-time circus has raised its tents. Beyond Dearborn, the flat land is ploughed into immense farms. A roadside produce stand looks as if it were designed by the W.P.A., the entrance flanked by two photographic murals. In the first mural, a larger than life-size boy drives a tractor. In the second, a boy works with a hoe.

I brake to a stop between acres of soy beans. A man in blue overalls trudges up the highway. "Who owns this land?" I ask him.

"Ford."

A mile or so further I come to a road sign: *Worship the Lord in the Beauty of Holiness.*
at Henry Ford School
Every Sunday 10:15 a.m.

In the distance, beyond FORD THRIFT GARDENS No. 9, beyond the corn and the cabbage, the ten smokestacks of the River Rouge open-hearth furnaces neatly divide the sky. Three young boys cross the highway from FORD THRIFT GARDENS No. 9 on their way home.

"Hello fellows," I call, getting out of my car.

They smile shyly, leaning on their hoes. The youngest is

ten, the oldest eleven or twelve. They wear no stockings, their ankles smudged the color of the earth. Blond, blue-eyed, they look like three Huck Finns.

"Are you fellows farmers?"

No answer.

"Do you grow those soy beans I passed?"

The boy in the center, the smallest of the three, answers. "No. That's Ford's."

"But you're farmers anyway?"

The boy on the right, the one with the most freckles, suddenly exclaims: "We're not farmers! We're gardeners."

Again, a smiling silence as if their mothers have warned them to hold their tongues with outsiders. They lean on their hoes, the sun on their cautious burned faces. They have also learned patience.

Tallest in the sky are the smokestacks. The three gardeners belong to their landscape.

"Did you ever see Ford?"

"I have." The smallest boy smiles. His eyes are a darker blue than those of his friends. "He wears a straw hat and gives us bushels of apples."

"What does he do with the soy beans? Are they good eating?"

All three smile with the half-scornful pity of very young boys who know some one fact better than a grown-up.

"He makes oil from soy beans," Freckles explains. "They make machinery from soy beans."

"Machinery?"

Freckles shrugs his shoulders. "Don't ask me how but they make machinery from soy beans."

I turn to the boy who hasn't opened his mouth once. "How long have you been gardening?"

"Three hours this morning."

"What do you get?"

The silent boy doesn't reply. Freckles does. "We got three cabbages and a bushel of beans."

"Do you get paid?"

"No," the smallest boy says. "And sometimes we garden all day like the time we planted the garden."

After this spurt of talk, all three are silent, smiling up at me as if to say: What next?

"Do your fathers work for Ford?"

Freckles nods.

"I'll bet you'll be a farmer when you grow up?" I say to him.

He laughs in a high shrill alto. "Not me! I'm going to work for Ford. My brother goes to Trade School."

"What about you two fellows?"

They smile. Somehow all three seem to be shyer than ever as if the warning to hold their tongues has become more urgent.

From the ten smokestacks, sheathed in silvery aluminum, black smoke and yellow smoke pour from the stack mouths, writing the name of power across the sky.

> "The River Rouge plant employs more than 80,000 men. It operates blast furnaces, locomotive repair shops, the largest foundry and largest industrial steam generating plant in the world, motor assembly plant, coke ovens, open-hearth furnaces, steel plant and rolling mill, paper mill, laboratories and a cement plant. There are 14 miles of roadways, 92 miles of railroad tracks. The docks are 1 and 1/3 miles and can accommodate ocean going vessels." Facts.

"LABOR CANNOT DO WITHOUT CAPITAL."
From the altar inscription in the Shrine of the Little Flower

The young man at the information desk in the Ford Rotunda calls out in a voice as smooth as a politician's: "All visitors to the plant will go outside to the busses." His manner is that of a junior diplomat.

Girls gaze admiringly at him and trail out of the air-cooled Rotunda.

Outside, the sun is hot as an open hearth.

The busses fill with sweating people, start off. "You are now entering Ford property," says the guide.

Inside gate 10, thousands of Ford employees' cars are parked, thousands, thousands.

The busses roll on. "The Canal Slip," the guide explains in a voice like an orator's, "empties into the Detroit River and so on into the Great Lakes."

The busses pass by the docked ore freighters.

"Coke ovens. . ." says the guide.

"Locomotives. . ." says the guide.

"Largest private powerhouse in the world." The guide

glances out casually at one giant component part after another of the River Rouge plant, describing them as if they were a series of children's toys.

The busses stop. "You will follow me and stay in a body," the guide says. "We will go through the Foundry Building. No smoking and no taking of pictures is allowed. There are 134. . ." He raises his voice "134 miles of conveyor belt and. . ."

Noise hammers his voice down. NOISE! The Foundry Building is full of NOISE. And men. The Foundry Building holds a strange world of men who somehow seem to be behind glass like fish in an aquarium.

Two abreast, we follow our guide down the narrow iron gangway fifteen feet above the vast tank of men below. Men in caps. Men with handkerchiefs knotted about their heads. Men in greasy pants. Sweating men. Working men. Yellow sparks, machines, endless machines. The machines and machine noise, and men are one . . . like fish and water.

I stare down into the below and watch the auto workers repeat themselves at the machines, repeating, repeating, repeating. One worker steals a look up at me.

I look at him. He has brown eyes.

He looks away.

I look at him. He has brown hair.

He looks up again.

I look at him. He has a thin mouth. He has a human face underneath his speed-up face.

The human face changes back into the speed-up face as he hooks a chain into an auto block, a rough sculpture of the motor-to-be. The chain lifts the block onto a conveyor belt. He uses a screwdriver once. He uses a screwdriver twice. Once—twice. Once—twice. Once—twice. The conveyor moves the block away from him. He hooks the chain into the next block. Lifts. Screwdriver, once. Screwdriver, twice. Once—twice. Moving belt moves moves moves in NOISE moves moves moves in men moves moves moves before men's eyes transformed into spots of seeing into fish eyes into spots into seeing into seeing into seeing. Seeing moving seeing moving. . . On the shirt front of every auto worker a badge gleams like an empty eye.

The next department is a square island bounded north, south, east, west by moving belts flowing like water. On the island, the auto workers try to turn their hands into running brooks. A man in a torn cap shakes sweat out of his eyes, does something quick with his tool, but not quick enough he pursues the moving moving belt flowing the block away. The belt brings up the next block. The next. The next next next. Another worker steps across the belt, a can of lubricating oil in his fist. He pours the green-yellow oil into a machine not on a conveyor. The machine stands still, fixed, motionless. The machine does not move. He stands in one place, calm, almost serene like a man who has awakened from a nightmare. He stands still, no conveyor in front of him, the conveyors all around him, the different faces of middle-aged men, young men, Negroes, whites, all speed-upped into one Ford worker's face with one pair of eyes.

Always eyes. Eyes glance up from the below. Eyes stare. Eyes cheat the moving belts. Or half cheat the belts, eyes looking up and also looking down as hands flick to their tasks as if hands had eyes, too.

Separated from the conveyors and the eyes by a partition wall, we follow our guide into a row of glassed-off offices. Behind glass, unhurried men study blue prints.

"The training school," says the guide.

No need to shout here. Numbered young boys of eighteen and twenty dressed in white aprons work in long rooms. They stand at their desks, tools in their hands, working contentedly.

"The Motor Building . . ." says the guide.

Here, too, the conveyors surround islands of men and machines, eyes and functions. A worker leaves the line on his way to the toilet. He walks rapidly, a lump of tobacco in his cheek. The tobacco juice spit marks on the floor are like a sign reading: SMOKING PROHIBITED. Here, too, noise, a clanging, clattering, screeching roar. There is no sign: TALKING AMONG WORKERS PROHIBITED but nobody talks. Overhead, conveyors carry parts and boxes of screws to the reaching hands. Eyes move. On the line, a big bald man follows a motor, wooden hammer in hand. Swiftly he taps down a part into the motor as if it were a nail. Big belly pulled in by a belt, he leans his body sideward, hammer raised over the motor. He looks about to fall as he tries to stretch his six feet into seven feet, eight feet. . . The motor moves beyond his longest reach.

His whole body shifts as he advances another stride. In controlled frenzy he taps, taps, taps with his wooden hammer. Again the motor moves beyond his reach. He tails after it like a little boy after a leader. At the same time, another worker reaches into the motor with the lightning fingers of a cardsharp, adjusts coiled spring one, coiled spring two. A bead of sweat hangs from the end of his nose. No time to brush it off. Coiled spring one, coiled spring two. Tap, tap, tap. Coiled springs, one, two, tap, tap, tap. Poles, Negroes, Italians, Texans, Missourians, Canadians, change into taps, into coiled springs, accessories to accessories.

The stench of gas fumes fills the air. In a row on the floor, completely assembled motors, chassis-less, wheel-less, are being run by machines.

A worker dips parts bright as silver flutes into a tank of cream-colored liquid. Dip, dip, dip. He reached for another flute.

"What are those parts?" I ask.

He hesitates. TALKING PROHIBITED. There is no sign but his eyes are the eyes of warning. He looks around him, to right, to left. "Shifting shafts." He looks behind him. "Boy, it's hot here."

Like the presto of a magician, the assembly lines shape all processes into the soon-to-be automobiles. Three conveyor belts move forward. On the main belt, the body frames advance. From the overhead shelf, gleaming enameled upper bodies are being lowered down into the frames to fit exactly like coins that have been cut into halves. On the two narrow belts that parallel and flank the main belt, two auto workers put the headlights on. The motors are hoisted down into the cars; the iron hearts are in. Steadily, the three belts move forward. A blond youngster sticks a gas hose into the advancing empty tanks. He fills up the brown tank, the black tank, the green tank. The wiring is adjusted. Each pair of headlights glares identical electric beams. Two. Two. Two. Two. One. . . The left headlight on the green car isn't working. The three belts move forward, forward. A worker unscrews the defective headlight's glass front. A second worker takes out the bulb, puts in another bulb. The defective headlight glares yellow. Two, Two. Two. Two. Two. Mechanics start up the brand-new cars. Under their own power they drive off the end of the conveyor into the adjoining garage. Each car bear's the owner's name: FORD. FORD. FORD. FORD. FORD.

> "Labor union organizations are the worst things that ever struck the earth, because they take away a man's independence. Financiers are behind the unions and their object is to kill competition so as to reduce the income of workers, and eventually bring on war."
>
> *From the sayings of Henry Ford.*

"I started out in 1922. I came here from Kentucky," Roy Davis says. He is a spare man with blue eyes under hooded lids. His nose has been broken in some accident. "I worked for the American Railway Express and then went to the Ford Motor Company. I was about twenty-seven. I worked steady until the depression came. When the layoff come, I was laid off. I was on the motor assembly line testing valve leaks. I worked steady for the last three years. Every day that job run I was on the job." Slowly, he assembles his words. "In 1937 I was subpoenaed by the Labor Board and I went down to testify. After I went back, they found fault with my work. Up to this time, they never found fault with my work. The Super come and stop right behind me and watch me work. After I would test the valves for leaks on the motor, I would okay the motor. The Super wouldn't say anything. But he'd take me down the line to make me recheck the motor, to find one with a leak. I watched the job so close he couldn't get anything on me. He went away after two days. Then, the foreman under him went down the line and rubbed the marks off the motors I had marked to be repaired." He pauses. "They send the motors down to block test and if they find any leaks. . . Too bad for us! I had never been called down on the block test in the three years I was in that department. Then, a fellow come and told me: 'Watch yourself, Roy. They're rubbing your marks off.' "

Nervously, he rubs his broken nose. "They took me off the job. There were leakers in the block test," he says without irony, without emphasis. "They put me on another job and I knew I'd be fired. I put the union button on and wore it inside the plant."

He smiles to himself. "They let me wear the union button four days and then they laid me off. 'Your job is open,' they said: 'We'll call you back.' That time Ford was scared to death on account of the Labor Board hearings." He laughs. "The fellows wouldn't talk to me when I wore the button. They thought I was a stool pigeon. Al Smith, the Building Superintendent, come down and looked at me for fifteen minutes and then walked away as far as he could go. I'd sit down at lunch time with the fellows and they'd get up and walk away. Even fellers I'd worked with all these years stayed away from me. Going in to work the two Service Men at the door, one Service Man looked at the other one!" He pushes out his jaw, imitating their amazement. "My foreman used to give me a dime to buy chew terbacker to keep in my pocket. He'd pass by, take it out of my pocket and take a chew. But after I testified down to the Labor Board, he wouldn't take another chew. He didn't like union terbacker."

He stops speaking for a second. "After January 17th, 1938, I went out to the River Rouge plant to pass out application cards for the U.A.W. I got there about seven in the morning. . ." He halts. "When the men was laid off December 23rd, they were told to return January 17th. Ford issued passes to the men coming back to work. They couldn't get in on the badge alone. . . Me and another feller started walking from Gate 4 to Gate 2 on Miller Road. In the meanwhile, we met a feller in my department who was trying to get back to work. A car pulled out from Gate 4. This feller walking with us was six to eight feet behind us. By seeing him walking with us, they suspected him too. They stop their car real quick and reached out and grabbed this man by the arm. I stopped and turned around to see what they were going to do. They walked around the rear of the car with him. 'Were you passing out membership cards for the union?' they ask him. He said: 'No, I'm not. I'm trying to get back to work.' They told him. 'Get the hell out quick!' They were good huskies those Service Men. . . They called to us: 'We want you!' I didn't go back.

I walked on. This feller who was walking with me said: 'I'll ask the police for protection.' There were several Dearborn police on Miller Road. I told him: 'They're all working together.' But he walked up to the Dearborn policemen and at the same time the Service Men came up. They started in to question him the same as they'd questioned the first feller. I stood there, expecting they'd question me. Nobody said anything to me so I started to walk away. They knocked me cold. I never did know when they hit me. I woke up in the Rouge Hospital. I was hit over the eye. My nose was broken in three places."

He fingers his nose. "It's still crooked. Three teeth were knocked out of my plate. And how they did that I don't know? Unless they knocked the plate out and then put the plate back. My upper lip has four stitches inside. Four outside. I told the doctor: 'That's a hell of a way to treat the man who belongs to the union.' He agreed with me although he said: 'We don't take sides in the medical profession.' After they got through with me, two Dearborn police took me to the Dearborn Police Station. Inspector Slamer, Detective Kretchman and another policeman I didn't know, they each took turns questioning me. After I almost collapsed they rushed me out to the Ford Hospital. There they asked me: 'Do you want to stay in the Henry Ford Hospital?' I said: 'I have no money to pay a hospital bill.' They took my watch, the plate out of my mouth and my billfold. I had seventy-nine cents in change. They put all that in an envelope, sealed it up and put it into a vault and rushed me up to the X-ray room. They X-rayed me and brought me out. Some photographer showed up from a Detroit newspaper. Then they rushed everybody out of the room in order to keep him out. 'A man has to have air,' they said." He shakes his head without laughter. "The U.A.W. doctor removed me to the Woman's Hospital. But the watch and things, they were holdin' at Ford. Then they sent me a bill for $33.60. My wife, she went out to the Ford Hospital to get the watch and plate back. They told her, she couldn't get it back until I paid my hospital bill. The U.A.W. attorney called the hospital up: 'If you don't release the watch and plate, I'll start suit against the Ford Hospital,' he told them. They notified him they'd release the watch and plate. My wife went out there and they wanted her to sign a paper. She wouldn't. They called three or four nurses for witness and gave her the watch and plate. Then I got a second bill for $33.60." He opens his mouth wide.

I look at the three places where the false teeth were smashed out of their plate by Ford's Service Men.

> "Industry Is Mind Using Matter to Make Man's Life
> More Free."
> *From the sayings of Henry Ford.*

> "United States of America
>   *In the matter of Ford Motor Company*
>   *and*
>   *International Union U.A.W.A.*
>   *before the National Labor Relations Board*
>   Order
> 1. Cease and desist from:
>   Threatening, assaulting, beating, or in any other manner
>   interfering with, restraining, or intimidating, directly or in-
>   directly, members of International Union, United Automobile
>   Workers of America.
> 2. Take the following affirmative action, which the Board finds
>   will effectuate the policies of the Act:
>   (a) Offer to George Onnella, Richard Weyhing, Clarence
>   Fleming, Percy Llewellyn . . . immediate and full rein-
>   statement to their former positions . . ."
> *From the* National Labor Board *Findings.*

"I come to Detroit in 1932 right in the midst of the depression." Percy Llewellyn clasps his square hands behind his head. A big man, he fills up the chair in the little room. "I was out of work." His voice rings out, a singing tenor voice. "During the coal strike in 1927, 1928, 1929, lots of the coal miners got jobs with Ford. So I came here to Detroit. I left my family home in Pennsylvania. I was a miner back home. My folks were miners on both sides of the family. . . During the first two or three days I was here, it was before a school board election, I was invited to a blind pig election party. There I was introduced to various politicians and one in particular asked me if I wanted to work. 'Where?' I asked. 'Ford,' he said. I thought it very peculiar, me being a new man in the city and thousands unemployed, that I could get a job. He told me to see him at the City Hall at Dearborn. He never gave me no name. I never run across the guy since then. I hung around the City Hall at Dearborn for two, three days trying to see him. While there I heard of men going to work through the Mayor, Clyde Ford, a cousin of Henry's. I scouted around to find out how you could get in there. I found you had to contact one by the name of Teddy Contori, and that he could fix me up with a job. I contacted this man. He gave me a calling card to the secretary of the Mayor. After making notations on the card, he told me to be in the City Garage at 9 a.m., the morning of June 20th, and to stay in the garage until he came. Contori was secretary to the secretary of the Mayor as far as I could make out."

Llewellyn's blue eyes are so light they gleam cold and chilly. "On the morning of June 20th I came to this garage. There were about twenty or twenty-five other men. About 9.30 a.m. Contori came in and we were loaded into automobiles and taken up to Gate 9 to the employment office. We were all given jobs. That struck me then as very funny, the way you had to get jobs. That the City Hall of Dearborn was the hiring office. And this was happening with the city full of Ford workers and their families who had lived there continually and were either in want or kept by public relief. I didn't think it was possible that such a system existed especially having read so much about the liberalism followed by Henry Ford." He shrugs his heavy shoulders. "I was given a paper badge and a time card, taken by bus to Department 435. An employee was placed with me to teach me to operate. I hadn't worked more than two or three hours when it occurred to me that the employees in and around me acted as though every move that they made was watched. It was quite a change coming from the mining country where although the muscular labor was much heavier compared with the work in Ford's, yet here. . . The men were continually under a severe strain! They were watching for straw bosses, for foremen. On the machine you were worried by the rules set up. If you chewed tobacco and wanted to spit, you watched for a chance. You were fired if caught spitting on the floor. Spit in the air!" He laughs bitterly. "Now a man in a coal mine could load coal all day, but still he comes out a free man. Coming from the coal mines as I did, that struck me. . . The speed-up at Ford's, the heavy strain, the little things like taking a smoke or a chew, the things a workingman wants to do. It was an altogether different world. I used to work with men that enjoyed their work. But regardless of how good a job you wanted to do at Ford, you can't do it because of the speed-up and the strain."

His eyes stare downwards to the right, to the left. "That's how the Ford workers look at something. I worked there until August 1932. I sent for my family. They were here about three weeks and then I had no job. I got by until the first part of 1933 when I inquired as to getting welfare. I made an application and said that I had lived eighteen months in Dearborn. I was granted welfare. Three months later, Leo Schaefer, Justice of Peace, sitting as a one man grand jury, summoned me in. He said that I had defrauded the City of Dearborn for the sum of fifty dollars because I had told them I had lived in the city for longer than I had. Schaefer says: 'Why did you tell this lie?' I answered: 'I'll steal before I'd see my family starve and I'll lie before I steal.' He gave me twenty-four hours to reimburse the city. I insisted on my constitutional rights and heard no more of the matter. But a month or so later I received a letter from the Probation Department of the City of Dearborn calling my attention to the fact that I had not appeared before them, such as is expected of those on probation. I didn't know I was placed on probation, not having been given a trial. I called this to the attention of the probation officer. He informed me that Schaefer had placed me on probation."

"What happened?"

"That was the last of that thing. I was able to place my wife in the Henry Ford Hospital for confinement. I was billed $143. Anywheres else it's $40 or $50. But I don't think I'd have had a job back if I hadn't a bill. . . July 1st, 1933, I was rehired as a seaman on one of their boats. I worked twelve hours a day, seven days a week and got seventy dollars a month. I received thirty-five dollars twice a month, less seven fifty which was checked out for the hospital confinement case. That left me not so much for the wife and family. But still there's an advantage having a hospital bill to get a job back at Ford's." His smile breaks. "They don't give you a Goddamn thing for nothing out there! They gave my wife good care but a man can't afford to pay $14 a day for a hospital. On ship. . . On ship the work was continually laid out for you. Never no time when you caught up with the work. And you weren't allowed to smoke. The first boat I was on, *The Chester*, carried a load of salt but we came back to Cleveland with a load of sugar. That's another one of his side-lines. Salt down. And sugar back. Then we hauled finished cars to Buffalo. All the time they were taking off that seven-fifty every two weeks."

"Did you ever see Ford?"

"I was on the *Henry Ford the 2nd* when Mr. and Mrs. Ford made a trip with us. We were given orders that every time we came out on deck, to have our best clothes on. We were continually changing clothes on that trip. We'd be painting, scraping down in the hold in our oldest clothes. But if we had to come up to the deck we had to change. He sat on the bridge. His wife would read the papers to him. He didn't mix with us but the day he came on, he said: 'Hello, boys.' That's all he said. He struck me as an honest sincere sort of person who might be duped by those under him. He looked like an old farmer, a very modest, a very common sort of man."

Llewellyn frowns, remembering. "I left the boats in the winter of 1933. I was placed on Final Inspection in the Motor Building. I worked continually except for seasonal layoffs until 1937. . . One morning at seven a.m. a foreman I knew came to my work table and said: 'Don't look around. Don't look surprised as to what I've got to tell you. They just had me up in the office. They told me that one of the inspectors is a C.I.O. organizer and to get rid of him. When I asked who this inspector was, I was told it was Llewellyn.' He then told me to watch my step, that he was sure they were going to get me that day. My Superintendent, Norris, did not start work until eight o'clock. This morning as on other mornings he spoke to me when he came in. He had not been to his office yet. However, about fifteen minutes later he came back to me and made accusations that too much scrap was getting into the Motor Assembly Department. Because of being warned, I was very certain nothing would get by me that day. I didn't chew terback or nothing that day. Norris continually walked by and had others watch me. About ten thirty a.m. he called me aside and said: 'I'm going to send you to the Employment Office. If they want to use you, they can put you on another

job. You're doing too much talking here to suit me.' He told
me to get my time card. I did and two Service Men marched
me to the Employment Office. The employment manager,
Miller, said to me: 'How long have you worked here?' I said:
'Five years.' He said: 'What're you doing talking to those men
and keeping them from working?' I said: 'No more than I've
talked in my five years here.' I was then told to come back
the next morning to the Employment Office and there they'd
find another job for me. The next morning when I called
back, Mr. Miller and his assistant, Mr. Brown, asked me why
I quit. I told him I hadn't quit and I didn't know what was
wrong. He told me we were having a little layoff. I then ap-
pealed to the National Labor Board."

"Were you a member of the union?"

"Yes. A week later on May 26th, within two blocks of my
home in Dearborn, I was attacked and beaten by a group of
five Service Men on the public highway for attempting to
pass out leaflets to Ford workers. Two of the Service Men I
identified for the Labor Board hearings but nothing was ever
done. This Ford myth!" he exclaims, leaning forward as if
about to jump out of his chair. "In 1933 Ford promised the
public that nobody in Dearborn'd go hungry. He then set up
a commissary where former Ford workers were withdrawn
from the welfare rolls and placed on Ford Relief. The only
difference between relief offered by Ford and that offered by
the City of Dearborn was that those upon Ford Relief were
charged exorbitant prices which were checked out of their pay
envelopes when they were called back to work. You'd get
cabbage and stuff in a bag and no bill. When you went back
to work, they checked it off. Yet he claims he's against Wall
Street and that he's a worker, too. That sold his automobiles.
I remember one of the things he said: 'The difference between
me and the capitalists is that I earn my living honestly. I produce. The capitalists loan out their money and collect interest
and let others do the work.' "

The ex-coal miner smiles. "This Ford myth! It's almost
funny. He doesn't let a Negro roost in Dearborn but still he
hires them. Why? He's building up the Negro for a break
sooner or later between the Negro and the white. That's Ford.
In 1933, the Service Men used to come into the departments
and fire a man if he was garnisheed. When the union came in,

workers were still garnisheed. But every time a man was taken out, the rumor was started that he was caught organizing. . . As long as Ford puts fear into the hearts of the workers, we won't organize them. But once we can convince the workers, he must organize to change his conditions, he'll sign up. Ford can be licked. He's no different than any other manufacturer, regardless of what he says about money meaning nothing to him. He wants to show a profit at the end of the year. And once we educate the workers of this country as to the real conditions these cars are made under, they'll refuse to buy the article until he agrees to recognize his workers. To stop us, he started the Ford Brotherhood, a company union. The motto was: 'Every man working for Ford should buy a Ford.' He'll do anything to stop unionization! He played ball with Homer Martin when Martin was still in the U.A.W.A. The trouble with Martin, he's not slick enough. He can give you a flowery tongue but he can't keep his mouth shut until he performs."

Llewellyn shifts in his chair. "I suspected Martin of playing ball with the Ford Motor Company around about the latter part of October 1938. The Company then had a company union known as the Liberty Legion of America. We printed up 2000 leaflets attacking the Liberty Legion. That was on a Monday, the day before the newspapers carried the news of the first meeting between Harry Bennett and Homer Martin. A couple of days later I was called into Homer's office and he asked me not to put out any more leaflets until I was authorized by him. Later on, a group of us were called into Homer's room in the Eddystone Hotel. He told us that he had a tentative agreement with the Ford Motor Company. I left something out. . . The day that Homer told me not to put out any more leaflets, I told him that the Ford workers were being coerced into joining the Liberty Legion. He said he had talked it over with Bennett, and Bennett said that if the foremen were coercing men into joining and if Homer could give him the names, he would remove them. I turned over to Homer quite a number of names and badge numbers of foremen but the intimidation did not stop. Nobody was ever fired even though Bennett said: 'Even if he's General Superintendent of the God-damned building, I'll fire him!' To get back to the Eddystone, Homer said that the Ford Motor Company would recognize us as collective bargaining agents for members. He said that Ford would do away with company unions, and foremen antagonistic to the U.A.W.A. would be removed or discharged. In return for this, Martin said we would have to drop all Labor Board cases against the Ford Motor Company."

He smiles broadly. "The next day Homer called us in again. At this meeting there was a man by the name of Gillespie who said he was a representative of Harry Bennett. Gillespie was asked if he was not the same Gillespie that had represented the Ford Motor Company in the oral agreements between the U.A.W.A. and the Ford Company in Kansas City and St. Louis in the summer of 1937. He said that he was. Gillespie was also asked if the Ford Motor Company didn't deny that he was employed by them at the Labor Board hearings. He admitted this. He was then asked by us how he could expect us to have faith in him after the part he played there. He said: 'Ask Homer.' Homer said: 'Bennett told me anything we agreed to with Gillespie would be okay with the Company.' We asked Gillespie if he could arrange a meeting with Bennett and a committee of Ford workers. He said: 'Absolutely not. The Ford Company has faith in Bennett. You must have implicit faith in Homer Martin.' I could see very clearly that the Company would be in a position to save millions of dollars in back pay to discharged workers involved in Labor Board cases. On the other hand we would have nothing but Gillespie's word and Martin's word. We refused the agreement." He stares out of the window for a second. "After the Pittsburgh convention of the C.I.O., the U.A.W.A. set up a committee of three, known as the National Ford Organization Committee. As President of Ford Local 600, the River Rouge Local, I took the position that we should cooperate with this Committee. But Homer Martin advised certain of my executive board members not to work with this National Committee. By these actions, Martin created factions in Local 600. I was slandered by members of my executive board, called a Communist . . . I have no politics . . . and accused of violating the principles of unionism, because I insisted on working with the union as a whole instead of one man. In January I came to my local union hall and found there Jack Swift and Walter Williams. Swift was the International Representative from Kansas City, Missouri, and Williams was Recording Secretary of the Kansas City Ford Local. They told me that they, along with Homer, had a conference with Harry Bennett at the Ford Motor Company the day before. They said that they were surprised at finding Bennett such a nice man to deal with. They said that Bennett told them that he realized that sooner or later Ford would have to recognize the auto workers, but he insisted that Ford would fight the U.A.W.A. for the next ten years as long as it was connected with the C.I.O. or had such leaders, excepting Homer Martin. But that he would recognize the U.A.W.A. and help organize the auto workers as long as Homer Martin was President. They said that Bennett told them: 'We have checked Martin from the day he was born and have found him to be honest.' That he was the man they wanted to deal with as representative of their employees. That Wall Street, through their competitors, would never be able to buy Homer Martin, to use him to start unauthorized sit-down strikes, that if Homer Martin wanted a meeting of Ford workers and could get a hall big enough to hold them, Bennett'd see to it that 30,000 Ford workers came."

Llewellyn grins. "That is all Bennett talking: 'My Service Department is at Homer Martin's disposal. We will settle strikes in Kansas City, St. Louis, and Long Beach. We will allow Martin to place back to work between 300 and 600 men in the Rouge plant. But these men must swear their allegiance to Homer Martin and his policy. And they must not be members or sympathizers of the Communist Party.' At this time Evans, a supporter of Martin entered the room and said: 'Llewellyn, you know that the Ford Motor Company has the greatest espionage system on the face of the globe. Every move that you made we have watched. We knew every time that you talked to the National Ford Committee. And if anything happens that will sabotage this plan, it's going to be too bad for you or whoever does it. Remember, the Service Department is with us.' Later, we had a local meeting. I chaired the meeting and introduced Homer Martin. He opened the meeting by describing the taking over of the Plymouth Local. He referred to this incident as 'storming the Bastile.' His talk throughout was concerning the activities of the Communist Party. He said: 'The Communists want a revolution, we will give them one. It's time for everybody to get a gun. I'm getting mine before my enemies get all of them.' He said that the Ford Motor Company may have fired us in the past because we were members of the U.A.W.A. but in the future we might have to be members if we wanted to work at Ford. That it was possible that the Liberty Legion might become part of the U.A.W.A. Then he upheld Henry Ford and Harry Bennett as progressive citizens of the United States. He said that they had always kept an open door to him to take up the problems of the Ford workers, while General Motors and Chrysler would have him hanging around in the hall. It was plain to see that the Ford Motor Company had hopes of dominating the entire U.A.W.A. through Martin."

"Dearborn, population 50,350.
Detroit, population 1,568,650."

"IF YOU STABILIZE ANYTHING IT IS LIKELY TO BE THE WRONG THING."　　　　From the sayings of Henry Ford.

"In order to get an understanding of the Ford atmosphere you've got to live in it, to work in it, to be in public life. You got to understand it from having contact with the people about Ford. They talk of Hague in Jersey City. But here it isn't the Mayor, it isn't the elected officials, it's Henry Ford. In the eyes of the people he's King of Heaven and Hell." The eyes of Mr. —— are those of a man surrounded, in a besieged city, as if Detroit's flat streets and avenues were in peril of sudden capture. "In Ford's political life as in his industrial life, he has organized two groups. He *always* has two groups. In the plant now, he has the Liberty Legion and the American Federation of Labor under Homer Martin. . . Mr. Bennett once told me: 'Never try to fight anything directly. Always fight it with another organization.' And there are two groups in Dearborn. The Mayor's on one side, the Chief of Police is on the other. Both are Ford men. But Bennett encourages the Mayor to curb the Chief of Police, and the Chief of Police to ignore the Mayor. Ford's idea of Government is to have two groups fight each other. It holds true right in the Ford Motor Company itself. Mr. Bennett and Mr. Sorenson are in conflict. At one time, Sorenson was Henry Ford, himself, the

General Manager of all Ford properties. Bennett was head of non-production, maintenance, the Service Men. Ford maintained this policy for years. . . He was never an exponent of democracy. Ford's whole life was feudal from the start. He's obsessed with the idea, and I mean obsessed, that the reds are about to take over the country. He's come to regard the veterans as the only thing that can hold the country together. That's why he's giving the vets a preference in jobs! One of the principles of Ford's life, more important to him than money, is to operate that plant without unionism."

Mr. —— wipes his brow. "He's enlarged on the policy of turnover. If a man gets security, he doesn't yield his best. . . There has always been turnover at the Ford plant, turnover right up to the executives with the exception of the big two, Bennett and Sorenson. Bennett came to the forefront due to the police power which operates production. Sorenson's position now is secondary. This obsession about the reds is greater to Ford than profit. He has increased this turnover. If the men don't have much contact with each other they won't unionize. This turnover policy is now replacing his foreign national groups. As a rule, Poles are not hired now because they're susceptible to the U.A.W. He is replacing the foreign groups with groups harder to organize. The Southerners are the predominant new group. Ford also hires Negroes for certain classifications of work where the white men cannot stand the heat and the pace. He's hiring Southerners and Negroes. That's no accident. You'd have to see Harry Bennett operate to really understand the Ford policy. It's purely a rule of force, otherwise Harry Bennett could never have come to the front. Consider Harry Bennett from that angle. Go into his office and talk to him like I have. He's one of the most moody of men. He's liable to throw a telephone at you. Nobody has ever exercised such control over Henry Ford as Bennett. It's not a direct frontal control. Bennett has placed in every position a Bennett man. Even Cameron fears Bennett. No letter goes to Ford but the contents are controlled. Even Ford's relatives recognize that Bennett is supreme. He's the Rasputin of the Ford dynasty! You ought to make a search of the press dispatches to analyze Edsel's position in the Dynasty. You'd find that Edsel is a figurehead because Henry Ford is jealous of the prerogatives Edsel might get. Ford loves publicity. He doesn't want anyone to occupy his place in the eyes of the people. Bennett long ago recognized this trait in Ford. And Bennett is supreme. . . Henry Ford has two thoughts, soy beans and Harry Bennett."

"What will happen when Ford dies?"

"Here you have Edsel rankling with resentment against Henry Ford. Bennett, himself, has said: 'It'll be a race to see who gets to the phone first. If I get there first I'll give in my resignation. If he gets there first I'll get kicked out.' I think Edsel will make changes but he isn't equipped by his training to carry on. But right now Ford does nothing without Bennett. Ford is as spoily as spoily can be. Yet he needs Bennett to keep the union out of the plant. They drive their men and machines to make the last cent of profit, but at the same time maintain this vast overhead of Service Men and spies. It's staggering. At every election in Dearborn, a group of men organized under Bennett's jurisdiction go out and line the people up. Ford has a program where they lay off everybody a month or so before elections. Then they are rehired through the Chief of Police. And the people don't buck it. The economic club is always held over their head. . . The make-up of the town is part of the scheme. The West End of Dearborn is anti-East End, and the East End is anti-West End. The codfish aristocracy live in the West End, the people who hold down the executive jobs, the clerical positions. The workers live over in the East End. There used to be two towns, West Dearborn and East Dearborn, but Ford merged them into one for his own reasons. And now the student has become the master of his former master. A study of Harry Bennett would reveal Ford's philosophy as it developed through the years. Bennett has used this philosophy to control Ford. The old man's up in the years. He hates unions. He's obsessed with the idea. He's afraid of reds. He's obsessed with the fear that the Jews will take his money. And where does Coughlin get his money from?" He shakes his head, stares at me. Wordless, he has named the besiegers. There are two of them. The old multi-millionaire in Dearborn. The priest in Royal Oak. Still, he shakes his head as if at the millions of Fords speeding out of Dearborn across all the highways of the land . . . the millions of high-powered words speeding out of Detroit and Royal Oak . . . one manufactured product.

"To hell with democracy. Big business is going to fight in another year, and God help the reds. The senators are scared of me, as scared as if I were a boa constrictor coming down the aisle. Once I went up to Senator Borah and I said: 'You started out as a fine upstanding man. Now, look at you. You're old and ugly. You're shaky and wrinkled. Your hair is thin; you have bags under your eyes. Your chest caves in, and your stomach sags. You're no good and why?—because of your evil Communistic ways.'"

From the sayings of Blanche Winters, head of the Legion of the Blue Cross in Detroit.

"Large industrialists are the involuntary tools of Communism, inasmuch as they do not crush Unionism."

From the speech of Mrs. Dilling at the Metropolitan Tabernacle in Detroit.

"You are running into a man who with a million other people will put you where you belong." *From the sayings of Rev. G. L. K. Smith of Louisiana now located at the Industrial Bank Building in Detroit.*

"The police department will continue to arrest people and search homes without warrants whenever, in the personal opinion of the Commissioner, such actions should be taken. Until Federal, State, and local laws are changed, this will continue to be our policy."

From a statement by Commissioner Pickert, Chief of Police, in Detroit.

Henry Ford: "Do you know the best police force in the world today? It's the American Legion."

From an interview in the New York Times, June 29, 1937.

"The principle of majorityism—sometimes called Democracy and sometimes Bolshevism—is not enough. The popular fallacy is that '50 million Frenchmen can't be wrong.' As a matter of experience and historical fact, 50 men are much more than likely to be right than 50 million . . ." The 1917 list of those who, with Lenin, ruled many of the activities of the Soviet Republic disclosed that of the twenty-five quasi-cabinet members, twenty-four of whom were atheistic Jews whose names I have before me, published by the Nazis and distributed throughout Germany—the list—a German list not mine—will be published in the pamphlet which I will distribute to all who request a copy of this address."

From the broadcasts of Father Coughlin at Royal Oak.

I lunch with Dr. ——. Slowly, he chews his sandwich, as slowly speaks. "The Church and the laity are divided on Coughlin. Coughlin goes back to Austrian political Catholicism, to a mixture of Christianity and modern fascism, the Christian Corporate State. When Coughlin came along as a strong radio figure, it fitted in. The line is there. Duncan Moore of WJR estimates Coughlin's Sunday hour broadcast at $19,000 to $25,000 a week. Who's paying for his time? He doesn't get that from ten cent contributions. Nobody knows how much he got in insurance when his wooden church burned down." He takes a drink of coffee. "The general idea among informed Catholics is that Coughlin has some special dispensation from Rome and that's why he can step out openly. The old fight of the Church and the State centers right here in Detroit, not in Rome. The Church has lost control in Germany, Italy, Mexico. The Austrian-Hungarian Empire is annihilated. The United States is the strongest Catholic country left and if Coughlin is listened to by ten million people, he can't be sneered at. The belief was that the present Pope, Pacelli, would curb Coughlin. But if Coughlin can help swing the United States into some form of Christian Corporate State with the aid of the Black Legion . . . Well."

He stirs his coffee. "Don't forget this is Ford's city. It's no accident that Homer Martin tried to smash the auto union. Ford as the biggest open shopper in the country has the most to gain by keeping his plant non-union. It's no accident that Ford was the recipient of a medal from Hitler or that Fritz Kuhn, the *Bund* leader, was an engineer in Ford's plant. As for Coughlin, the real fear among liberal Catholics is that he not only is working for a Christian Corporate State but that he is also working for a schism in the church." He studies me calmly. "That is why liberal Catholics feel that Coughlin should be allowed to talk himself out. If curbed, he'd create a schism. Coughlin wants power more than anything else. He's hobnobbing with Protestant fascism. That's no tall story. William Pelley, the Silver Shirt leader, wrote that Coughlin delivered the prize Silver Shirt speech of the year. This appeared in the November issue of his magazine *Liberation*, last year. As far as that goes, only last winter *Life* Magazine ran a picture of the head of the Klan shaking hands with one of the Cardinals. The word, *schism* . . . You can hear that in certain intellectual Catholic and liberal Catholic circles. You may have heard that Coughlin has precedent for a schism right here in Detroit. A branch of the Polish Catholic Church broke away and created the National Polish Church, and after they achieved independence they went back to Poland to proselytize." He pushes his unfinished sandwich away. "The point is that the hierarchy is afraid of Coughlin. Is he working to bring clerical fascism to America or to become America's first Pope? He probably is working in both directions. A short time ago, he was friends with Frank Murphy. But now they've broken and yet I don't think Murphy is investigating Coughlin, or investigating Detroit, the center of fascism in America. Murphy's ambition is to be the first Roman Catholic president of the United States. Is that why he isn't touching Coughlin? The biggest issue here is not auto but political Catholicism! Detroit is the center of fascism in the United States!" he repeats. "The union-haters are here! The Jew-haters are here! Ford hates both the Jews and the unions. And Coughlin is one of the most effective of all baiters. A small fighting minority is much better than a majority and that's what Coughlin has here and is organizing nationally. The masses think that if you give Coughlin enough rope he will hang himself, but the masses do not count."

He finishes his coffee. "The Jews are not the only ones who are worried. The liberal Catholics are worried too. There is a tendency, a corporate state tendency among some important Catholics to quote from Pope Alexander the Sixth, the despot of the church, a great anti-Semite in the time of the Spanish inquisition, instead of quoting from the latest Pope. It's no accident that Detroit has the largest Catholic population of any city in the country. . ." He pushes away his coffee cup. "Perhaps Coughlin, himself, doesn't know whether he wants to be the first American Pope or to bring clerical fascism to America? But if there is a schism or plans for a schism, the K.K.K. would be for it. They used to fight against Roman popery but a Nationalistic American Catholicism under an American Pope. . . Well."

"KING. WORKER."

From the altar inscription in the Shrine of the Little Flower.

The highway out at Dearborn divides agriculture and industry. On one side are Ford's truck gardens, on the other Ford's mountains of sand and scrap iron. A barbed wire fence protects the River Rouge Plant with its acres of foundries, steel mills, paper mills, tool shops, motor and car assembly buildings.

The Ford Rotunda is a long distance away from the River Rouge Plant, a long distance away from the miles of belts, the speed-up, the eyes of the auto workers.

Tourists park their cars and stroll up to the Rotunda between the green lawns. Inside they smile pleasantly as the cooled air washes the summer heat from off their brows and cheeks. They sit down at little desks, fill out cards that will later passport them through the plant. Above the desks, immense photographic murals show the auto workers at their collective tasks . . . making steel . . . making lightning out of their hands on the conveyor belts.

The sayings of Henry Ford circle the Rotunda's walls:

THE AUTO MADE ROADS AND ROADS MAKE COMMERCE AND CIVILIZATION.

THE FARM AND THE SHOP EACH NEEDS WHAT THE OTHER PRODUCES.

NEVER HAS ENOUGH OF ANY GOOD THING BEEN PRODUCED FOR USE.

On the Rotunda's floor, dioramas show tiny miners digging out zinc, copper, iron.

The center of the Rotunda is like a penny placed on the middle of a silver dollar. Unroofed, open to the sky, the sun burns down here. Yet many people leave the air-cooled outer circle to lean on the railing, impressed by what they see. Silent pilgrims of the twentieth century, who have traveled here in Fords, Chryslers, Buicks, Pontiacs, Packards, they stare in front of them. Like true pilgrims, they have read Ford's streamlined Ten Commandments on the walls. They have looked at the men captured in the photograph murals and dioramas, those holy images of Ford's power. Now, sweaty of face, entranced, they stare in final worship. Inside the railed circle, a huge illuminated globe, the earth itself, revolves majestically. Africa, Asia, North America, South America, Europe, Australia! On all the continents, Ford properties and Ford lands and Ford factories and Ford mines and Ford forests are marked off in yellow. Here, in the Rotunda's dead center all that is Ford's spins before awed eyes.

Marked off in sacred yellow, the color of gold, this globe is both the altar-shrine of the Ford Motor Company, and the image of the Shrine's god, the great god: MONOPOLY CAPITAL.

U. S. Route Number 12

The highway is like a conveyor belt. Brand new automobiles move in twos at a fixed unchanging speed, the second automobile in each pair, driverless, as if the movement were controlled by a technician in Detroit.

The procession rolls between hay and corn fields. The wind waves the young corn into one dancing weather vane; the cows in the fields milestones between Detroit and Chicago. On this green land of farms, the cities shine like steel disks.

Ahead is Lake Michigan, blue and spreading, another Atlantic scooped out of the Middle West.

A signboard reads: BACK IN OLD INDIANA
             MICHIGAN CITY 4 MILES

A car honks its horn, a blue-sleeved arm signals me to pull over.

Mr. Indiana Cop steps out onto the highway. "Don't leave your door open," he cautions in a neighborly way. "You don't want it wrenched off. You crossed the yellow line." The yellow line divides the four lanes into east-west and west-east. "Back there at the hill. You kind of straddled that line."

I trail him back to the Justice of the Peace's office, a

wooden structure off the highway like a wealthy farmer's chicken-house.

Justice of the Peace, Raymond C. Edgerly, a man of thirty-seven, sits at his desk, his straight blond hair brushed back from his sandy red forehead. His blue eyes, curved nose and thin-lipped smile are the law. He listens to both of us. Mr. Indiana Cop leaves and Edgerly examines the documents on the desk. "I'm going to fine you one dollar for reckless driving and five dollars for costs."

"Can't you give me a break? I really didn't cross that yellow line."

"I'll waive my dollar as presiding judge."

"Thanks." I pay out five dollars and read the itemized list of costs on my receipt:

Docket *Township*	.50
Affidavit	.25
Warrant	.25
Trial	1.00
Judgment	.50
Record	1.00
Final Judgment	.50
Index	.25
Receipt	.25
Seal	.25
Hearing Judge	.25
Total Costs	5.00 (handwritten)

"I'm in this Justice of Peace business part-time." Edgerly pronounces *part-time* like paht-time.

"You practice law, too, I suppose."

"I read law for seven years in different offices." He nods at his shelves of law books. "You're looking at a fine library. That *Cyclopedia of Law* set's bound in red morocco leather and India Bible paper and is supposed to be worth six hundred dollars. I became a Justice of Peace because of my being an avid student of law. Some of the most famous lawyers never went to Law School. The only reason I'm not admitted to the bar is because of the P.D. or post-depression. I've attorney friends in Gary and at the end of the year, my steel mill earnings will equal their income."

"Steel earnings?"

"I work four days a week in the mills."

The traffic placard on the wall reads: YOU CAN'T BEAT THE LAW OF AVERAGES. STOP.

"I come from Maine," he continues. "You see I was in the Service and I worked West to meet this lad I was in the Service with. I'm half-Hoosierized by now. I got into this Justice of Peace business by being appointed to fill a vacancy. But now I'm serving a four-year elected term. I'm also president of the Justices of Peace Association of Indiana."

"Why do Justices of Peace need an association?"

"We formed our association because of the recent session of the legislature. Legislation was enacted to deprive the justices of peace of all criminal jurisdiction. It delegated authority to the Circuit Judges in the State to appoint magistrates on the petition of forty free-holders. As soon as a magistrate would be appointed at a salary of one hundred dollars a month, the justice of peace lost his criminal jurisdiction, which includes traffic violations. The burden fell on the taxpayers to pay the magistrate's salary and rent for the same work we do without any expense to the taxpayer." He smiles. "The motorist who breaks traffic laws pays the overhead and expenses as the Justice of Peace is on a fee system. This Magistrate's Act was so unconstitutional that no judge in the state appointed any magistrate. It's on the books but it's not lived up to."

"And you're a steel worker."

"Clarence Gorman of East Gary and myself are the only two Justices of Peace in Indiana in the C.I.O. I've worked in the Gary mill for six years. When that plant's running full time, six days a week, they'll employ fifteen thousand men. It's the largest steel mill in the country, the largest in equipment and acreage. We have fourteen blast furnaces and that's the answer, by golly. The first steel rail rolled by electricity was rolled in the Gary Works in 1908. We roll fender steel for auto. Body steel is rolled in the plant west of us." He is the steel worker now, not the Justice of Peace. "Working conditions are better than they used to be. I'm Republican though." The gold teeth in his mouth show in quick flash. "They say that Maine and Porter County, Indiana, are still Republican." C.I.O. man and Republican, he smilingly straddles the two Americas.

Men

CHICAGO

"Loop:—a fold or doubling as that of a string or rope so as to form an eye or a bend through which something may be passed; a noose."   *Dictionary definition.*

"The Loop: the name of Chicago's business district."
                                                   Fact.

DONALD STEVENS GLANCES AT ME through his horn-rimmed glasses as we walk up the Loop's streets. "You won't find out what the people are thinking if you read the newspapers here," he says solemnly. Tall and gaunt, in his middle forties, the organizer looks like a college professor. "Most of the papers here are pirate sheets. On the Chicago River shore, you have a Barbary Coast along which have looted such beauties as McCormick, Hearst and Knox." Traffic jams each side-street. Overhead the Els form a noose of steel tracks. "Long before the New Deal, C.I.O., American Newspaper Guild, Chicago was the arena of violent repression of labor organization. The battles of the Chicago publishers against the A.F.L. mechanical crafts, coupled with their circulation wars, were among the prime developers of modern gangster methods. The leaders of the Guild knew that the nation's runner-up news center was a center of reaction. They realized that work must be started to neutralize a Chicago as a company union fink fortress of industry-wide influence. Accordingly, the first organizer of the A.N.G. could afford was sent to help Chicago's newspapermen. In late 1935 the first A.N.G. organizer arrived. What was the attitude of the publishers? 'Some monkey trying to muscle in,' " Stevens imitates a mobster's lingo: " 'Have the boys case the joint!' Our Guild office was broken into and rifled three times. That was done by a few Hearst reporters and office boys. We know. Because since then they have joined the Guild. In late 1936, while Chicago's big-shot publishers were reeling in knockout defeat with their usual front disunified under the shocks of the election results, we organized the majority of all Chicago editorial workers. Early in 1937 the Guild was on top. What was the attitude of the publishers? 'Look Butch,' Stevens monotones: 'Those muggs'll get us down. Let's cut out the private beef and figure the pay-off!' The Chicago Newspaper Publishers' Association pulled together and rushed the concession of the highest printers' wage scale in North America as anti-strike insurance for a two-year contract term. Now they were free to give us the Dion O'Bannion handshake. That is, they pretended to agree to organization just as O'Bannion's killer shook hands with O'Bannion before pulling the trigger. In the middle of 1937, the publishers shifted to open offensive: 'Okay, Butch, give'm the works!' The city unmasked as the headquarters of a press-led bloody reaction from the South Chicago steel massacre to the Washington social-legislation massacres. The Newspaper Guild also was terrorized and decimated. The Barbary Coast along the Chicago River was in all its glory with Hearst acting as muscleman number one. But we've doubled salaries and won the five-day week. Still we have no contract with any of the large papers. But we'll stay in Chicago until we get one."

"Health is Wealth. Take Care of Yourself."
Armour Company advertisement slogan.

Lake Michigan borders Chicago on the east, a blue endless water, a blue look into the future. The blue of water, the iron ore boats in the distance and the skyscrapers on the shore, preview the city of tomorrow.

Along the lake's edge, men turning handles manipulate contraptions that resemble ancient catapults. Nets, supported by long iron pipes, lower and submerge below the surface. Again they turn the handles. The nets rise, the sun and a few fish caught in their scoops.

A middle-aged man watches the fishermen. "They're catching perch. That's all they get. The gill nets get all the big fish. But they're getting something to eat." He is one of those short strong Italians who looks as if he has marched straight out of the Roman past. "You working?"

"How about you?"

"Same as all over. Nothing doing."

"What do you do?"

"I used to be a plasterer. W.P.A. now. This place, a man can't start a business. You need a couple hundred dollars to open a place and how you going to keep it going? Now they're cutting people off W.P.A. It's like with Hoover now with Roosevelt. What do you think people do? What's going to be?"

Away from the lake shore, away from the concentrated business district of the Loop, Chicago changes into the North Side, the West Side, the South Side, a flatland covered with apartment houses, two-story stuccos, factories, frame shacks, empty lots.

The market on South Halsted Street is a poor man's market. The pushcarts sell shoes, pants, women's wear. On the sidewalk in front of a butcher store, live chickens and ducks are prisoned in tenement-like wooden cages. This butcher store also sells puppies. A sidewalk merchant specializes in watch faces and clock parts. Store awnings shade the streets and in the shade, the Chicago of the poor, Poles, Negroes, Jews, Italians, Irish, Slavs, Germans, trudge up and down between the stores and the pushcarts. Everywhere the tenement smell of hot dogs, hamburgers and frying liver sandwiches cooks in the air.

The secondhand clothing proprietors pull at the sleeves of the men.

"What do you need today, feller?"

"Need some pants, Bud?"

"What can I do for you, Doc?"

In the adjoining streets, down-and-outers mind the cars parked along the curbs.

"Hello." The down-and-outer hellos me back. His hair hasn't been cut in months. His old clothes have the faded dead color of an unpainted slum shack. His breath smells of booze but doesn't stink. It's too early and anyway he hasn't picked up much change yet.

"What kind of city is this?" I ask him.

"This town is the railroad center of the country," he declares as if he owns a thousand shares himself. "It's the packing-house center. If a man can't make a living here, he can't make a living anywhere." He pulls a rag from his pocket and begins polishing the windshield of a big Buick.

Blocks of frame houses surround the square mile of packing yards. A thick smell, a smell not sour, not sweet, a smell as if from compressed fat, stuffs the air like meat in a sausage. A barbed wire fence guards the Armour plant.

I walk through the gate. It is lunch hour. The men in overalls, the women in white caps and aprons who belong to this city within a city, chew on their sandwiches. The various Armour buildings are connected at their second floor levels by a series of brick terraces. The buildings, the terraces, the freight trains on the street level are all as inter-related as a bunch of guts.

Inside the Visitor's Entrance, the blackboard carries the day's diary:

7/18/39

LIVESTOCK RECEIPTS

	Hogs	Cattle	Sheep
Chicago...........	14,000	4500	3000

At twelve-thirty, the Armour guide leads the visitors into an elevator and up to the hog-killing room. We stand on a platform high above the killing floor, high above the red pouring of death.

Upside down, two parallel rows of hogs travel up into the killing room, big hogs, smaller hundred-pounders, black hogs, brown hogs, chained by one rear leg to the overhead conveyor. Squealing, they toss their fattened bodies from side to side in seal-like throes, squealing, squealing.

Two hog killers, a white man and a Negro, stand at the entrance like doormen. They stand in complete calm, in utter poise. The white hog killer reaches one hand forward, grips a throat, digs his knife into the jugular. The Negro hog-killer reaches one hand forward, grips a throat and digs his knife into the jugular. Poke and turn. Poke and turn. The blood pours. The floor is blood red. The boots of the killers are blood red.

Already, the overhead conveyor is moving the slaughtered hogs forward. New hogs are coming up. New throats are slit. New blood. Lunging their bodies from side to side, the hogs writhe, twist. Their blood spills out. The conveyor never stops. The squealing never stops. The hogs keep arriving, each chained by one rear leg.

One of the hog killers sharpens his knife with slow steady ease, not a movement wasted, incapable of any sudden or abrupt movement. Only the hogs are sudden, smashing their heads and bodies from side to side. Even after their throats are cut, they try to escape from their death chains.

"I've been around these yards seven years." Herbert March shifts his good arm. One arm is in a sling. He smiles as if he had said: I've been around the campus seven years. Good-looking, intelligent, he has the appearance of a college man. "I've always been considered a radical. I was fired out of Armour's twice. I was a common laborer. I was in the boiled ham department. I was in the salt cellars, the second job. In the smokehouse. I worked all over. I was active in the Stockyards Labor Council when it was formed. This is the second time they've tried to shoot me." He glances at the sling. His bright blue tie might have been worn by a college senior. He frowns as if thinking: Suppose they don't miss the next time. . . "Rough stuff around here—it's dirty. The packers use violence. I set out to expose Martin Murphy, who ran the Stockyards Labor Council. I set out to expose Murphy and his Ada Street gangsters. Finally, the workers were united on Murphy being no good and then we had all kinds of threats. We got together and decided to go into the A.F.L. Amalgamated Meat Cutters and we ran into trouble. Collins was the big shot in the A.F.L. He was drunk all the time. He went into a tavern to bump Julie Link off. Julie Link was a hoodlum protecting one of the company unions. Collins was carrying a shotgun in his pants. By accident he shot himself in the knee. Gangrene set in. Collins died of pneumonia." He pauses, smiles. "He died of pneumonia of the knee. To get back to Murphy. He had several bodyguards, the remnants of the beer running days. But the union grew in spite of Murphy's splitting tactics. We organized Armour's and organized it well!"

He glances toward the door. "I have to go soon. The doctor has to dress my wound. My shoulder doesn't hurt. I'm supposed to keep my arm in a sling but when I telephone, out it comes— The A.F.L. Union consists of stool-pigeons and hoodlums. I mean that. We had an election and 237 men out of 5000 voted against the C.I.O. Those 237 men are in the A.F.L. After the election, a carload of hoodlums came into the Armour plant at lunch hour. The next day we had a committee of one thousand to meet them. We ran those hoodlums, guns and all, out of the yards. They came back the next day and our committee was up to three thousand men. On the way back, one of our fellows, Sykes, passed the Armour Employment Agency and was stabbed. A few thousand workers wanted to tear the place down. Simmons, who did the stabbing, ran into the building. Armour's police force of about a hundred were there. The workers lifted me up to their shoulders and I said: 'Quiet.' Everyone was quiet. That was when Armour's saw I had too much influence with the men. The next day, three men in a car pulled up alongside my car as I was coming to union headquarters. They emptied their automatics at me. I let the car run and jumped out. I lay flat on the sidewalk. I got away clean, just scraped my face. . . This second effort was on Friday night. They got me when I was going home. Their car got alongside of mine and they fired. Thought they'd killed me because my car caromed. The bullet entered my shoulder and went up to my neck. The glass deflected it a little or I would be pushing up daisies. . . Armour wouldn't kill a man. That's why they use the company union with its stoolpigeons and hoodlums. Simmons, who stabbed Sykes is still working for Armour. Armour put in a fix somehow."

In the killing room, the hogs keep coming forward. Armour's can handle 1200 hogs an hour. Back in 1867, Armour could only handle 30,000 hogs in an entire year. One by one, the slaughtered hogs are dropped into a long trough full of scalding water. Five men push the hogs up the trough with long wooden poles, working in a cloud of steam. Out come the hogs, chained to the conveyor. They move into a de-hairing machine. Painted with a resin preparation, the white hogs move through a roaring gas flame. Lifeless, squealless, hairless, bloodless, like porkers in an advertisement only lacking apples in their mouths, they approach the processing line. At one end of the room, the hogs are alive, the two hog killers wielding their knives, cutting through the fraction of an inch separating the living from the dying and the dead.

The white porkers are de-headed in the next department, gutted, cut into two. Each half with its gleaming bony structure moves forward on the conveyor, moves out of death. The hogs become meat.

Outside, the Armour refrigerator cars, big yellow iceboxes on wheels, wait for their shipments. Above the freights, almost covering the side of one of the buildings, a big sign shows two black money bags against a green blackground; printed letters stating:

HEALTH IS WEALTH
TAKE CARE OF YOURSELF

"I came from the south of Ireland in 1928." William Joseph Mooney's brogue is Americanized. He has the determined, wary face of a boxer who knows how to box. "I was in the *Fianna na h'Eirrean* when I was sixteen. The idea was to train the youths of Ireland, mentally and physically, to fight for the Irish Republic. I carried dispatches. We felt we must have the Irish Republic. . . My mother though was born in this country and naturally, she kept up a correspondence with her brothers and sisters in the United States. And all the kids I knew were lavin' for Australia and America. When I first come to Chicago, it seemed very big to me. But I expected it, too. We had been getting Chicago papers in

Ireland. My uncle got me a job at Armour's through a friend of his. I worked with the construction gang ten years and six months. I was a carpenter's helper. We worked inside and outside. Floors to be repaired or scaffolding, we done it. Ten years and six months, I done the same thing. We carried the lumber to the carpenters, then start the tearing up and tearing down, cart away the rubbish and clean up after them. There was little promotion in our gang. Men are still laborers who started as laborers. Yet they go home and put in window frames and hang doors. A child could lay floors! I joined the C.I.O. in 1937—I know for a fact that the carpenters and laborers have made one hundred and thirty sections of fence in the lumberyard on Packers Avenue to be used as barricades in case there's a strike. Thousands of workers on the way home, saw them."

Outside Armour's beef dressing floor, the semi-opaque wired window has been left open. Down below, a worker sits alone in an empty yard. The walls surround him. In the distance, the walls belong to Swift. . .

The headless beef carcasses enter the dressing floor on the overhead chain system. One tug on the iron-ringed guide ropes and the huge carcasses descend to the skinners and their knives. They cut, pull with both hands. The hides peel off three feet. A second tug on the suspended guides and the carcasses lift off the floor. The skinners grip the ends of the loosened hides, pull, their bodies arching backward. The hides come off like gloves off hands. Continuously, the carcasses enter the one-hundred-and-fifty-foot-long dressing floor, carried forward by the machinery near the ceiling, machinery like a thousand pulling horses and mules. And on the floor the skinners begin the job of converting the cattle of the West and mid-West into sirloin steaks.

The sheep room is like the hog killing room. But the sheep do not squeal. Herded outside the room itself, the flock waits to be hooked up to the overhead conveyors. In they come from the sheep states, upside down, their woolly pelts dark brown. The two sheep killers reach forward, clutch handfuls of wool. Their knives dig into the throats. The conveyors carry the sheep over the blood red iron grate, a grate like that over a subway. The machinery clanks. Forty or fifty dying sheep bunch up together, shaking their heads from side to side but without the violence, the convulsive terror, the energy of the hogs. As their blood floods out through their nostrils, the sheep shake their heads almost gently.

The semi-opaque window outside the sheep room overlooks a yard of cattle. Massive, alive, the brown steers are trapped inside a fenced-in passageway, their great heads and soft brown eyes all facing in one direction; the direction of the stunning sheds and the sledge hammers. Above the steers, an old man walks up and down an elevated wooden platform, calling a special word to them, a farmer's word, a word the steers can understand: 'Come on,' the word urges. 'Come on. It's all right.' The passageway is packed so tight, it seems all movement has been frozen but the steers do move, move backwards, then forwards in the direction of the stunning sheds. The old man continues to call his special word to them, his shoulders hunched as if absorbed in his own thoughts.

"I'm Walter Stabbers," Stabrawa smiles with full red lips. A man of twenty-five, he has a butcher's pinkish meaty complexion. "The name is more of a nickname. It's been in the family." We walk along packingtown's gray streets. On vacation now, Walter Stabrawa is wearing a green gabardine suit and a straw hat. "I was born and raised here right back o' the yards. Me, I've been in the union back in '33. You take me. I started in working when I was sixteen. I scale and pack pork loins. It felt like a prison when I started, the boss yodeling— I got two bits an hour and I worked as high as eighty-five and a hundred hours a week. I scale and I pack and I throw the box on a conveyor. Those boxes weigh from fifty pounds to one hundred and forty pounds. All the time I have to keep up to the speed of the table. The butchers cut over nine hundred hogs an hour and that means we had eighteen hundred pork loins an hour. There was eight of us on the loin gang. Four packers, two nailers, two scalers. Always it was

thirty-five degrees in that room. All day, the pork loins kept
coming through. You could work up an appetite after that. I
carried a lunch that looked like a laundry bag. I averaged
ten sandwiches a day."

He laughs. "They don't let you smoke so I smoked in the
washrooms. Scale and pack and holler at each other when we
want to talk! Talk about baseball, about women, how drunk
you got last week and how drunk you were going to get. But
in them days when you got through, you were too tired to
get drunk. I'd go to work around six o'clock when it was
dark. And get home when it was dark. At eight, nine or ten
o'clock. Only saw the light on Sundays." He shrugs. "All
lousy conditions until the union come in. Now I get sixty-five
and a half cents an hour instead of two bits. I've been nine
years on that same job. All the time I live here in Packingtown, just back of the green fence. They have a green fence
around the yards. It used to be the old saying: 'Where do you
live?' 'Back of the green fence.' That's where I still live. Me
and the wife. We live in a frame house, four rooms. She works
in the Campbell Canning plant. We got married when the
union came in. We couldn't get married before. We didn't
make enough. It's luck I got married. . . When I was a kid,
I go with a gang of fifty kids. The old man wouldn't give you
no money, so we grab apples, nibble around for what we can
get. The cops chased us. We sell junk to the ragman, copper,
brass. There was fifty of us. Now, about six are dead, killed
by cops. Ten or fifteen are in the penitentiary. Others are
rolling around in the streets. Others are married like me.
We was part of the Ada Street gang, the Murderer's A.C.
That was us from one generation to another. I was just
lucky. . . I went to work because the cops got too rough.
You couldn't stand on the corner. 'Let's see your hands,' the
cops say. You got blisters on you, you were working. Otherwise you was loafing. First, I was too young to get a job. Then
there was no jobs. I was lucky. . . Now I get sixty-five and
one half cents an hour. They tried to frame me. I got the
blame for stealing hams. They fired me, blackballed me at
ten A.M. At ten fifteen A.M. the bunch I work with sat down.
The General Super came around but the bunch said they
wouldn't go back to work until I was taken back. Next day
there was a committee from ten different departments to meet

with the Supers. The committee said if I didn't go back
there'd be another sitdown so I did get back. Since then we
don't get hounded so much from every slaphappy boss."

Room empties into room at Armour's, a maze of special-
ized activity. Rows of girls line both sides of a long table.
Down the center, at easy hand reach, a tiny conveyor, almost
toy-sized, carries empty glass jars and trays of sliced wafer-
thin beef. Hands reach for trays. The slices are packed into
the jars.

Another room. A time clock, a wall file of cards, a NO-
TICE: PUNCH YOUR TIME CARD IN YOUR WORKING CLOTHES
BOTH COMING TO AND GOING FROM WORK.

Rooms of bacon and frankfurters. Coolers with sawdust
on the floors and sides of beef on hooks. Rooms where girls,
in white uniforms and white hats like nurses, wrap and toss
hams onto the conveyor in front of them, rooms where the
work is twenty and thirty removes separated from the first
knife thrust, where young boys stamp cardboard boxes for
shipment, boxes that will contain farm-packingtown's
products. . .

The railroad enters the yards like a private trolley line.
The warning sign is printed in many languages: Polish.
English. German: GIE UEBER DIE BRUKE ES IST VERBOTEN.

Packingtown's frame houses hold a city of people, peopled
from Germany, Poland; Mexicans, Irish, Swedes, Iowans,
Nebraskans, Missourians, Oklahomans, Alabamans, a prairie
city of LIVESTOCK RECEIPTS where steers are changed
into jars; a prairie city of HUMAN RECEIPTS.

On Sunday, I board the Cottage Grove Avenue trolley in
the South Side. The trolley clangs north past the stores used
as homes by the South Side's Negroes. Every tenth store seems
to be a Baptist church. DANIEL, THE TAILOR. THE LOUISIANA
STORE: Red buffalo and silver bass for sale. It is half-past

eight, the summer's sunstreaked sky still bright. To the east, the railroad tracks of the I.C.—the Illinois Central—border Lake Michigan's shore. The trolley cuts between blocks of business and slums, the MORGAN LAUNDRY SERVICE, beer taverns, the Exposition Apartments, slants across Cermak Road named after the Mayor who died from the bullet aimed at Roosevelt. On South Indiana Avenue, the large ugly buildings of light manufacturing alternate with former mansions converted into furnished rooming houses. Greek poolparlors. Auto wreckers. Garages.

Rows of cops stand outside the Coliseum on South Wabash Avenue. Inside, there isn't a seat left. Huge red and white banners are strung along the balcony:

MILLIONS IN THE C I O DEMAND A NEW DEAL FOR THE PACKING INDUSTRY.
PACKINGHOUSE WORKERS WELCOME JOHN L. LEWIS.

The platform is at one end of the Coliseum. John L. Lewis is seated in the middle of the speakers' row, his head like a gray stone, his eyebrows like coal streaks.

Bishop Shiel is speaking to the people of packingtown, to the Poles, Negroes, Irish, Germans, his churchman's voice magnified by the loudspeakers: ". . . You need every ounce of strength you can muster, for in union there is strength, in division there is weakness. Every friend of organized labor, from the President of the United States down to the humblest worker in the land, is hoping and praying that the breach in the ranks of organized labor may soon be closed. . ."

Applause in handclapping thunder.

A woman sings: "My Country 'tis of thee, Sweet land of liberty, Of thee I sing. . ."

The people rise, in shirt sleeves, in summer dresses. A middle-aged worker doffs his gray cap and puffs on a large pipe. He belongs to the South Chicago Steel Workers delegation; the delegation's placards are their own industrial flags. There are many such placards.

The speakers follow one another, the flashlights of the cameramen repeatedly highspotting the platform with its Bishop and C.I.O. President. The woman singer renders "Let me call you sweetheart" as the bandmaster, in white hat and blue uniform conducts a band who look as if they belong to the German bands of Chicago's past. Music thumps and blares. A Negro woman comes down from the balcony with a little wide-eyed boy.

Van A. Bittner, Chairman of P.W.O.C., speaks. "The frontiers have not passed. Labor has a great frontier in America and that is to organize every unorganized worker in this Republic. When that day comes and only when that day comes, will we have economic and political justice in America. Three years ago we came to Chicago to organize the steel industry. They told us United States Steel was too strong. Today in Chicago and in the Calumet area, we have one of the most powerful unions in America. Armour's isn't stronger than the steel corporations. . ."

Thousands of lips become one: "BOO!"

"Tomorrow when you read the Chicago Tribune. . ."

"Boo! Boo!"

"You will find that there were about a hundred people here at this meeting."

The people laugh. Near me, a six-footer with close-cropped yellow hair doubles over with joy, his mighty shadow on the wall also doubling over.

John L. Lewis gets up out of his seat. Vestless, he wears a dark suit and a white shirt. He is whiteness of shirt, grayness of face, blackness of suit and blackness of eyebrows.

The band bangs out a marching song. The union delegations parade up and down the aisles in front of the speakers' platform as if at a presidential convention. The man with the close-cropped hair laughs a giant's laugh as the people rise to their feet, the banners, the flags, the placards of the delegations gyrating and waving, the colors of the workingman.

"Down in front!" voices shout.

An auto horn honks, honks, honks.

John L. Lewis begins to talk. "Labor's patience is not without limits, however, nor am I convinced will the American people generally continue to tolerate a condition of industrial serfdom when Congress has decreed through the National Labor Relations Act that democratic rights must be accorded to American workers. Packinghouse workers are now serving notice on Armour and Company that their patience is nearing an end, and that if the company continues to refuse collective bargaining, it must accept the conditions of its own action. . ." His voice rolls even more slowly as he recalls the Memorial Day Massacre. "The cause for which those strikers died has not been stopped by the bullets which laid them low. It has gone marching on, until even Tom Girdler and his associates can now see the determination of the thousands who have joined the union to take the places of the martyred dead. . . Through the nation, twelve million unemployed have been dispossessed from our national economy. What are we going to do about it? We aren't going to do anything about it until the workers, in their might, rise and demand that something be done about it. Who are the people of this country? Those who toil constitute the overwhelming majority of our population!" He booms out. "Organize! Organize! Organize! Capital is organizing. Finance is organized. Everyone in our national economy is organized. Organize! Organize!"

The meeting ends. I leave with a newspaper reporter. "Good speech," he says. "Hearst is losing ground here. All of his policies have been against him. In 1931 or 1932, he tried to make his papers respectable whores by doing away with large type and that also helped destroy his circulation. The strike hasn't helped any. I think his *coup de grâce* came when he allowed the Newspaper Guild situation to come to a strike. I doubt whether Hearst'll ever recover. . . I wrote editorials on the damn thing and the orders would come in to write up the American Legion crow drive down state. That's the sort of editorial Hearst considered safe. During the gangland days, the Hearst papers sold the Capones to the public as Robin Hoods. That's Hearst. Naturally, he fought the Guild right from the start."

"How did the strike start?"

"Last November, they fired forty in a lot and about a dozen others were given notice. That brought about the strike. Some of us had the state of mind that this was a matter we had to go along with. Working for Hearst was a miserable lot and perhaps we might improve it. We've had enormous support considering the kind of city Chicago is. The majority of the people here once wouldn't get excited about anything. The Germans, the Poles, everybody here has been conditioned by the general nature of the town. That is—not to bother about anything except their own private affairs. The people were lethargic. The politicians stole forty or fifty millions raised to build a subway, stole year after year, and the people weren't interested. Now they've gotten around to the subway. One line will run north, the second line south. . . Hearst hasn't helped make Chicago a large town. He never took a stand on transportation. Chicago has worse transportation for its size than any city in the country. That helped the trend of the large racial groups to continue living by themselves. But I think the C.I.O. is our entering wedge."

He walks rapidly, excited. "Of course, I'm a typical newspaper case. Most people drift into it. I graduated from the University of Illinois in Romance languages. I thought I'd teach but I fell into a job as a press agent in a farm exposition down in Kansas. Through that job, I got to know the newspaper men and the usual bull that it was an interesting life. I came to Chicago to work for Hearst in 1927. What I'm getting at, is the change here. The people came here first to make money. Chicago draws from the provinces and in the past from the poor European stocks. New York gets the restless young folk. We get the rest. . . And yet our strike has been a surprising force in awakening people. Newspaper men I know who used to think that active Guild members were agents of Joe Stalin, have changed their minds. They've gone through a crucible and will come out good strong union men and liberal men. Some of us saved money and we can coast along. Others are in hock to the loan sharks. But they've gone on relief without a murmur. That's a wrench for white collar workers. And the C.I.O. is the wedge! Years ago, the worst place in the country for a mass meeting was Chicago. The people would stay over in their own neighborhood and not budge, but now. . ."

The people who attended the meeting are now waiting for the trolleys to take them back to their own neighborhoods.

"Some crowd!" the newspaper man says. "Imagine the possibilities if the two and half million farmers who raise livestock were organized. . . If the farmers cooperated with the packingtown workers. . ."

U. S. Route Number 14

Chicago's Lake Shore Drive connects Lake Michigan and the resort lakes to the north. The city strides into the country with its hot dogs, Bar-B-Q's and vacation hotels. At Phil's Beach a sign is stuck into the ground:

MODERN COTTAGE FOR RENT
GENTILES

The barns and silos of Wisconsin duplicate into the far distance. Herds of cows crowd together under the green umbrella shade of trees.

Fort Atkinson.

Cambridge.

Deerfield.

Sun Prairie.

Columbus.

Beaver Dam.

Everywhere the sun is a hot golden rain upon the cornfields.

THE PEOPLED PRAIRIE

Emery's Eighty Acres

COLUMBUS COUNTY, WISCONSIN

*"Once upon a time, the world was a berry patch and then
somebody put a fence around it and said: 'The patch is mine.'"*
Old grandmother's story.

THE BIG WOODEN HOUSES on Park Avenue in the town of
Beaver Dam are lit by electricity. But in many of them the
brass gas fixtures of an earlier America curve out from the
walls. Outside, the maples green-roof the gutter down to the
railroad crossing. Here, Park Avenue becames treeless Front
Street, the business center. Rows of modern electric posts
stand on the roots of the old maples.

On Saturday night, Front Street's parking spaces fill up
with farmers' cars. The neons of Zweck-Wollenburg Hardware, Veling's Boot Shop, Newton and Wenz Department
Store, the Odeon Movie house, J. C. Penney & Company,
flash on for the cash customers. Big blond farmers' wives stare
with admiration at the porcelain girls kneeling in prayer
inside the Reier Floral Shop window. The taverns get the
men. The bars are crowded with beer drinkers, the music
boxes singing a song of Saturday night.

The sidewalks become open-air parlors as families gossip.

"Think we'll have rain?"

"My corn needs rain."

"So does mine."

They talk of friends, relatives, neighbors, populating the
town with the names of hundreds, the names of the Wisconsin people.

Fat wives corral their children whose corn-yellow hair
must have once been the color of their own faded brownish
blond marcels. Blond couples walk by the blue, red and green
neon of the Farmers' State Bank.

A little boy of four tugs at his father's hand. "Let's go to the circus, Daddy. Let's go to the circus, Daddy."

"There is no circus now. The circus is tomorrow," the father explains.

The boy rubs his teary eyes. "Will we go tomorrow?"

All night long, outside my furnished room on Park Avenue, the circus wagons rumble past. I get up and listen to the noise of wheels, the clip-clop of hooves. Outside the two screened windows, it seems as if the America of fifty years ago is on the move between the maples.

Emery Lenz's eighty acres are four miles outside of Beaver Dam.

The Sunday sun hangs in the morning sky, a burning sermon on the land. The Lenz family, my wife and I sit outside the house in the pine and maple shade. Strong-jawed Emery is dressed in his Sunday suit, a tall man of forty-two with straight blond hair and blue eyes bloodshot in the corners from the week's work. His wife, Lora, smiles often. Good-looking, with curly dark brown hair, blue eyes and freckles, she seems Irish. On the lawn, two-year-old Lorraine chases after one of the cats, her pretty face contorting with delight as she runs on bare feet, her little belly round and cute as a kewpie doll's. Lawrence Lenz watches his sister. He is about twelve, the blondest in the family with a face as innocent as Lorraine's, his strong hands smaller copies of Emery's huge ones.

"My, it's hot," Lora says.

"Lawrency, take Lorrainey to the swing," Emery calls out. The green and orange swing is near the unbarbed wire that fences the house and lawn.

Emery nods in the direction of the unpainted toolshed, the pump and its windmill tower, the barn and the silo farther away. "Today we rest," he says solemnly. "Only Lorrainey don't rest."

The red paint is fading from barn and silo. The new addition to the house has never been painted, the white boards still clean looking. Lawrence's cousin, Dougy, a boy of about his own age, comes out of the house.

"The Cole Brothers Circus came to town this morning," I say. "Are you fellows going?"

"I was going to take them in to see the parade," Emery answers.

Lawrence trots over toward me. "After church this morning before you got here, Dougy and I went over to the Fair Ground. A man told us he'd give us tickets if we helped him put up the poles."

Dougy grimaces as if he'd swallowed medicine.

Lawrence shakes his head sadly. "We'd do anything to go to the circus. But those poles. . . Break your back on those poles. Let 'em put up their own poles." He smiles, his discolored teeth, separated one from the other now making him seem more boyish than ever. "So we ain't going to the circus."

"I'll take you and Dougy."

"Will you? You're fooling!" Lawrence's smile drops from his lips. "But Dougy hasn't any money neither."

"I'll take you both."

Again, he smiles. And again, he mourns. "It'll cost a lot of money."

"Do you want to go?"

"Yes."

"Well, then I'll take you."

Convinced now, he stares at me, then hurries over towards the pine trees on the lawn. He returns with a glass jar. "You want to see my arrow heads? They're flint." He places two arrow heads on my palm. "Ain't they nice? I know where there used to be an Indian mound. It's a secret but I'll show it to you."

We leave in the early afternoon. The windmills are as still as their towers, the gravel roads dry as old bones between the cornfields. The oat and barley fields have been shocked, the shocks like endless rustic miniature houses. The near fields have been shocked, and the far fields on the hill slopes, and the fields beyond the hill slopes.

In Beaver Dam, traffic is jammed because of the circus

parade. Lawrence and Dougy get out of the car and dash to the street corner. Under the spangling sun, the grown-ups and the kids crowd the sidewalks.

The parade!

All is red and yellow, blare and gilt. The wooden carvings of women on the wagons are like the figureheads on ships, the carvings of birds like ancient temple gods. A row of slobbering spitting camels stride up the street, advertisements hanging like blankets from their sides:

PURINA FEEDS SOLD BY HARTZHEIM FEED CO.
LEADERS OF TODAY, ZIEGLER'S PILOT BEER

Behind the last circus wagon, the cars follow the parade out to the tents.

The only shade at the Fair Grounds is the shade of the barkers' colored umbrellas. "The circus is here today and won't be here tomorrow!" A barker shouts. Behind his swaying shoulders, the towering lurid canvases of the Side Show flank the entrance:

MAURICE, SWORD SWALLOWER.
ZORA, QUEEN OF SERPENTS.

"Nobody's going in there," Lawrence says. "It costs 25 cents."

Tickets to the Big Show cost 75c for adults, 40c for children.

Shoe leather slithers on the dry faded grass as farmers walk over to the stable tent to stare at the circus horses. Equestriennes come out of the tent, their shapely legs, hairless and dead-white, their faces movie-ishly pretty. Lawrence shakes his head over the horses. "Boy, they're beauties."

Back at the Side Show, the barker has become frenzied in his appeal: "Maurice will swallow his sword in the most reckless and careless manner!"

But the people continue to enter the Big Show. "Seat chairs, 75c!" a ticket seller hawks.

All the seats paralleling the three rings are reserved.

Our tickets are good for the unreserved section of backless wooden benches behind the three rings. "They charge too much," Lawrence says. His blue eyes swerve to the three giant poles supporting the big tent. Like ship masts they climb up and through the canvas.

Suddenly, pitchmen yip at the customers from all sides. "Win a camerah!"

A pitchman holds up a pair of ladies' hosiery. "Lady wins silk stock-ings."

"That's the guy who wanted us to put up the poles." Lawrence points. "That one there. I'll bust him one."

I buy one of the candy boxes the pitchmen are selling. *The Aloha Hawaiian Health Confection, Rich in Vitamin D. Helps to Prevent Rickets. Promotes sound teeth. Helps to build strong straight bodies.*

The ringmaster's whistle!

A chain of elephants, trunk to tail. Clowns, one clown leading a tiny white dog disguised as a horse with an artificial pony head and a white flowing tail. Acrobats and tumblers. All pouring out as if from some immense box, living toys. Seals catch balls and clowns with faces painted white as skulls, death-faces forever painted with grotesque smiles, cavort around the track. Waiting their turn, the solid-thighed, velvet-caped women acrobats stand in a group at the entrance.

Three horsemen gallop around the ring. The ringmaster announces: "The West is fast fading from the American picture. See the Wild West Show after the performance! Bucking horse riders! Everything that makes the real Wild West."

Dazzled, Lawrence and his cousin stare in silence at the living fairy tale before them.

Back home, Lawrence shows me his cardboard box of baby rabbits, "I ran them down," he says, taking one out. The warm ball fits inside his hand, a tiny cottontail, its ears flattened down in fright. "I have my pets. I have doves, too."

Emery puts Lorraine in a home-made go-cart. "Lawrencey built this for baby." As he pulls the cart, the iron wheels, salvaged from some junked machine, squeak on their wooden axles. "Wood and iron don't mix." He lifts the laughing baby high in air, her body fragile between his calloused hands, his fingers fitting the palms like spokes their wheels.

On the lawn a dozen pullets search for food. A yellow-legged White Rock and a bluish-green legged Giant peck at a rat Muttsie the cat has brought in. The cat has only left the skin. "They ain't hens yet," Emery says. "Around seven months they become hens and begin laying eggs. But already they want to be strong. It's good you come Sunday so I have time to explain tings." He leaves out his h's now and then. "Come, I show you the farm. Lawrencey, you watch Lorrainey."

Muttsie glides up the lawn, a young rabbit in her mouth. She drops it to the ground and eats off one ear, the second ear, the bloodied face, the head.

"She likes that rabbit," Lorraine says. "That kitty nice."

Emery smiles.

The cat eats out all the guts. Three or four pullets come up to the rabbit, waiting their turn like crows. One of the White Rocks pecks at the vanishing meat. Muttsie growls, a sleepy gorged growl. The White Rock pecks down, seizes the rabbit's hindquarter and leg in her bill. Off she runs through the picket fence chased by the other pullets.

"They're not afraid of the cat, Emery?"

"Friends are not afraid of each other. They each have enough."

We tramp to the first shocked field. "That's velvet barley," Emery says. "We plant it just as quick as the ground is fit, when you can take the ground and it don't make no mudballs. I got fifteen acres in barley. If it went for a dollar a bushel, the livestock wouldn't get it. You can take all the good kernels out and feed the junk to the stock."

The sun lowers in the sky. Emery nods at his barley crop. "To produce this, we need a binder, a seeder, a disk, and a drag to smoothen off the ground. That's four machines besides your hosses for power." He pulls out a barley stalk from one of the shocks, crushes the head against his palm. He smiles. "I like to thrash this way." He bends his head and mouth over his palm, blowing the chaff away. "See dat." He shows me the seeds in his palm. "Dat's the malting barley for beer. See those shocks? You build up a house, and on top, the clothes-pin pinches everything together." He picks up the top bundle of barley. "See that t'istle in there. That's Wisconsin cactus, those Canadian t'istles. The binder has no heart. It bind the barley and the t'istle together. But we'll take it right home and let the chicken do their own thrashing. They pick out the seed." He breaks open a thistle with his patient fingers. "You've seen men go down in parachutes? Here are the parachutes." He drops the fluffs, watches them descend to the ground. "The seeds are the men. These seeds will not grow. It takes a healthy t'istle seed to grow." Squatting on his haunches, in his blue overalls, he raises his tanned face. "See that twine on the bundle? They treat the twine at the factory so bugs won't eat it off the bundle."

We climb down into a hollow. "When water runs downhill, it gathers together at certain places. We plow the ditches smooth to do away with the ditch. The less ditch the longer your machines'll last." Emery points to a young tree. "I carried that tree over there. He was a little thing and he growed. That's what I like. Plants and machinery."

A partridge booms up ahead of us and into a clump of trees. "This is a hickory tree grown here by itself," Emery says. "You don't see them all over. Up above is a robin. He knows no depression."

The sun is sinking on his barley acres. He shakes his head at a place where the wind has blown the bundles out of their architecture. He almost seems maternal now. "See what the baby cyclone's done to our nice work? All over, we got enemies." He smiles. "The t'istle's our enemy and the wind's our enemy. When it don't rain and we need rain, that's an enemy too."

"You act as if you like your enemies?"

"The farmer can handle all the enemies but one. The price. Over that we can do nothing. We got two dollar milk in 1926. The tin holds eighty pounds. That's two dollars a hundred. Now we get ninety-five cents a hundred."

He pauses at the edge of the field. Great boulders lie in a scattered pile, the blunt teeth of the earth itself. "Those pessimists were all over. See that old windmill? That was built in 1895. A new windmill cost one hundred and twenty-five dollars. The more tower, the higher the price. That grass over there is our hay. We have six acres in grass. We feed the cows first, then the hosses get the cleanup. In other words we cheat the hosses out of what they work for."

"Emery, do you own your farm?"

"It was this way. I work three years out west in Minnesota

and three years around here and I have six thousand dollars and a Ford car. I bought this farm fourteen years ago but it still ain't mine. I got a mortgage on it." He frowns. "It was last year . . ." His forefinger charts a circle on his flat palm. ". . . I think of the year as round. It was here I'm supposed to pay interest. A farmer ain't nothing but a slave to the interest." He is silent. When he talks, his voice is boyish again. "You're about three feet above water, the sweetest kind of water. This new grass takes its time. Babies have to grow. Two, three years before the hay comes in."

We skirt a patch of land grown to horse nettle and full of stone boulders. "In fourteen years I couldn't tame this corner. So each year I did a few of those pessimists. It was a spare time job and only when it's dry in the fields. As you farm the pessimists come out. Erosion'll wear them out. I like to work with them cripples. One man from North Dakota says if they were supposed to be moved, they'd have handles on them." He laughs. "The great big he-ones we load with dynamite. Now, we come to the corn."

Indian file we walk between the green rows. "This corn grow two foot in thirty days and it'll go eight feet. It's silo corn. I have six acres of this young corn. We plant it late to keep it green. Start with a manure spreader, then the plow, then a drag, then a planter, then the tractor cultivator or hosses. When you harvest it, you use the corn binder." He stoops between the rows. His brown hand spades into the dry earth. "If you let the ground crack open you lose all the moisture. See that?" Below the powder brown surface, the soil is wet brown. "Some of the farmers need rain in ten days or their corn'll die. I can get along without rain for a long time." He scrutinizes one of the stalks. "This one, I cut his toes off. He had reserves on the other side. But you can't rob them of all their roots. A man can't walk far on one leg either." He plucks out a handful of grass. "Pigeon grass. It's a weed to us here because it shouldn't be in the corn." He digs into the earth with his fingers. "It sure is a lovely corn land."

He straightens up. "Now I show you twenty acres of the corn I plant May twentieth."

The tall corn is between five and six feet high. He kneels to earth. "I got to show you cultivation again. Big as this corn is, it could last thirty days. I need rain in two weeks for this

corn so the ears can grow big." He shakes his head, smiling a
little. "Out in Minnesota, I sat in a one hundred acre corn
field. That's pretty. Corn on all sides of you." He breathes
deep of the sweet corn smell. "This is planted with a wire
with knots on it. The wire strings out the length of the field.
You turn around. You look both ways and you get square
rows both ways on account of the wire planting. This is the
center of the field. We have no corn here. When you plow,
the plow turns the earth to the right and to the left and in the
center you got the dead furrow. . . The machine drops pretty
near three wherever you want it. Human hands couldn't do
better. Here we try to drain the water by making a ditch because it's a hollow here. The rains come and take advantage.
We can control the water but we can't control fire. After you
have the crops in, lightning will hit the barn and take all with
one shot."

We enter a field of yellow sweet clover. Emery lifts his
blue eyes to mine. "Eighty acres is too much for one man, but
two men can handle one hundred and sixty. They can double
up and help each other. Like when we go thrashing, you'll
see how all the men help thrash and that's how you get done."
He stoops, uproots a thistle. "The t'istles, they have a root
goes through for all of 'em like a city sewer system. I killed
this one and the others know it. They can talk to each other.
Nature sure is wonderful. Now we go over there to hell's half
acre."

At the edge of the corn field, the corn in even rows, we
enter a tangled wilderness of willows, wild hemp and wild
cucumber vines. "It's too wet and it's full of rocks. But when
you don't cultivate, nature does her own." He points to a furrow in the earth. "Nature do that. I've seen furrows six feet
deep when it gets dry enough. The rain come and it got to go
in the crack."

We tramp over to the alfalfa. Emery plucks off a few of the
tiny purplish flowers. "That's the relish for the cows, the appe-
tizer. I got six milk cows, three hosses and fifteen pigs. Two
acres of alfalfa ain't enough. I should have at least ten. Over
there we have six acres in oats." The oats, like the barley, have
been cut and shocked. "That's pig-feed but when we get
smut . . ." He holds up a shriveled stalk, the smut like black
pepper. "That's no good for nobody. We can contend with

the smut. We farmers can get along. We help each other out with the thrashing and the corn harvest. But the one we can't contend with is the price. When we go to the counter we ask: 'What do you want for the stuff?' But when we got pigs to sell or milk, we take what they gives us. My milk, I sell to Joe Schmied. He's a *Schweitzer*, a Swiss. He has twenty-two cheese factories from Watertown to South Beaver Dam. He pays the cheese-maker, pays for the coal, and takes some for his management. He's very fair." He smiles quickly. "But farmers don't trust each other enough. They like it better if a stranger skins them."

The one acre of white-flowered buckwheat seems like a garden after the oats, corn and barley. "We use it for hog and chicken feed. Or we can sell it for a cent a pound. That's the price. We truck our pigs to Milwaukee and they pay us according to the amount they want and according to the run coming in. They buy the most pork when the price is lowest. A two-hundred-pound pig can bring you twenty-four dollars or eight dollars. That's the gamble in farming. The price."

In the darkness we come to the grain binder with its elevated driver's seat, giant wooden reel and cutting platform. Emery reaches down into the binding side, the steel rods shaped like fishtails. "That presses the bundles when full enough, up to the big needle." The big needle is curved like a bird's bill. It holds the twine, ties the knot. "That's the knotter under the needle and that's the knife that cuts it off. I'm taking care of the machinery of three or four of the neighbors. I can always get it to work. That sounds like bragging, but the truth is the truth. Since John Kant left his farm, I've got his customers. He was a good machinist but he gave up farming. I could fix the Model T's but the new cars, them're too fine. I can do anything on a farm except fix teeth. But all I can make is a living."

The first stars are out as we walk home along the road. "I wake you up five-thirty tomorrow. This week we go thrashing. We help each other out. Just a bunch of neighbors."

The next morning, Emery and I meet in the kitchen. Our two wives, Lorraine and Lawrence are still asleep. Smiling, Emery tosses me a pair of rubber boots. "Put them on. It's wet in the fields. You take Billie and drive the cows in from the pasture." He is wearing his blue work shirt and blue overalls with their smell of stable and field. "That reminds me of the boss who wakes up his hired hand. 'Wake up,' said the boss: 'It's daybreak. We've got to cut the oats.' 'What's the matter with them oats?' the hired man said. 'Are they wild oats that we got to sneak up on them in the dark?'"

Laughing, I follow him outside. The sun has come up but the new day is almost twilight. Barn, silo, the shocked fields beyond them, the barns and silos and fields of the neighbors, all seem to be part of one beautiful farm.

"Billie goes for his walk in the morning, and not like other dogs at night," Emery says as I untie the half-shepherd, half-collie. "Don't let him get too close to the cows."

Far down at the end of the dew-wet cow path are the six cows. Billie tugs at the rope knotted to his collar. The cows lumber forward, all six, the black ones, the brown Guernsey with the big ring in her nose. I turn my back on the lemon sun and drive the cows to the barn in the bird-singing morning.

Inside the barn, Emery has already put the cows into their stanchions, the big metal collars that hold their heads in place at milking time. He hands me a three-legged stool and a pail, and then demonstrates the proper milking technique. "You open and squeeze. Hold the pail between your knees."

Pail between my knees, I sit down under the black and white Holstein. She turns her horned head around to stare, leaning her warm body against my shoulder. I clench my fists around two of her four teats. I pull. Nothing happens. I squeeze. Nothing happens.

A pullet picks off the flies on the Holstein's legs.

"Don't pull so hard. You've got a good cow. That's a good healthy cow you got there but they get sick when the boss don't watch his business. Open and squeeze like this."

I follow orders but my hands aren't the jack-of-all-trades machines of a farmer's. At last a white dart of milk jets out of the right teat.

Emery leaves. When he returns, he says. "I fed the pigs."

"I got her milking but now she's drying up."

He takes my stool. "You got to understand cows. Sometimes they stop their milk from coming. But we won't get much milk now. They're on vacation. When the calf is born, there is a waste material and sometimes that stays stuck. I wash my hands in a solution I got in the chest there and take out the waste by hand. The veterinary give 'em medicine and let it go at that." He stands up. About one fifth of the pail is full. "Another thing about milking, you have to get it all out or the milk thicken inside and the cheese-maker say: 'What's the matter with your cow?' One cow can spoil the whole tank of cheese. Now we eat breakfast ourself."

There is no running water in the kitchen. In turn we fill a tin basin with water from the bucket on the faucetless sink. We soap and rinse.

At the kitchen table, Lorraine is already sitting in the high chair that was her brother's before her. In front of every setting, there is a bowl of oatmeal. Lora comes to the table with a platter of fried eggs. Emery clasps his big brown hands and Lawrence clasps his. Lorraine imitates Lawrence. Head lowered, Emery says grace.

"Amen," Lorraine says.

"Lorrainey knows." Emery smiles at my wife and me. "Now you and the lady help yourself."

"Why don't the cows give more milk, Emery?" I ask.

He picks at his teeth. "The heat and the flies. It bothers them." He rubs his eyes. "Everything has its season."

As the women clear off the dishes, we three men go out. Emery stops at the pump, drinks from the tin cup, tilting his old straw hat back on his forehead.

Lawrence rolls his head like a puppy. "Did you like those circus ladies?" he asks me.

"Did you?"

"No. They're all French and Polish."

Emery finishes his drink, finds a rake for me and a scythe for himself. "The grim reaper," he comments, the words religious, almost biblical on his lips.

We cross over into the orchard behind the barn.

"I paid one dollar seventy-five for ten of these apple trees," Emery says. "They're eight years old. Now we work."

He swings his scythe, the long curved blade cutting through the alfalfa.

I rake the long low wave of alfalfa and timothy grass in his path. Following behind me, four or five of the pullets gobble up the bugs and grasshoppers cut out of their homes.

Emery drops his scythe, leaps to the ground. He rises, a baby cottontail between his palms. "You bring that back to Lawrence and tell him you catched him. There's the cheese-maker's truck!" Emery squints at the car pulling up to the barn. "Lawrencey, pull the weight cans up! Lawrencey!" he calls.

"All right, Dad." Lawrence shouts back.

I return to the house with the rabbit. "Your dad caught him."

"You going t'rashing." His face saddens and he forgets the new rabbit. "I wish I could go."

"Wait'll you get stronger."

"I'm strong enough for t'rashing."

I return to the orchard and take my turn with the curving scythe. The sun climbs in the sky and we finish the chore.

Lawrence is sitting with the women in the shade on the lawn, a harmonica in his hands. The yellow sun surrounds them as if they were on an island. He plays:

> "Home, home, on the range,
> Where the deer and the buffalo play,
> Where seldom is heard a discouraging word. . ."

"How'd you get that wart on your knuckle?" I ask when Lawrence finishes.

"I had twelve warts on my hand when I was a girl." Lora smooths back Lorraine's damp locks. "I rubbed my hand on a stone until it bled. Threw the stone away! And I got rid of all those warts."

"Was that when you were going to school?"

"My, yes. There was a boy there, they called Donkey Ears." She laughs with recollection. "They stood out so. But they called me Curlyheaded Jew on account of my hair and that was worse." She pouts like a little girl.

Emery returns with two pitchforks. "You and Lawrence go cock the hay."

Lawrence puts away his harmonica, jams his farmer's

straw hat down to his eyebrows. We march out into the heat. A bird's repeated song sounds as if it were perched overhead in the glaring empty sky. "That's a bob-white!" Lawrence exclaims, whistling back. He studies his shadow on the ground. "It's about half past nine."

"How can you tell?"

"When your shadow points straight north it's noon. But it's a long way from noon." He sighs. "We can't use the hay loader to pick up the hay. There's too many holes and the ground's too soft. The horses would sink in." He begins to rake the cut hay into piles with his pitchfork. Methodically, like an old farmer, he builds a sweet-smelling hay cock. "I like to farm." Lawrence smiles. "Do you?"

"Yes."

"Do you like the city better?"

"I don't know? I didn't know you played the harmonica."

"I can play the accordion, too."

"How'd you learn, Larry?"

"Picked it up by ear."

"Maybe you'll be a musician?"

"No. I like farming better. I wish I could go t'rashing. But I have to stay home and do the chores when you and Dad go."

When all the hay is cocked, we go back. Lawrence pounces down to earth like a cat. "I got a mole!" He shows me the prisoner in his fist. "They ain't bad little fellers. He has eyes but he don't see. I like pets, do you?"

I nod.

He climbs the garden fence. "That sugar cane's for my doves. Most all the kids around here have doves. But mine are mostly blue ones." We walk between the cane, between big green cabbages and yellow starry pumpkin flowers. "That green lettuce is like in the stores but I like the red lettuce, too. Best of all, I like the watermelons. I let them grow. Then I cool them and go out in the field. I slice the watermelon in four parts and eat them all up. Sometimes, I drink the watermelon water. At night, I have to go out all the time. That's what I like. Watermelon. Once I ate five whole watermelons. No supper, only watermelon." He stares down fondly at the green watermelons.

At the house, my wife is scraping off the skins of newly picked potatoes. "We just dug them up. Lora's inside with the carrots."

Emery calls. "Come on. We got to pitch the t'istles to the chickens."

In the rear of the house, I find him standing on the top of the hay wagon load, his feet planted down on the mixed bundles of oats and thistles. "Whoa!" he calls to King and Queen, the two Montana seven-year-olds hitched to the wagon.

I climb up and we start dumping out the load. "It's a long way to twelve o'clock, Emery."

He smiles. "In two, three weeks, those chickens pick out the seed. They do their own thrashin'."

We reach the floor of the wagon. Emery takes the reins. "I'd let you drive but the horses, they know. Come on, Queenie," he coaxes in an almost comradely way as if he were telling her: I know all about you horses. The wagon jounces forward down towards the barn and silo and out onto the road. "It's a knack to learn how to stand right on a wagon. It's all knacks. And the farmer must learn them all." The branches of the roadside trees swish by.

Emery guides the team into the hay field. "Whoa!" He jumps off, attaches the hay loader to the rear of the wagon, climbs back. "I invented a corn loader to take the fifty-pound bundles from the corn binder to the wagon. I saw a man in town but he said there was nothing in it. Three months later, it was for sale with a big farm machinery company. I was only eighteen years old. Come on, Queenie."

The horses pull up to the first long swathe of hay where the hay raker has piled it, a narrow long sweet-smelling mound. "You take the pitchfork and when the hay comes up in the loader, you push it forward all the time."

The two horses reach the swathe, the diagonal belt of the loader picks up the first hay, carries it up above the highest wagon bar. Faster, faster, faster, the greenish-yellow hay forms clouds above my head. I work the pitchfork as fast as I can. A wind blows. The pile of hay, released from the belt, seems to hover in air between wagon and loader. I leap out my pitchfork as the wind leaps. The hay falls to the ground.

"Whoa!" Emery shouts. "The wind's our enemy, too. You take the reins. Don't let them pull too hard and keep the hay between the two horses."

"Giddyap King, Queenie." The freshly cut sun-yellowed hay piles up knee-high as Emery forks it forward.

"Step on it! Put it underfoot," Emery calls to me.

I swap the reins for the pitchfork. Standing on hay, I stamp the new hay from off the belt into the mass underneath.

When we get a load, Emery drives to the barn.

I climb up the iron ladder into the hay mow, the wagon below me, the fields of shocked oats and barley stretching to the hills.

"You look out for the grapnel up there," Emery warns. "That critter's dangerous."

Lawrence takes out the truck, the five-passenger car with the rear seat out. He ties the end of the pulley line to the rear of the truck, drives forward.

The silver-colored hay grappler, pointy-legged like a giant spider, rushes down the overhead cable in the middle of the barn's ceiling. Stops, jammed.

"Lawrencey," Emery calls. "Get the fishing pole. There's a sparrow nest in the way of the grapnel."

A minute later, Emery reaches up the tip end of the twelve-foot bamboo pole, the line in a spiral, the hook in the cork. "The enemies are all over. Poke it to the right."

I push at the nest. Like a tenement hit by dynamite, the ramshackle nest tumbles down. Emery pulls the grapnel rope. The grapnel jumps from the barn to the top of the wagon, digs its pointy legs into the hay. Climbing up in air again, the huge load blocks out the sun as it enters the barn on the cable. The grapnel whizzes down to the rear, a mechanical spider, dropping the hay. Quickly, the wagon empties and the mow fills.

At noon, we walk to the house for lunch. "I like the birds." Emery points up to the orange and green birdhouse on top of its pole near the windmill. "I made that myself for the birds. That's my ideal. Some day I live in a house like that myself."

We all sit down to plates of yellow carrots, boiled potatoes, cold fried eggs left from breakfast, hard meat from the pig slaughtered a year ago. Emery clasps his hands at the table, his hands a church, and says grace.

"Amen," Lorrainey sing-songs. "Amen."

Lora turns on the radio to the hog market broadcast. The announcer in Milwaukee calls off the prices: "260 pounds to 325 pounds, 5 cents to 6 and 1/4 cents. . ."

"Hogs are low." Emery smears butter on a piece of bread. "I'd like to get 10 cents. After dinner, we go for a drive. On Mondays, I take it slow. The whole week's ahead of you on Monday."

After lunch, a neighbor's car pulls up alongside of the lawn. "Are you going to thrash tomorrow?" the tanned woman at the wheel asks Emery.

"I think so."

The neighbor shakes her head. "Here you go thrashing the other side of the county. You ought to thrash closer to home."

"I always thrash with them boys."

"We need a good worker."

"You get Paul. He's a good worker. You find him home now. Sorry."

The neighbor drives off.

"Can I go t'rashing?" Lawrence coaxes.

"You have to take care of the chores, Lawrencey. Now I'll get the car."

Lora laughs happily. "They'll be thrashing up to our place next week."

Lawrence and I sit up front with Emery. My wife, Lora and drowsy Lorraine sit in the back. Emery shifts into first, second, high. We pass a big red barn and silo.

"That's the John Kant farm. Tom Powers has it now. It's a 160 acres." Emery explains. "Two Nebraska boys run it on shares. One's married and one isn't. They got twenty cows. They was burned out in Nebraska. Tom Powers gets half."

The blue sky holds a few clouds. "Maybe it'll rain?" I guess.

"No. That's Wisconsin weather. The clouds come out and then they back up. I show you a neighbor with a combine harvester and after we go thrashing, you tell me what you think is better."

We see an orange-painted combine harvester in action even before we park. It's left cutting side devours the edge of a field of oats. The oats pour inside the machine, seed and straw are separated, the oats sacked, the straw whirling out in swathes on the right.

"They have to pick up all the straw," Emery says. "And they have to work longer thrashing with the combine."

He parks the car at a second farm. Here, the combine harvester isn't in use, the sun tropical, on the orange paint. The owner, a pale man with glasses, and his wife a strong woman in men's overalls, greet us. The woman laughs. "We have a combine here. But we only have my boy to help. And my husband. That's just one man and a half on this farm."

"She likes to ride, that lady," Emery remarks.

"Did you see the horses in the circus?" I ask her.

"We saw the circus come in at half-past four in the morning. Oh, they have riding horses!" she exclaims enviously. "I've got a horse half western, half native. He's broken in to harness and I'll ride him yet. I'm not afraid of him."

"Did you see the circus?"

"No. We just saw them unload. Then we went fishing and caught some bullheads that we fried for lunch."

"When are you going thrashing, Emery?" the pale man asks.

"Soon, I think." He smiles at me. "This man's going to tell me which is better, the combine harvester or the thrashing crew."

Dentists, doctors, lawyers have their offices above the stores in Beaver Dam. I sit in a lawyer's office, between bookcases full of tomes with titles like Bryant's "Wisconsin Justice." The blond neat lawyer grins a neat grin. "This talk of a lawyer requiring a needle mind is all poppycock. It's a business like any other."

"Have you always lived here?"

"Practically. The biggest event that hit me was when I entered the Army. I trained in the State of Washington and in San Francisco in the heavy artillery. I was about twenty-three then. After I got out of the Army, I went to the University of Wisconsin. I was terribly green out on the West Coast, a boy who'd go a block out of his way to avoid meeting an officer because he didn't know how to salute." He grins at his youth. . . "Before that I was a theater musician but I wanted higher and better things so I entered the legal profession. I wanted a more regular life than you could get as a musician. I began to practice in 1925. My clients are mainly plain people who work in the stove factories, in the cheese factories. My work revolves around small claims. Some probate work, some criminal practice. I served two terms as a prosecutor." He stares out of the window at Front Street below. "You see things very clearly in a city like Beaver Dam. The few remaining factories are working on a part-time basis. The cheese factories work full time but are affected by the low retail price. One textile hosiery factory that had been located here, moved out to Gary, Indiana. Now, the manufacture of hosiery requires air free from dust. They have their troubles in Gary on that air problem and yet they moved. All these things tended to give me a larger view. I suffer from insecurity when my clients suffer. As for the other lawyers, we are all friendly with one another, but each man tends to move in his own social orbit. There's enough friendliness but there's little social contact. As the years go on, the bulk of your litigation revolves around automobile accidents."

I enter the dentist's office next door. The dentist is a tall man dressed in white, with brown eyes that give his gaunt face an intense look of concentration as if he were constantly peering through a microscope.

"How are the teeth of the farmers here?"

"There's a family I know. Ten years ago, the father came in to see me. During the course of the year they had run up a bill for three hundred dollars for the family. I told him the sum and he wrote me a check without questioning it. But about a year ago when I gave him his bill, a small bill of eight or ten dollars, he questioned me about the price I had charged for cleaning teeth. That's the difference. He paid three hundred dollars, ten years ago and didn't make any bones about the charges. But when things got hard, he asked me how much I charged for cleaning teeth: 'Two dollars,' I said. 'That's high,' he said. 'I don't think so,' I said: 'That's a fair price for cleaning teeth.' I've been here in Beaver Dam eleven years. Ten per cent of the people here are on relief. Forty per cent are on the ragged edge of nowhere. The stove workers have averaged three days a week for a year and a half. That's bread and butter and leaves no money for dentistry. The Home Relief people can't get an order for dentistry except to have a tooth extracted. Many dentists feel as if they're a group apart, the professional class. But I don't. And yet I was chairman of the Republican County Committee up at Lake Superior. I was Mayor of Washburn, Wisconsin. That's in northern Wisconsin. This may explain my attitude. When the depression came, I began to wonder why the wheels of industry should be thrown out of gear. . . I was the son of a lumberjack. I began to remember the past."

Jack's Tavern is on South Center Street. Inside, John Kant, the farmer turned tavernkeeper, a big man with the precisely cut features of a doctor in a movie, is serving small beers to his customers.

"I can't talk to you now," he says. "You come around my house tonight between six and eight when I'm having supper. I'm on Madison Street. The white house."

Outside, the sun seems to flow between the rows of buildings like water in an irrigation ditch.

The blacksmith sits on the couch in front of me, a big man of fifty with a chin like a stone. He wears no shirt, his old-fashioned underwear suit buttoned down the front. His wife smiles from her chair. In the kitchen down the corridor, I can hear the blacksmith's daughters washing up the supper dishes.

Opposite the big stove, a picture of three white horses' heads hangs on the wall.

"A pretty good friend of mine wanted me to learn the blacksmith trade about twenty years ago." The blacksmith speaks in a ponderous voice. "The job wasn't bad. We used to have a lot of horses from 1912 to 1920. Now there aren't many horses to be shod. Years ago the farmers used to drive their milk to the cheese factory with horses. That the blacksmith hasn't got to do. They use trucks. There used to be a lot of repair work. That the blacksmith hasn't got to do. They have rubber wheels on the wagons which before we used to put a new felly on . . ."

"What's a felly?"

"The circle around the wheel and then we put a metal tire around the wheel. In 1912, three men would put on one hundred and twenty-five shoes from six in the morning to late in the evening. That continued that way for four weeks." Slouched on the couch, his shoulders don't seem broad. He looks like a length of narrow steel. "I worked eight years as an apprentice. Then I ran a blacksmith shop of my own until the cars took away the business. In the fall of the year, the farmers couldn't plow when it was dry for more'n two days. There used to be a lot of plow work in the fall. . . It takes twenty-five minutes to sharpen a plow. The cast plow we sharpen on the emery wheel, the steel plow shares in the fire. Now the implement man in Beaver Dam will send the plow share to the company. There used to be seven blacksmith shops in Beaver Dam. Now there's two. Right alongside of the blacksmith shop, there'd be a wagon shop to build wagons and sleighs. Factory does all that! The way it is now, the farmer goes to the hardware shop. They got the hayrack irons, the horseshoes right from the factory! I had my shop in Woodlawn about thirty miles from here. . ."

Two blond girls enter the parlor from the kitchen. The older heavier girl remarks. "I remember the shop. I remember when the horse kicked him that time. He come in all bloody."

The blacksmith doesn't seem to hear her. He is back in the past of clanging iron. "Them outlaws from Nebraska and the Dakotas! Take you all day to shoe one of them. Some horses you couldn't whip. You'd have to get along without whipping or you couldn't shoe them! We used to make everything by hand. When these garages come out, they knew how to make a lot of money repairing. But not the blacksmith. It'd cost the farmer one dollar for a shoe complete. We put on a new toe calk and fix up the heel calk, dress the horse's foot down, maybe with a pad under the shoe, eight new nails in it. One dollar complete."

"Too bad the blacksmith went to pieces like that." His wife's steady blue eyes shift from her daughters to her husband.

"If I had a dollar for every shoe I put on, I wouldn't have to be on relief." The blacksmith sighs. "I used to put on six hundred shoes myself in about two months."

"The trouble with him," his wife says, "he nailed them on too solid. Some blacksmiths put them on loose so the horse would come back."

"I had to quit the work. It was coming in so uneven. Some weeks I had to wait for a job and I had my rent to pay. I went to work for the Monarch Range Company. I did blacksmith work. I made wrenches there. I sharpened tools. I did brackets of all kinds."

"Oh dear," his wife says. "I helped him put tires on the wheels. When you're first married like that, you don't mind anything."

"You'd have to make the steel tire smaller than the wheel," the blacksmith explains. "Steel will expand. Always did that job in the evening. We piled up those tires and piled wood around them to heat them. I then got them on tighter than a drum." He pauses. "I been on relief on and off since 1934. I was working for the C.W.A. doing blacksmith work. The local people used to do the blacksmith work for the W.P.A. But now a wagon comes from Madison and takes all the tools, picks and bars to be sharpened there and brought back. We had that to do here."

A third girl enters from the kitchen, a child, blue-eyed like her sisters.

"I don't know what the future holds," his wife says. "I have three girls here. Years ago I was on a farm. I liked to milk cows. Put on overalls and pitch hay, but now . . ."

"I want to be a school teacher, a nurse or a beauty cultur-ist. The main thing, I'll be a nurse," the middle girl frowns seriously.

The child smiles. "I want to be a dancer or go out in Texas and be a cow-girl."

Her mother laughs. "She pestered the head man out at the circus to ride a horse. She likes all animals, cats and dogs, any kind of animal."

"Except skunks!" the child exclaims.

"Seems as if we're scum." The blacksmith's face is un-smiling, cast in the pale metal of his hopelessness. "In the heat, iron throws the scum. And that's what they want to do with the poor people."

"It's discouraging," his wife agrees. "But what you going to do about it?"

"Father Coughlin's telling the world the truth," the blacksmith mutters.

"No," his wife contradicts him. "People think with all his talk, something'll happen and now it don't happen so they don't listen to him. He's all talk."

Later that day I hurry down Madison Street. But the door of John Kant's house is locked. "He's watching them fish," the next door neighbor calls over to me from his porch.

"Thanks."

The sun is setting, a reddish golden splash on the narrow winding waters of Beaver Dam Lake. On the concrete dam, boys are fishing with cane poles.

"Hello, John Kant."

"Hello."

We walk between the rails on the dam to the opposite shore, sitting down on the points of two rowboats pulled up on land.

"Well, God dang it, I did have a little money at one time before and during the war and I finally thought I had plenty of money to buy a farm." John Kant smiles. *"Ja!* I bought that farm up near Emery's and paid fourteen thousand dollars for it, and the boys all said that I stole it because it was such a bargain. Along came the depression and the drought, paying six per cent interest there on my mortgage, so it finally got to where I couldn't pay the interest and the tax. Finally I decided to quit the whole damn works. I was offered a job by the Reeseville Implement Company selling farm equipment. After working two years, I had a chance to get into the tavern business. I've been in it a year and a half. It's a hard life. It's worse than farming ever was in some respects and that was bad enough. You got to put up with a lot of riffraff that a man don't enjoy. It's eight in the morning until one at night, time off for meals." The golden lake colors red. "You know what I think! The whole damn country's absolutely shot. A man can't make a decent living these days. Farming's a lot of grief. I was the hardest worker ever lived over there. I like hard work, but the interest! The interest was bad enough and then I had the drought. One year, I had forty acres of peas and all I got back was the price of the seed. There was a time this town was booming. That was before and after the war. Just ten years since all this was shot. I don't blame Roosevelt. I don't blame the Republicans. I don't blame the Democrats. They're both to blame. They're all we've had for seventy-five years and look at the mess we're in. There's no difference between the two parties and here we sit. The people are holding the bag. A man can barely exist."

He slaps at the mosquitoes. "You've got a wonderful farming community. Why, go north of Beaver Dam. Go east from here to Juneau. You'll see the prettiest land you laid your eyes on and still we can't cut the buck. Even there they're slipping. Listen here, less than twenty-five years ago, you could buy a grain binder for one hundred dollars. At that time the farmer was getting a dollar forty for milk. Today, that same binder costs two hundred and sixty-four dollars and the farmer gets ninety-five cents for milk. Figure that out and then they wonder why the farmer's going broke. The farmer should get two dollars a hundred for milk. It cost a dollar sixty to produce it. And he should get ten cents a pound for hog. But he doesn't. That's why ninety per cent of the farmers are broke. I sold farm machinery. I know. Sell a man a tractor and you'd have to finance it. You went and looked up their record in the County Court house in Juneau and found out they were in bad shape. *Ja.* That's how I know how broke the farmers are."

Another day ends on Emery's farm, the many tasks fitted exactly into the many hours. Still the leghorns dig for worms in the garden, the pullets climbing up the hill of last year's straw hunting for grubs. But Emery is through working for that day. We go into the repair shop shed. The wooden vises are home-made. The metal drawers were once old oil cans. The anvil is a block of wood in which Emery has whittled out a space to hold a flatiron placed upside down. He rubs his finger across the triangular steel surface. "I know a good trick. Can you drive a needle into a penny?"

"No."

"You put the needle into a cork and cut the top of the needle off so the whole needle is just inside the cork. Then you put the cork on a penny, on a wooden block and if you know how you can drive the needle right through."

I follow him out to the pump for a drink. He plucks a stalk of ragweed out of the ground. "Horses like that. We don't go to college to learn how to farm. All I'd have to learn in college is salesmanship to get my share of the cash. All the rest I could handle." He laughs, pleased at his humor, walking over to the barn.

I stroll over to the pig pen. The pinkish-white Chester Whites and the black Berkshires are gruntingly busy, shoving their snouts into the corn kernels. Two pullets slip through the wire, robbing what they can. One of the Berkshires suddenly seems to remember better food. He scampers from the corn to the troughs, the pigs in a herd after him. The troughs are empty. They return to the corn. Emery strides up to watch with me. "Why have they got rings in their noses?" I ask.

"Pigs will dig holes in the ground if you don't stop them. They're good pigs. When pigs are active they'll be pigs. All animals, horses, we are all the same."

Grunting, the pigs gulp up the corn.

"They're noisy neighbors," Emery says. "Generally, your neighbor's your worst enemy. That's not true of mine. It reminds me. . . The Sunday of the circus I went to church and the preacher said: 'People are like porcupines. They can't stay together, but when it gets cold the porcupines come together to keep warm. But they stick each other so they move apart. But it's still cold. They come together and try once more. They find a way when they have to.' "

I squint up at the near twilight blue sky.

"No rain there," Emery sighs. "The leaves of the four o'clocks by the house, they hang down. They pray for rain. Tomorrow, we go thrashin' and you see how the porcupines come together. Lawrencey!" he calls. "We take the car out!" He lowers his voice. "This man we go to see, he has ten children and they all work with him on the farm and yet he don't own the farm. He's a renter."

All of us pile into the car and we drive up the road for two or three miles, stopping at a big brick house. Lawrence sprints

over to the barn. Our women folk join the renter's women
folk on the lawn. The renter, a black haired man in overalls,
walks over to Emery and me. "How do you like my barn?
That barn's one hundred and four feet long. It's sixty years
old. You don't see many barns like that any more." His voice
has Sunday's rhythm, the easy speech that a farmer speaks
between the last chore and the night's sleep. "Emery, I want
to show you my pigs."

"How long have you been here?" I ask the renter.

"This year." He leans on the pig fence. "I've got ten kids,
five boys and five girls. The oldest is eighteen. I employ a
hired man. No sense working the devil out of the kids when
they're young. Yes, and I still don't own this farm." He snaps
himself out of his thoughts. "They're healthy pigs, Emery."

Emery peers at the pigs. "I think so."

"I had worms in my pigs but this year I gave them some
lye and that cured them. I give my pigs good care. But I work
hard all year to get something to eat and don't get enough at
that," he says gloomily. "In the city they can't buy what we
produce and we don't get the prices we should. It's all wrong.
All my children work on this farm. The oldest graduated from
high school. She's going to Training School to be a teacher in
the fall but she's working on the farm now, too."

The stars shine in the night-deepening sky. We walk back
to the lawn, sitting down on the concrete walk, the wives in
front of us in the rockers. The renter's wife, a stout woman
with glasses, rocks among her daughters, the two in overalls
lounging on the walk.

Light gleams in the black barn's tiny window. "Lawrence's
playing in there with your boys." Emery's face is shadow, his
strong body a longer shadow. "What are those boys up to?"

"We need rain," the renter's wife says.

"Once, you'd go out haying and it'd be sure to rain,"
Emery remarks. "But that don't hold true no more."

The renter laughs bitterly.

"I hear you're travelling West," the renter's wife calls to
me. "Your wife was telling us. Are you going to Yellowstone
Park? Before I die I hope I can go to Yellowstone."

The silver moon cuts the corner of the brick house, silver-
ing on the women in the rockers. The sprawling young girls
are silver on the silver walk.

"I'd like to travel myself," the renter says. "But I'd need two cars or a trailer. I don't know when I'll be able to travel. I've two brothers farming down in Tennessee and they write me that it's worse there. The land isn't ours any more."

"I've worked fourteen years," Emery says. "I paid for my farm two, three times but it ain't mine. This way my car's my bank. The finance company'll lend me money on it. The interest though is sixteen per cent a year."

"A farmer doesn't get the prices," the renter continues. "The worker in the city can't pay. They can't buy. The way I think something has to happen. I remember hearing old Bob LaFollette before the war. He said to some of those Republican bluebelly farmers: 'You have money now but you're going to be devoured in twenty years.' And it came true. He said: 'The old Morgan has a diabolical brain.' And that's true. What's going to happen? I don't know! It's all a muddle but the younger folk'll be easier to organize than the older folk. Something has to be done. It just can't go on." A little girl of five runs to him, clings to his strong arms.

"I'd like to go West before I die," the renter's wife half whispers. "Well, will one of you girls bring out some refreshments. The moon's right over the pines."

"Those big banks own everything," the renter says in a thick constrained voice. "They're the hidden hand behind the government."

One of the girls in overalls comes out of the house with the refreshments. Emery picks up one of the powdered doughnuts and mumbles: "I'm going to the barn."

Munching on my doughnut, I follow him.

The electric lights are bright inside the barn. Balancing on the wooden beams the renter's many sons seem to be putting on a boy's circus. Pigeons and English sparrows whirl up and down the barn's length, pursued by the boys on the beams. Lawrence climbs a ladder to one of the tiny windows, his hands snatching at the birds trying to escape.

"What are you doing?" Emery demands anxiously.

"We want to catch the young blue pigeons."

The barn with its smell of hay and shrieking of boys' voices is like something read about in an old yellowing country newspaper.

"You come down here!" Emery orders. "You'll get hurt."

Down they come, all of them.

"We caught three," one of the renter's boys boasts.

"Poor dove," an older brother says pityingly. "Look there's blood on my hand. Poor dove. He must've torn himself on a nail."

Lawrence glances at the injured pigeon. "I'll take the other two home to my coop."

"They could make pigeon pie out of them, Lawrencey," Emery reminds his son.

"We don't want them. Lawrence can have them."

The boys march out into the moonlight. "Let me have the hurt one," Lawrence says. He takes the bird in his hands, wrings its neck, flinging the body over the fence.

"We go home now," Emery says. "We have to go thrashing tomorrow." He strides over to the car.

"Good night," we call to the renter and his family. We all pile into the car. The headlights flash up the road between the shocked fields.

"Good night," Emery says back at the house. "Tonight we don't talk."

My wife and I climb up the flight to our room, with its silhouettes of owls, rabbits and a witch on a broomstick all kept from school and tacked on the walls. Lawrence has given us his room to sleep out in the tent on the lawn. Emery's framed confirmation certificate also hangs on the wall:

Grinnerung an den Tag der Konfirmation
geboren den 21ten June 1897
konfirmiert den 9ten April 1911 in der E. Luth.
Salems Kirche zu Lowell, Dodge Co; Wis.
                                        Aug. Kircher
                                             Pastor

The next morning after breakfast Emery carries a homemade stool and a cardboard box out to the lawn. "I give everybody haircuts. I'll give you one." He motions me to sit down on the stool. He takes a white apron out of the box, tying it around my neck. "You need short hair for thrashing."

He guides his clipper as if it were a hay cutter up the back of my head.

The family stand around and watch.

"Now that's nice and short," Emery says, finishing. "I'll get the car and you get your pitchfork."

"Good-bye," Lawrence calls sadly as Emery drives off.

"Now's the cooperative rush," Emery smiles. "The thrashing. Then the silo filling and the corn harvest." He nods as we pass by the farm John Kant once owned. "John, he see a deer go 'round the haystack once and he bend his rifle so he can shoot in circles. That what he say." Behind the car the road dust streams white and opaque. "See over there? Up a half mile. That's a cheese factory. I show it to you."

"What about the thrashing?"

"Plenty time." Emery pulls up in front of a white wooden building. On the ground floor, the cheesemaker is firing the big boiler, his hands dipping into golden light up to the elbows.

The next room is long and cool, two narrow tanks in the center. One of the tanks is empty, the second white with curdling milk. The cheesemaker returns, raking the milk up and down with a long wooden rake. As he works, two silvery double spoons, driven by coal power, churn up and down the length of the tank like fins in water.

"This was milk this morning," Emery explains. "They work on a cent a pound commission. Handle a lot of milk, they get a lot of money."

"We get the milk in the morning and we're through by twelve. *Ja*," the cheese-maker says.

"They make the cheese in bulk," Emery adds. "They sell it to the Kraft Phoenix who process it for the fancy trade. I can make cheese, but the art comes from making cheese out of all kinds of milk."

We leave and don't stop again until we reach the farm where we will thrash. Emery parks under a catalpa tree. He breaks off a few of the snake-like green fruit, tossing them into the back of the truck. "For Lorrainey."

We walk towards the big red barn. Behind the red walls, a spinning leather belt, thirty or forty feet long, joins the chugging tractor to the huge threshing machine. The threshing machine looks like an alligator. On either side of its long metal head is a hay wagon with a hill of yellow barley bundles. On each hill, a farmer stands digging into the bundles and pitching them onto the metal head with its conveyor belt. The bundles move up the head into the body of the machine. Down at the opposite end, the blower, like a long funnel-shaped tail, excretes the flying yellow straw. The barley seed pours out of the machine through a diagonal metal tube into two attached empty bags, the bags filling with seed as if with water.

Beyond the threshing machine, the yellow fields are being emptied of their yellow shocks by other wagons. The two-horse teams stop at the rows, the drivers jumping down to the ground, pitchforking the bundles up into the wagons. Loaded, they pull up to the threshing machine. Never stopping, the funnel-shaped tail rains out the yellow straw.

I climb up with my pitchfork into an empty wagon. "Who owns the thrashing machine?" I ask the driver.

"Al Winters. Al, he pays for the oil, the farmer pays for the fuel. He gets 2½ cents for each bushel." He drives out into a field where two other wagons are already at work, the sun lighting up the endless shocks. "You go help them up front. We do 'em in rotation."

I get down, hike up to the wagon ahead. It is about half full of the yellow bundles. A boy of twenty in a white shirt and old felt hat is pitching by himself. He jabs his pitchfork into a bundle. The beautiful stalks silhouette against the blue sky. Neatly, he slaps the bundle down on top of the barley wall he's building inside the wagon.

I dig my pitchfork into the clothespin bundle on top of the next shock, lift and place it on top of the rising yellow wall. Dig. And up. . .

"Giddyap!" My partner guides the horses to the next row of shocks.

Now, we are almost alongside the first wagon's driver, a big handsome fellow. Like the other younger members of the threshing crew, he doesn't wear overalls. "It's raining down where you are," he smiles at me.

Sweating, I toss the bundles up. The barley walls seem a mile high in the sky. I dig and toss a bundle over the wall down into the center hole. Loose straws dance in air, getting into eyes, nose and throat.

Handsome squints down at his partner, a hatless dark-haired boy with a prominent thin nose and a downy upper lip that has never been shaved. "Up to the dances?"

"No." The hatless boy laughs. "But I got a date tonight at eight-thirty."

"I'll keep it for you," Handsome offers.

"No, you won't. How much do you get a month?"

"Forty a month and if that isn't top pay for these parts, I'll eat all the barley you give me. I don't have to worry about spending my money on girls. They'll go with me without spending money."

My partner drives off with his loaded wagon. I start pitching bundles into Handsome's wagon.

The boy with the downy mustache grins. "Hard work, isn't it?"

"Yes. Do you go to school or what?"

"I've got one more year of high school and then I'm going to Milwaukee. I've got an uncle there."

"Don't you like farming?"

"No. Don't like it." His brown eyes confront me almost angrily as if I had insulted him.

"Are you from around here?"

"My folks run the cheese factory up the road. I don't like that either."

Handsome up in the wagon waves his hairy arms at him. "He's the son of a cheesemaker turned farmer."

"Yeah, only for a while," his partner retorts.

We get our load and drive back towards the threshing machine. I jump off at the pump where ten or twelve farmers are resting in the tree shade, taking turns with the tin cup.

A stout man of fifty-five with an unshaven face and eyes bloodshot in the corners rolls his head stubbornly. "The Government's going to take over the farms. We got to go in debt. And the Government'll have to run the whole works sooner or later. It'll have to. It's no use buying a farm, you young fellers. It'd be no good in the end because they'll have to take it over. The Government's loaning more and more money on credit and they'll have to take it over."

"The money we got now'll be worthless," another farmer mutters. "If you got some money, somebody'll try to beat you out of it. We're slaves."

"Have to deny yourself of all things," the first speaker scowls. "Why, when the depression come I said: 'If the government would give each able bodied man twenty-five hundred cash money instead of relief, we'd pull out of this depression.' Look at all we've spent and we're still where we were. A lot of farmers who owed twenty-five hundred or three thousand were foreclosed. That happened to me. That's why I'm a renter now. The money I get, goes to the man I owe and he don't spend it. He banks it. I've been through ten years of hardship and I ain't seen a change yet. I've saved all my life and was roped in on mortgages."

"So was I."

Polish and German and Anglo-Saxon, they all look the same in their straw hats.

A little man with bushy eyebrows passes his tin cup to a waiting hand. "I'd go to work in a factory if I could."

"So would I. Rather than starve to death on a farm," the first speaker agrees.

They look at each other in silence.

I walk over to the threshing machine. There are another ten men here. I begin to recognize them as separate individuals. The old hired man with the lantern jaw. The bantam farmer with his pointed little nose and his jokes about tailing. The young fellows who either work for their fathers or hire out. Handsome. The cheesemaker's son. The three sons of giant Al Winters, all brown of eye, brown of hair, all working at their father's machine. The middle son, a lanky six-footer in a sun helmet, stands on top of the thresher, directing the angle of the blower. The oldest son, the machinist of the family, is busy with the motor and spinning belt. He steps near me, takes off his sun glasses. "You're from the city?"

I nod.

"We're better off here." He rubs his chin with his work-calloused hand. "In the city you got to buy everything you put in your mouth. But we don't know either what's gonna be."

Two loaded wagons drive up, waiting to take their places at the conveyor. Al Winters' oldest son and I sit down, our backs against the silo, straw from the blower whirling before us.

"There's Emery." I glance at the bagger man, tending the bags.

"That's one of the toughest jobs there is thrashing." The oldest son sneezes. "It's no snap out here. I've canned corn eighteen and twenty hours at thirty-two and one half cents an hour and sometimes a bonus to bring it up to thirty-five cents. There was no time for school. . . I never learned to swim, and that's what I would want to do." He smiles suddenly, almost pathetically.

I stare at the muscled beauty of the scene, the men, the horses, the machines.

"If the farmers had money, you'd see things move." The oldest son shakes straw ends out of his neck bandanna. "This way we run our old tractors and old grain binders. Patch what we can. The wealthy farmers have money from years back. But not many around here own their land clear. This farm is owned by a man in Beaver Dam."

The cheesemaker's son examines his hands intently, holding them up in front of him as if they were goods he might buy.

"What's the matter?" The oldest son winks. "Don't you like callouses?"

"I can't pass a football when they're too calloused."

"You want nice hands for your girl!" The oldest son ties his bandanna around his neck and returns to his machinery.

Al Winters now drives up the small wagon with its load of eighty pound bags of barley seed. Silently, his youngest son, the cheesemaker's son and I, follow the wagon into the barn. "Whoa!" Al Winters cries. Four or five yellowed teeth remain in his mouth. He spits a stream of tobacco. "Whoa!"

He clambers down from the wagon towering over all of us, his grizzled gray head like an old bear's.

"What's wrong with farming, Al?"

He blinks at me. "I'm a farmer just as I ever did." He blinks again. "I think credit's the worst thing in this country. Some fellows don't deserve credit but a white man should have credit for thirty, sixty, ninety days. I used to get credit at the banks for three thousand dollars. Now I can't get a hundred dollars. Believe it? I'm no kitten. I'm sixty years. I've worked forty years and I've paid for my piece of land three times over and still don't own it." He spits tobacco juice. "If all the farmers would quit, say for two months, the Government'd help us. Every farmer should have credit from the Government and no interest to pay, no mortgages to pay. Indians used to live here in Wisconsin. Why can't we make a living?" He lowers his head towards us. "We're taking what we can get and got to get by with it. The banks are no good to us. The farmer got no credit."

He climbs into the wagon and lifts the first eighty pound bag as if it were empty to the top of the low wagon side. His son receives it chest-high, carries it four steps and dumps the barley out into the bin.

My turn. I carry my bag to the bin, grab the bottom corners and heave. The yellow seed rivers out.

The first shift of eaters, twelve in all, sit down to lunch in the farmhouse. Hands washed, lips cool from long drinks at the pump, the twelve men smile at the bountiful table before them. Plates of brown savory baked beans. Newly chopped cabbage. Potatoes. String beans. Carrots. Towers of white bread. Brown beef stewing in brown gravy. In front of every seat, a huge slice of elderberry pie and cup of hot coffee. The thrashing-time meal becomes a swift passing of heavy plates.

"Want some torpedoes?" the bantam farmer with the pointed little nose asks his neighbor.

Emery takes the chair next to mine. "The vegetables are from the garden. The beef's their own. Everything but the coffee, the sugar and the toothpicks is theirs."

The pitchers of gravy sluice down on mashed potatoes. The brown beef vanishes. Already, two or three farmers have finished, the new shift taking their chairs.

"My corn won't last if I don't get rain in seven days, ten days maybe," Bantam is saying.

Outside, five or six men are gathered around the pump. "It's 91 degrees right here," one of them says. "Right here in the shade."

"The corn's so advanced, it's sucking up water like a tree."

"More than a tree."

"What job will you get this afternoon, Emery?" I ask.

"A feller takes the job he gets. The loader, he loads. That was you before. The bagman, he bags."

The old hired man leads up his team to drink out of the trough. One horse sticks his nostrils under the water.

Al Winters spits a stream of tobacco juice out into the sun. "I've seen horses do that but not often."

"There's the owner," somebody remarks. "That's Ernest Klatt. He's half-German, half-Polish."

Everybody stares.

Over near the barn, a man in town clothes and panama, shirt and necktie, pressed jacket and trousers, is talking to Al Winters' oldest son.

I go over. The owner is a pale man of about fifty-five with a nose hooked almost in the center, a bony little man who looks like a strict priest.

"Are farm conditions improving?" I ask him.

"They're not getting worse. It's not very fast but on a slow order. I've been in Beaver Dam thirty-five years, in the Beaver Dam Silo Box Company. Business is not as good as it should be, but it's good as can be expected. I farmed up to twenty-five years ago myself." His blue eyes seem to be flaked out of blue stone. "One trouble is that Roosevelt lets the breweries import barley from Canada and that's knocking the price. We got to put up with Roosevelt, work with him in harmony, and hope that someone will spring up to take his place and do a better job. That's what we're all hoping for." He walks into the barn, scoops up a handful of barley from one of the bins. "Those kernels are plump. Good as the average. The breweries like it plump. Good barley will sell for $1.25 a bushel but this will sell for 60 cents."

Al Winters and two or three other farmers come into the barn.

Klatt smiles nervously. He buttons up one of the unbuttoned overall buttons on Winters' chest. "You always leave it open, Al. How's your pea crop?"

"Fine," Al Winters says, unsmiling.

"Glad to hear it." Klatt smiles from one to the other of the overalled men. "Excuse me. I've got to see my partner." He hurries from the barn to the farmhouse.

Nobody says anything. Al Winters gets into his wagon and drives down to the threshing machine.

The working afternoon begins. Again, the straw flies out of the blower. The bags fill with barley and Al Winters is back again. His youngest son, Bantam (substituting for the cheesemaker's son) and I follow each other like the elephants at the circus to the bins. In turn we empty out the bags.

Klatt's partner examines the kernels. A genial man, he feels he must tell us a story before leaving. "There was a horse in Columbus, he broke his neck. The doctor reaches into his rectum and cut his jungular. He was as dead as a hammer in two minutes. But that's where his jungular was. Speaking of horses, I was two years out west in Montana. The fellows there practice creasing. They aim at a horse and hit him behind the ear. Just enough to stun him. Then they go up and tie the horse up. There were wild horses then."

He leaves. Al picks up the reins in his wagon. "The oats are coming in now to be thrashed. I'm no big business man," he grins, his yellow stump teeth showing. "Take Governor Heil. Heil's no good for the poor man because he's a big business man. The LaFollettes was good for the poor man. But one thing, there won't be no big business man president in 1940. There'll be a president for and by the people."

All afternoon we dump the oats into the oat bins. Each time we clean out the wagon, we gossip for a few minutes. Standing on the ground, Al Winters leans both elbows on top of the wagon's side. "Last week I took four hogs into Milwaukee. That's as far as I go in Milwaukee. Into the stockyards. . ."

"Ever been to Chicago?"

"No. Never got time. Those hogs weighed 195 pounds each. Just five pounds short of 200. I got six dollars and eighty cents a hundred. The trucking cost me twenty-five cents a hundred. What can I make?"

"Who bought your hogs? Armour? Swift?"

"One of them. Who owns all them places anyway? The Jews?"

"I don't care about hogs," Bantam says. "I want to buy eight more cows."

"He's got twenty-seven. With eight more, he'll have a

corner on the cows in Doyle County." Al Winters leads the laughter.

We walk to the pump, drink again for the hundredth time, it seems, out of the tin cup. "If you can buy eight more cows, you got no worry. You're a rich man," Al Winters teases.

"What am I going to do?" Bantam demands. "Things are bad. I got a hired man and I pay him twenty-five a month. I can't pay wages. But if I pay wages, I can't use the tractor. I use horses. I have to use the horses. I can't pay wages and pay for fuel, too. I just make out. I got two children living, two dead. I couldn't make ends meet if the two dead were living."

Handsome drives his big grays to the pump. "Give me a drink."

Al reaches him the tin cup.

Handsome gulps the water, wipes his flushed face. "I wish I was up in North Wisconsin. All we do there in the summer is fish and tail."

"Why work down here?" Bantam grins.

"When he's up there, he wears his new clothes and they get a little old, so he comes down here to wear out his old clothes, farming," Al Winters says. "Then he'll go back."

"Give me another drink," Handsome demands. "We'll be through here soon. Most of the oats are thrashed."

"We go over to the next farm and begin to thrash there." Al refills the tin cup.

North and south, the fields are empty of the shocks. The mountain peak of straw has lengthened out into a shining yellow range.

At the next farm, the shocks line the fields in endless rows. The owner of the farm assigns each man his task. The cheese-maker's son becomes the new bagman.

The loaders drive their teams out into the hot afternoon. Already the first loader has begun to pitch barley bundles onto his wagon.

Al Winters gets his old job. Emery, Bantam and I are picked as Al's assistants.

The first load comes in to the threshing machine. . .
The bags fill with barley seed. Emery and I hop off. Together
we grab the top flap ends of the first bag and half-lift, half-
heave it up to the wagon where Bantam drags it back to Al
Winters.

"Don't grab by the edge," Emery counsels. "You make
handles like this."

I watch his two hands swoop down on the next sack, digging in about four inches from the top, compressing the barley
between his finger-tips and wrists.

One by one we swing the bags up to Bantam. Like headless pigs, they cover the wagon floor in plump rows. Bantam,
Emery and I sit on the tops as Al drives the team back to
the barn.

"Can you make cheese?" Bantam asks Emery.

"I get three five-pound cheeses, brick cheese, out of two
milk cans. I show you sometimes."

"All right. I was thinking of it. For a long time I don't
like cheese. I was snowed in and I ate American cheese." He
laughs. "American cheese and snow. American cheese and
snow."

The bins in this barn are full of last year's grain. Emery
climbs up to a wooden platform ten feet above the bins as
Bantam places a plank board across the top of the wagon. I
lift up the first bag to Bantam on the plank. As he grabs the
top, I push up on the bag's fat heavy bottom, elevating the
bag up to Emery. He grabs the eighty pounds in his two arms
as if it were a baby, walks four steps and empties the barley
down into the bin.

Al Winters smiles at Bantam and me. As we labor to raise
the bags up to Emery, his smile becomes fixed, a perpetual
joshing smile.

"You're stronger than I am," he teases me. "But I'll show
you." He takes a bag between his granite thumbs and casually
as if there were a hole in it, lifts the eighty pounds up to
Emery.

He waves Bantam and me aside. "You're stronger than I
am. And they're two of you." Again, the seemingly effortless
lift. . .

All afternoon we ride up and down, from the barn to the
threshing machine, the sun blazing into four o'clock.

"What I think," Emery says as we return again to the threshing machine with the empty bags. "Nobody should get interest or own a farm who don't work it. No insurance companies or banks should own a farm. Only a farmer who works it. Like one of the boys on the renter's farm last night said: 'Two tits of every cow belong to Dad, two belong to the landlord.' "

At the thresher, two drivers are pitching the barley bundles onto the conveyor belt. Above their heads, the clouds of summer dot the blue field of sky like immense white shocks.

Again Emery and I hop off the wagon to the loaded bags. The cheesemaker's son smiles at us from his place near the diagonal tube.

I sneeze, a straw from the blower up my nose.

"Your nose'll build up a resistance," Emery's hands reach for a bag. I race my hands to match his. "Nature's wonderful." The bag takes off from the ground into the wagon. "You can tell a farmer by the bristles in his nose."

A voice sings: "Organize you farmer boys . . . and join the milk pool gang. . ."

"Is that all to the song?" I shout to the voice at the other side of the threshing machine.

"There were five stanzas. I forgot the rest."

"There was a milk pool in 1933, 1934 after the strike." Emery grabs the last bag. "But it faded out."

I climb up into the wagon after him. "Giddyap!" Al shouts.

At the barn, Emery and Al find stones which they throw into the bins. "That'll take the moisture out," Al says. "If a mold sets in, it's all wasted. Now come on you strong men. Let's see if you can lift these bags."

Bantam places the plank, gets on top of it. Again, with cracking muscles, we tote the bags up to Emery on the platform. Al shakes his head. "I guess you fellows don't know how to use your thumbs proper. It's all in the thumbs. Let me show you."

He finishes up, each time whispering as if to himself, "It's all in the thumbs."

The cows come into the barn for the evening milking, the black and white Holsteins in a long file, the owner of the farm behind them.

"He has to milk the cows," Emery says. "They can't wait. . . The whole thing's out of balance. I'd go fishing if I could afford a hired man. We'd both go. I'd like to work five days only. But the farmer's slave to his job. Why, I'm just as changeable as the weather. Give me a price and I'll work my head off, but when there's no price, I feel like doing nothing."

The wagon returns to the threshing machine in the blueing day, the setting sun streaking the clouds rose and orange. The cheesemaker's son frowns at us. "I'm leaving this soon. I've got a date at eight-thirty in Beaver Dam and I'm going to keep it."

Bantam haw-haws. "I'll take your place. What do you want a date in the night for? I like it an hour before I get up." He jumps down from the wagon, picks up five straws from the ground, arranging them on the wagon floor into a square, the fifth straw a handle to the square. "Now can you make that into a sucker?"

"I give up," the cheesemaker's son answers.

Bantam grins. His fingers move. The square and handle become a word: TIT.

"Put these bags up!" the cheesemaker's son says, sulky but grinning.

We travel back to the barn for the last time. "War'll raise prices," Emery says.

Bantam sighs. "I learnt my lesson. I'll sit on my pile until it freezes. Boy, if I ever make money like hay again!"

We empty the bags in the light of two electric bulbs. Outside, the silver moon is on the land, the wagons in the fields and the men on the threshing machine charring black against the sky.

"We finish here tomorrow," Emery yawns. "Now we go home."

At the farmhouse, the drivers attach kerosene lanterns front and rear to their empty hay wagons for the trip home.

"Goodnight," Emery calls.

"Goodnight."

"Goodnight."

We get into the truck and head for home in the chirruping of the crickets. "I told you I'd ask you which is better, combine harvester or the thrasher?" Emery turns to me.

"The thrasher."

He laughs, pleased. "Here's another picture. Those fellows who like to live alone shouldn't sell to people. They work separate, let them stay separate."

Hot water is ready in the kitchen when we get home. Emery places a big washtub in the middle of the kitchen floor. "That's our Wisconsin bath-tub. You wash. Your missus help you." He shoos his wife, Lawrence and baby Lorraine out of the room.

I strip. Barley and oats and straw ends rain from my clothes to the floor.

After Emery washes, we all sit together in the sun-parlor. Near her father, Lorraine plays with the catalpa fruit. Barefooted, in a fresh change of overalls, Emery stretches out on the floor.

"Was it fun?" Lawrence asks eagerly. "I'll bet it was fun. I was hunting when you were thrashin'."

"What'd you get?"

"I shot some English sparrows."

"The cats followed him like dogs," my wife says. "They waited for the sparrows to tumble out of the trees."

"Lawrency, play something," Emery says.

Lawrence takes his accordion. Smiling, he plays: "Home, home, on the range. . . Where the deer and the buffalo play. . ." The music has a deep sweetness now after the day of harvest.

I shake hands with Emery after our last breakfast together.

"Names I forget but not a face," he smiles boyishly but Lawrence looks sad, his eyes on the ground. "A farmer's whole world is five miles. When the stranger come out, he try to sell us oil stocks. Now we're broke, he don't come out. But you weren't afraid to work. That's what the boys told me on the thrashin'. They were all glad to have you see how we work."

Lora smiles. "Good-bye."

I tousle Lawrence's head. "So long, Larry."

"Maybe Lawrency see you," Emery says. "There might be war. So maybe he come to New York before going abroad. He'll stay with you then."

U. S. Route Number 16

Shocked fields of oats and barley, and green standing corn. Counties of oats and barley and corn. The tourist haven of the Dells where the Wisconsin River has sliced the sandstone into nightmare carvings.

North of the Dells, the wooden cabins and tents of the Winnebago Indians ambush the highway at intervals with their wares.

I park in front of one of the cabins. The Indian woman behind the roadside counter of tom-toms and bead bracelets, smiles. The outer corners of her eyes slant down.

"Do you farm at all?" I ask her.

"No. Too sandy to grow crops here. We have no corn, no chickens. We buy everything we have to eat."

A boy of fourteen comes out of the cabin. His hair is jet black, his skin copper brown. He smiles shyly as if he had never seen an automobile before.

"He draws the pictures on the drums." His mother picks up a tom-tom stick, hits the hide-wrapped end against the drum head. Indian sound echoes. . .

A car drives in off the highway, and a paunchy Indian with a blotched reddened nose gets out, his feet sockless in his old sport shoes.

"Do you hunt here at all?" I ask him.

"Years ago before our time, Indian hunt with bow and arrow. Plenty game. Now city people come out with high-powered rifles." He shrugs his fatty shoulders. "I wouldn't live in the cities. I've seen the cities."

"What cities?"

"Madison, Milwaukee. Milwaukee's too dirty. And Chicago!"

Again the wheel, the empty miles. . .

Eau Claire, Wisconsin.

Chippewa Falls with a huge red white and blue banner hung over the street: PLEDGE YOURSELF NOW TO USE MORE DAIRY FOODS.

The farms between the towns on the flat land seem to belong to another country, endless and wind-blowing, their walls of trees palisades against the north wind.

Rice Lake, Wisconsin.

Minong, Wisconsin.

In the distance, Lake Superior is like a pale blue hill of water. . .

The city of Superior's iron-ore docks trestle out into the lake. On the opposite shore, the windows of Duluth, Minnesota, glint in the sun, a city of gold specking light.

Duluth. . . Grain elevators full of wheat from the Western states and Canadian plains, piles of lumber hewn from the wilderness, iron-ore docks for the ore from the ranges, steel warehouses, railroad tracks, all line the water's edge with the wonder of arrival and departure. Superior Street in the east end of town. . . Flop houses, third-rate hotels, taverns, missions, idling men on the streets, sailors, vagrants, drifters, the men from nowhere and everywhere.

At night, the moon grows a rippling silver grain on the lake. A cold wind blows in and we feel hungry.

I reach for the menu at Gustafson's Restaurant as soon as we sit down. "It's cool here," I remark.

"It's always cool here. We have no summers," the blonde waitress answers.

"Any crops?"

"The crops are ruined. Too much rain." She laughs. "The only crop is iron ore anyway. I wear a suit or a coat to work every day. It's too cool."

"How are things here?"

"Slow. The boys finish in the C.C.C. camps. Twenty-three, twenty-four's the limit, but nobody hires them. And they're big families here. The French and the Slovenians have the biggest families. There's seven in my family and my mother says that's small compared to the French and Slovenians. One family here has eighteen. Another family has twelve."

She takes our order, returns, lingers to talk.

"You've got a lot of boats here," I say to her.

"That's funny, I don't know one sailor. I wouldn't mind if I could meet them in a decent way. I'd like to meet a sailor. All the girls here have sailors as boy friends but I don't know one. One girl's engaged to a sailor. He was to China. Now he's in Panama. They start in as sailors on the ore boats on the Great Lakes and end up on the ocean in China."

THE BLACK BEAR COFFEE SHOP in Hotel Duluth has a mounted bear in its window. A front page newspaper story mounted on cardboard informs the passerby about the bear. It weighed three hundred and fifty pounds. It came down starved from the woods because there were no berries in the drought year of 1929. It broke into the hotel kitchen and was killed by a policeman. . .

In the morning we leave the city, climbing slope after slope to the top of the height, Duluth far below with the two steel structural legs of its aerial lift-bridge straddling the ship canal, and out on the lake, an ore boat, white superstructure up front separated from the smokestack in the rear by the long red ship hulk.

To the north, a wilderness of young trees. Lake after lake, strung in sunlight, in swift cool wind. To the north, the iron towns.

THE BIG SPACE

Miners of the Iron Wheat

VIRGINIA AND HIBBING, MINNESOTA

"Points of Interest in Virginia

Mesabe Open Pit—Largest ore producing pit mine in the world.

City Hall—Large elaborately decorated arena, curling rinks, rifle shooting target range, and other conveniences.

School Buildings—Among the best in Minnesota.

Municipal Hospital—Recently erected at a cost of $250,000.

Olcott Park—A true garden spot. A large zoo including a monkey island. Band concert every Sunday evening by Virginia's 60-piece Municipal Band.

Golf Course—Beautiful 18-hole course with Minnesota bent grass, bluegrass fairways.

Tourist Cabins—Situated within a mile of the Post Office on the banks of beautiful Silver Lake.

All utilities, recreation buildings, hospital, tourist cabins, golf course and tennis courts are all municipally owned."

From the Virginia Chamber of Commerce brochure.

I RENT ONE OF THE BROWN wooden cabins on Silver Lake from the caretaker, an old man of sixty-five. "It's a dollar and a half a night without linen and blanket," he says. "If you stay more than one night I can let you keep your bedding and it will be a dollar and a half. It'll cost you fifty cents for bedding just this once. These tourist cabins are owned by the city. You can't do better. Hot and cold water, electricity and gas for cooking, shower bath, good mattresses. And the swimming's free."

The three rows of cabins, separated by driveways and green lawns, overlook the kids splashing in the lake. In ten minutes I get out of my clothes and into swimming trunks.

Down at the pier, another old man is staring at the divers out on the float. He wears a big brown felt but no jacket or vest, his suspenders crossing his shoulders. His brown felt and his big mustache make him seem all dressed up.

"Ever work in the mines?" I ask him.

"Plenty work in mines. I work thirty year in mines. Copper mine Michigan. Iron mine here. Twelve year ago, stop working. No good now." He breathes heavily. "I work for city, clean cabin."

"What's the matter with you?"

"Rheumatism. Dust in lung. No good now. In mine, one week I work day. One week night. People no eat right when work night. People no sleep right. Noise all the time."

Virginia's main thoroughfare, Chestnut Street, ends on the west with the railroad station of the Duluth, Winnipeg and Pacific. On the east, Chestnut Street drops off into the vast hole of the Missabe Mountain Open Pit Mine. Four hundred feet down in the earth, the horseshoe-shaped pit has a floor, railroad tracks, locomotives, electric shovels and miners.

Down below, a locomotive is pushing five loaded ore cars ahead of it. Black smoke banners up against two hundred and fifty feet of iron ore, a black vertical cloud against the lemon, dark red, ochre and bronze pit walls, black against the terrace hewn out of the wall, black against the one-hundred-and-fifty-foot thickness of brown rock above the iron ore, black, black against the sky. The slower locomotive chugs towards the surface on the circling tracks.

Above, a yawning cop stands near the gate to the mine; long flights of wooden stairs descending to the bottom. His badge shines. It is initialled O. I. C., the initials of the Oliver Iron Company. The cop passes a miner through.

The miner walks to the steep diagonal of the first flight. The miner climbs down. The ore train climbs up, the locomotive in reverse now.

The miner . . . down.

The ore train . . . up.

Down.

Up.

On the looping tracks below, a second locomotive hauls five empty cars to an electric shovel. The shovel pivots around on its square carriage, digs its pointed iron mouth into the bank of ore, dumping the scoop into the first car. Three scoops fill the seventy-ton ore car. Near the shovel, two machines also powered by electricity are drilling blast holes. The drilling rods, iron masts on the earth, pump up and down. . . . The dynamite boxes are tiny yellow spots, the miners blue straws.

The ascending ore train is higher, the descending miner lower.

He is halfway down the last flight of stairs.

He is all the way down.

He is out of sight, hidden by a ledge.

Fifty feet above the drilling machines and the shovels, two blue straws on the terrace are trimming bank. They have picks in their hands. The picks are invisible but their bodies have the shape of men driving steel into the earth. Small landslides of ore roll from their feet, the wind blowing the dust away, a yellow wind. Now and then, the trimmers uncover the bone-breaking rocks and ore chunks they are after.

The O. I. C. cop nods down at the men in the pit. "Drill, blast, and shovel. That's all there is to it. The mine here covers two hundred and forty-five acres. Millions of tons of overburden material had to be moved out before the ore could be mined. There's eighteen miles of railroad track down there. We pump out twenty-six hundred gallons of water every minute."

The ore train pulls up to the last incline, life-size, the locomotive lettered O. I. M. Co. 609, the five cars loaded with black ore, yellow ore, red ore, loaded with iron, loaded with steel America, with typewriters, saws, steel girders, cans, railroad tracks.

The wind parachutes hundreds of milkweed seeds out over the pit. The electric shovel has filled up four of the five ore cars. Three more scoops and the train is ready for the haul up. Black smoke pours out of the locomotive.

Iron ore.

Steel.

Skyscrapers of Chicago, Detroit, New York City.

Grasshoppers leap up before me as I stride down the walk of gray wooden boards to the door of John Pribonich's house.

John's dark brown hair is thinning but he still seems younger than the solemn bridegroom with heavy mustache and thick hair who stares down from the wedding picture in the parlor. Embroidered pillows line the wall. A red, white

and blue flag waves on the biggest pillow, above a motto:
AMERICA, I LOVE YOU.

"John, when did you start mining?"

"I started work in 1909. Most time I work underground.
I work in the copper mine for a while in Michigan. I do ever'-
thing in mine. I was a motorman. I was track man. I was ever'-
thing but civil engineer and boss. I was seventeen when I
work for Oliver Mine Number 6 in Eveleth. I go there from
Jugo-Slavia." He laughs. "First time I get job I paid ten dollars to the shift boss. Because I was too young, they won't have
me in mine. When I come underground and see the timbers,
I feel they come down on me. I was kind of scared. I start
work cleaning track, helping the motorman, helping with
timber. I work ten hours a day. Dust didn't bother me but
the smoke from the dynamite when blasting!" He laughs
louder than ever. "I never did get hurted to have bones
broken." He smiles hugely as if his years in the mines were a
game between himself and a hundred potential accidents.

John's son, a tall powerful boy of twenty, brings in the
mail. He reaches forward his tanned arm, the forearm thick-
ored with strength, the letter between thumb and forefinger.
"Here you are, Pa."

John slits open the envelope, pulls out a check. "W.P.A.
check for $13.33," he reads. He puts the check away. "That
time in mines, we use an auger to get in five, six feet. That
time no jackhammers to drill hole." He slaps his knee. He acts
younger than his son. "We use candlestick, too, that time. Use
five candles a day. Sometimes it melts on your head, you pull
it off with your hand. But when I go coal mine in Iowa in
1911, we used oil lamps. I worked mostly in low veins of coal,
three feet high. Bend over all the time. Some places we didn't
even blast. We take out all the coal. Take out the clay. Take
out the slate above the coal. They closed down the mines so I
come back in 1919."

"The younger generation will all be bums." His son's
eyes flash angrily. "I went to Virginia Junior College in Hibbing for two years. I threw the discus on the track team. I've
never had a job yet."

"What did you study?"

"Agriculture. But I'm taking up chemistry this fall. I
won't get any credit but that's what I'm interested in."

"He was born in Iowa," John says. "He was a year old when we come back. You see my garden? I got some cabbage, some onions, tomatoes. I used to have a cow but I had to sell her. She go uptown and the Chief of Police after me. She used to give rich milk, too. One time I go to see if Chief put her in jail." He bursts into laughter. His son smiles. "I don't like starve. I work on W.P.A. Most of them on W.P.A. want to work for private industry but what can we do? I want to work, too, for private industry. You're not sure you work tomorrow on W.P.A. That's the worst thing. You're not sure."

"Well, I'll take my car and drive off." Jokingly, John's son taps the sides of his thighs with his broad palms and walks out.

"Down there when I was in Iowa, I know a rich farmer, Harmon. Always he look up the prices for cattle. He raise cattle on his farm. Prices going up, Harmon load up the cattle for Chicago. But he come to Chicago, the prices go down. Always he look up the prices. That's the thing. . . Nobody's sure." He laughs the laugh of a boy whistling in the dark.

"In 1891. Captain Nichols discovered iron on the Missabe range. Wilbur Merritt was in charge of the work at Bibabik. The winters were freezing cold. The office was a log cabin. The logs were full of frost which melted in the day time and froze at night. John C. Cohoe, a gold miner, who had spent years developing gold and silver mines in Nevada and California, worked for the Merritt brothers. He tramped over the hills on snowshoes. At last he located a pit, and started two men digging. Later, he went down into the pit and drove a pick into the dirt. He brought up iron ore on the point of the pick. The pit was thirteen feet deep. John C. Cohoe found the first ore at the Missabe Mountain. Men rushed in, taking up claims. The townsite of Virginia was laid out. There was a population of five thousand in three months. In 1893 there was a depression. The Merritts could not sell their iron ore. There were no buyers. The Merritts had borrowed money from Mr. John D. Rockefeller. The Merritts waited for the depression to end so they could sell their ore. In 1894, the Rockefeller interests owned the Merritt properties. The Rockefellers sold the Merritt properties to the Morgans."

From the records.

"I work in one of the underground mines," the miner says. "Where it is I won't tell you. I don't want no trouble. The dust isn't bad. We have electrical fans down in the passageways, the drifts like we say. Some drift is seven feet, some three feet, some twenty feet. We climb down ladders to work. I work in a mine three hundred feet deep. That's plenty of ladders. My partner and me drill eight, nine holes in the set and put the dynamite in. We buy the dynamite from the Company. It costs us six dollars a box. We're contract miners and we get paid according to the car. If the ore comes easy, the price is lower, a dollar sixty, a dollar eighty a car. If the ore comes hard, we'll get two and a half dollars a car. I average one hundred and fifty dollars a month, twelve months a year. In the open pits, the miners only work from May to October. That's my pay, one hundred and fifty dollars a month. We fill twenty-five ore cars a day. Each car holds five ton. A hundred-and-twenty-five ton in all. A ton worth four dollars. My partner and me mine five hundred dollars worth of ore every day in the month. We make three hundred dollars a month between us for a whole month's work. The Company rich?"

Mountain Iron, west of Virginia, is an iron town surrounded by the farms of ex-miners blacklisted in the 1916 strike.

Buhl is west of Mountain Iron.

Godfrey is west of Buhl.

They are all iron towns. Near the mines, the grassgrown hills of ore, red-colored from paint rock, lump into the sky.

Iron towns.

Ore.

Steel tracks.

The little woman in the blue and red checked housedress wears her graying hair in a bun. Her eyes are an odd murky blue.

"This Hibbing?" I call to her from the street.

"Yes. Hibbing is the Ore Capital. Virginia is the Queen

City." She comes towards me down the plank walk between her flowers.

"Do you like living here?"

"Yes. The reason I like Hibbing is that we have five or six nationalities on the same block. That wasn't true in Michigan."

"No?"

"I don't mind telling you that years ago, we were more or less within our own nationality. My parents came from Finland to Michigan. We had our clubs and we used two languages, Finnish and English. But now the children have gone to school together and intermarried. Years ago, it was the Finns against the Italians, the Finns against the Swedes, the Slovenians against the Finns, and all against each other. I remember the Scotch miners in Michigan, the Cousin Jacks. . ."

"Is your husband a miner?"

"He works for the railroad. He started as a section laborer. They were building new roads then for the Duluth, Missabe and Northern. It'd be rough sledding but I do housework here in Hibbing. I really don't see how people get along on the W.P.A. I don't think we live extravagantly. We need everything we have and we bought our car and frigidaire on time. We had a second-hand radio and that went on the blink so we got a new radio. We're paying it off on time. In case you're from the census you can put that down. You can put down that we have fine schools and cooperative stores in Hibbing because the people are not against each other."

Inside the CONSUMERS CO-OPERATIVE STORE, canned goods line the shelves. At the counters, shirts, socks and other department store items are for sale. On the wall a placard reads:

CO-OPERATE! LOOK AT THE BANANA!
EVERY TIME IT LEAVES THE BUNCH
IT GETS SKINNED.
BE YOUR OWN GROCER
JOIN THE CO-OPERATIVE.

"How do these co-operatives work, Miss—" I ask one of the blond clerks, a girl in her early twenties.

"Miss Macki." Her apron is lettered CO-OP BRANDS, her eyes the murky blue of so many Finns.

"These co-ops are all affiliated with the Central Wholesale Co-op in Superior. That's our central buying organization. Each co-op, in each locality, is owned and controlled by that particular locality. We sell general merchandise, hardware, clothing. We're also affiliated with the Co-op Federation in Virginia and they go into farm machinery. They have a sausage factory and a creamery. Now in this Hibbing Co-op, the most shares anybody can own is two hundred dollars. Each stockholder is entitled to one vote. Right now we have between four hundred and fifty, and five hundred stockholders. We give a ticket to each purchase and the customers save their tickets throughout the year. At the end of the year, they turn them in and at the membership meeting, we hear about the profits. Although we don't like to use the word profits." She smiles. "The members decide how many dividends will be paid back to the customers. That's how we determine our rebate. This co-op is paying three per cent rebate for 1938, half in trade and half in shares. We have this store and the service station around the next block. We entered the coal business a couple of months ago. *The St. Louis County Independent* had an article about us."

I drop in at the International Tavern, Peter Lubina, Owner, for a beer. The bartender, a man of about fifty, with straight gray hair and octagon-shaped eyeglasses, cuts the foam. He wears an A.F.L. button in his lapel.

"That button's the bartenders' union?" I ask him.

"As a bartender I'm in the A.F.L. As a miner I'm in the C.I.O. If they start the mine again I mine. The trouble is the mines don't need many men. That's the situation. I talk yesterday to accountant from Chicago. This situation. . . This drive people to fascism or to communism. Another thing, Washington got to change the country. One way or the other."

"Are you Peter Lubina?"

"He, my brother."

Tacked over the cartons of cigarettes and boxes of Baby Ruth candy, the motto proclaims:

No One Can Please Everybody
But We Try

Two miners, their boots reddened from the iron ore, clump in for a beer.

Arnott Widstrand, one of the publishers of the *St. Louis County Independent*, sits back in his living room. A small man with a baldish head, he is still in his zipper-front gray shirt and work trousers. "Now, I've been in the A.F.L. Typographical Union since 1917. So when the printers' strike broke in 1921 we had the idea of starting a labor newspaper. Every newspaper on the range went scab. We began our paper in March 1922. It's been an uphill fight all the way through. There were personal grudges against us. Not that we weren't right but we were too right. We depend entirely on our job work, letterheads and so on. That's our real livelihood. We have three job presses and a cylinder press. Machinery makes it possible to get by with less men. It's all machine work practically. We don't set by hand any more. Things have changed since I started in as a printer's devil in 1912."

His curved spine straightens. "And it's machinery in the mines! Three men go on an electrical shovel. They can produce! They used to go down with mules and now they pull it up with locomotives. Over in Eveleth, they're trying out a conveyor belt. They've spent a half million experimenting. Why, the belt takes it right up from the mine and dumps it into the ore cars. No need to figure out the circles for the trains. Soon, all they'll need will be the men on the shovel. It's a fright the way they can do it. And you're going to see more consolidation of newspapers. The small country paper is doomed. Half the people right now are getting the nearest big town paper." He pauses. "The people here have absolutely nothing. There's no future to invest here or make something of it. The only thing we can depend on are the tourists. A lot of men have gone into tourists. But you can over-ride a good horse. Everyone with a little money has put tourist cabins out on the lakes."

He grins wryly. "We're taxed on a per capita base in Hibbing. The lower the per capita tax on the people, the lower on the Steel Corporation. At one time it was a hundred dollars per capita. The Steel Corporation pays about eighty per cent of all taxes. Well, they got the per capita down to seventy and we got in debt to about three million dollars. The individual taxpayer paid less of course. But so did the Steel Corporation, and there wasn't enough money to keep the town going. In 1935 the North Hibbing Bill cut our taxes to fifty per capita with a provision that the Corporation buy North Hibbing property with the amount the Corporation saved in taxes. The idea of the Corporation is to lower the per capita tax until the town won't be able to take care of its needs and the people will have to move out. They want to drive the people out of here by 1942. They want to depopulate the range. All they want here are a few miners to go on the electrical shovels. They don't need the towns."

Most of the houses in North Hibbing have already been demolished by the corporation, street after street depopulated. Here and there people live in the ghost of their old neighborhood as if there were no iron ore under their cellars, as if they were not bounded by the largest open pit mine in the world. Almost four hundred feet deep, two and a half miles long, a half mile to a mile wide, the yellow, red, brown and black ores of the O. I. C. Hall-Rust Sellers Mine tongues into the solid earth under North Hibbing.

Minnesota State Route Number 3

4 Reel Sport
Joe's
Pike and Muskies

Young evergreens, ten feet, fifteen feet and twenty feet high change the land into a summer Christmas. Here in these Minnesota woods the Mississippi River has its source in lake Itasca.

Miles of shocked oats, barley and wheat.

Immense cornfields, the outer sheaths of the corn brown from lack of rain, brown as the Indians. The Indians. . . How they stalk the reservation of memory, the people before the wheat and barley, the people of the corn.

The rolling land curves, rises, falls from summit to hollow, from hollow to summit. A hawk soars above a clump of trees, an island in a sea of land. "A sea of land"—so said the hunters, the guides, the first settlers.

Farmers are cutting and binding oats, and in the next mile they are threshing, the blower spouting yellow straw like a whale spouting water. The blue cloudless sky ascends, a deeper unfathomed depth.

The three wires on the telegraph posts are snow-white in the sun. Space flattens: The next river is the Buffalo.

The Seedsmen

FARGO

ON FRONT STREET IN FARGO, North Dakota, the seedsmen
have their buildings, the railroad in their back yards. In the
cool office of the Magill Building I meet a medium-sized man
with blond hair and blond mustache, a man in the prime of
life. He leans back in his swivel chair. "Fargo isn't very big
but it is the largest town in a good many miles. It's the biggest
town between the Twin Cities in Minnesota to Butte, Montana, a stretch of seven, eight hundred miles. Therefore it's a
good commercial and seed center. The seed comes in from the
farm unclean. We run it over the cleaners. The dirt, the chaff
must be cleaned out with three, four different types of mills.
We have a gravity mill for example that floats the seed across
a table or deck. Air is blown up from below and the vibra-
tion of the deck separates the heavier seed from the lighter
seed. In the spring, there's quite a sale to farmers in the territory. In every town, the local elevator will sell the seed. I sell
the *Magill Brand*, of course. There's nothing dull about a
seedsman's operations. We buy our stock in the fall and hope
we can dispose of the seed in the spring with a profit. It is a
seasonal business. There's always that uncertainty whether
there will be a demand in the spring. In recent years, the Government soil conservation program with its required planting
of soil conserving crops such as alfalfa and clover, before the
farmer can qualify for soil-building and soil-conserving pay-
ments, has helped the seed business. But it has created an
artificial demand. And occasionally, the Government program
is changed in the middle of the season and that creates an
upset in the normal flow of seed."

The sun burns like metal on the windows. "Our agriculture is changing up here. This Red River Valley is an old

glacial lake, fifty miles wide and running up to Hudson Bay. This entire valley is developing into a live stock feeding center. Cattle and sheep are brought in from the ranges of western North Dakota and Montana. We raise very fine feed crops here and can do so more economically than in Iowa. Our land values are lower than in Iowa. And then this is one of the most fertile valleys on the face of the earth. The land is flat and easy to farm." Magill's voice is almost rhythmic now. "In the big drought in 1934, this was the only section that had any crops. Of course, wheat is the biggest crop. North Dakota is the largest durum producing wheat area and the largest hard spring wheat. The average farm is a half section or 320 acres. Yet, the corn crop is increasing all the time."

He rises from his desk and walks across the office to a board hanging on the wall over the seed counter. "We're getting into hybrids. Hybrid corn will yield from ten to twenty per cent more than the open pollinated corn." He nods at the board with its labeled corn specimens as if to say: There's the future, the future of planned scientific farming.

C 16 and C 20, two small white corns are shown side by side. Below them is their larger cross, Single Cross I. Two other small yellow corns have been crossed to produce the Single Cross E. Single Cross E and Single Cross I have been crossed in turn to produce the largest corn of all, a corn with both yellow and white kernels, Minhybrid 402.

"The use of these hybrids will result in more corn acreage. We'll get the yields to make it profitable to grow corn commercially." He returns to his desk. "A seedsman isn't interested only in hybrid corn. Our sweet clover seed is shipped to Iowa, Missouri, Ohio, Pennsylvania, Indiana. We ship three or four hundred carloads to the central states alone." He smiles. "Yet I didn't intend to go into the seed business. I graduated from Princeton in 1913 but I didn't enter law school as I had intended. My father came up here from Clinton, Iowa, in 1887. His father was in the grain business before him and it was natural for me to go into this business with my father. The farms then were mostly settled by the homesteaders, by Scandinavian immigrants of the previous generation. In the early days there were quite a few Scotch and English. . . Now, farming conditions have become about the same. Iowa is an older agricultural area. But South Dakota,

Kansas and Nebraska. . . In general their farming practices
are the same as ours. Southern Minnesota, Iowa and Missouri
have smaller farms and are more diversified."

Again he leaves his desk. "I want to show you the soy
beans." At the seed counter, he dips his fingers into the round
white beans. "There's been an effort to develop interest in
these. As for wheat, the acreage isn't increasing any. That was
because Triple A required a reduction in wheat acreage. New
varieties have been perfected to combat rust. We had tremen-
dous rust losses a few years ago. The Durum wheat is used
primarily for making flour for macaroni. This Thatcher
wheat is a bread wheat and rust resistant. We sell a lot of
sorghums."

The origin of the different seeds cover the continent, the
black amber sorghum comes from Nebraska, the Sudan grass
from Texas. . .

Near the buildings of the seedsmen are the Employment
Agencies. Fifteen or twenty men linger outside the plate-glass
of the NATIONAL EMPLOYMENT AGENCY and the next-door
rooming house. They aren't the cooks, dishwashers, waiters,
carpenters, electricians of the city. In blue overalls and heavy
work shoes, many of them with knapsacks, the farmers without farms linger on the sidewalks. A young woman in slacks
steps out into the street from the rooming house. Part Indian,
her round squaw face, scratched on one side, is like the unsee-
ing face of a blind woman. A sniffling little girl comes up the
street and the woman in slacks stops. "Don't cry," she says,
taking five pennies out of her purse. "Get yourself an ice
cream cone."

I enter the agency. To the left, a bartender is filling up
beer glasses at a bar. In the rear, there are several pool tables
in a row of green baize . . . the click-click of ivories, cigarette smoke. To the right, a section of floor has been railed off
from the bar and pool parlor. A few farmers stand near the
rail and inside it, the proprietor of the NATIONAL EMPLOY-
MENT AGENCY presides over his corner of the premises. His
eyes are brownish green, his complexion pale white under the
brim of his felt.

I nod. "I didn't know there were employment agencies
for farmers?"

He gives me his card: NATIONAL EMPLOYMENT AGENCY

BEN H. SCHMAING. "I hire on the average of twenty-five to thirty men a day for farm work. It starts the middle of March, right through the first of November. I send them in and around one hundred miles of Fargo. It's transient labor." The tanned farmers listen with the intensity of men waiting for work. "The women and girls get down by train. The men hike in. I ran two advertisements in the *Fargo Forum*. I figured up this morning, I sent one hundred and forty-eight men this week. They get two dollars a day for shocking and two-fifty for thrashing. They're thrashing everything now." The listening farmers edge closer. Schmaing smiles cautiously, the smile of a man who has always been careful. "I was never a farmer myself but I was a foreman on a farm up in Mapleton about twelve miles from here. I operated a seven-section farm for four years and a four-section farm for six years. My folks were farmers down in Ioway. I came up here in 1910. . . It's went down the last year and a half. More combine all the time. Business has gone down fifty per cent. But more people are looking for work, more men looking for jobs. . . It's been a tough proposition the last year and a half. It's been kind of a tough proposition for everybody. But a feller experienced in that line can get a job the year 'round."

Behind the rail on the wall, a card warns: IF YOU CANNOT DO THE WORK, DON'T BOOK UP.

One of the farmers, a middle-aged man with a snout nose and light blue eyes the color of his faded Oshkosh overalls, mutters, his whiskey breath rising in my nostrils. "I been in this Red River Valley a long time, a long time. It's the combine! It's a lot of machine work! I'm an American. I was born in this country but it's a lot of machine work. I was born in this country but it's very little for the working man." Near him a big man is leaning against the rail, a battered brown hat on his head. "Are you looking for work?" I ask him.

"No. I come down here to hire men. So far t'aint been so bad. We've got three hundred and eight acres in small grain, one hundred and eighty in corn and sugar cane. We've been gitting good prices for hogs and cattle. We sell 'em into West Fargo. Used to sell 'em in St. Paul." He scratches his chin with a black-rimmed nail.

"It's a lot of machine work!" the man in the Oshkosh overalls shouts. "It's the combine! It's the machine work!"

Outside, on the sidewalk, they are listening in silence to the shouter's voice, sober and tongueless. On this street in front of the NATIONAL EMPLOYMENT AGENCY, their blue overalls are not the uniforms of free men.

"A great deal of machinery is shipped out of Fargo." The salesman lowers his voice although there are few people on the hot street. "All the big companies, the International Harvester, the Case Company, they're all located here. This machinery is handled through local dealers who handle it on commission. These local dealers are forced to pay cash for the stuff and their commissions are small. They stand all the expense of distribution and collection. The company that makes a contract with a dealer compels him to handle just their line. And these machine companies have foreclosed on many farms due to their implement deals. The machine companies, the big banks and the insurance companies own most of the foreclosed farms. Let's go down to the railroad. I want you to see some of these foreclosed farmers. I'd estimate that about forty per cent of the farms are rented. It's the companies and the grasshoppers. In the last two years, the grasshoppers have been very bad. A few years ago what the drought didn't get, the grasshoppers did. Grasshoppers are very effective machines. A cloud of hoppers can go into a field and clean it up in a day. Those hoppers will eat everything green."

He nods emphatically. "The farmers have used a lot of poison this year, arsenic, molasses and sawdust. They use a two-car arrangement. They spread the poison with a homemade spreader. They cut the top and bottom out of a gasoline barrel. Then they build a funnel arrangement in the bottom which allows a small part of the poison to drip through onto a revolving drum which has blades on it. The blades throw the poison off in about a twenty foot swathe. They attach the barrel to an old car. I'll have to explain that. They take an old rear axle and cut about three feet off the shaft, leaving the gears working on the car. They then attach the shaft to the plate on the bottom of the barrel. Then they attach a truck behind an auto. As the truck moves, the axle revolves, turning the drum. It's been in use the last two or three years. Evidently, a lot of farmers thought of the idea at the same time. The machine companies haven't invented it yet. The farmers are ahead of them!" he grins, taking a personal pride in the skill and ingenuity of the plain American farmer. "Look! There's one of them come in on a freight."

"You can see them all day," the salesman says. "Farmers' sons and farmers foreclosed off their land. They follow the harvest up through Kansas, Nebraska, Iowa, into the Dakotas and Canada. There are almost as many of these harvest hands as the hoppers. You'd think that with all our machines, we would manage better."

The gasoline station attendant at Standard Service runs out to the three pumps, Standard White Crown, Standard Red Crown, Standard Blue Crown. Blue-eyed and apple-cheeked, the attendant has the coloring of a storybook fox-hunter.

"Are you of English stock?"

"Yes. My name's Robert Tomlinson," he speaks formally, pleasantly. His smile is younger than his years. He is about twenty-two.

"Ever farm?"

"I liked farm work very well. Spring seeding and thrashing were the two busiest seasons."

"Did your dad homestead?"

"My father was a homesteader. He was born in Canada. My mother was born in Iowa. I left the farm to attend the Agricultural College here when I graduated in 1936 from Tokio High School."

"Tokio?"

"Nobody knows why it was called Tokio! It's right on the Indian reservation, the Sioux reservation. They make very nice neighbors. They do beadwork and basketwork. Well, I didn't like farming all by myself when my father passed away. I rented the farm. It was about four hundred and twenty acres. As a side-line we raised poultry and turkeys."

A car pulls up to the three pumps. Robert trots away from

me, inserts the Red Crown gas hose. The owner of the car scowls at his tires. "Give her a little shot of air."

The car pulls out and Robert returns. "I like to sell and to meet the public very well. And it's a means of earning one's way at this time. I'd like to go into some selling line connected with agriculture." He smiles in the reek of gasoline. This North Dakota seed of England seems as honorable and innocent as Tom Brown of Rugby, as if no centuries separated him from the famous legend, England.

U. S. Route Number 10

West Fargo, the International Harvester Company, Armour's plant . . . the earth beyond a plain of wheat and barley.

West . . . the farmers are thrashing, yellow straw clouds cycloning out of the blowers of their threshing machines, the yellowest yellow in the world. Each farmhouse stands lonely on its half section or section of land, American baronies of red Hereford cattle and corn. Who owns his section? Who rents? Who is lost, who forgotten? In the burning sunlight, the farmers' shadows are on the land like the shadows of the buffalo hunters and homesteaders before them.

Parked on the highway ahead an old Ford. A man signaling.

I brake to a stop. The Ford has Minnesota plates. "You're a long way from home."

"I'm from Fergus Falls, Minnesota. I'm looking for thrashing work. Have you got a tire pump?"

"Yes." I get my tire pump. Grasshoppers on the highway collide against my legs.

"Thanks," he says, pumping up his tire. The inner tube shows in the worn center. "I just patched it. I have a spare but it's worse than the one on the wheel."

"You're liable to get a flat in the next mile."

"I know. Here you are. Thanks for stopping."

West . . . the huge American land of a thousand promises, the towns of five thousand and eight thousand population.

Valley City on the Cheyenne River.

Jamestown on the St. James river.

Endless wheat farms . . . so large that the farmers drive out to work like city commuters, parking their cars among the shocks of wheat.

For no reason at all I drive onto a ridge of dirt and gravel in the center of the highway. My car stalls. I press on the starter. Nothing happens. The silence of the land hums like a vast motor.

An old Chevrolet comes alongside. It has Missouri plates and three young fellows in overalls and red polka dot handkerchiefs.

"What's wrong?" one of the Missourians asks.

"My battery's shot."

The Missourians swing up the hood of my car with enthusiasm.

"Do you know much about motors?" I ask them.

"I've fooled around with these some," one of the Missourians answers.

My wife is skeptical. "I'm going to the farmhouse on that hill and telephone for help."

"It must be the feedline's blocked," a second Missourian diagnoses.

Aided by his friends, he unscrews the feed lines and sucks in a mouthful of gas. "It don't taste good," he says after a good spit.

I sit down at the wheel. They hop into their car and bump me in mine off the highway onto a dirt road. The motor starts, throbs, stops.

The three young fellows come on the run. They lift up the hood. The motor is wet with gasoline.

"I wouldn't drive that car if I were you," they advise me.

They push me back to the highway and then hold a final consultation.

"We better go. We're looking for thrashing in Montana."

A road tractor is leveling out the ridge where I first got stuck.

My wife returns. "There was no telephone there."

The tractor's driver walks over to us.

"Is there any telephone near here?" I ask him.

"Nearest telephone is in town and that's ten miles away."
He examines the motor. "If you have gas coming through the
carburetor it's because a washer's worn out. Have you any
tools?"

"Yes." I tell him about the three Missourians.

He takes apart the carburetor. "I never took one of these
apart before because it's cheaper to buy a new one if the old
one goes bad." He examines the component parts. "They're
all right." His voice rises. "Here's the jigger!" He picks up a
metal part shaped like a bullet. "When those fellows took
the gas feed off they let this slip out. This jigger stops the gas
coming into the carburetor when the carburetor is full. That's
why you have that overflow. If I would've seen this before I
wouldn't have to have taken the carburetor apart. But I'll
get her together."

He does. I start the car. The car starts. No gas pumps
through the carburetor. I pull out my wallet.

"No, thanks." He smiles.

"Please take some money for cigarettes."

"I have a pack."

"I want to give you a present."

Reluctantly, he accepts a half dollar.

I drive off. My wife laughs. "I can still see you on that side
road with those three boys from Missouri. At one time you
weren't even in the car. You were trotting after them while
they were pushing it. And all our belongings, everything, in
that car . . ."

It is seven o'clock now, the birds diving for grasshoppers,
the shadows of the haystacks lengthening, the dried-out ponds
battleship gray in color, the living land westerning ahead
of us.

In this hour, the towns are legends, the sun slanting long
shadows across the streets, the white puffy clouds golden
tawny, a ghost herd of buffalo in the southern sky. The horses
have been let out to graze in the pastures. Without harness
or halter, they stand carven in the light, the colts near their
mothers. The sun sinks in the West. Space colors twilight
blue. Near Bismarck, the grain elevator is lettered CUSTER
BRAND FEEDS, the huge drawing of yellow-haired General
Custer on a white horse galloping into life again.

The store windows in neon-lit Bismarck are museum show-cases for the approaching Golden Jubilee. Arrowheads of all colors and sizes have been arranged as if they were mounted butterflies. Saddles, pistols, tin satchels in which money was carried in the old western days, are on display up and down the main street.

The Golden Jubilee . . .

The early day stretches into the distance, a plain of light. A farmer's boy in cap and blue jeans rides out into his father's fields on a big brown horse towards a small herd of mares and colts. He reaches the herd, separates four mares. He drives them back to the distant farmhouse, each mare followed by her colt. The herd begins to graze again as the saddle-less rider brings back the animals picked to work.

West . . . the bad lands, a hole in the earth, floored with knolls and buttes of clay, sandstone, red-colored scorio rock, yellow stone, all cracked and fissured, tent-shaped and house-shaped, a petrified stone encampment.

Medora. Houses. And a monument to Theodore Roosevelt, who ranched here long ago.

The badlands wedge west into the wheat and oat fields of Montana.

The Yellowstone River at Glendive flows yellow. Herds of cattle graze right up to the blunted mountains in the distance. Sage brush and sweet clover grass. Cottonwood trees along the unseen rivers, their courses marked by the green flow and curve of leaves.

I brake to a stop where four Montana Highway Repair Department workers are fixing the shoulder of the road. "What kind of country is this?" I ask the oldest man.

"It's nothing like it used to be," he answers. His cheeks are leather, his eyes blue, his nose a big hawked one. He looks as if he had stepped out of the 1890's. "It's Durum wheat, that's macaroni wheat through here. I've seen macaroni on one side and blue on the other and the bearded wheat will always stand the drought better. Irrigation's the only hope we have out here. The Government's taken a lot of the people out to Fairfield where they have a big irrigation project. If it's the old West you're interested in, that's gone. There are still one thousand and two thousand acre ranches and the railroads still own every other section. The Government give them that land for building the railroads in. But the old West, that's gone. This year, the towns are going Western for the tourists. They all are wearing silk shirts and big hats. That's because people were beginning to say Montana wasn't no different from the East. When I came out to homestead, it was so late I could only get a quarter section. That was about twenty-five years ago. Only part of the land was breakable. I couldn't raise enough for my family." He gazes beyond the barbed wire to the meadowlarks over the land. "When I was a young sprout I used to lumberjack in Wisconsin and I got homesick a few years ago. I got homesick for the lice in the camps. But when I got back there there were no lice and not much logging."

Dead jack rabbits and gophers spot the road, blood-pasted by the tires. The buttes in the burning bright distance seem like huge colored pots in which heat cooks.

Billings, Montana. Streets of men wearing cowboy hats and plains Stetsons, green, red and blue silk shirts. Streets of cafés, restaurants, and jewelry stores selling **Montana agate** rings.

I go into a shoeshine parlor. The shoeshine boy, thin and bright-eyed, rubs polish into my shoes. "We have a nice town here the tourists say." He smiles the sharp wise smile of all shoeblacks.

"Do you like it?"

"I'm leaving next spring." He jerks his thumb as if asking for a lift. "I'll get out somehow. I'm going somewheres and see something."

In the new morning the Beartooth Mountains are one shade bluer than the sky, the snow fields on the peaks cloud-color.

We climb.

Between the mountain forests and mountain brooks, the

summer air cools into spring, into autumn. The sudden angles of this world freeze into stone.

Ten thousand feet high.

Winter. . . The snowfields seen hours ago in the summer, level out with our eyes. . .

Cooke City at the base of the mountains, below the peaks and the hawks, is a carnival of tourists, women and girls dressed like Hollywood cow girls, men like cowboys and Alaskan trappers. Half of them are liquored up, their laughter either booms or gurgles.

Beyond the bars on the main street, a white frame house displays a sign: HOME COOKING. The proprietress serves us. The biscuits are homemade, the beef good. She sits down at a nearby table, her brown eyes and long face solemn as a minister's wife's. "There's a lot of fake Wild West outside," I tell her.

"There's the fake and the real," she answers. "I was a lone woman from Iowa when I came here. But I'm making a living." She has the quality of silence about her. Her forehead wrinkles a little as she thinks. "You can't grow a fuss on some of the sections. The Government just bet you the thirteen dollars you paid for your deed that you couldn't stay on three hundred and twenty acres for three years and put in the improvements you had to put in. It was a bet. The first man put something into the land and he had to go. The second man fixed it up some but he had to go. The third man maybe could stay with it. As I see it, we're glad to make a part living. It ain't a full living exact. But what can we do? We have sixty days for our season to make a year's living in. The Government shouldn't have homesteaded this land. Should have left it for grazing. The homesteaders didn't have enough grazing land on their half section to raise much stock. Yes. . . There's the real and the fake wherever you are, in Iowa or back East or out here in Montana. You're going to Yellowstone, ain't you? The tourists go there and many of them are fake but just the same it's wonderful to see. Some people and some things are real wherever they are."

The Photographers

YELLOWSTONE PARK

AT THE END OF THIRTY MILES of wilderness, Camp Roosevelt in Yellowstone Park is like a modernized pioneer camp. A cabin rents for a dollar and a quarter, blankets for fifty cents, a bundle of wood for ten cents. In the twilight, we drive out to Tower Falls. Between the darkening pines, white water plunges down one hundred and thirty feet. The basaltic cliffs smell of sulphur, the earth's ancient smell, the smell of volcano, fire and geyser. . .

Back in camp, I park between my cabin and the cabin next door. The garbage pail in the rear has been knocked over and foraging inside like a city tomcat, head out of sight, big, black end jutting out, a bear. "It's a bear, a real bear!" I exclaim.

The bear comes out of his metal cave, blinks and ambles off into the woods. The first rain drops patter down. . .

A morning of sunlit mountain peaks rings the camp.

"Did you hear the noise last night?" my next door neighbor asks me. His plates are from Illinois. Although he isn't more than twenty-six, he has a two-year-old son.

"No."

"Well, one of the bears smelled some trout in a car and he ripped open the canvas roof to get the fish in it." He smiles joyously as if talking about the feats of his baby son. "I wish I had my camera with me."

"Oh, dear," his wife calls from their cabin. "Have your breakfast. And you're not taking another bear picture. Three rolls are enough."

"All right, honey. If you're going into the park," he advises me, "be sure and have your camera ready!"

The smoke of many fires rises from the tin chimneys.

After breakfast, the young couples, the honeymooners, the

middle-aged folk, pile into their cars, climb up towards snowy Dunraven Pass. Last night's rain was snow in this higher altitude. The pines and spruces are Christmas trees. The cars drive through an enchanted Yuletide forest, the melting snow drip-dripping, the pine-green and snow-green winter strewn with pink and yellow wildflowers.

Up ahead, forty or fifty cars are parked all over the highway. Corps of cameramen and camerawomen have surrounded a glossy black bear with a white spot on his throat. The bear wants food. The people want pictures. A giggling woman tosses the bear an orange. As the bear crunches it into a pulp, the photographers snap his picture, feverishly turn levers for the next shot, squint into finders, grimacing like children playing a game in which the bear is the adult. The bear gulps down the last of the orange and casually like an experienced panhandler appraises the crowd for the next touch. He lurches forward. "Oh!" the woman shrieks.

"Watch out!"

"Here he comes!"

Mothers pull away their children. Men pale and heroically snap another picture.

The cars move on. A half mile up, the highway again looks like a parking space. Like a wave of infantrymen the photographers are advancing on a tall brown animal in an alpine field.

The man near the Idaho car explains to the two girls with cameras leaping out of the New Jersey Chevrolet. "That's a female moose. A young one."

The New Jersey girls join the line of stalkers. Close, closer . . . every man, woman and child peering into their finders. The elk feeds like a cow.

"Get the sun over your shoulder, Daddy," a girl of ten whispers to her father.

"Sh! Go back! You'll get your feet wet in the dew."

"It's my camera," the girl complains. "You let me take a picture, Daddy."

"Sh!"

The moose raises her head. The hunters snap her picture. The moose runs from the field into the woods.

"Give me my camera," the girl demands in a loud plaintive voice.

The caravan of cars drive on until the next adventure a few miles up.

Deer! Five big brown deer with beautiful antlered woodland heads are staring at twenty-five or thirty humans walking towards them with little black boxes.

Effortlessly, the deer leap out of camera range.

"Go slow everybody," a man with a Brownie whispers.

"That's right, slow." The photographers creep up to the deer.

A branch cracks.

"Sh!"

"I didn't break it! I'm a Boy Scout," the accused cries out.

The photographers advance. The five deer retreat into the woods, stop. They stand there a second then leap away . . . into the bloodless and rifleless wilderness of Yellowstone Park.

The photographers return to their cars.

"Your shoes are soaking wet," a mother reprimands her son.

His eyes shine with joy. "I got them!" he cries.

The morning is like a fairy tale in which the wild animals have become the friends of man. . .

A few miles from the deer, a brown mother bear and her two cubs are begging for food on the highway. From inside her car a woman tosses out four or five slices of bread. In quick gobble, the mother and cubs finish the bread. All three stand up on their hind legs, begging the bread woman for more. She winds up the window in her car as the photographers circle the bear family, snapping picture after picture.

The mother bear drops to all fours. One cub chases after her.

"Oh, get those baby bears to stand up!" a woman begs.

A blond boy of six or seven approaches the cub left behind. He and the cub are about the same size.

"Don't go near the bears!" his mother shrills.

"Aw," he mutters scornfully. He picks up a stone and holds it high over his head. The cub gets up on his hind legs, reaching with his toysize paws and claws.

"Hold it!" two or three voices exclaim. . .

At the Grand Canyon, cameras are aimed at the blue-green river seven hundred and fifty feet below, at the white

white pools. Below are the trees, stub-sized, and above the trees a fish hawk soars. The photographers frame the world below the hawk in their finders.

"If this platform were to break," a girl in riding breeches whispers to her friends.

"Ooh, you make me nervous."

A sightseeing farmer in overalls stares intently as if at a five-legged calf. "It looks like a big hole to me."

"But it's pretty," his wife says.

A blonde brittle lady of forty murmurs. "It's grand. It's grand."

The yellowish earth slopes down to a desert of gnarled rock and shipmast pinnacle. A peninsula of green pine spears up into the multicolored red, copper, brass, yellow, green lava walls.

Yellowstone Park . . . the mud volcanoes, the geysers, the Morning Glory Pool with its sky-blue flower of boiling blue water, the black glass Obsidian Cliff, the glittering expanse of Yellowstone Lake, and its Fishing Bridge with a hundred lines, a hundred Colorado spinners, worms and grasshoppers down stream, the cut-throat trout colored like the volcanic rock, the Continental Divide, the starry night at Old Faithful Camp, the people waiting and the steam rising out of Old Faithful's stone nozzle, rising, rising and then bursting, hosing power, water and steam against the black night, billowing into a steamy ghost, the ghost of the pre-Indian upheaval that colored and carved, and burned out this wilderness.

U. S. Route Number 89

The Absaroka Mountains are grim and black, but the land is used by man.

A ranch hand follows his two horses, reins in hand and walking like a horse himself. Herds of red Herefords graze on the miles, their white faces shining like snow patches.

Over the Continental Divide, into canyoned Silver Bow County. . . Placer gold was discovered here on Gold Creek, silver, copper.

Through Pipestone Pass, pass of the old-time prospectors and the bearded mountain men driving their mules into the secret canyons.

West . . . the world's greatest mining camp, the richest hill on earth, the copper city of Butte, Montana.

Westerners

BUTTE

"You two go left, I'll ride right. Start shooting when I do. And hope we can scare 'em. If that don't work, I'm going to rush in whooping and try to stampede the herd! (To be continued)."
From the serial "Phantom Ranch" appearing in THE BUTTE STANDARD.

"Its Butte properties consist of 1662 acres of mineral claims at Butte, including all the claims at Butte and other properties formerly held by 15 other companies. The Company operates the following mines, located in Butte: Anaconda, Alice, Anselmo, Badger State, Belmont, Berkely, Colorado, Diamond, Emma, East Colusa, High Ore, Leonard, Mountain Con, Mountain View, Never Sweat, Nettie, Elm Orlu, Poser, Moulton, Evelyn, Original, Orphan Girl, Pennsylvania, Poulin, St. Lawrence, Silver Bow, Steward, Tramway, West Colusa, West Grey Rock."
From the pamphlet published by the Anaconda Mining Company.

THERE MUST BE THIRTY OF US, old gray ladies, fat men discussing copper and steel futures, all dressed up like copper miners as if for a masquerade (costumes supplied by Anaconda), all wearing the hard brown miners' hats, the men in blue jackets and overalls, the women in brown coats. At the lamp house, electric lamps are attached to the fronts of our hard hats, the batteries suspended on the Company belts underneath the blue jackets.

The Leonard mine is 3680 feet deep. We are going down to the 2800-foot level.

The guide hurries over to the shaft with its three metal cages, one above the other, a vertical train down into the earth. He pokes his hard hat back off his sweating face and one by one, ushers the passengers into the cages.

Each cage holds seven or eight men and women, the beams from their lamps criss-crossing.

Down we go.

Down.

The cable whips from side to side. Down through the thick earth, massing around the shaft like flesh around a vein.

Hurling down.

Down.

2800 feet below, we step out into the underground station hollowed out of the copper earth, a cave entered through the shaft. Up and down the shaft travel the miners, the tonnage of rock and copper ore, the air and water columns, the electric power, the tourists.

Two miners grin at us.

"How do you pump the water out?" I ask them.

"Pump the water up from the 3300-level to the 28-, to the 12-, to the surface."

The guide walks out of the station along one of the cross-cuts intersecting the ore veins. Under electric light the granite drift walls, streaked with the parrot-colored blue-green ore, seem too massive to be broken by man.

"It's hot," a tourist complains. "These hats are heavy."

"We shouldn't have come," his wife says. "How do the miners stand the heat?" she calls to the guide.

"Fans supply fresh air to them."

"It's a half mile down," an old lady whispers in an awed voice.

The guide picks up a long drill.

Sudden terrific noise as the drill bites into the drift wall. Cooling water trickles through the hollow iron bit. "We drill a round of holes before we blast!" the guide shouts. "The water keeps the dust down. Before a man goes to work he wets down everything with water. That is how we avoid the lung disease, silicosis. . ."

The drift wall is hard with eternity, but the drill penetrates, fraction of an inch at a time.

The guide puts the drill down. "We'll go to a stope now."

A stope is like a small room. "Nothing is nailed," the guide explains. "The timbers are brought down, cut and wedged into place, wedged as tight as can be with blocks of wood."

The timbers pry open the earth's huge dense mouth, supporting a plank ceiling.

The tour ends. Hard hats in hands, the lawyers, doctors, business men and their wives wait in the station to go up to the surface. "I wouldn't want to be a miner. Not I," the old lady exclaims.

"It's hard work even under the best of conditions." The guide smiles. "There are ore souvenirs in that compartment over there."

The tourists dash for their souvenirs, their hands grabbing at the heavy chunks of ore as if they were gold nuggets.

Sweaty, hot and tired, they wait impatiently for the cages to carry them up to the sun and fresh air.

Above the drifts and stopes, the hill city of Butte towers one mile above sea level, Main Street running north and south on the hill's slope. Bisecting Main, Park Street divides into West Park's stores and East Park's miners' rooming houses. Everywhere the old West and the new West and the West of legend . . . the two-story red brick buildings carry gilt inscriptions near their roofs: *1890. Marchesseau and Valiton.* The mineral ore specimens in the windows of the Assay Offices are monuments to the strike-a-million dreams of the old-time prospectors. To the south, to the east, to the west, the Rocky Mountains peak into the sky. The shafts of the copper mines mark the fortune buried under the streets. On a side-wall an artist has painted a huge advertisement: BLACKBEAR OUTDOOR CLOTHES RUGGED AS THE WEST. The painted bear growls at the out-of-work miners in blue overalls and old clothes who parade up and down East Park Street. . . The window of the Owl Loan Office is full of fishing reels, clocks, bright trinkets made of copper, old jewelry, horsehair belts woven in the Penitentiary. The Silver Moon Café, and the State Café with curtained-off *Booths for Ladies,* once private to the men who struck it rich and their girls imported from Chicago. . . Mounted elk, deer and moose heads hang on the walls of saloons, cafés and drug stores. The sporting store window displays a mess of cut-throat trout in a big tin pan. Hued like the western legend, the trout are strewn on lumps of melting ice. The neat card against the pan reads: CAUGHT BY ART KORN, POP KORN AND BILL WILSON. CAUGHT ON BIG HOLE AT GLEN WITH POTTS' LADY MITE FLIES.

"I'd like to have one," a sandy-haired man remarks. "There are thirty-five trout in there. I counted thirty-five."

"One would be enough for me," a lean blond boy says. "I know the holes where you can pull them out."

"You do?" I ask him.

"You're a stranger here!" The boy smiles. "I've been East myself. I like the East. I'll take you fishing with me. I live in Butte but I've been all over!" He nods, hinting at his adventures. "You won't need a fishing license either. These Montana hicks won't catch us."

"What's the matter with Montana?"

"There's nothing here!" the boy retorts.

"Not so many trout as there used to be," the sandy-haired man says regretfully.

West Park Street is any shopping street in a hundred cities, Woolworth's, Symons Department Store, dentists' offices, stores of shoes, dresses, hats, the Metals Bank and Trust.

Yet, across the street from the bank, the Arcade also offers a return for every invested dollar. The Arcade is one of Butte's wide-open gambling establishments, a silver-dollar business, the names of horses racing from Saratoga, New York, to Del Mar, California, listed on the walls. Omar Khayam's and Abraham Cowley's rhymed sentiments hang over the long bar:

> *Come, fill the Cup, and in the Fire of Spring*
> *Your Winter-garment of Repentance fling.*
> *Ah . . . fill the Cup that clears*
> *Today of Past Regrets and future Fears.*

IF HE IS NOT AT THE ARCADE HE ISN'T IN BUTTE. This is the motto of the house.

The slot machines wait for nickel investments, the gambling tables on the big floor for quarters and dollars. Men in battered felts, in old suits, in overalls, play poker. The house gambler at the roulette wheel appraises each newcomer's face as if asking himself: 'Sucker?' 'If not, why not?' The white ball spins around the rotating wheel, drops into a red number. The gambler rakes in the quarters bet on black. At all the games, towers of silver rise round and gleaming. The banker at the twenty-one table throws out kings, eights, fours to the men betting against the house, and then tosses down a king (ten points) on his own open four, for a total of fourteen. Adds another card, a trey. Total of seventeen. He examines each opponent with shrewd eyes, takes another card, a second trey. Total of twenty. He uncovers the hidden cards of the players. His twenty tops everyone else's score. He rakes in the silver. Other men surround the green baize at the craps table, flinging their silver onto the Do Pass section, betting against the house, betting with the man shooting the dice. The point is eight. The house gambler places the wooden marker on the number eight. The dice tumble out again: Five. Again: Eight. He makes his point. The house gambler pays out silver as if the Arcade were the mint. A young fellow takes a five-cent pick in one of the pickboards but doesn't win the prize, a pair of ten-dollar shoes.

I leave the Arcade and visit its nearby competitors, the Board of Trade, the Crown, the M. & M. The gray-haired old-time gamblers wear eyeshades, their hands beautifully manicured. The younger housemen look like cow hands just off the range. Homeless drifters watch the play, the house boosters gambling with the house's dollars, the tight-lipped miners, workers and business men losing, winning, losing.

Out on the streets, the shopping women walk by the gambling establishments without excitement or interest as if they were no different from any other business.

Whitehead's Grinding Shop is on 15 North Wyoming Street. The man in overalls behind the counter, a pair of scissors in one hand, looks up as I enter.

"Are there any other grinding shops here?"

"We're the only grinding shop in Butte." He laughs, surprised but friendly.

"Were you born in Butte?"

"I was born in my dad's grinding shop in '99. You're

curious but I don't mind. The typical westerner'll tell you anything. My dad is a typical westerner. He was a farmer back in Irwin, Pennsylvania, if you know where that is. They were original settlers in Pennsylvania. They had their rights on a sheepskin. It showed their land from post to post, from mark to mark. Dad's seventy-six now. . . When he was seventeen he went to work in one of those Pennsylvania tube mills. He used to tell me their feet got so hot they were always sticking them in tubs of water. He made enough to get to Iowa and then he went to Colorado for silver mining. He struck it rich and came to Butte. The first night in Butte, he slept under a livery stable on Park and Main. That was the busiest corner in Butte and it still is. It wasn't much of a town then. Butte was going from gold to copper. Why, they used to haul the copper concentrates to Brigham, Utah, and reship them to England to refine them. And they still made money."

He nods, almost awed at how easy money could be made in the old days. "My dad started mining. He'd run into a good pocket and make money. But after a while he got disgusted. That's the trouble with mining. If you get big enough, the companies would squeeze you out in some way. Well, my dad wanted to get into something everybody else wasn't in. And that's how he got into the grinding business, filing keys, making razor blades and pocket knives. He got a few tools and all he had left was enough for a loaf of bread."

He points at a narrow rectangular showcase against the wall behind the counter. "That's dad's first showcase. He kept his cutlery in there. That's four by eleven and six inches deep." He laughs, proud of his dad and yet a little amazed at the ups and downs of his dad's life. "He kept building and he kept building. He figured the town would go up the hill but it didn't. They put the Post Office all the way on top of the hill just below the statue of Marcus Daly. . . Daly was one of the first big operators, but the town wouldn't climb up." Young Whitehead glances down at his trays of knives. "My dad is a typical westerner. I've seen people come in here to buy a razor. If my dad knew a man wouldn't take good care of a razor or a pocketknife, he wouldn't sell him one. 'You'll tell your friends I don't make good knives,' he would say. But I'd sell anybody anything. I don't care. I don't spend hours making knives like dad. I'm a typical American. I'm here for what I can get out of it. I want a job done right but I want to make money." He shrugs. "Butte's changed a great deal. Where I live now, you hardly know anybody. It's a funny thing how the old-timers have drifted away. The people who have come in have that stick-to-themselves feeling. My dad used to say: 'Anybody who wants money to eat, give it to him. He'll pay it back some day.' My dad. . ."

An old woman enters the shop. She hands young White-head a pair of scissors. "I can have my scissors ground. My man's back in the mines."

"I'll do it right away."

The woman leaves.

"The whole town is underworked." Young Whitehead walks to the door. "See that Hotel Finlen across the street. That's Butte's newest hotel. See where the corner's breaking? They put the concrete posts down to bedrock but everything's shifting in Butte. Park Street, South Main Street, the whole town's honeycombed with mines. There's a vein here—starts at Rocker west of here and comes right through here, several miles to the east side of town. They can produce a million pounds of copper in one day!"

"How many scissors can you grind in one day?"

"We used to be busy from morning to night, but now it's slow. People don't use expensive knives for show. They use just what they need." He shakes his head. "The old West is gone. Your western spirit is leaving. Everything's the same now all over. It's the same old thing. A man comes in to buy a pocket knife and I'll sell it to him. Not like the old days when my dad would say: 'The hell with you!' if a thing wasn't right. And the day is coming when you'll say today's a good day."

A sign on the wall reads:

VILLAGE BLACKSMITH
HOLLOW GROUND
STEAK KNIFE

"Let me ask you something?" Young Whitehead smiles. "Three quarters of the people here are on P.W.A., W.P.A. and Federal stuff. . . The mines are operating on account of the war scare. Copper's just struck ten and one half cents a pound and Butte's good. It'll go higher if there's war. But what's going to happen?"

"God's country? Any place is God's country if you got the iron men."

From the sayings of the people.

Standing on East Park Street, in the distance . . . a spur of the Rocky Mountains like a huge showpiece fills the eyes. Here the out-of-work miners linger outside the café windows, the sun on the backs of their tanned wrinkled necks.

Arizona is in his sixties, a short door-wide man with the large domed head of a 'typical' professor and the chin of a truckdriver. His dead white face is all wrinkles and hollows. He leans on his walking canes, one in each hand. "I'm not much of a guy for looking back but I'm a great guy for looking ahead. I've seen a lot. I was in Cœur d'Alene when Senator Borah prosecuted Bill Haywood, Moyer and Pettibone. That's when they were trying to break up the Western Federation of Miners. But that's all too far back. It doesn't concern the present generation. Where are we going from here? I'll go ahead in spite of hell and high tide." Arizona grins but his lips have been clenched together from too many hours of suffering for any grin of his to be humorous.

"I heard you were in an accident."

"I put five years on my back since 1929. Previous to that I had put thirty years underground as a miner. As a miner and not a dodger."

"What happened?"

"One day, lifting timber I felt a sharp pain in the side. They told me I could walk it off so I walked it off . . . on my back. It just hit me in the side! A stinging pain! I'm more a victim of poor medical care than anything else. I was walking for nine weeks when I should've been on my back. Those were the nine weeks that crucified me. You have no choice of hospitals here. You go where they send you. You're contract patients. You pay the dollar a month and they rush you out as soon as they can." His big hands tighten around the heads of the two canes. "I'm not a home guard. I happen to be a tramp miner. I came in here from the State of Arizona in 1926 and this accident happened in 1929. This is a story without a parallel in western mining history." He glares at two old miners shuffling by. "Most of the doctors are dominated by the Anaconda Copper Mining Company, the A.C.M. Both newspapers are A.C.M. papers. The *Standard's* Democratic, the *Post's* Republican. The A.C.M. doesn't care what your politics are as long as you're for them. They're non-partisan." He grins contemptuously. "I've fought these birds ten years." His voice deepens, becomes heroic. "I've fought the A.C.M. for ten years and I'm not through fighting yet! I'll take my case to President Roosevelt! I've been no good since the fourteenth day of June, 1929. From the fourteenth day of June to the twenty-first day of August I was walking. Then I came down again. They decided to railroad me to Galen. . ."

"What's Galen?"

"The state T.B. San. I put nineteen months in Galen. I walked out of there without my sticks. . . In all these ten years I haven't received one cent from the A.C.M. The best thing they offered me was a donation of three hundred dollars. For that I had to sign on the dotted line I'd never bring suit against the A.C.M. and its officers. They told me they'd hike it up to five hundred if I found a chicken ranch. I told them I couldn't try to do business without the cash in my hand. After I came out of Galen, I took my case to the Industrial Board. I was turned down on this Statute of Limitations. I hadn't filed my claim *legally!* I didn't make a claim to the A.C.M. in thirty days! They had *no* knowledge. Yet I was taken to Galen in an A.C.M. private car! I've been fighting them by taking it up through different Congressmen and different Senators. I've taken it through the State Supreme Court. I'm independent. I'm independent all times!" He grins again, apologetic. "This is a squawk. . ."

"What is wrong with you?"

"My back. Three vertebrae are gone. I'm fighting paralysis. My pains are girdle pains, burning pains, contraction pains.

Any damn thing a nerve can produce. Your back is like these
knuckles of mine. And three of these knuckles are crushed,
fused together. There's pressure on these vertebrae. Until the
nerves adjust themselves I'm no good. I came out of Galen
feeling fine. . ." He nods sadly. "A man who's never stopped
or disabled in his life doesn't stop. 'Take it easy,' they tell you
in Galen. But when you come out, you're out. I figured I'd
go to Galen for a week or ten days but I was there nineteen
months. The hospital here took a picture of my lumbar region and said the pain was a rheumatic condition. Galen said
it was the dorsal region. You're not supposed to be admitted to
a T.B. San unless you have T.B. But it relieved A.C.M. of
obligation, having me in Galen. But, I'll fight them!" Leaning
on his two canes, his dead white face the chart of all his
sufferings, he seems like a figure out of a legend, the colossal
tonnage of Anaconda's mines and smelters on his crushed
back.

One window of Judd's Sporting Goods Store on East Park
Street is crowded with beaded Indian moccasins, claw neck-
laces and feather war bonnets. Small boys and old men are
always stopping to take a look. Sometimes they talk.

"I've seen the Indians make them," the tiny old man says.
He is about five foot three, his suit a pair of ragged overalls,
his stockingless feet in old cracked shoes, his big white mustache discolored from chewing tobacco.

"Where did you see them?" The boy is about twelve, his
eyes constantly shifting from Judd's window to the old man's
left ear. Cut in two at one time, the top half is missing.

"Yes, I seen them make them." The old man's breath is
foul, not from liquor, but from some organic disease. The
sun beats on his ancient face. He might be seventy or eighty.
There's no telling. "That expedition was made up of men
from Bozeman. Trappers and hunters and miners from all
parts of the territory. They wanted gold. They thought it was
in the mountains. My cousin was one of them. They began
to have trouble with the Indians. They were mostly Sioux.
They killed fifteen hundred Indians. That was another
time . . . I remember. I was just a boy." He measures off a

height of four feet or so with his hand. "They killed them in Utah. I remember." His eyes gleam as if he had somehow taken a drink out of the empty air.

"Where did you see them make bows and arrows?" The boy stares at the Indian war bonnets in Judd's window.

"They dug graves but they didn't bury the bodies in them. They buried sticks of gun powder. My cousin was one of them. They had it fixed to explode as soon as the Indians came near. The whole territory was full of hostile Indians. They couldn't look for gold until they killed the Indians. I'm a Mormon. No man should deny what he is. No man!" He mutters unintelligibly. His voice clears. "I've been in churches of all denominations but I'm a Mormon. Joseph Smith prophesied . . ."

"What?" I ask. The boy has lost interest in the old man.

"I know a canyon where I can get all the Indian root I want. That'll cure a cold in your chest. Cure any sore. I'll find that root." He shakes his head up and down many times as if to impress me with the bonanza value of Indian root. "The Indians knew where it was. . . They killed the Mormons like they did the Indians! I'll bring that root back and sell it for a dollar a piece. I know where it is. It'll cure anything that ails you. . . Sores. . . I know the Indians. I know them. Speak their language. I'll sell you a piece for a quarter."

Like Judd's, the shelves of the Ideal Bargain Store hold the West, not the Indian West, but the new silver dollar West. "Every type of person in the world comes here," the proprietor informs me. "Cowboys and farmers come in for drinking money. Working in the mines is no snap. They drink to stand up under it. They sell their hard hats." Yellow cowhide riding belts, broad and tough, horsehair belts once worn by ranch hands, tools, all are for sale.

The names of the streets are like remembered lines of the forgotten song. West Agate Street, West Ruby Street. . .

"I come into the world bare-ass and I'll leave it bare-ass." His voice is husky, his brogue from the eastern seaboard.

"Where were you born?"

Under his cap, his craggy face slits into a grin. "I come into the woild back in New Joisey. My father was an Irishman and so was my mother."

"How did you get West?"

"It's a long story. My first li'l adventure was as a coal passer on the old Merchant Marine back in 1910. In those days a coal passer's life was as bad as living in a slum. Your corned beef was dished out in a dixie. You ate with dirty hands and face. Now to jump from the indignity to the sublime, unionization cleaned things up." He pokes at his cap, his gestures like a New York taxi-driver's, his gray eyes steady and wise. "I'll jump from this to the World War. I went over on a cattle boat. We hugged the coast along Barcelona and Portugal. We were takin' over western horses and I was a butler to the horses. I served my time with the English Royal Engineers. The war, well . . . I couldn't make head or tail out of it. Shoot a guy down you never saw before. . ." His lower lip juts out in quick wonder. "I went in mostly for a t'rill. After the war I made a trip inland to Sudbury, Canada. I worked in the mines. Then, I drifted into the hay fields of Winnipeg. Then I made a free shipment of my carcass from Winnipeg into British Columbia. In other woids I hopped the freights."

He smiles. "In those days, working my way troo, I was enjoying life. I took out of life what life was givin' me in return. I paid as I went along. It was rough and ready. I was a lumberjack for the Canadian Railroad. Four of us slept in a bunk. Our bed was pine needle leaves and you can imagine the lice. Then I went up as whistle-punk. That's a sort of stationary engineer who controls the logs with a net that come down from the river. Your hours were eight hours, seven-fifty a day. Living conditions were very good. We had mattresses and bedsheets because we had the one big union boys, the I.W.W.'s. I landed in Butte in 1922." He scowls. "Anaconda's the octopus of Butte! But I don't know who to blame? I think it's the handicap of our parents. If their education was poor in body and soul, if their living was just an existence, so no child had a chance to get the right kind of thinkin' . . . and then we guys come along and foller the same line our parents did. We can't think for ourselves. When I went into the Army they handed me a rifle and bayonet and

said: 'There's the dummy out there. Keep diggin' into him.'
The Sergeant, he was doin' the thinkin' for me. I was just
an automatic machine. I remember when I was a kid, I used to
ride the subways in New York and the biggest sign was—
Sloan's Liniment. If I bruised myself I thought of *Sloan's
Liniment*. That's what I mean. I can think. Yes. But it seems
that ninety per cent of what I think is the wrong way."

He shakes his fist. "The only thing to improve the conditions of this country will be technocracy. Big business knocked
over technocracy because it's more dangerous for the working
stiff than the Townsend Plan. There's more unemployed people than people to retire on pensions. The principle of
technocracy is wonderful. Four hours a day, ten months a year
work, two months with vacation and pay. But the biggest
thing in technocracy is where they do not believe in nego-
tiable bonds being transferred from one country to another.
And when you eliminate the creed of money, you'll eliminate
hate, greed and selfishness. I'll take a chance with a bunch
of scientific nuts rather than with a bunch of selfish nuts.
But the average stiff thinks it's all a pipe dream. He'll never
wake up."

He lights a cigarette. "When I came up here as a copper
miner, we had to contend with those mines. They were hot
boxes. The ice and drinking water were in one tank. The
average stiff would come along and dig in with his dirty hands
for a piece of ice to put in his water bag. I'd come along and
want to drink and I'd have to drink this dirty water. Through
unionization that has been eliminated. We have separate
tanks for the ice and separate tanks for the drinking water.
Here I am, a copper miner! Every day I report in when I
hit the mine. Then I hit the dryer and change my clothes to
put on a dirty shirt, dirty overalls, dirty socks and my hard
hat. I go to the lamp room for my headlight. Then I go to
the surface station where the cages are. You go down with
about ten men in a deck. The quicker they can get you down,
the quicker you get to work as a contract miner. We trust to
fate going down and going up. If a cable breaks ten men get
killed. . . Down on my level, I fill my water bag with ice and
hit for my hot box. It might be in a drift or it might be in a
stope. The first thing you're squawking about is the night
shift, if you're the day shift. It's because they didn't clean up

right. The next thing, you're shouting to the motorman for empty cars to start mucking. Mucking's filling up the cars. . . Soon as the cars come in the drift, you start barring down, taking down all the loose rock so you won't get killed. Then your partner or you starts with the mucking machine, that's a miniature of a steam shovel. The other feller starts with the drillin' machine. You drill at least eighteen holes in a drift. You have to hit the ball! You got to move every minute while the other feller is mucking up! A snowbank is easy but drillin' in hard iron will take six hours. You eat your dinner on the fly so you can finish drillin' by four o'clock when you go off. You got your primers to set up. . . A box of powder, that's one hundred and sixty sticks, is what you need for eighteen holes. When you're ready to blast, you strip down your machines and air hoses and set 'em 'way back out of harm's way. Now you start loadin'. One man uses a loadin' stick while the other feller throws the powder in by hand. If it's a wet drift, you use a battery charge. You come and look your wires over to see there's no breaks. You pull the switch at the end of the drift. Off she goes!"

"It's no soft picnic on that job," he says. "You're on edge. When you hit the station at the end of the day, it's a relief. You're a cave man in the drift. The heat wears you down. It could be improved by putting down the hours. Six hours is enough of that kind of work. This way you have to finish your round and blast before you quit work. If you don't, you're out on the snow. The contract prices have been chiseled. One day's pay is five and a quarter, and if you're lucky to make seven, you're lucky! Aw, don't forget they crucified Christ. He was alone. If the average feller instead of follerin' the footsteps of his father. . . This way, the average stiff thinks he's a smart guy if he can pull a fast one over on me. But there's always the big guy on top pulling the fast one on both of us."

East Park Street, street of miners.
He wears a gray shirt and brown canvas suspenders. His face seems hewn out of ore, his sharp blue eyes shaded under

the brim of his black felt hat. "Hiram G. Beasley is the name," he introduces himself with an antique courtesy. "Kentuckian by birth. Entered into the lead field in '98 in Missouri. Worked for the National Lead Company and for Guggenheim. Then helped to re-timber old shafts the same as new." His mouth is shaped like an upside down U. He considers each word carefully before speaking. "In 1900 we were working twelve hours per day, 90 cents for shoveling, one dollar for running a machine. A few years later the miners consolidated into a union body under the Western Federation of Mineral Mine Workers. They elected J. L. Bradley of Farmington, Missouri, to the State Legislature. By his work we obtained the eight-hour law, without penalty. Then we placed J. L. Bradley into the State Senate and obtained a penalty in the law which forced the companies to honor the State Law and work eight hours per day. At the same time, wages were increased. These locals were sponsored and assisted by Eugene Debs. Eugene Debs in person was one of the most sympathetic men in America in his day and one with foresight of the future needs. He lived a half century before his time should have been. He was the foundation agitator."

He pauses, his blue eyes shifting from face to face of the passers-by. "After coal mining in Indiana, I came to Butte in '26. Entered into the stope mine work and general repairs. In '26 and '27 we were required to drill and blast and muck out. At that time it would figure from three hundred cubic feet per shift. The Anaconda Copper Company paid me three cents per cubic foot for drilling and blasting, two cents per cubic foot for timbering, two cents per cubic foot for mucking. A total of seven cents per cube. Now the same contract forces the men to break from four hundred to five hundred cubic feet and muck out and timber. And receive in pay one dollar and four cents per hundred." He half winks, his eyelid lowering to the point just above his pupil, as if even while winking he must be on the look-out. "Last week, we drilled and blasted and mucked out three thousand cubic feet in one five-day week. My partner and me received five twenty-seven per day. That was with a bonus of two cents per day. Ten cents bonus for five days. Twenty cents bonus for two men. In the '26 and '27 time, copper was selling for nine cents. It's ten and one half cents now."

He begins again after a minute of silence. "There's from three to four to five accidents a day. I'm in the 3600 level in the Anselmo mine. I got one of these fans but it takes in hot air and lets out hot air. The shift bosses say it's too hot to work in. You've got to wring your shirt out two or three times a day. You pour from a pint to a quart of water out of each boot several times a day. It's hot work. The Anaconda Company is trying to cool it but have failed so far. These accidents could be avoided if they changed the system of operation. They use the cut and fill system in the stopes. The cut and fill system leaves too much open ground without timber to hold it."

"I saw careful timbering in the Leonard mine."

"That's the show-mine. They're using the cut and fill system to save timber." He half winks again; one corner of his mouth twisting up as if in appreciation of the Company's economy. "Mr. Weed of New York, he established the cut and fill system. Accidents have increased ever since. They had to have timber on the vertical stopes. But they don't use the timber system where they can get away with it on the diagonals up. Now after you pull the copper ore out of a stope to a space fifteen feet high, you fill in by pouring waste down one chute and filling the bottom of the stope plumb across to the other raise. The raises are empty holes going through. The raise on the right is for the waste. The copper goes down the raise on the left, or whichever is convenient for operation. It's hot hard work. . . The reason I haven't got silicosis is because I shifted around from mining to mining. If I had stayed steady in the mine I would've had it. This way, the change from job to job, and getting into the open air, gave my lungs a rest. . . Mining is a natural trade of itself but the mine industry is profit for the stockholders and none for the producers. The testimony the Anaconda Copper Company gave to the Senate Committee, and this is according to their own paper the *Montana Standard*—in nineteen months' operation in '37 and '38, their clearance was forty million eight hundred thousand dollars in the four towns of Butte, Anaconda, Helena and Great Falls. None of the miners cleared much after he paid his board and expense. If we get a two bit raise, the roomin' houses raise their roomin' rent. I've been mining a long time. . . I was born in 1878. I'm sixty-three. But one thing about the people where I was raised. If they haven't got a meal ahead, they'll still be independent. The Anaconda Copper Company is a rich company but the people where I was raised are independent."

Further up on East Park Street, the Park Movie is featuring THE PURPLE VIGILANTES.

On Saturday night, the idle men always loafing in front of the Arcade corner and the adjoining M. & M. on Main Street, multiply. Inside, the two-bit gamblers are playing Chinese lottery. For twenty-five cents, each man receives a paper slip numbered from 1 to 80. Frowning or analytical or playing hunches, each man inks out the ten numbers he likes best. At the Lottery Booth, the house man in the eyeshade duplicates each set of numbers on a second slip which he keeps. The players take their copies to a long high desk like a desk in a post office. They wait, their eyes on the lottery cage of eighty numbers marked on eighty celluloid balls. The house man rotates the cage, and one by one picks up twenty balls. The twenty lucky numbers are flashed in turn on the overhead electric board. If five of the numbers on the board correspond to five on a slip, the investor doubles his investment, If he has six, seven. . . Twenty-five cents can win as much as forty-five dollars! One investor wins fifty cents. The other speculators in this poor man's stock exchange dig into their pockets for another two-bits plunge. Twenty-five cents can win forty-five dollars!

The *American's* two features are Ronald Coleman in IF I WERE KING and BLUE MONTANA SKIES. Inside, the movie fans sit up, grin, whisper a few words when the plains, canyons and buttes of "Blue Montana Skies" flash on the screen. "It's real so far," a fellow remarks to his girl.

ADVENTURE flickers before the eyes of Butte. Fur smugglers cross over into the Canadian wilderness, robbing honest trappers of their valuable pelts. The leader of the fur smugglers is also the part-owner of a dude ranch. His partner, innocent and beautiful, is a blond fashion plate who wanders starry-eyed from peril to love in a series of stunning riding outfits. The hero is a singing cowboy, who also has a partner, an old tough but goodhearted son of the West who gets knifed by the fur smugglers. The singing cowboy will not rest until he tracks down the killers, until he clinches with the fashion plate. . .

The show ends. The fans exit. Every sidewalk is a paved ceiling a half mile above the copper streets below.

"BUTTE COUPLE IS FOUND DEAD
Authorities here today figuratively painted a tragic picture of privation and desperation in connection with the deaths of Jesse Malin, 56, and his wife Della, late Saturday night . . . Malin, they said, sent a bullet into his brain, in desperation and resignation against the cruelties of life, because he was unable to work and provide food and other necessities for his wife and himself . . . The woman, who lay in bed screaming in terror as her husband fired the suicide shot, had joined her husband in death by the time the authorities came. She died of a heart attack, apparently brought on by shock, according to Coroner Con Sheehy . . . Malin worked as a miner for a number of years, but was physically unable to work during the last few years."
From the August 14th edition of THE POST.

On Sunday, the Columbia Gardens, situated at the base of the Continental Divide, fill with the people of Butte. Today is the annual Pioneers' Picnic. The youngest descendants of the pioneers skip across the green lawns to the carousel. Men swap stories. Scores of families climb the slopes to the picnic tables. Shaded by cedars, the mothers rest on the benches.

A young blond woman of thirty in a blue dress, leads her blond brood to an empty bench. Her face is still youthful but her body has been blown up into fat middle age by her many childbirths. Her oldest, a girl of nine, carries the youngest, a baby of seven or eight months. Another girl of about seven guards an army of little brothers like a watchdog. There are four of the boys, the oldest about six, the youngest about a year and a half. All four of the little boys have had their blond hair clipped close to their skulls as if the barber had agreed to a special wholesale price. Their downy heads shine golden. As they tumble and fall, they look like clumsy little ducks. Two elderly women waddle up to the young mother, meaty ladies with big jowls. They sit down on the bench and seem to take up all the space.

"That was Ryan for you. That was Ryan indeed," one of them says.

The young mother says nothing. Her four sons scatter over a half acre, one of the younger ones running around with a mouthful of dirt. The youngest wears green pants. All he does is fall and cry, his dirty smudged cheeks wet with tears. He either is falling or being left behind by his older brothers. Patiently, he gets to his feet and tries to catch up with them. His feet aren't strong enough. . . All afternoon he tries, sniffling and weeping. When he gives up, he is too tired to climb back up the slope to his mother. "Mama! Mama! Mama! Mama!" he sobs in anguish. The watchdog sister retrieves him. His shoes are much too big for him, a pair inherited from one of his older brothers.

"That was Ryan all the time!" The bigger of the two elderly ladies smokes a cigarette.

"He was a man just the same," the second says.

"That was Ryan."

The young mother says nothing, still preoccupied, thinking, perhaps, about the baby in her womb.

Down on the level lawn, the picnic officials, two aging men, have roped off a track. The crowd jams against the ropes. There are pioneer great-grandmothers of eighty with worn stone faces, too near death to bother with the make-believe of their daughters. Many of the women between fifty and sixty are dressed in long pioneering dresses and sun bonnets. Underneath last century's bonnets, their faces are the made-up faces of the twentieth, their dry lips bright red, their hollow or fatty cheeks rouged. The stoop-shouldered old husbands are dressed in their ordinary Sunday suits.

An official swings the bag of prize money. "The first race will be for men over sixty. The first prize will be a dollar and a half. The second prize will be a dollar. Come on you men over sixty."

"Come on," a matron urges her husband. "You enter."

"I don't want to. My running days are over." He smiles at the smiling faces.

"No, they're not."

"My heart's not what it used to be," he says. "They have enough there without me."

Seven or eight men line up down at the end of the lawn.

Hatless, coatless, they glance sideways at each other and at the starter. . .

The signal! They race for the tape with long strides like fast walking.

The winner pockets his silver dollar and half dollar, the second winner his silver dollar.

"The next race will be for all ladies over sixty." The official waves his straw hat. "Where are the ladies over sixty?"

None of the ladies steps forward.

The official grins. "The next race will be for all ladies over fifty."

Two women in sunbonnets accept the invitation.

"He should say for all women over forty," a man remarks.

Happily seated on a nearby see-saw, one of his brothers on the other end, Green Pants is riding on air, a smile on his lips.

At the signal, the ladies over fifty raced for the tape. . . Winners and losers stroll out of the limelight back into the crowd. The young mother of the duck family has seen enough. She leaves the laughing spectators, calls to the see-sawers. The older boy toddles off but Green Pants doesn't budge. His mother drags him off and the tears stream down his cheeks.

"My two boys and myself, we're still operating that gold mine," a man of sixty-five says to another old man on the fringe of the crowd. Both of them are well-preserved as if they have a little money in the bank.

"It's a waste of time." The second man shrugs his shoulders. "Now Helena was a great placer country back in 1890. Helena had more millionaires in the early '90's than anywheres else. It was pure gold, too. I remember how we washed out the gold."

The gold mine operator listens impatiently, sucking in his hollow cheeks. "Haven't you a good word to say for quartz mining?"

"Ledges and rocks and hard work. How deep's your shaft now?"

"Five hundred feet deep."

"It's a penny ante business. You've been working your claim for three years, haven't you? I'll bet you haven't made expenses yet?"

"It's working on a small scale, a small capital mine," the

gold mine operator half-agrees. "My father-in-law located those claims. I have no thought that we'll make a fortune. We're just poor people, my sons and I. The two boys are baching it in a cabin with an older man. He's an excellent cook. And that's fortunate. We're poor people and they've got to be near all the time."

"Near for what? Ham and eggs?"

"Why, we have two or three tons of high-grade ore out that's worth two hundred a ton. If you're gone—and they're all people like that near a mining camp, they'd come and sack it. That ore's worth twenty a sack!"

"Twenty a sack?" the skeptic asks, smiling.

"Twenty a sack," the gold mine operator repeats.

"Five hundred feet! That's labor and timber and food." The skeptic frowns as if counting costs in his head. "There's nothing in quartz mining but hard work. You would have gotten a better return on your money if you would have bought A.C.M."

"No!"

"Copper's just struck ten and one half," the skeptic persists.

> "You can search this wide world over
> As you travel up and down
> You will never find another
> Like this old Montana town.
>
> I struck the mining city
> In the spring of ninety-nine,
> It wasn't very pretty, but things were going fine,
> With countless thousands toiling
> In mill and mart and mine.
>
> Butte really is two cities,
> One above, one underground:
> It would startle all creation
> To compute the wealth they found.
>
> And they spent it dime and dollar
> Spent it with a lavish hand,
> Everything, the very latest,
> Came to Butte from out the land.
>
> In closing, I will state a fact
> That you will not dispute,
> There will never be another
> Like this great old town of Butte."
> *From Mike J. Rowan's "That Butte, Montana, Town."*

"I come here in '98. It t'was a country, a land of enchantment," Paddy's voice is as solemn as his eyes. A small wiry man with a thatch of blond hair and blond furry eyebrows, only his eyes are unusual, blue wonderful eyes that look as if they can never age. "It t'was a land covered over with foliage. The hills were green. The whole state was a green carpet. There were springs and brooks running then that are dried up now. The railroad companies brought in people to settle this beautiful land." His voice is lyrical as if he were a young man again in Montana. "The world was a very small place in my day. Each man lived in his parish or town and was afraid to go on to the next. So when I come out here I felt I was in a country I had dreamed about. The streams were full of trout and grayling like sardines in a box. It was a Garden of Eden. The Indians knew what was here and they knew what would happen. They knew. Montana was like a young woman of sixteen or seventeen. Montana had always been like that. Now, she's haggard. People say Montana is pretty. But it's nothing like she was."

His blue eyes seem to be gazing past me into the green canyon of his youth. "There were intense feuds then between the copper companies and the original locators. The independents were battling monopoly even then but nobody could foretell what has happened. Monopoly came in here in Pullmans and crushed the original locators. In those days, there were men who had been working in the mines from the age of nine and ten. They couldn't read or write. I used to read their letters for them. I was a boy and they were men of fifty and sixty and even seventy. Now, in the mines, a man's motor plays out before that. Why didn't the people fight?" He answers his own question. "People planned to go to Idaho, to California, to Nevada, to Alaska, to Mexico. People were fascinated by the other places. Like cows in a rich pasture, they'd feed awhile and go elsewhere. And when they come back, they found Montana under the heel. We never realized how rich Montana was. Come to Montana and you'd hear of the mines in Mexico. . . The mines in Oregon were better. . ." The names of the virgin Western states with their mineral mountains seem like a land in sunlight as he speaks them. "The mines had such fancy names. Silver City . . . Gold Field . . . Tombstone in Arizona. . . They were all alluring but when you got there, you wondered why you'd left."

His blue eyes stare into mine. "The mining companies began to merge. Henry H. Rogers, he was the president of the Standard Oil then, he had his agents here propagandizing. But the people always voted against the monopoly candidates. But they kept per-sisting. They divided Heinze and Clark, two of the multi-millionaire locators. Marcus Daly was the third of the early locators and Marcus Daly opened the gates to Standard Oil by giving Rogers an interest in his mines. He thought he'd be the big dog." His voice is slow and angerless, his words carven out of stone, words on stone lost from human mouth and human passion. "For awhile, that solidified Heinze and Clark. Heinze would go down to the Butte balcony and people'd listen spell-bound as he turned the heat on monopoly. He was a man of twenty-eight or thirty then, a big good-looking fellow. He had a blond sweetheart, the envy of all the women in the State. They raised the moral issue against Heinze. His blond sweetie and he should be driven out of the State. Standard Oil was virtuous! Heinze had a vice-president in his company by the name of McGuinness. McGuinness bought four hundred shares in the Boston and Montana, a monopoly mine. McGuinness wanted an accounting of the B. & M. books. They refused to give it to him. McGuinness got an injunction and the B. & M. was closed down. Rogers then said: 'We'll close all the mines and bring the people to their knees.' He as much as said: 'To hell with Montana.' He tried to take the litigation out of Silver Bow County into the counties where he had puppet judges. But at every session of the Legislature, the monopoly bill was snowed under. To win the people, he arranged a big barbecue at the Columbus Gardens. They slaughtered a lot of steers. They had beer. Thousands went out there. A week later, Rogers sent a telegram: CLOSE DOWN THE BUTTE MINES. That was in the fall of 1903."

His voice is the voice of a prophet, speaking not only for himself but for all the bottom men. His eyes seem to see them all, the dead and the living. "Heinze was the spearhead of the independents. Heinze was the locator of the big leads. The real bonanza was down deep and he found it. Clark had gotten to the United States Senate and Daly was dead. Now,

Rogers threatened to have Clark expelled if he didn't break with Heinze. Clark didn't want to break, but he did. Heinze was still strong in the election of 1904 but the ballot boxes were stuffed. There was bribery. The corrupt wings of the Democrats and the Republicans were welded together. The Democrats used to put up two candidates for Judge, the Republicans two. But now the Democrats put up one Judge. The Republicans put up one Judge. Like lice they welded themselves together and elected two puppet Judges who decreed that all the mineral in Silver Bow County belonged to the Amalgamated, belonged to monopoly. Heinze and his Fusion party, consisting of the silver Democrats, the silver Republicans, the trade unionists and the Populists, won the rest of the offices, which proves the corruption. . . That was the day Montana committed suicide. They drove Heinze out. Butte had three shifts then. The saloons and cafés stayed open twenty-four hours. You couldn't tell night from day. But the ten-hour corporation won! Heinze and Clark gave the men eight hours. The Amalgamated gave the men ten hours. The ten-hour corporation won! In 1905, they kidnapped Moyer, Pettibone and Haywood in Denver. They took these three men to Boise, Idaho, and Senator Borah, a puppet then for the Mine Owners' Association, tried them. Monopoly wanted no unions in its territory, which was the whole West. Between 1914 and 1934 Butte was unionless. . . The politicians are very small men, here. They puke up what they're told. They're hatched in the monopoly incubator. . . Rogers was never here in Butte or within the State of Montana, to my knowledge, and yet this man and his corporation have changed a land of enchantment into one of their banks. . ."

U. S. Route Alternate 10

The Anaconda smelter, the tallest smokestack in the world, is circled by the deforested mountains.

Named after trees, the streets of Anaconda, Cherry Street, Cedar Street, Oak Street, glare in the sun.

West of Drummond, forests cover the slopes, trout brooks silver alongside the highway. The Bitter Root Mountains with stone ridges like immense bent ribs are green with trees.

The signs warn: DON'T BE A FLIPPER.

USE YOUR ASH TRAY.

YOUNG TREES ON FAMOUS 1910 BURN.

Small green pines grow among the blackened masts of the 1910 burn, mountains with dead tree trunks needling against the sky like porcupine quills.

THE 1910 FIRE WAS 25 MILES LONG.

Through the Glidden Pass into Idaho among soft mountains round-shaped like Indian faces.

The lead-silver mining towns of Idaho, Mullan, Wallace, Kellogg, the mine shafts cutting into the mountains, the gulches of Slaughter House, Terror, Rosebud and Little Terror, are all on the twisting Cœur d'Alene River.

West, the sinking sun smelts its own gold, the burning gold of the sky.

Through the forest darkness, I drive along Cœur d'Alene Lake, its miles of water lit with the moon's electricity.

I rent a cabin on the lake among red firs rising up sixty feet into the stars.

The Lumberjacks

COPPER CREEK CAMP

"But no sooner was the first sawmill erected than the axemen began their devastation. Trees one after another were, and are yet constantly heard falling during the days, and in calm nights the greedy mills told the sad tale that in a century the noble forests would exist no more."

From the life of AUDUBON.

ON THE BEACH THE SUN BURNS the bark ovals washed ashore. In the shallows, the sixteen-foot barkless logs escaped from the booms or rafts gleam white through the green water.

Two miles west, the town of Cœur d'Alene is a pedalling place for tourists on bicycles. At lunch hour, the insurance men leave their offices, the walls decorated with the heads of Rocky Mountain goat and sheep. The waitresses in the cafés hurry to the tables with menus.

Outside town on the northern loop of Cœur d'Alene Lake, the Winton Company sawmill workers are eating lunch. They sit in rows along the lake's edge, chewing their sandwiches, their eyes squinting against the bright noontime water, their bodies turned to the red-painted mill with its piles of sawn pine boards.

"How do you like sawmill work?" I ask a worker in blue cap and blue jeans.

"Most sawmill men want to go farming and on the farm they talk sawmill. I've been on and off it for twenty-five years." His eyes are set wide apart in his smiling face. His hands are small.

"What do you do?"

"I'm on the carriage. I'm a setter. We've got to judge the size of these logs and spot our blocks according to that. We got a set-works. That sets the size of the board. The sawyers call for the size of the board. . ." He shrugs his shoulders. "It's pretty hard to tell. You come up after lunch and see for yourself," he says with the natural friendliness of many Westerners.

"So you've been in it twenty-five years?"

"I started in when I was eighteen and I've been trying to get out all these years. We feel we're underpaid for the work we do. They're two setters on a carriage, two carriages in this mill. We setters get eighty and a half cents per hour, eight hours a day, four days a week. But, I've got a farm, a couple cows and chickens. Sooner or later, I'll make it I believe. I got a lot of cherries on my farm. My boys run the farm. I've got two hundred acres. I've been hoping to be a farmer since I got married. I started with forty acres and then I bought the nineteen laying below me. Then I bought a hundred more and the other day I bought forty-three more. It's benchland at the foot of the hills, sloping down to the lake."

He stares out on the water at the hundreds of floating logs penned inside a floating log corral. "Those are the booms. They store 'em there. The logs cut too green will sink. This lake is about covered with second growth logs. But there's quite a lot of virgin timber. Idaho has the largest stand of white pine in the world. The Winton people think it the only thing. It's a white pine mill. That's why I've got a farm. Mills always shut down about the time you save a little money. Originally, there were four mills in Cœur d'Alene. Now there are two running part-time. The Blackwell's out. The Winton and the Rutledge are left. It's not reliable enough for a man with a family to make a living."

The mill's whistles shrill of the afternoon ahead. The setter and the other sawmill workers hurry back to work, the whistles like a more piercing alarm clock.

Suddenly, noisily, the mill begins operations.

Two boom men with pike poles walk out on the wooden pier alongside the boom. They javelin their iron-pointed pikes into the pig-round logs. The logs jam together. The taller of the boom men leaps from the pier to a floating log, skipping from one sinking sliding footage to another. The second boom man, a stocky fellow in a sailor hat, lunges his pike pole into the freed logs.

One by one, the logs move down the side of the pier to the conveyor that rises from the water in a diagonal up to the second floor of the mill. One by one, the logs ride up the conveyor under a jetting shower that rips off entire sections of bark. Like spearers of fish, the boom men heave their pike poles into the endless shoals of logs, the incessant whine of the saw inside the mill whirring in the hot air.

The first floor of the mill is a dark belly of huge wheels and belts, the second floor a teamed muscle of men and machines.

There is the farmer-setter I spoke to! Quicker than a dancer, he balances on his carriage. Like a flat railroad car, the carriage speeds up and down on a hurling repeated journey of forty feet. Another setter rides the carriage with him. Two pairs of hands grip on levers, make adjustments. Two pairs of knees hold other levers in place, as up down, up down, up down, the carriage races on its single track.

A log enters the mill on the conveyor. The carriage speeds for its cargo. The two setters receive the log, hands and knees performing their complex tasks, bodies in rhythm with the up down, up down carriage. Metal fingers reach for the log, a vertical bar like a metal thumb lifting and setting it. Up down. Up down. The saw flashes . . . the whizzing cutting sound of steel in wood. Already the bark edges have been sawn off. Up down. The metal fingers, the metal thumb and the two setters toss the log into a new set. Up down. The round log has been sawn into a rectangular square. Up down. The boards slice off like cheese onto a series of revolving bars that like conveyors carry them into the middle of the mill, to the finishing operations.

I edge along the wall, the carriage a thunderbolt of danger on my right. Up front, the raised platform that receives the logs from the lake also separates the two carriages. Dripping wet, the logs keep coming into the mill, a young fellow in a red baseball cap pushing off the last clinging sections of bark with a stick. At the same time, an old man measures off the butt ends with a ruler, noting his findings in a ledger on the desk before him. He also controls the lever, which flings the log to either the right or the left station. There the logs wait. The left carriage is empty. Up, it speeds. The old man tugs back the lever. A log on the left station rolls down a metal skidway. The vertical metal thumb shoots up. The log is clamped to the carriage.

"What are you doing?" I shout in the old man's ear.

"I'm scaling. Measuring off the board feet in each log."

Up the carriages race as if they'll smash through the platform and mill wall and go flying out into the lake.

The sawyer near me is also an old man with a long face, deep brown intent eyes and hands beautiful because of their calm. He faces the up down carriage from the inside, estimating the boards in each log. The rotating saw is controlled lightning but the sawyer's woodsman's eye is just as swift. Calmly, he holds up one finger.

The setters manipulate their levers. The saw cuts off the first one-inch board, the second. Another signal from the sawyer. Two fingers. The setters and their metal thumb knock the log over on a different side. The boards slice off thicker.

One finger.

Two fingers again.

The white rectangle whittles down to a plank four inches thick. One last whizzing slash. Two new boards. And no more log.

The boards travel down on the revolving bars to the edgers and trimmers, and then outside the mill to the corrugated metal sheds where they are piled up by the green chain men.

In the yards, the boards are drying, stacked up into houses without doors or windows. The sun shines on the railroad tracks, the red freight trains.

I go into the Winton office building, a white painted frame structure about a hundred yards from the sawmill. "I'd like to go up to one of your logging camps," I explain to the stenographer.

"I'll have Mr. Ball see you. He's in charge of logging operations."

Mr. Ball is friendly, a man in his late thirties who looks as if he might be a trout fisherman. "I'll write you a note to Egan, the Copper Creek Camp clerk," he decides. "But I want to warn you about the road. It's our own road. It climbs up into the mountains. It's one way and you'll meet trucks coming down with logs. You'll have to reverse when you meet one of those trucks or you'll go to kingdom-come."

"Can I get up with my car?"

"Oh, sure. But watch those trucks. We can't give you permission to stay over. That's up to Mr. Brown. Mr. Brown's contracted to deliver that lumber to us. It's his camp."

"Thanks. I'll go up the first thing tomorrow morning."

"This is how you get there. Wait, I'll draw you a map. . ."

The next morning I drive east on U. S. 10. It's the first left-hand road just before the tunnel through the mountain, I think to myself: the first left before the tunnel.

The highway climbs above Cœur d'Alene Lake with its second-growth forests. And up ahead, waiting for a lift, a thin elderly lady stands off the concrete, her suitcase at her feet. I brake to a stop. "Where are you going?" I ask her as she sits down in the seat next to mine.

"I'm on my way to Missoula. I left Spokane two-thirty last night." Her face is tired under her blue straw hat. She looks like an ex-nurse, her wrists the fragile wrists of the old. "You're not going to Missoula by any chance?"

"No, I'm turning off about fifteen miles from here."

"I have friends in Missoula to keep me. I'm a telegraph operator for Western Union, you know. And they've promised me a job in Butte the first of September."

"Have you been a telegraph operator long?"

"Have I? I only have one year and eight months to get my pension. When I began in 1904, you had to work thirty years for your pension."

"That's some stretch of time." The green forest miles check off on my speedometer.

"I was left a widow in 1908 with two children to take care of."

"Where are you from?"

"California. But I haven't been home in six years. I was picking beans in the Spokane valley last week. I picked fifty-eight bushels in seven hours. I received a penny a bushel. But one woman, a tiny little woman got down close. She was tiny and she scooped the beans in." The telegraph operator laughs demurely. "I've always made my living with my fingers but picking beans was hard. I hate to admit it but I am getting old. I've picked those Kentucky Giants in my garden but not for a living."

I let her off at the tunnel. "I have to turn back. I'm past my turn. But motorists kind of slow down before the tunnel. The tunnel's new out here and you'll have a better chance for a lift."

"Thank you very much." She walks to the edge of the highway, her back as straight as the young pines behind her.

I drive back to my turn, to a broken asphalt curving around boulders to a junction of two narrow dirt roads. I wheel to the right and the brown dust smokes up. I raise my window to keep the dust out. The road just seems wide enough for my car. I think of the log trucks coming down and nervously honk my horn at the next curve. The road is all curves. I shift into second but even at the slower speed the brown dust is a fog in front of me. The trucks? Where are Mr. Ball's trucks? A pheasant flies from the road into the pines. I drive around the side of a mountain. Below, the forests slope down into the wilderness before man. Where are Mr. Ball's trucks? Suppose something happens to my brakes? Suppose something goes wrong? I creep along the side of a second mountain. Below, in the giddy beautiful below, Lake Cœur d'Alene is a small pond, a broken mirror. Where are Mr. Ball's trucks and how can trucks travel on this road and what will I do if I meet a truck?

The turn-outs are few and far between. A new idea hits me. I must have taken the wrong fork.

I come to a crossroads in the wilderness. I stop my car in a still world of evergreens. One fork leads to Killarney Lake, another to Cœur d'Alene Mountain. I wonder if I should go back the way I came? The sign on the fourth road reads: 6 MILES TO U. S. 95.

I take the fourth road down mountain and up mountain, through a ghost wilderness of abandoned miners' cabins falling apart, abandoned shafts like forgotten doorways into the mountains, into the ghost fortunes of gold, silver, lead. . .

Two-car wide U. S. 95 skirts the blue waters of Cœur d'Alene Lake. I come to a log boom, hundreds of logs floating inside the huge circle of chained trees. A boom man of fifty in high logger's boots sits on the side of the road.

"This Winton's?" I ask.

He stares at me. "Yes."

"Are those logs from Copper Creek Camp?"

"Yes."

"I got lost. I took the right fork . . ."

"You should've taken the left. You wait here. A truck'll be along soon. And you can follow the truck up to camp. You came out t'other side of the lake. This is Wolf Lodge Bay. They dump the logs here and the tug rafts them down to the sawmill." Impassive, he waits in silence.

A truck thunders down the highway. It pulls up, six-wheeled with its log trailer, loaded to the sky. The truck driver manœuvres the truck to the edge of the road.

He hops down, a burly six-footer with a round face a size too small for his heft. He sets up a tall lever pole, chaining it to the truck's shaft.

The boom man glances down at the three skid logs leading from the bank to the lake. He swerves around, glaring up at the load, fixing his eyes on the big end log. "That's a wild sonofabitch!" Cursing, he dives under the truck with iron chains.

He comes out, the sun on his stubborn face. "Let 'er wheel!" he shouts at the trucker as he knocks the hook-end out of one chain.

The truck's two top logs roll off, smashing against the skids, plunging into the lake.

"You bastards!" The boom man jumps out of the way.

He returns to the truck, knocks out the next hook-end. The bark rips off as the logs collide against the skids.

The truckdriver now uses a peavey. He digs the point in, the movable side-hook forking into a log's side. His back curves. He jumps.

More logs roll down the skids into the water, drifting into the boom. . .

Logless, the truck is just an iron platform. The truck driver chains the log trailer to the frame off the ground.

I walk over. "I'll follow you up to camp."

"Okay."

He drives like mad as if fleeing a forest fire, steering off the highway to a roadside eating place. "I'm having my lunch before I go back," he says as I come out of my car.

We sit down at the counter. "Lunch!" he orders.

The red-haired waitress brings us platters of fried bacon and eggs, potatoes, cucumber salad, bread and butter, lemon meringue pie and coffee.

"I always get my gas and lunch here," he remarks, breaking the yolks of his eggs.

"Don't you eat up at camp?"

"Not me. It costs a dollar thirty-five for board and bunk up in camp. I've got a farm near here where I can sleep."

"A farm?"

"My brother and I. It used to be worth one hundred and fifty an acre but you couldn't get fifty for it now. It's high prairie between the mountains and can grow anything the frost won't kill. But it's too far away from markets." He smiles. "It's all on the gyppo."

"What's that mean?"

"On contract." His smile widens. "On the gyppo!"

"I don't understand?"

"Brown's on gyppo for Winton. The cook's on gyppo for Brown. . . The cook's contracted to feed the camp for a price. He buys in big lots and has to make his profit above the gyppo." He drains the last of his coffee and stalks out to his truck. "I won't drive so fast up the mountain. There's ten miles before we get to camp."

I tail his racing truck. For the second time that day I come to the turn off U. S. 10, to the broken asphalt, to the junction. He swings onto the left fork. The brown dust rolls in clouds from his rear tires. The leaves of the roadside trees are brown. I drop behind the truck, bumping along at ten miles an hour.

The truck I'm trailing stops.

I stop.

A loaded truck is coming down.

There is no turnout on this stretch.

My truck driver reverses downhill. I reverse behind him to the turnout. Inch by inch, his head out, his eyes unblinking, he crawls out on the turnout, his two outer wheels separated from space by inches.

The loaded truck slowly drives down. The empty truck crawls back out the road from the turnout. My turn. I crawl out. The loaded truck grazes my inside mudguards. I quit thinking of where my right mudguards are. . .

Up we go around mountains, where the slash of the road seems narrower.

We meet another loaded truck on the top of Copper Mountain. But the turnout is summit-wide here. The truck driver going down, pokes his narrow red-head out of the window. "Wait here. There's another truck behind me."

I get out and stand on the ceiling of the wilderness. Below, white pine forests climb the V-shaped mountain slopes.

"They opened it up for the first time last year." My lunch companion spits a stream of tobacco juice into the dust.

"How many trips do you make up this road a day?"

"Two. Three if you're lucky." The second loaded truck comes into sight. "You keep to the right all the way and you'll miss the trucks. The trucks don't use that stretch. It was put in last year. From this point on it's clear if you keep right."

I climb back into my car, brown as the road now, and drive to the right, to a place where the roadway is made of logs. But the logs haven't been wasted. It really isn't a roadway but a tireway. Between the twinned logs on the left and the twinned logs on the right there are no logs, but a log-bounded hole of varying depth. Almost a bridgeway, it leads into the dusty road.

Ahead, Copper Creek Camp is a dusty square and a dusty street on the bottom of a narrow wilderness valley. The V-angled slopes are green with ninety-foot trees. It is three o'clock. The air smells of pine and tamarack.

I park my car among the cars of the lumberjacks behind the mess shack and walk up the camp street into a hundred years ago. . . Past the mess shack and the bunk houses on the square, the row of log buildings ahead belong to the forgotten architecture of the frontier. The forgotten West, solidly hewn out of logs, is only a dozen steps away. . . The dust kicks up brown and thick with each step forward. The creek seems unbelievably crystal pure, the trees unbelievably tall, the air unbelievably fragrant.

"Mr. Egan!" I call outside the first log house. "Egan!"

A head juts out of a window, the head of an Irishman with a snub nose and gray-blue eyes, and the sunken cheeks of a man no longer young. "I'm Egan. What do you want?"

"I have a note for you from Mr. Ball."

Egan tilts back his old felt hat. "Come on in."

I climb a short flight of stairs and hand Egan the note. He is standing inside a wooden-barred cage like a bank teller.

He reads the note quickly. "Brown isn't back yet. There was a shortage of blankets and he drove into Spokane for them. I don't know whether you can bunk over until he comes." Behind his narrow shoulders, the shelves are full of blankets, soap, gloves, candy.

"I'm not going back today. I'll sleep in my car if I have to."

"How do you like our roads?" He grins, walking around and out of the commissary to me. "Come on. I'll show you the camp."

We cross the street to a small log shack. Inside, the five-and-a-half-foot saws line one wall. An iron bed is near the window. "Here is where the brain work is done," Egan explains. "If the saws don't cut right, we don't get much timber. Ain't that right, Filer?"

The filer, a young man of about twenty-five, smiles. His head is long and narrow, his hair curly red, his little mustache reddish. "They have to be sharpened just so," he says with the withheld speech of the South. "See those four cutting points? And the drag teeth?" He runs his fingers down the cutting points. Miniature bayonets, they alternate with the fish-tail drag teeth. "If the drag teeth are too long, the sawyers can't pull the saw through."

A medium-sized man with crow-black hair steps into the shack, his eyes two black shining spots in his Indian-dark face.

"That's the blacksmith," Egan says, smiling.

"The boom's cracked off the jammer." The blacksmith doesn't smile. His lips aren't smiling lips.

"The boom loads the logs into the trucks," Egan explains as the three of us go out.

Four lumberjacks in high logging boots, blue jeans, blue shirts and dusty felts are standing around the jammer, an apparatus like a derrick mounted on a truck.

"See where the boom's cracked off?" Egan points to where the long derrick-like pole joins a metal plate.

The jammer's crew doesn't say a word, glaring at the crack.

Egan leads the way down the street until the camp is behind us. The huge cedars across Copper Creek are so thick no two men could loop them with their arms. The silence almost rings its silence, the voice before voices. . . "The men will be quitting at four o'clock." Egan shrugs. "The trees are sawed down first and then sawed into different lengths. Then they have to be skidded down to the road. That's done by horses. Then they deck the logs to a height of eight or ten feet in great big decks. You could go up to where they are." He nods at a rough trail snaking up the slope between the trees at a sixty-degree angle. "That's the short cut to where they are." He seems to forget me. "Another day," he says to himself.

"Do you come from these parts?"

"I'm from Superior, Wisconsin. I worked fifteen years for the Great Northern Pacific. . ." He nods as if contemplating his trek west. "One of these decks will hold a couple hundred thousand feet of lumber. This is Government timber. The Government's spotter picks out the trees to cut down. They're instructed to leave ten per cent of what we're cutting for seeding. They put red tags on the seeding trees." He grins, his eyes flickering youthfully for a second. "I guess we can bunk you if you don't want to drive back."

The road curves into a stretch built of logs. "Why log roads?" I stamp the dust off my shoes.

"See those rock faces here? Pole roads are built where it won't pay to blast out the rock. There's rock on each side. It'd cost fifty thousand a mile to build a road here."

"How did you get out to Idaho?"

"I made too much money railroading so I bought a bakery." He stares down at the creek. Every pebble shows clear on the bottom.

"Many trout?"

"Yes, but they're meat-eating fish." His head tilts back on his neck, his eyes slanting up. Three trees climb straight, pillaring the sky. "White pine. See how far up they go without knots or branches. That's the main building material in the United States. Over there are some culls they cut last year." Two logs lie on the ground. "They're no good. They have punk knots or hollow rot. The Government scalers mark them. The butt ends are crayoned: *Cull*. We'll go back now." He sighs. "Soon as the rains come we're done. The early rains knocked the huckleberry blossoms off and the bears are getting hungry. They're raiding our slop hole. . . Soon as the rains come, we're done. You see the roads here! Not even the

truck drivers would travel them. If it's a wet fall we're done!
Once, we used to saw and skid and deck all winter. Now they
just cut and skid what they can haul out. The old lumberjack
used to go in for the season. Now Saturday noon, they drive
off in their cars. You never saw a car in a camp in the old days.
They used to walk in in the old days." He grins. "The way
they tell it, there'd be one bed, twenty-five men long, and one
blanket twenty-five men long. If you had to turn over, the
man at the top turned over and then everybody followed him,
one by one. Hard tack and sow belly and beans, that's what
they ate."

Back in camp, the jammer's crew are still studying the
cracked metal plate. Felt hats pulled low over their eyes,
mouths clenched, gloved hands on hips, they concentrate on
the problem.

Egan walks up to the steps of the commissary. I wander
into the blacksmith shop. The blacksmith is banging away on
the iron point of a peavey. Hammer in hand, he works
steadily.

"How long you been blacksmithing?"

"Ever since I was seventeen. I'm fifty-four now."

Clang clang.

He looks up. "I've been all over the West."

Clang clang.

"Hell, the West has changed!" he growls.

Clang clang.

"It's all becoming modern. It used to be horses. It's machinery. We got a bulldozer out here, a caterpillar with treads.
It'll take stumps out and do more'n fifty men in a day."

I walk out. In front of the commissary, a young fellow of
about twenty-two is filling up a row of gasoline lamps, Egan
watching from the top of the commissary stairs.

"That's the bullcook. He chops kindling, sweeps up, does
all the odd jobs around here." Egan winks.

The bullcook smiles shyly, two gold teeth shining in his
mouth, the large Adam's apple in his lean neck rising and
falling.

"I need a towel to wash up, Egan," I say.

"Come on up."

I climb up the flight. From behind the wooden bars, Egan
flicks a black and white towel through the bank teller's win-

dow. "They're thirty-five cents but you can have it for two bits. Take that soap over there on the sink. But don't forget to bring it back."

"Thanks."

The sun slants over the trees on the big dusty square, over the mess shack and canvas-topped bunk houses, burning on the barricade of fire logs and kindling piled up in front of the washing shack.

Inside, long wooden sinks like troughs for horses are built along two walls. Washing basins, upside down, are part of the troughs' equipment. A medium-sized lumberjack with eyes sky-blue in color turns one of the basins right-side up, twisting the hot and cold faucets above it. He dips his hands in the basin, soaps his tanned forearms, rinses. Clean, he up-ends the dirty water. It runs down the trough, a dirty brook. He steps over to the barrel-shaped stove in the middle of the floor. The shower stalls are behind the stove's stacked four-foot logs. He smiles. "Just come up?"

"Yes. Logging long?"

"Up here?"

"No. Right from the start."

"I commenced to log when I was eleven. I'm thirty-six. My dad lumberjacked all his life."

"Where from?"

"Michigan. Back there, they'd have nothing but pork and beans three times a day. At night there was a big fire. All the lumberjacks would lay down with their feet to the fire. They were never dry. I've seen triple bunks myself, one man on top of another, with straw in 'em for mattresses." He rubs his neck with the towel.

Bullcook enters. "Hev you got hot water?"

The lumberjack nods. Bullcook flings open the stove door and tosses in a few logs.

I strip, piling my clothes on a bench near the hot stove and step into one of the shower stalls. My feet are brown as the road. When I come out, the lumberjack and the bullcook are gone but an old man of sixty-five is sitting on a bench, undressing. He yanks off his sport shoes and socks. His ankles look as if they're made of yellow brittle bone, his bald gray-tufted dome and face white as fish belly. He points his bony nose at me. "Who are you?"

"Who are you?"

"I'm the chief chef." He pulls off his duck trousers. "She's a tough racket. Cooking, it's not the cooking," he mumbles. "It's the surrounding and the long hours." Naked, he steps into a shower stall. As I towel myself dry I strain to hear what he is shouting above the splashing water. "Twelve hours . . . fourteen . . . I've cooked in hotels. . . In. . . . In mining and lumber camps and I find. . . You take like myself . . ." He rushes out of the shower to the hot stove, toweling himself methodically. "You take like myself. After all a man gets two months, three months work. Then I hustle another job. I've got a job up in Spokane to cook for an old man's home. That's about all I have in view." He reaches for his socks. "It's the gyppo system, the contract. If I can't fill my job I'm through! Life is just what you make it?" he asks and scurries out before I can answer.

A snub-nosed man who looks as if he could be Egan's son or nephew marches into the shack. Walking over to the trough, he rolls up his sleeves.

"What do you do?" I call over to him.

"Me?" He pivots around. "Are you the new timekeeper?"

"No."

"I'm a scaler. I measure the feet in a log." He grins. "In other words, I screw the sawyers. If you're a new sawyer I'll screw you."

"You sound as if you mean it."

He whistles for an answer.

I leave the washing shack. Outside, three lumberjacks are talking, one of them the jack with the sky-blue eyes.

"Scaler says he screws the men."

The three lumberjacks smile.

Sky Blue nods. "That's right. The sawyers are on gyppo. They get a dollar a thousand feet. Scaler scales all day long and they get paid on what he reports." We stroll over to his bunk shack, sitting down on the flight of stairs, the square in front of us.

Bullcook carries out eight or ten water pails to the hose attached to the water pipe. He fills up the pails and then packs two at a time up to the mess shack.

"He keeps up the buildings," Sky Blue says reflectively. "He works all day and gets all the dirt. He ain't independent and neither are the lumberjacks. Used to be you couldn't find a more independent bunch of men than the lumberjacks. I'd take a job and quit it the same morning. But now you can't be independent. The season's too short. There they come. We eat at five."

Up the long street into camp, the lumberjacks tramp in from the forests. Between the giant trees, they seem lonely and lost, toting their double-edged axes, holding their saws like rifles, one end in hand, the bending almost living steel on their shoulders.

"You better see about your supper," Sky Blue advises me.

I hurry down the street to the commissary. "The men are coming in now. Do I sleep here?"

Egan smiles at me from inside his cage. "We're housing about ninety men, truckdrivers and all." He examines a box of Star Brand Gloves. "Running a store comes natural after my bakery."

"Where was your bakery?"

"I bought this bakery in the old section of Hibbing, Minnesota. Back in '23, the depression had hit there. I was there when they were building the new High School. I lost my rights when I quit railroading to buy this bakery. You need twenty years on a railroad to have any rights. Then I came out here to be in a better climate." He chews on the end of a match. "When I got married, it was fifty-three below for three days." The sun has sunk behind the trees, the light shadowing into cool forest light. "McDonald's back there." Egan nods towards the rear of the commissary. "He's the road builder."

I walk back to a middle-aged man in a khaki suit. "I traveled up your roads today."

The road builder glances up from the map on his desk. "I've got the map of this logging job right here."

I look down over his shoulder. "What are the red lines?"

"The roads constructed. We're hauling this timber at an adverse grade, against the load. When you came over the top, over the hump, well, that was forty-two hundred feet." He consults his map. "These shaded-green areas are privately owned forests, Winton owned. The orange-shaded areas are also owned by Winton but they were formerly the property of the Mountain Iron Company. The white areas are Government owned forests." His fingers slide north on the map. "We're logging up through here now."

He gets up. We sit down on the commissary steps, the street below, the skidders leading their teams of horses into the big stable near the filing shack. "Horses are getting to be a thing of the past," McDonald remarks. "Five or six years ago you could see horses worth five hundred a team, horses that were horses!"

The brown teams and the blacks plod into the stable.

"Logging has changed in the last five years." McDonald yawns. "Trucking started two years ago. We used to log-drive down on the water before that. This camp was built for a flume camp. Down from Copper Creek to Little North Fork River and into Cœur d'Alene Lake. But under the driving system, the logs are in the river a year. Under trucking, logs cut here today can be in the mill tomorrow. You see the rivers would get low, and the logs would blue, and wind up in Number Fives, and ordinarily we get Number Twos and Number Threes."

"What do you mean the logs would blue?"

"They would get blue streaked in the water. Trucking's coming in all over this country. We started trucking here just this year!"

A musical ringing sounds, resounds through the camp. "Supper!" Egan says. "Come on!"

From all over camp, from the bunk shacks, from the washing shack, from the stable, the lumberjacks, hair combed neatly, leg it for the mess shack. In twos and threes, partners, friends, rush up the board path towards the music. On the mess shack landing, a tall limber boy in a green sweater tinkles off the symphony by banging on a suspended metal triangle.

Egan shows me my place at one of the long tables. I sit down between Bullcook and a lumberjack of about thirty-five. The first arrivals have already begun to eat.

At each of the two parallel tables about forty men face each other. Everywhere, their arms reach out for the platters of hot dogs and sauerkraut, fried crisp potatoes, brown beef in gravy, pale white macaroni. Everywhere their polite voices are calling: "Please pass the bread."

"Please pass the potatoes."

"Please pass the butter."

I turn my tin plate right side up. "Please pass the hot dogs."

Opposite me, a young lumberjack with a wedge face and straight blond hair has about cleaned out his plate. To the right, to the left, and over at the second table, the hungry men are packing it in. Faces stand out, a middle-aged jack with a mouth slashed as if by a knife, a redhead with red brown eyes, warm and soft as a dog's and unusual among the cold blue and the chill gray eyes of the majority. Forks and knives rattle on the tin plates. Third helpings follow second helpings.

The swiftest eaters are up to the tin cups of hot coffee, watermelon, canned fruit and slabs of cherry pie. "Please pass the melon."

"Please pass the milk."

The chef's assistants sprint in and out of the kitchen with new platters, snatching away the empty plates as if fighting a personal battle with the ninety hungry men.

The first man finishes. He gets up from the bench, walks down towards the door. Here he pauses a second to select a toothpick in the door box. Others follow him out. No man skips his toothpick.

Outside, in the late afternoon, the lumberjacks talk but a few of the older men are already clomping up to their bunk shacks, through for the day.

I walk down the street past the filer's shack and the stable, the smell of horseflesh rising domestic and homelike in the wilderness air. Down by the creek, two lumberjacks are grinding an ax.

The short solemn-faced one holds the blade to the grindstone. The tall one revolves the wheel. Lank, with the build of a cartoon Uncle Sam, his ears jutting from his closecropped, reddish-blondish head, he spits out whole rivers of tobacco juice. Head to foot, he is homespun and gangling.

He squints his bright blue eyes at me, cackle-laughs. "This grindstone's lopsided. Old Winton brought it in from Minnesota. Are you sleeping in one of them open-air bunk houses?"

"I guess so."

"That's where I am. But it's good enough for a sawyer."

His wide mouth splits into a grin. "We sawyers only work half-time. Ain't that so, partner?"

His partner smiles solemnly.

"Where are you from?" I ask the solemn one.

"I'm from Washington."

"And you?" I ask the lanky grinder.

"I'm from thutty-two states." He laughs his wild laugh again. "You know why we sawyers only work half time?"

"No."

"I pull the saw back and then I hain't doin' nothin' while I'm waiting for my partner to pull it forward. Yes, sir, no sawyer works more'n half-time but when night comes you feel as if you've worked all day." Round and round the grindstone spins. "This is the first white pine I've logged. I used to be a swamper. It warn't bad."

"What does a swamper do?"

"You take your ax and cut out a trail up the mountain wide enough for a team to get through, so they can pull down the logs to the road. Along the Missouri River, it was hardwood. We even cut the walnut stumps out for furniture."

"Are you from Missouri?"

"No, sir," grinning. "I hain't from Missouri. I'm from damn everywhere. I hain't got no home. I'm just here on a visit." His laughter pours out.

I laugh but Washington only smiles as if he has decided to let his partner do the real laughing for both of them.

Thirty-two States wipes his mouth on his sleeve. "I'm working on my first million. They tell me the second'll come easier. But let me tell you, stranger, that the lumberin' business is shot to hell. It's back in the hills and hard to get out."

"I started in 1917 out in Everett," Washington says. "And it's all out, the Douglas fir, the spruce. That country looks like a prairie."

Thirty-Two States takes the ax from his partner, sights down the handle. "You take a crooked handle, it'll throw you off. Yes, sir." He grins. "I used to farm in Nebraska and in western Oklahoma. I never needed an alarm clock because I go to sleep on time. You won't find me burning a hole in the night."

"What time do you go to sleep?"

"About eight o'clock and get up at five."

"I'm going out with you tomorrow, if that's all right."

"Hit's all right with me. I think I saw Bullcook fixin' up your bunk in my open-air bunk house."

I go back along the street and drop into the filing shack. A gasoline lamp, still unlit, hangs from a hook in the ceiling. Sprawling on the bed in his corner, Filer is puffing away on his pipe. In the shadow, his red hair seems black. "I sure eat up the files on them sucking lice," he says. "Take twunny minutes to file a saw and got to file 'em every day. Them sonofabitch saws are the worst sucking lice!"

Scaler steps inside, waves his hand at me. Cocky, he confronts Filer. "How much should a saw saw?"

"A saw should cut a million and a half."

Scaler leans against the wall. "That's an awful pile of timber."

"The nicest God-damn timber's eight-log timber." Filer's voice is soft, almost gentle. "Eight logs to a thousand feet. That's the damnest nice timber a man could want. It's easiest to handle all the way 'round."

"I see the whole bunch from Eagle Creek Camp down here." Scaler lights a cigarette.

Filer smiles. "Any sucking time I can't see the money I'll quit."

A handsome lumberjack almost fills the door, one of the tallest in this camp of compact men. He stalks inside.

"Want some chew terback?" Filer offers.

"I wouldn't chew that for nothing. Of all the world's things . . . chew terback!"

They both smile as if they've been friends a long time, friends in other camps.

Scaler laughs at the newcomer. "You sawyers ain't humans. You're animals!"

The sawyer tosses his long hair out of his eyes. "You couldn't saw," he says contemptuously. "There's plenty to sawin'. A tall man and a short man won't work right. If one man don't feed right, it won't work. Anybody can scale. Anybody at all. It don't take much to walk around like a mountain goat all day."

"I've got to see about my bunk," I say.

I find Bullcook near the commissary, a roll of blankets hugged tight to his chest. "Where's my bunk?" I ask.

"The last shack over, the one with no door. It's a top bunk. I put your beddin' in." He speaks more boldly in the twilight although I can see his Adam's apple gulp. "You can't miss it."

"Thanks, Bullcook."

"You bet."

I climb the short flight of stairs up to the doorless bunk shack, one of two with a tent canvas top. Inside, two rows of double-deck bunks line the walls, four uppers and four lowers to a wall. Sitting on the wooden benches in front of the lower bunks, Thirty-Two States and two other lumberjacks are talking in low voices. And listening from inside their bunks like sleepy children, who don't want to miss anything, five or six other lumberjacks follow the conversation, leaning on their elbows.

"I had a good day today," Thirty-Two States says.

The wind blows in through the space where the door should have been. The iron stove between the two rows of double-deck bunks has no pipe.

"I got some bunk here!" I nod at Thirty-Two States. "Where's your partner?"

"He's in a bunk not so airy." He laughs but not with the daylight gusto of an hour ago.

I climb to my bunk and spread out the pile of blankets Bullcook has left for me, using one blanket as a sheet, rolling up my sweater for a pillow.

Finally, I jump down to the floor, sitting next to Thirty-Two States. The double-deck bunks, the darkness of this last hour before sleep, is like that of a ship, Copper Creek Camp a forgotten hulk in the white pine forests, the lumberjacks womanless and childless sailors.

Across from our bench, the last of the bluing light, cold and lonely, pours in through the doorless space on the lumberjack in the first lower bunk, scooping out the hollows under his half-closed eyes. His head, massive and whitehaired, shows above the blankets pulled up to his chin. "I'd rather chop yew wood rather than hemlock," he says like an oracle.

"That's Old Willy, the skidder boss," Thirty-Two States says to me.

The heavy lumberjack sitting on our bench smiles to himself, his shoulders sloping like a wrestler's.

"We'll have to work like a bastard!" says the stump-headed lumberjack in one of the upper bunks. He tugs off his boots, drops them to the floor. "Woodwork is bastard work! 'Twas always the same. Always be the same."

From the outside, Bullcook's ax, cutting kindling, sounds as if a thousand miles away. More than ever, the camp seems to be anchored for a few hours, only for a few hours in the pine wilderness. . .

"Today, we had damn good luck," another voice says. "Forty-three hundred feet in the morning and forty-three hundred in the afternoon. But that Johnson goes at it like killin' snakes. I don't like to saw with that bastard."

The heavy lumberjack smiles, his features blurred now by the darkness but his teeth flashing. "If a man holds a saw straight, the saw cuts twice as fast." He speaks in a deep guttural voice. "But many a man hangs on a saw to keep from fallink down. You can tell a goot sawyer by the stump. It's just as straight. . ."

"That's the bohunk," Thirty-Two States whispers in my ear.

Old Willy mutters. "Young fellow I knew once, he sawed with one hand and looked up in the trees. He cut himself bad once. He bled like a hog. I had to stick a couple pins into the cut to close it up."

"That should learn him a lesson, by Jesus!" Heavy declares with approval. "Anyway, a sawyer only works half the time. His partner works the other half."

Sleepy laughter greets this classic.

"I learned to saw when I was eighteen," Thirty-Two States declares. "He was an old man learnin' me. 'God damn you, I'll break your neck!' was how he taught me."

Still another lumberjack comes in to go to sleep. A slender man in a red and black plaid shirt, he smiles at all of us. He sits down on the bench across the floor.

The darkness is almost complete. Heavy's guttural voice rises. "Frenchman was driving an ox team pullin' logs. Only could make one trip a day. So the push . . ."

"Who's the push?" I ask him.

"The feller with the brass nuts, the boss."

Laughter at my greenness.

Heavy continues. "The push, he wanted two trips. He

kept after the Frenchman. This day, the Frenchman got one log on and he drives up to the landing on the lake. He didn't have time to unload because if he stopped he couldn't make two trips. So he just wheeled back into the woods. Then he wheeled back to the lake and unloaded. He got back into camp pretty late and the push said: 'How many trips today?' The Frenchman says: 'Two trips today.' And the push said: 'How many logs?' The Frenchman says: 'One. One big one. Trips you want and trips you gets!' "

In the middle of the laughter, somebody sneezes, curses. "God damn this refrigerator!"

The lumberjack in the red and black shirt scratches a match and lights the gas lamp hanging from the central beam near the stove.

Thirty-Two States crawls up into his bunk and stretches out, leaning his head on his elbow. Only Red and Black Shirt, Heavy and myself keep sitting on the benches. In the light, Heavy seems even huger. His hair is brown, his face white, his small eyes the homeless eyes of a man who has always hunted for a home and friends.

"They're making buildings out of asbestos and steel," he remarks to me.

Smiling gently, Red and Black listens, his face like a country minister's. The burning gas makes a steady flaring noise. Old Willy seems to be sleeping, rolled over on his side.

"I came across an old homestead today, and it wasn't made of steel," Red and Black says. "The two women who had homesteaded wrote their names in blue chalk on a slash in a big tree. The year was 1905."

Closed eyelids open. Old Willy stirs like a man in his sleep.

"And out on Eagle Creek, there's a grave and a cross cut on a tree," Red and Black continues. "He was a claim jumper and they shot him and his dog and his horse."

"What'd say?" Old Willy grunts.

" 'Joseph Bulliet,' " Red and Black recalls. " 'French Canadian by birth. A good woodsman but a poor neighbor. Turned to claim jumping and here paid the supreme penalty. August 5, 1905.' " He smiles at the silent men. "That was all cut out on the inside of a tobacco can, right on the tin and nailed to that tree on Eagle Creek." He shrugs, as if to conclude his sermon. "Stranger," he addresses me, "did you know that lumberjacks are turning into Christian Scientists?"

"I didn't know that."

"See that stove. There's no fire in it. We have to imagine fire."

Laughter and a lumberjack shouting: "And imagine there's a door on this shack to keep the wind out!"

"It's just a big spittoon, that stove!" Heavy remarks.

Old Willy smiles in his sleep.

Heavy grumbles. "The food you get here's put up in a can. The God damn milk's put up in a can. The sweet stuff's good but a man should lay off that food. Take a man on a ranch, his complexion shows color. But a man who follers the woods is like nicotine." He spits on the floor. "The lumberjacks started out as rugged people. They couldn't stay to take the orders in the factories. They're too high-strung. They went on the tramp, lived in the jungles. Most independent class of people if he had five cents in a pocket or a penny."

"That's why he ain't got a thing today," Red and Black states. "What'll be when the trees go?"

Old Willy snorts awake. "We'll all be dead."

"When the trees are cut down," Heavy says, "we'll go to California and be California tramps in trailer houses."

"We'll go to South America," Old Willy says, his eyes shut.

Heavy's head lowers. "I'm about twenty-four years in the woods. Minnesota, Michigan, Montana and Idaho. I go out to California and back here again."

"I started fifty years ago in Maine for the Diamond Match in 1892. I was thirteen." Old Willy tugs his blankets up to his chin.

Red and Black climbs up into his bunk. "I'm just a colt. I've been in the woods thirty years." He strips off his shirt. "I was never hurt except one day I reached for a biscuit and a feller got me with a fork and put it between two pieces of bread."

Again the lumberjacks laugh.

Heavy smiles. "Then that feller, he got to the woods and was he surprised to see nothing between the two slices." He spits again. "But the biggest liars in the world's the placer miners. They know where the gold is but always lookin' for a grubstake. I was a placer miner. I quit before I turn into big a liar as they are."

A black dog trots into the bunk shack. Old Willy pats him. Clouds of dust rise from his fur. "He's dirtier than the roads," Old Willy growls.

"That dog's got coach dog in him. He likes a horse," Thirty-Two States declares, leaning over his bunk.

"No way to live," Bohunk puts out the light. "Three months work a year. How you live rest of year? Years ago, you plow out in a prairie with a woman, kids and a couple ponies. Get up a section of land! They t'ought it was no hend to that. Roosevelt, what's he done? The C.C.C.'s git a dollar a day. Everyt'ing Roosevelt put out is in that line." He too, gets into his bunk. "The blankets!" he scoffs. "You wash them blankets once it's like a gunny sack. Them blankets a Jewish invention."

"H'aint you comin' to sleep?" Thirty-Two States calls down to me.

"I'll take a good-night walk."

Outside, the stars have been pushed up into the highest blackest sky by the tree-tops. The bunk shacks are all dark. The only light is in the wash shack.

Yawning, I go inside. Seven or eight of the younger lumberjacks, Egan and the blacksmith, are sitting around the stove. The blacksmith's dark cheeks seem more leathery, the camp clerk's wrinkles deeper among the many young faces.

Bullcook gets up, opens the door to the stove and heaves in a log, his eyes never leaving the faces of the two men washing at the wooden sink. These two are the center of a sly laughing atmosphere like that of a street corner. One of the men belongs to the broken-down jammer crew, a wide-shouldered jack of twenty-eight or nine with a hooked nose and a hard, defiant eye; the other is the redheaded trucker.

"Come up all the way in the dark!" one of the admiring young lumberjacks exclaims. His voice lowers. "Where were you, Bill?"

Bill the trucker grins at his audience, rubbing his towel on his red glinting hairy forearms. "Where you think?"

Two or three of the baby jacks and Bullcook laugh joyously, as if also adventuring in Bill's boots.

"How about you?" The eager faces swerve to the jammer man.

Solid on his two thick legs, he combs his wet hair straight back, smiling at the questions. His eyes shine. "Bill took her. Then I took her. Then we took her together. All these damn waitresses in the inns! She was drunk but we got rid of her boy friend."

"How?"

"How?"

The jammer man only grins.

"How, Bill?"

"Bill!"

Bill the trucker laughs at the baby jacks. "Never mind how," he grunts. "I'm worried about my tires. Those God damn bears are so hungry they'll chaw up my rubber and exhaust pipe. They're hellcats when they're hungry."

"How, Bill?"

"Tell us how."

The jammer man and the trucker explode into laughter, a laughter of pride and accomplishment. They stand on top of a mountain of laughter, the white pine woods, the broken jammers, the brown dusty roads, the turnouts far away in the morning.

A half-hour before the five o'clock wake-up bell, I climb out of my bunk. "Why don't you stay in bed?" Thirty-Two States asks drowsily. "You'll freeze gittin' into your clothes."

Teeth chattering, I dress and hurry out of the bunk shack. The sun hasn't slanted yet into the draw or valley, the new daylight flowing like a bright river between the slopes. Only the blacksmith is in the washing shack. Stooped over a big basin, he is scrubbing his dirty underwear and socks. "Good morning."

"Good morning."

A lumberjack follows me inside, a little man with a head gnarled like a root and a broad broken nose. "I hear there's a fire int' Wallace, Blackie. I don't want no fire."

Blackie wrings out a soapy shirt. "This draw is a good fire trap."

"Bet it is."

"There's no money fighting fires!" Blackie declares.

"Bet there ain't." He walks to the wooden sink.

"We might be packing out of here by tomorrow. One of the Government men went over to Wallace." Blackie wrings out a pair of socks.

"Fires all over. Over to Spirit Lake. Over to Athol." The little lumberjack grunts.

The big dog, the friend of horses, comes into the washing shack. He sniffs at each of us and then sprawls on the floor near the hot stove. I notice a red and white sticker on one of the windows. Somebody has pasted it up since yesterday:

JOIN THE I.W.W.
6 HOURS
BETTER CONDITIONS

The five o'clock wake-up music rings through camp. In a few minutes, the first sleepy lumberjacks, towels over their shoulders, clomp into the washing shack. Basins fill with water. Men sneeze, cough, stretch. More lumberjacks pile in. Middle-aged, young and old, they all seem to have been cut out of the same log. There aren't enough wash basins for all. They wait their turns, yawning, rubbing their eyes, scratching their chins. Nobody appears to see the red and white sticker. Nobody walks over to read it. They pay no attention to it as if it were a calendar.

Breakfast is a swifter meal than supper. Wheat cakes in big stacks, pans of scrambled eggs, oatmeal, bacon, hot coffee, are devoured in the rush of morning. Morning! The working day is ahead!

I finish and join Thirty-Two States and his partner. I take the ax sharpened the night before. Washington has the saw on his shoulder. Almost solemn now, Thirty-Two States carries the bucket of oil.

Like an army, the lumberjacks tramp up the camp street, past the commissary, the filer's shack, the stable, tramp tramp up the brown dirt, up the pole-road stretch and the culls near the uncut pines. Nobody says much. Breath isn't for speech now. Breath is for the long stride, for the steep short-cut trail. One by one the sawyers climb up. A squirrel leaps from rock

to tree, beady eyes curious. Tramp tramp up the winding
trail between the tamaracks and pines. Ahead of me, Thirty-
Two States climbs like a deer, no surplus fat to lug along on
his hips; behind me, Washington, the saw on his shoulder
rhythmic with his stride. And behind him, the lumberjacks,
their hard breathing like a little wind. Up into the stillness,
into the virgin land.

On top of the draw, the logging road is strewn with the
sixteen- and fourteen-foot logs cut yesterday, each log slashed
with the Winton turtle mark, a square blaze with four cuts
like four feet. Thirty-Two States tight-ropes along the line of
fallen logs. I tail after him, slipping now and then. I have no
calks or hobnails on my shoes. But the land is level here, a
land of sawn logs, of pine smell, of mountain sides. Slanting
up from the log path, the white pines seem without end, un-
surrounded by cities and towns but by other forests, endless,
endless. . .

Pairs of sawyers drop from the line to clamber up the
mountain side to their strips.

"A man needs water." Thirty-Two States grins, stopping
at a little wooden bridge across the road. He drops down to
the creek, picks up a cached canvas water bag and an empty
Union Pipe Tobacco tin. "Water, hit's a man's oil." He holds
the tin under a tiny falls, fills it, emptying the tin into the
water bag, filling and emptying.

A short blond sawyer watches him. "How do you like it?"
he asks me.

"I like it fine."

"I come from the East, myself. I heard you talk yesterday," he smiles. "I'm from Chicago. I worked in Chicago until the depression pinched me out. Then I prospected in
Nevada for gold. . ."

Thirty-Two States again leads the way.

"So long. I got to go," I call to Chicago.

He smiles. "There's no gold any more."

"This is our strip," Thirty-Two States says as he cuts up
the mountain side from the logging road.

"Who gives you your strip?"

"Sawboss. Hit's all the way up to the top of the hill." He
pauses suddenly, turns around, his blue eyes steady, a grin on
his wide mouth. "Think our country'll go to war?"

War. . . The word seems unreal among the hundred-foot pines.

"What do you think?"

He rubs one of his ears. "I had a couple uncles killed in every war since the Rebellion." He nods as if he had fought in the Rebellion himself.

War. . . These pines were big trees when the battles of Bull Run and Gettysburg were fought, were straight and strong when the Revolutionary soldiers were freezing to death at Valley Forge. . .

The silence is slashed by the sound of an ax on the strip below us. Thirty-Two States takes the ax I've been carrying and begins to clear out the undergrowth and brush around the first white pine to be cut. His ax and the ax below us peoples the wilderness. Already, Washington is sprinkling oil on the saw. He scrambles down to his partner. Each man takes his end of the saw, the bark giant between them.

"Low enough?" Thirty-Two States cries out.

"Low enough."

Together, the two men saw, their steel biting into the trunk. They work steadily as if keeping time to a steady drum beat. White sawdust covers the mouldy leaves, spat out by the drag teeth.

They straighten and reach for their axes. There are two axes (one of them had been cached here.) Down flash the two blades into the pine! Swing and swing, all their muscle in each blow, the white shingles splitting from the trunk, the notch slanting down to the straight saw cut.

Thirty-Two States rests a second. He blinks uphill with his careful woodsman's eye like his forebears before him. He measures the depth of the notch with his ax just as they must have done. The blade fits snugly. "Think it'll clear the hemlock up there?"

Washington nods.

Satisfied, Thirty-Two States stares up at the notched pine. "Next to Christ's work, I like Coulee Dam best," he says simply.

The partners pick up their saw and start the back cut on the opposite side of the under cut. Their oiled saw bites into the wood. Bites, bites, bites.

The tree stands immovable, bearded with green moss, two

hundred years old, mighty in this draw where no man has ever lumberjacked.

Thirty-two States straightens up, chews off another chunk of chew tobacco. Swiftly, he picks up three steel wedges from the ground, drives them into the back cut. "Reckon we ought to trade these God-damn wedges in for new ones!" he exclaims.

Again the partners stoop to their saw, deep-buried in the pine. "About six inches!" Thirty-Two States warns.

"I got more'n that. I can't see the under cut yet."

The sawdust thickens. The cutting points teeth in. The drags plow out.

"About five inches now," Washington says.

"That's about what I got."

"About three."

"About four, I guess."

"About an inch now." A flicker of excitement sounds in Washington's voice.

Thirty-Two States pulls out the wedges and leaps away, shouting: "There she goes!"

The pine topples over, falling upslope, smashing through the branches of the living trees like a meteor, the thunder of its passing singing in air.

Washington walks over to the butt end and axes the Winton turtle out of the top thick bark. The smell of pine, the smell of the deep forest, rises from the cut. Thirty-Two States hammers a stake against the butt to keep it from skidding down slope. "About an hour," he says, consulting his watch. "That's good time for an old one like this."

The rings of its two hundred years have been cut in two. Butt-end and stump show the severed centuries. Washington searches for the four-foot measuring stick, finds it, and measures off four lengths up the trunk. The first log will be a sixteen footer. Again, he sprinkles oil on the saw.

Thirty-Two States spits tobacco juice. The partners brace themselves and begin sawing straight down. They cut the first log off in five or six minutes. Washington axes the Winton mark on the top of the new butt end. They each drink a swallow of water out of the canvas bag.

They saw off a second sixteen, a fourteen. From a nearby strip, the crash of another pine echoes.

The partners clean out the underbrush and saw off a twelve-footer.

Tiny black flies spot my hands and neck.

Thirty-Two States laughs, the first full laugh of the morning. "The gnuisiums are after you."

"The gnuisiums?"

"That's an Indian word. It means hard to see. This one'll be a sixteen," he says to his partner. "And the next looks like a ten."

They finish up the tree and then relax for a few minutes.

"Out on the Coast you don't see a horse in the camps," Washington says dolefully as if he's been brooding about it while working.

"But it's gyppo all over." Thirty-Two States grins. "Here we got to pay a dollar month insurance. Figure it out. A man hasn't much left. Here we get one dollar a thousand feet for two men. We count the logs we cut but just the same the scaler can cheat us if he wants. We pay a dollar thirty-five a day for board and bunk." He grabs his ax. "We got six logs out of this tree. You need about eight logs for a thousand feet." He stares at the next pine. "How about that sonufabitch there? Quite a nest of 'em there."

"Four of 'em." Washington counts.

"I'm going to find the skidders," I tell him. "If you want to go into town Saturday I'll take you in my car."

"Thanks, but I live in Spokane." Washington shakes his head. "I couldn't get a ride in from there."

"I'll go with you," Thirty-Two States says. "And thank you. I live about six miles off the highway. I can walk that. Just let me off on the highway."

"I'll take you to your door."

"I h'aint got no beer." He laughs. "But don't you get lost here. We're goin' in together Saturday."

I hike downhill to the logging road, following it into the forest. The road U's around the mountain. Behind the curve a skidder and his team are kicking up brown dust, horses and man ankle-deep in dust as if in a brook. The skidder is about fifty, a small man in overalls and calked boots. Hatless, his sweating face reflects an arrow of sunlight shot down between the trees.

"Whoa, Buck!" he calls to the buck-colored horse, pulling

on the reins. "Giddap, Chub!" he urges the dark brown horse. His voice, deliberately soft, seems horse-ified, as if speaking a language, not neigh and whinny, but the closest human thing to it.

The team climbs off the road up the slope to the sawn logs, to where the swampers have already axed out a trail. Now, higher up, Heavy among them in an old panama hat, they are extending the trail up to the highest log.

"Whoa, Buck!" Skidder calls.

"Those horses know their work," I shout, keeping abreast with them.

"They've been at it four years. They purty near know. You can do it without lines almost. Back, Chub! They keep their wind."

I goat up to where Heavy is chopping knots off the sawn logs.

"Hello, swamper."

He smiles. "Sixty cents an hour I git. Skinner gits sixty-five. We both strike it rich. Why don't you work? Own the camp? Help that taildowner."

Below us, the skidder or skinner is circling his team around, their heads turning down slope. As Buck slips, he implores. "Back, Buck! Back, Chub! Giddap! Whoa, Chub!" The circle completed, he chains the first big log to the team, a second log attached to the first by the two-toothed "dogs," one metal tooth driven into one butt and steel-looped to the tooth driven into the second butt. "Giddap, Buck! Giddap, Chub!"

The horses plunge downhill, dragging the skidder after them. Tightly, he holds onto the reins, stepping high like a pony as if the ground were baking hot under him, the sun burning in patch and square down the trail. "Whoa!" he cries out loudly. The logs are skidding too fast, the horses are moving too fast! "Whoa, Chub." The horses slow down. "Giddap."

I follow them up the road to where the logs are rolled off or decked. The taildowner, a tall man in overalls and a black hat, is whistling *Sweet Adeline* to himself.

The skidder shouts: "Whoa!" Now, the chained logs parallel the decked logs stacked in the hollow below. The taildowner, still whistling, picks up a pointed iron wedge and knocks off the dogs biting the logs together.

"What do you call that?"

"That's a skipper. And that tool's a hoedag, a mat-ax they call it in the store. And that's a peavey." He digs the movable hooked fork of his peavey into the second log, rolls it over and over to the road's very edge. Once more he lifts. The log rolls off into space, downhilling to the logs in the deck.

I help him deck all morning . . . the deck becomes log-house high.

A man in a military felt hat, dressed in khaki and looking like one of Theodore Roosevelt's Rough Riders tramps up the road.

"That's the Government man, Pruett," the taildowner says to me.

Pruett smiles at both of us. "This is the nicest pine in the State."

"I hear you tag the seed trees?" I say.

"We tag the seed trees that are to be left to grow a new forest." He climbs down to the deck and numbers each log in his book: *Log 51. Log 52.* "A checker comes by and checks on us." He climbs up the road and I accompany him. "Stump rot kills many of these trees." He points his scaling stick at a roadside log with one scarred end. "Those catfaces are caused by fires in younger stages of the tree. And if you find punk knots, that means when the knot rots it extends right inside."

"Were you always in the woods?"

"No. I homesteaded in Clearwater in 1914. I had a quarter section of land. I cut down quite a lot of timber to start a garden. I went home one day and the packrats had the knives and forks packed away in the stove." He smiles recalling the past, the unpleasant past. "I stayed up all night and killed packrats. Fifteen of them. The following summer I needed extra money to live on the homestead and I called up the Forest Service if they needed a man. I worked for them. I've been a lookout. . . Live in a tower and locate the fires. Usually there are two lookouts. We may have to send one man down. . . The last few years I've worked for the Government on timber sale work. After it's all logged out, we pile up the brush. We burn it after the first heavy rain so the fire won't run through the timber. Once one of those fires get started, they'll go to the top of the trees and crownfire. . ."

"I think I better go back." I return to the deck. "I just spoke about fires with the Government man."

The skidder tugs back on his reins. "Whoa! Whoa! The God damned fire up in the Yak River up in Montana! That was that God-damnest fire I ever did see. Whoa, Buck! I went up there to fight fire back in '31. When that fire went through it burned black. It drawed in the spruce trees at least a hundred yards away. The God-damnest fire! It had such a draft, it uprooted the spruces on the lower side and drawed them into it. That God-damn fire burned on a seven mile front! Giddap, Chub. Giddap, Buck."

The taildowner now is marking the butt ends of the decked logs with a stamping hammer. The stamp is a horseshoe with both ends turning left. He stamps five horseshoes on each butt. "Government'll stamp on U. S. to show whose timber it is. Talk of timber. Five, six years ago you'd see three hundred and fifty men in a camp. But the last few years it's been no good. Nobody's got money to build houses. Sure as hell slacked off! I worked with the Cascade Lumber Company in Washington. Six hundred men. Christ, what a crew! Used to work all winter. But now you have to figure out what you'll do when it shuts down. I used to work eight, nine months, miss three months in the middle of the winter when the snow got too deep. But them days are gone." Steadily, he marks the butts with the symbol of luck.

Saturday morning, the last working stretch of the week, I'm at another deck. The skidder, here, is one of the baby jacks, a boy of twenty.

Old Willy stalks up the road, his felt hat over his eyes. In the sun, his cheeks show the mottled red color of a man past his prime. "Good morning," he says. "You didn't see Babe, the blue-eyed ox? Eleven feet tall and fourteen inches?"

"I didn't see Paul Bunyan either."

The taildowner doesn't show a grin as if he's heard every last story a dozen times.

Old Willy stares at me. "I used to work for Paul Bunyan. . . I can talk from now until tomorrow morning and I'd tell you the same story twice." He smiles with just one corner of his mouth. "He had a hell of a time when he lost Babe. Babe broke through the ice one hundred and fifty miles up in the woods. Bunyan drove in one hundred and fifty carloads of peas and took the drive out in pea soup." He pushes his hat back onto his white hair, hooks one thumb inside his suspender strap. "Paul Bunyan showed them how to log." He nods at the skidder, who, reins in hand, rides on the first of his three dogged logs as if on a sleigh. The skidder balances easily, the muscles in his young legs synchronizing to each bump on the road. "He showed them how. But he lost money through bad management the first winter. So he told his boss that if he quit crossing his *t*'s and dotting his *i*'s he'd save nine barrels of ink the second winter."

The taildowner bursts into laughter.

"He's from Maine like me," Old Willy says.

Unlike massive Old Willy, the taildowner is lean and long. "I came West from the East Coast. . . There must be awful poverty now in those big cities back East."

Old Willy nods. "You come along," he says to me. "If we don't find Babe nobody leaves this camp this afternoon."

At the next deck, the taildowner holds up a buzzing horsefly that he has caught, and tied to a horse hair. "I put a slipknot around his neck. He can't fly with the string." The taildowner grins, his eyes like a schoolboy's.

Buzz, buzz, the horsefly buzzes.

"Horses are getting scarce," the taildowner remarks. "When they go, the horsefly'll go out of business. That reminds me of the two fellows in Chicago. They were talking about a big parade. A big fat lady with no clothes on was going to ride a big white horse. 'Are you going to see the parade?' one fellow says. 'I am,' the other fellow says: 'I'm going to that parade to see that big white horse.' " He bursts into laughter, swinging the horsefly from side to side. "I tied up a dozen horseflies once and put 'em in a bed with a fellow scared of yellow jackets. He ran to beat hell. Yellow jackets'll sting the shit out of you."

"Well, I still got to find Babe," Old Willy hurries up the road.

"I'm going back to camp," I say. "It's pretty near dinner time." Ahead of me, the road is blocked by a jammer and truck. The empty truck has just reversed up to the jammer, the sun gilding the brown dusty air. Already the jammer's crew have speed-upped their eyes and bodies. Standing on the jammer, his felt hat thick with dust, his face like a driver's in a speeding car, the hoister pulls at his levers. Like a giant fishing pole, the boom pivots over and above the deck of logs and the two hookers down in the hollow off the road. The hookers dart like trout for the two hooks attached to the boom, speeding over to the nearest log in the deck, digging the hooks into the two butt ends. As they hurl away from the log like fish in a pool disturbed by a pebble, the hoister pulls on another lever. The boom lifts. The hoister stares at the teetering log, wets his dry lips with his tongue and swings the log up to the truck where the top loader spears at it with his peavey. Log after log moves from deck to truck.

Again, the two hookers dig in their hooks, their gloved hands snatching at the ropes dangling from each butt end. Running from the ascending log, they tug on the guiding ropes as if on reins. The cable from boom to upslope tree quivers, the tree whipping up and down as the log rises up to the truck. Supervisor of all cables, engineer of the levers, the hoister keeps the jammer crew in simultaneous bird-circling sight. A cable might snap! A log might slip from its hooks! The sweat shines on the hoister's forehead and cheeks. He wets his perpetually dry lips. Never pausing, he floors the truck with logs, floors the floor. . . The jammer's motor thrums, thrums, thrums like a million buzzing horseflies.

I continue down road to camp with one of the Government men who also has been watching, a young fellow of about thirty-two with eyeglasses and the devout healthy appearance of a Boy Scout master.

"Dinner's at eleven and I'm hungry," he says. "I'll show you a short cut." He jumps off the road, downhilling along a pine-needled path.

"How do you like the woods work?"

"All right. But I would've gone into private business. . . You make four times as much in private business as with the Government. . . But that's in good times. I was in the class of '28." He tightrope-walks down an ancient barkless log, as

if on a stairway. "There are twenty thousand forestry graduates and they can't get placed. Not enough openings." He
leaps from the path to the pole road, the camp a hundred
yards ahead of us.

As we pass the commissary, Egan calls over to me, "Come
and meet Mr. Brown."

The big six-footer near the camp clerk smiles. Solid and
thick through as a pine, Brown isn't any older than the
forester.

"You're young, Mr. Brown," I say, shaking hands.
"Thanks for letting me stay here."

"I'm the youngest contractor in the country. I started out
with two portable tie mills, cutting ties for the railroad in
1933."

He sits down on the commissary stairs. "The bank at
Sandpoint backed me. I followed the business about three
years. I was in the Pack River for the Winton Company from
1937 to July 15, 1939. Then I contracted this job here."

"What kind of job is it?"

"Just a logging contract. Trucking, skidding, hauling. I
take a job for so much and dump the logs in Cœur d'Alene
Lake." He smiles shyly. "We're timber beasts, cedar tigers.
All kinds of names."

"How long have you been in it?"

"Since I was fourteen. I was a lumberjack back in Wisconsin around Ladysmith. I drove a skiddin' team. As you
grow up you learn it all if there's any git in you," he says
with the fervor and sincerity of a Horatio Alger hero.

The dinner music peals. All conversations end in Cooper
Creek Camp.

After dinner, Thirty-Two States and I drive for home, the
dust billowing behind us. "Listen," I half turn my head.
"Now, you tell me what state you were born in?"

He laughs. "My father was a doctor in Tennessee. He
homesteaded in Oklahoma in 1890. . ."

"So you're from Oklahoma."

"Yes, sir. From Oklahoma and thirty-one other states."
His laughter booms in my ears, the laughter of a man at the

end of the week's work. Below, the forests extend for green miles.

"I left home when I was thirteen. There was a cow, a mean one to home, and Dad said: 'You milk her or pack up your duds.' I left home that same night. I followed the harvest up to Canada." He laughs reflectively. "A man's life goes and he remembers the damndest things. . . I was drinking once and a big fellow pushed me. I pushed him back and we stepped outside. 'I'm Cyclone Jim from South Dakota!' he says to me. 'I'm Glenn and Herrick from Oklahoma!' I hollered back." He rubs his chin. "I don't know why I remembered that? But Glenn and Herrick are my given names. And believe me, we shook hands and had a drink. This is dust, hain't it? There's no dust on my farm." His bright blue eyes shine at the thought of home-coming. "I'm married twenty-six years and for twenty-five years I've been looking for a home and I found it here in Idaho." He speaks with pride, his face with its wide mouth and jutting ears good to look at. "A land agent comes up and said to look at this farm. I wanted a quarter section and this was a half section. 'Take a look at it,' he said. I took a look at it and soon as I got out of the car I knew it was the home I'd been lookin' for all my life. A mountain in my front yard across the road, and a creek runnin' by in the back. I only got six hundred to pay off and she's mine. That hain't so much," he speaks softly. "A man has a right to his own home," he says, as his forebears must have said before him.

On the highway again I step on the gas. The wind whirls through, lifting the dust. We both sneeze. "There's my turn," he says. He sits very quiet now, staring at me anxiously. He is hoping I'll like his home. "There she is."

I park the car on the dirt road in front of Thirty-Two States' little wooden home. His wife, a dark-haired woman in overalls and his son, darkhaired like his mother, come down from the shady porch. The good-looking boy grins from ear to ear. "How was the cuttin', Dad?"

"I told this man there warn't no beer but he said he'd take me to my door," Thirty-Two States explains to his wife. He takes off his hat, the sun on his reddish-blond hair.

"Let's sit down!" his wife exclaims, smiling. We walk to the porch and Thirty-Two States narrates the week's events up at Copper Creek Camp.

He sits down on the floor of the porch, facing the mountain across the way.

"Do you like our place?" his wife asks eagerly. "I seen here what I always wanted to see. A faun. That's what I seen here. It's little spots. . . It was right on that mountain over there, stretching its little legs. Once I saw fifteen deer at one time."

"There's a black bear with two sets of cubs, one set this year's and t'other set last year's," Thirty-Two States adds. "And the boy here, he calls up the kiyotes right to the door."

"Do you use a whistle?" I ask his son.

His wife taps her son's chest. "He has his whistle right in here."

The boy grins and grins, his eyes on his dad. "How was the cuttin'?"

"This mornin' we cut two big ones, all holler inside." Thirty-Two States frowns. "But yesterday up to forenoon the scaler measured five thousand feet for my partner and me."

"That ain't bad," the boy says.

"I'll have to be going," I say.

"You wait here." His wife runs inside her kitchen, returning with two bottles of sweet cream. "Now, that's not beer. . ."

"Do you have to go?" Thirty-Two States asks. "Hit's early."

"I've got a wife, too."

He grins. Father and mother and son watch me go. I look back at them, at their little home and cows. I look back at the mountain in the front yard. . .

U. S. Route Number 10

WELCOME TO SPOKANE VALLEY—THE VALLEY
THAT HAS EVERYTHING

The valley of fruits and vegetables like an opening door leads into the rolling plains of Washington, into the sagebrush and the wheat.

Lincoln County. Grant County.

The Civil War has marched its leaders out into the Pacific Northwest. From town monument and county nameplace, the Civil War cannons into memory even here among the coulees and dry canyons. . .

Far away the foothills of the Cascades, like huge bald skulls, dome into sight, and the land, the wonderful American land, becomes an orchard of apple, peach and pear, endless as the winding Columbia River. The tangy smell of fruit carries in its fragrance the history of man's harvests. . .

Up through the forests of the Cascades, among the Douglas firs, their bark the red of the Hereford herds, through a wilderness burned black from fire, the mountain slopes strewn with charred trunks. Sawn by flame, the stumps are higher than those left by the lumberjacks. Here in this dead land, the Pacific Ocean seems close and even the American continent rolling forever west on the wheels of the sun will soon end.

The Collectors

SEATTLE

"Juneau, Alaska
April 22, 1939.

L. W. Baker, Traffic Manager
Alaska Steamship Company
Seattle, Washington

Unemployment and relief situation is such in Juneau and other
Alaskan towns that I am asking your cooperation in disseminat-
ing information that there is no employment available in
Territory.

That unless people coming to Alaska have return tickets and
funds to take care themselves while here, or employment already
definitely secured they should stay away.

Only the seriousness of conditions here prompts me to make
this appeal which I am also making to other transportation
companies.

John W. Troy
Governor of Alaska."
From the Governor's Letter.

Seattle, city of freighters and sailors, fish smell and sea
smell, city of the waterfront Alaskan Way, is one of those harbors where the sensation of *port* waves like a flag on a ship.
Port, where the continents and nations meet in the people
drifted here through chance or for business. Port of Scandi-
navians, Latins, Chinese, Filipinos. Port of the waterfront
men, of rooming houses and sailor hotels that seem to have
drifted onto the waterfront like the men themselves, hotels
without permanence as if made of driftwood and masoned
with seaweed.

At night, this city jutting into Puget Sound, lake and
sea bounded, seems like a black-shored ship, its prow pointed
to the Orient.

At night, Washington Street and Second Avenue South is a neighborhood without a woman, the streets a tide of sailors, loggers, cannery workers, fishermen, vagrants, bums. The Gospel bands trumpet their message from all the corners. Fifty men, a hundred crowd each corner, listening and not listening to the hymns. The only women in the street play in the bands.

Here comes the Salvation Army, men and women, solemn soldiers of Christ in dark blue uniforms, two little girls in ordinary dresses. The drum bangs. The Army executes a turn with military precision, occupying the corner where the Green Spot Tavern does business. The Chinese cook in Jim's Café next door, steps to the entrance for a look. Silently, he stares. Two men with the price laugh and enter the Klondyke Café.

The tamborine player steps forward to speak, a tall erect woman with regular, almost pretty features under her Salvation Army bonnet. She frowns with righteousness in this world of taverns, flophouses and pawnshops. She talks of Jesus Christ as if He were her neighbor. "Let each one come unto Him," she concludes.

The band takes up in music where she leaves off in words.

The neons of the cafés and taverns flare up to Occidental Avenue. Traced in blue neon outline, mighty Paul Bunyan guards the Loggers' Tavern.

The tamborine player hits her instrument with elbow and hand. The drummer removes his officer's hat and steps forward a pace. His bald head lowers to his Bible. He reads and the strong heroic words, *Salvation* . . . *Mercy* . . . fall from his lips.

The faces of the listeners reveal no spark as if the bald soldier of Christ were saying: Why listen? Why listen? over and over again. Concertinas, tamborines, drums and trumpets manufacture their religious tunes and the listening men, the hungry men, break off and shuffle up the sidewalk past the hash houses with their signs: BEEF STEW 5 CENTS.

Antiques.
We Buy and Sell Any Old Thing.
M. Gold.

The plate-glass window is full of old silver, beer steins with drinking mottos in German, Chinese swords, miniature ships in bottles.

The door opens only four inches when I try to enter, chained from the inside, chained in broad daylight. I knock. A round fat man unlatches the chain.

"Dont you want to do business?" I ask him.

M. Gold ushers me into his store. About forty-five, he has the antique manner of a man of eighty who has determined to stick to a forgotten fashion. He wears a stiff collar, a black bow-tie, and one of those green and black striped silk shirts that were last popular twenty years ago. Now, he pushes his spectacles down his short straight nose until he can peek at me over their tops. "I want to do business but I have reasons for keeping the door locked." He leans on his display counter of silver spoons and cut glass.

"What reasons?"

"I have reasons. They talk so crazy when they come in."

"Who?"

"I don't want to say. Maybe you're of their nationality?"

"No, I'm not."

He hesitates, his brown soft eyes searching my face. "Swedish?"

"No."

"I'll tell you. Those Swedes come in. They're crazy a li'l bit. I keep it hooked here to keep them out. Swedes mostly come into antique shops in Seattle."

"Are you serious?"

He won't talk now. I have hurt him, this mild old-fashioned Jew.

"How's your business?" I glance at the tray of rings under glass.

He shakes his round head sadly. "Some money power allows such a poor grade of thing to be produced," he says philosophically, easily as if he has had the thought a hundred times. "Why not give people something for their money? Why not give them the good things of life if they're to be gotten?

I'll tell you. Something made by hand is fine. The touch and the use of the article! It's a different life, see? It gives you more satisfaction. It's wonderful! Made by an artist. . ." Words fail him. "Anything made slow'll last a long time." He takes out a tray of rings and picks up one of them, a weave of gold string. "Anything fine has a life to it. Here's a ring I made. It took me a week to make. Sixty-five stones could be put into it. Those are little flowers, and little stones can be set into it."

"Where'd you learn your art?"

"I worked for Goldsmith." He laughs. "On Gold Street in New York at gold and my name is Gold. I was raised in New York thirty years ago. I been around. I been around half of this world and some more." He selects a second ring, one with a ruby supported by the upraised arms of two pairs of tiny nude Adams and Eves, their golden faces expressing fear or distrust. "I made one half of this and a Japanee made the other half. When he made the faces look like Japanee faces, I grabbed it away from him. I made it when this war came out in 1914. I thought so much more of the animal, I put the lion over the men and the women. The ruby's the lion."

"And business is bad?"

"The five-and-ten-cent store!" he blurts. "The general and natural use of it. . . As long as we're here, why get rotten things? Why allow such a thing to exist? That's what they call progress!" He flushes angrily. "The machine age! That's going backwards. Bullets are going backwards! And the movies! The movies are an imitation of live people, of actors. They turn off the lights and sit in a cellar! I like anything that's fine and that isn't phoney. *Phoney*," he laughs at the slang word. "I'd rather travel by stagecoach than auto. We only have a few years to live on this earth so what's the hurry? The less you see the better. The hurry and the rush and the bustle hurts people's health. I've been out of the jewelry business ever since I've been out here. I worked in six different countries as a jeweler. I could sit down and make fine jewelry if there was a market. But they go to the dime stores. The people are too busy buying gasoline to buy good stuff." He shrugs. "I come out here to find a certain man, a doctor. When I come out here he wasn't alive. He didn't wait for me. So I've been wanting to go back. Oh, gosh," he sighs.

"Tell me about the Swedes."

Immediately, he becomes a man with a chip on his shoulder. "The Swedes are the only race in the world who have no variety. They come in and say: 'How long did it take you to collect this stuff?' Or: 'My, where'd you get all this?' They get me so down I started locking the chain. A Swedish girl comes in and says: 'I want some ash trays.' There are millions of kinds of ash trays!" he cries out as if to say: Isn't that so? " 'What kind of ash tray you want?' I ask. 'Have you anything in mind?' There she stands and stands and stands in the middle of the floor. 'I can't see anything,' she says. So I say: 'Why don't you whistle for it?' So she whistles. I'm not fooling. She whistles and then she says: 'I want something in metal.' But she didn't want anything. When I don't answer them, they come back and start acting silly. If I make them think they're Roosevelt's daughter, they'll buy it." He shakes his head, baffled. "They'll buy it because a Swede always has a friend. They're such a make-believe people." He points at a big red and white cat in the rear. "That's a Swedish cat. A Dane, a friend of mine, comes in here and calls him Oscar because he's so blond. Now, they might be different in the street but get them into an antique shop and all Swedes are the same."

Down on the Alaskan Way, the plate-glass window of YE OLD CURIOSITY SHOP is a hodgepodge of sea urchins, shells, Indian clubs and totem poles. Inside, the scores of people gaping at the counter displays are being waited on by half a dozen sales clerks. The oldest member of the selling force is a little stooped man wearing a black silk skull cap. He stands in front of a pile of Indian baskets answering a fat lady's questions. "We correspond with fourteen different countries and it's the same thing all around this globe. The old people are passing away. They'd sit and do the work for the love of it. The young pople don't care about the art. It's the money and get it quick!" His shoulders have caved in with the load of age on them but his eyes and voice are spry and gnome-ish.

"How did you get into this business?" I ask him.

"I'm eighty-six and many people ask me that! I was born in Steubenville, Ohio. My dad had a steamboat store, selling supplies on the Ohio River. I come home from school and I had to work around the shop. I had to carry things to the boats down on the river. The foreigners used to land in New Orleans and go up the Mississippi by steamboat on their way to Pittsburgh for the steel and coal. The boats couldn't go further than Pittsburgh which is on the junction of the Allegheny and Monongahela Rivers. I would get the foreigners' coins. I had a great collection. My dad would throw the coins into a tobacco box and that's how I got my start. Also, I had the cleanest desk in school and I got a storybook as a prize. It told about the wonders of the seas, the wonders of the heavens, the different animals. And being on the Ohio River and seeing all the lumber floating down, the steamboats and the rafts, I got the experience to like nice things and different things. I'd go across the river to West Virginia to the Indian mounds. That must've been way back in 1870."

He nods briskly as if he really has no use for introspection. "I was eight or ten when the Civil War started. I saw Abe Lincoln, himself, dozens of times in Steubenville addressing people, old Abe with his English broadcloth shining like a ribbon. It was a fine weave. He had sunken cheeks and he was tall. They called him a rail splitter. I saw General Grant, too. Steubenville was a passageway from the eastern centers down into the South by way of the Ohio River. All the trains had notable people." He speaks and the stone and bronze memorials speak with him. "The soldiers had no commissary in the Civil War. They'd cut out windows in the freight trains, throw in a couple of bales of straw and go from one town to another. The bell-ringer would ring the bell as they neared a town and the town people would come out with washboilers of hot coffee and loaves of bread and feed the soldiers. Girls would go to the soldiers for souvenir brass buttons." He chuckles. "The soldiers had to borrow pins to fix their breeches. It was worse than the autograph craze today. My brother was killed in the war," he remarks casually with the indifference of a very old man to whom all memories are on a par. "And my father advertised for a substitute. He offered a hundred dollar reward to the man who took his place." Above his head, hanging in a row on a wooden plank, ten or twelve Indian war masks, fierce and aboriginal, glare out at the shoppers.

"How'd you get West?"

"When I was twenty-one. . . 'Go West, young man!' was all you could hear. I went to Denver and stayed twenty-five years. I sold curios, agates, shells and confectionery. It wasn't so wild either. The Indians came in the fall to buy gunpowder and stuff in those days. In 1899 I came to Seattle. I opened up right here in a li'l bit of a shack. A hobby, I call it. I had no capital." He pauses, becomes solemn. "Don't let other people affect you. Pick out your destiny and stick to it. Fight it out! Use your own judgment and head." Among the totem poles and carved walrus teeth, he too seems carved, the chisel marks of a young America shaping his words. "But now the hobbies of the people are eccentric! Today, they go to the cheap stores. Every month, a new fad comes up. Cheap shoddy work! Now you go and see my cradle up there."

Between a kayak and the vertebrae of a whale (80 OF THESE IN A WHALE, the sign reads) a cradle hangs from the ceiling and a sign:

DADDY J. E. STANLEY was rocked in this cherry wood cradle in 1854. All my relatives for the past 175 years were rocked in it. 3 daughters and 1 son in here, and my great-grandchildren will keep it rocking.

Washington State Route Number 5

South of Seattle, glacial Mount Rainier's white peak spears through the mist. The mist thickens, the peak vanishes. Burned forests and burned mountain slopes, with the surviving trees straight and topless like giant toothpicks, stretch up to Mount Rainier National Park. The Douglas firs and cedars, four and five hundred years old, unravaged by fire raise their mighty symmetrical trunks into the sky.

At Longmere, the Park Superintendent, Mr. Tomlinson dressed in forest-green uniform sits back in his chair in his office. "I'll tell you what my wife said about Mount Rainier. It was several years ago. She and I were out late in the fall and stood on the rim of the chasm. The Alpine glow faded immediately after sunset. She turned around to me and said: 'Daddy. . .' She calls me Daddy. 'I feel like I've been to church.' And neither one of us is religious. That expresses my feeling. I've heard some say that it depresses them. I hope that the mountain talks to you."

The road climbs. The Douglas firs give way to the Alpine firs.

And there is Mount Rainier again. . . Seen from one of the Park trails it seems eternal to a living man. The Nisqually Glacier starting from the summit, ribbons out into frozen ice and snow rivers.

The clarity of stone mass and glacial mass changes after sunset. . . The eastern ridge becomes a man, an Indian. He is either sleeping or dead, still wearing his bonnet of stone. His nose juts out, his upper lip clear as clear can be. But his lower lip hangs loose and irregular. He is either sleeping or dead under a blanket of stone wearing his ornaments on his chest. They bulge up, stone within stone. The blanket sheers down to the pointed ridge of his toes.

West of the eastern ridge but lower, one of the tributaries of the Nisqually shapes into the head of a huge wolfish dog, the ears long and stiff, the eye space marked by stone. The Indian is either sleeping or dead but his dog seems to live, its head facing east.

The western slope of the mountain becomes a second man, a man huger than the Indian and looking, not east but west. His great brow curves down to his nose, his lips and chin one round curve. His gigantic body stretches for miles, his knees a mountain peak. Now, the setting sun lights a pale red band over the sleeping western man. The red deepens, deepens . . . almost it seems the sun will stir the sleeper into life, almost it seems that the western man will wake from the mountain.

The Cowlitz River, gray-colored from its glacial flour, empties into the broad Columbia.

In the early morning, three people trudge down the main street of Clatskanie, Oregon. A procession of the dispossessed, they attract the eyes of the few shoppers. First in line, a young woman, who, brown pack on shoulders, is carrying a two-months-old baby in a pink blanket. She looks away from the curious, hiding behind her brown eyes as if she cannot admit that this is *herself* in a strange town. Behind his mother, a boy of three or four follows, his hands in the pockets of his overalls. Behind him, the father of the family staggers after, his thin body bent in two under a huge burlap sack, his two fists clamped around the sack's loose ends. A smaller bundle hangs from his hands. It holds the family's barn, two chickens, just as the sack holds their home.

A shopper gives the little boy a coin.

"Thank you," he smiles, shoving the coin into his pocket.

"Thank you," his mother says.

"We went to the Coast but there wasn't anything," the father explains to the coin giver. "We're going back now."

"Where was your home?" the shopper asks.

"Oregon. We had a farm. My brother wrote me he heard of something." Again the dispossessed file by the food stores, an inch of glass, an inch of civilization between them and plenty.

Gill-Netter

ASTORIA, OREGON

ASTORIA'S CANNERIES SQUAT ALONGSIDE the Columbia River, boundary of salmon between Washington's forested mountain shore and Oregon.

The gulls wheel over the red wooden buildings of the Union Co-op Fisherman Cannery, the drying nets on their racks, the fishing boats at anchor.

Inside the cannery, down at its northern water end, workers are beginning the process of shaping the freshly caught silversides into chunks that can be fitted into cans. Already gutted, their sides bloody, the silverside salmon arrive in boxes, their solid torpedo bodies, streamlined for speed through water gleaming and iridescent, their backs, blue, green, purple. Chinese butchers cut off their heads and fins and toss them still sea-wet onto the conveyors.

I walk down the damp stone floor with its puddles of water to the big blond worker at the gangknife. He reaches for the top salmon in a box on wheels, swings it up to the gangknife. One whirl and the big fish is sliced into many parts. The worker throws the tail cut into a separate tray, dumping the other pink cuts into their own wooden box. Another salmon. Another slice. Salmon. Slice. Salmon. Slice. When the wooden box is full of pink cuts, he swoops it to an inclined slide. The box moves down to two Chinese cutters who chop off the collar bones of the head cuts on round butcher blocks.

"I'm in charge here," a man says behind me. "I'm the Assistant Superintendent." In this thirties, the Assistant Superintendent wears a gray felt hat with two pencils stuck inside the hat band. His mustache is neat, his clothes a fisherman's.

"I'm just looking around. I hope you don't mind. What do you do here?"

"I have to act as the shock absorber." He smiles. "The Assistant Superintendent is the go-between. He takes the rap for lots of things that go on. We put out quite a few brands. Ninety per cent of our packing is sold in the New York and Boston markets."

Together we walk away from the gangknife. Rows of white-gloved, white-booted middle-aged women workers, dressed in pink hooverettes, rubberized cream-colored aprons and cream-colored caps, are cutting the salmon cuts into smaller pieces and fitting them into cans. As they fill up a can, they place it on a conveyor.

The Assistant Superintendent nods at the women. "They get a ten-minute rest every two hours. With pay," he emphasizes. "We provide the uniforms and we launder them."

The packed cans move down to the capping machine, looping inside. Coming out with new golden tops, they roll down a metal incline like endless wheels into the steaming tank.

The noon whistles shrill.

The cannery workers leave the conveyors and the tables. The clever machines, unmanned, stop.

Wild ducks with round black heads skim across the Columbia in gathering flight for the southern migrations.

I walk along the river with a salmon fisherman, a stocky man in his twenties. The wind rips through his blond hair and his fair complexion reddens. "Gill-netting's done right here on the river," he says. "Why, Columbia River is fished from the Bar where the ocean and river water meet, up to the Dells, one hundred and fifty miles from Astoria. . . On Sunday you mend your net. Then, after the weather has dried it, you pull it into the boat. Around six o'clock the grand rush starts for the river. Each boat scatters around. Some boats have one man, other boats have two. I fish in a boat with two. I'm the operator. The other feller's the boat puller. You should see the grand rush! Each boat goes to the place where they think the school of fish will be. But when we get to our place, we find others have the same idea. In the fall of the year for evening high waters, we would hit for Point Alice." He squints up at the gray sky. "We find our favorite place at Point Alice. . ."

"Why Point Alice?"

"There's a hole there, sixty fathoms. My partner throws the buoy out and then throws the net out as the boat goes forward. The net takes fifteen minutes to throw out. But some other fisherman's corking me. . ." He laughs uproariously. "That means another feller's putting net in front of me. The fishermen's fight begins. I holler: 'Can't you see my net's here? Our nets'll go together and neither one of us'll get fish!' Then he hollers at me and then we begin to call each other dirty son-of-a-bitch. One or the other, got to take up his net and find another place. Then you start waitin' for the fish to start strikin', especially when the sun sets and it gets dark. Maybe you cook some coffee but before you can take a sip you are disturbed by the salmon strikin' into the net. The water splashes. The boat puller drops his cup and pulls the boat along the cork line to where the fish are strikin'. When you get one gaffed, one of you will say: 'This is the first one for tonight. I see others are jerking.' "

"How big a boat have you got?"

"A twenty-eight foot motorboat. Now with the fish strikin', the boat puller keeps on working along the cork line and before he gits to the other end, he has about twenny royal chinooks into the boat. That's when I'll say: 'Looks like we got the right place.' " He grins at the habited sayings, those trademarks of any man's work. "But now the river's becoming very restless. The water's boiling a lot of eddies. It's the sign the tide's turning and there's still a chance to get many more fish. We leave the net in an hour, or an hour and half more. The tide has already taken us down below the lighthouse, miles below Point Alice. Can you see our boat?" he asks, smiling. "It has two white lights on the mast, the drift light. . . All the boats are drifting. Some have picked up their nets and are going upstream. If we got many different sizes in the hold one of us'll say: 'There's still sign of a run. Small fish and big fish are coming in.' "

Again, he grins at the folk speech of the gill-netters. "You start picking the net up soon. One pulls the cork line, the other piles the net into the boat. Maybe we got another twenny in the boat. The tide's too strong now and around ten-thirty we go and anchor at McGowan's Wharf and wait for morning. We sleep about two and a half hours and are up at one o'clock. It's now low water slack. That's just as the tide settles before it goes up. We get five fish. It's beginning to be light. We pick up and start for the cannery. The other boats are heading in the same direction. There's the Columbia River Packers' Association, the Union Fisherman where you was, Anderson's Cannery, Bobbie's Cannery. . . But the Columbia River Packers' Association's the largest and they're the ones that set the price. They decided to pay ten cents a pound for fish. We was asking thirteen cents. But all the canneries have to be in unity with the C.R.P.A. because it's connected with bankers. The other canneries need the banks."

"How do you sell your fish?"

He isn't cheerful now as when he was describing the night's work. "We go behind the last boat and wait our turn to deliver the fish. The catch averages a half a ton. You get paid at the end of the season. You bring the boat to your mooring lines and meet the other fishermen headin' for home. Each one is very anxious to know what your catch is." He smiles a little. "We find out Bill is very unlucky. Only got ten fish. And Jack. . . His net went into the beacon and tore and he wasted a lot of good fishing time. You find another brother, who had his net in the ship channel and a ship had gone over the net but they had kept on fishing by tying the ends together." He chuckles. "We go home and sleep until the afternoon and go out at six again."

"What's the season?"

"The spring season starts May first and ends August 25th. Nobody can fish from Saturday evening at twelve to Sunday at twelve. The best fish is caught in the spring. This spring, a ship ran over a boat driftin' in broad daylight. One man couldn't swim and grabbed the lifebelt. He went clean under the ship. The other fishermen see him and save this feller. Many fishermen can't swim. A fast tide'll take a boat into the jetties or capsize the boat. There's the danger," he says stolidly, his face strong and big-chinned like the faces of his Swedish seafaring ancestors before him. "There's hardly any conservation. The only conservation's the fish hatcheries. Without them, the Columbia River would have few salmon. This is about the only river without a deadline where commercial fishing isn't allowed. We lower river fishermen can't see the sense of valuable fish ladders being built to take the fish up over the Bonneville Dam . . . these same salmon are counted on the ladder . . . and then the upriver fishermen can catch these same salmon for commercial purposes. It's not doing good for anybody. It's just ruining the fish runs. The river is controlled by Washington and Oregon but so far there's been no way for these states to get together to fix any definite rulings on fish conservation. All fishermen are strong for fish conservation. The Federal Government ought to step in."

He breathes in the river air, inflating his big chest. "Fishing's healthy but a lot of people think it's a great profit. The best of us'll catch from ten to fourteen tons. The average'll be five ton. And that looks like a great profit. Only lots of boats are rented from the cannery. So the cannery gets one third, the boat puller one third and the operator one third. It takes a good fisherman to keep square with the cannery even if he owns his own gear."

We walk by the trawling boats of the ocean fleet. "The fisherman's life is not so hot." His voice is less and less cheery. "Tuna's the latest fish entered into the market. Tuna was right out here at the mouth of the river but nobody knew it was there until a few years ago. It developed a new industry and is developing Astoria into a greater fishing port. But the salmon in the ocean's almost completely gone and the salmon in the river's getting less. Four years ago there was large traps on the Washington shore. They're not operating any more. They voted those out in the State of Washington because they were taking all the fish. In former years, the seines and fish traps could take part of the run and leave enough for the gillnetters to make a go of it. But now if the traps were operating, we would be through. The fisherman's life is no good. A few years ago the pack dropped to the lowest in the history of the Columbia River. Tully Thompson of the C.R.P.A., he tried to put in on the fisherman this!" Anger twists his words. "He was picking the tullies out . . . those are the poorer fish, from the better grade bright fish . . . Thompson with his great plan of grading the fish! Lowering the general price! Tully Thompson! That's how he got the name. In 1923 we got twelve cents a pound for all salmon. But Tully Thompson started to grade. Royal Chinook is ten cents up to August first, then it drops to eight cents and the last two weeks, six cents . . . Tully Thompson!" he cries. "That's how he got the name and he don't like it!"

U. S. Route Number 101

Along the Oregon Coast, the land of long logs, the great Pacific washes into the American continent. The ocean fog cottons around the coastal trees.

A truck roars up the highway, its load two spruce logs. The next truck holds one immense log, its sawn butt, a map of the last six hundred years.

South into the redwoods. . . Serene and beautiful, the giant trees stand in peace, calendars of forest centuries marked by no disasters. South into the vineyards of California the purple grapes heavy on the vines, south into the orchards of figs, peaches, prunes.

And below. . .

San Francisco Bay, and above the Bay, the San Francisco-Oakland Bridge hurling east to Oakland and the continent.

South, across Golden Gate Bridge into San Francisco. On the road ahead, forty or fifty anti-aircraft trucks move in an olive green procession.

Descendants of the 49'ers

SAN FRANCISCO

Madera, Calif., Oct. 21.-(AP)—
Cotton growers and striking pickers fought hand to hand
in a melee at the county park Saturday until the crowd was
scattered by police using blank cartridges and tear gas bombs.
Lieut. Col. Charles Henderson, aid to Gov. Culbert L. Olson,
said highway patrolmen moved in at the request of Sheriff
W. O. Justice as growers rushed the strikers' mass meeting
and were driving them out of the park.

Alvy Shores, a cotton picker formerly from Oklahoma,
said, "Men came from everywhere, carrying shovel handles
and pick handles."

The Meckfessel home is Spanish in its architecture, the
street floor occupied by the garage, a flight of stairs leading
up from the sidewalk to the medieval alcove on the second
floor. The foyer with its print of Venice gondolas empties
into the living-room.

Light pours through the living-room's wall of windows,
on the three Meckfessels, father, mother and son. William
Junior, tall and blond, built like the 'typical' Californian
tennis player sits on the couch. His small features, neat and
northern, are set in a long face that still retains a suggestion
of childhood roundness at thirty-five. "We'll have to show you
San Francisco," he says, smiling.

"You bet we will." William Senior nods. "You and your
wife stay here as long as you like." He is a man in his sixties,
much shorter than his six-foot son, but with the same neat
features. His even teeth are white, his skin pink. Soberly
dressed in a dark blue suit, his shoes the high old-fashioned
ones of twenty years ago, he looks a little like a jockey who
has left the horses and aged into a solid citizen.

"We'll take them out tomorrow." Emma Meckfessel smiles from my wife to me. Emma is also in her sixties, taller than her husband, with a strong blue-eyed head that might have come off an old Roman coin, with firm lip and curved nose. More than her husband or her son, this living room seems hers: The maize wallpaper, the blue Chinese Buddha on the radio, the big couch with its two end tables both exactly alike, both white-lamped and blue-parroted.

The next morning, after William Senior departs for his club, we drive out in the green Meckfessel Packard, Emma and my wife in the rear, Bill Junior at the wheel.

The powerful motor easily climbs the steep streets.

"This is Grace Cathedral, our most aristocratic church." Emma stares through the Packard window as if San Francisco were suddenly new to her.

Bill parks the car in front of the Mark Hopkins Hotel. The street hills down to faraway Market Street.

Serenely Emma explains: "South of Market Street, we have the Mission District. All the poor trash live there." She speaks without animosity as if reading a weather report in the newspaper. Her back turns on the city below. Her blue eyes swerve to new landmarks. "All these four corners are prominent. There is the Union Club and the Stanford Court Apartments named after Leland Stanford, one of our famous Californians. He made his money in mining. . ."

Again, we enter the Packard, looping down on Geary Street into bright sunshine, red, white and green flags waving between the buildings: WELCOME SONS OF ITALY IN AMERICA, up Grant Avenue with its department stores and well-dressed women in furs, into the bright commotion of woman's town, the windows displaying the latest styles in clothes, hats, gems.

"Bill, I want to show them Podesta and Baldocchi's place," Emma says.

Bill brakes to a stop. Emma ushers us to a plate-glass full of flowers. "Look at those dahlias!" she exclaims. "This is one of the finest stores anywhere in the world for beautiful flowers." She leads us inside, pausing before a tree of heaven.

"Look at the shades! Greens, yellows! Oranges to brown and magenta!"

"Why do they call it the tree of heaven?"

"I don't know but Mr. Baldocchi will." She hurries off, returning with a sleek gray-haired man in a gray plaid suit. He bows his head like a diplomat when Emma introduces us. "These are friends of mine from New York." Already she is scampering away, arm-in-arm with my wife. I can hear her enthusiastic voice: "In Dresden, itself, you never saw such lovely figures as he has there. Last summer when we were in Dresden. . ."

I glance at the shelves of porcelain dancers and strolling musicians. "Do you grow your own flowers, Mr. Baldocchi?"

"No, We buy in the open market and buy the very best. These growers specialize in growing these flowers. They devote all their time to growing one certain flower." He strolls over to a big bowl, a miniature garden with a figure of the god Pan piping near a clump of cactus. "We're the ones who bring in the changes in style. We arrange flowers entirely different than years ago. Years ago, flowers were all the same length with some green, some ferns between. We never had such arrangements years ago. Here's another arrangement." Suavely, he gestures at a second miniature garden in which three musicians are playing near a lamp-post among plants arranged like a park. "Christmas comes along and we make snow scenes with skiers and such. They look very realistic."

When we go outside again, the well-dressed women are still coming out of automobiles and taxicabs, Grant Avenue, itself, an animated display inside a sky-topped case.

"Grant Avenue becomes Chinatown," Bill says. We stop in front of a red brick church.

"This is old St. Mary's." Emma's head tilts upwards. "As old as San Francisco itself. You're in another world down here. See all those turrets up the street? They're Chinese temple tops. My friend and I used to come here after school. It was the real old ancient dens in those days. We never thought of anything such as white slaving. But I remember how all the

Chinese looked down at my friend's feet. They like small feet. This was around 1880. I was married in 1889. . ." Her sharp observing eyes fix on two Chinese high-school girls. "Are the Chinese girls American? They're dressed in the height of fashion!"

VISITORS WELCOME
THIS IS A CHINESE STORE.

Emma studies the statuettes and vases inside the window. "Oriental goes with any kind of room. You take people like Barbara Hutton, with lots of money. She spends lots of money on oriental furnishings. But Mexican's coming in rapidly. With conditions like they are in Europe, many people are travelling to Mexico."

We drop into Fong Fong's ice cream place for Chinese fruit sundaes.

A young Chinese boy walks by the ice cream counter. "Hello, Slug," he greets one of the Chinese clerks. He smiles at the young Chinese girl who is making up our sundaes. "Bottle of milk," he calls to her. "And I don't want it sour."

"Oh, you!"

He sits down at the end of the counter next to a quiet Chinese boy. "Hello, Doc? How's everything? Can you loan me two bits?"

The girl clerk slides down the bottle of milk.

"What do you want two bits for?"

"For lunch."

"Why don't you go home?"

"Home?" He plunges two straws into his bottle of milk, yelling over to the clerk he greeted as Slug. "Hey Louey, got two bits for lunch?"

"Broke!" Louey retorts.

"Say, Doc, can you loan me two bits?"

Doc smiles. "All right."

At the long crowded counter, no Chinese has ordered a Chinese fruit sundae.

We drive out to Telegraph Hill. Below, the piers of the Embarcadero finger out into San Francisco Bay. The stone island, Alcatraz, is obscured by fog. White chains of fog stretch from Alcatraz to Golden Gate Bridge and the north-western section of the city. "There's our Fair sitting out in the Bay," Emma announces proudly.

Treasure Island, a brooch of land on the water, is north of the San Francisco-Oakland Bridge. Span on span, the bridge leaps the Bay like a magnificent steel grasshopper. . .

The Packard speeds home. All of us are tired but Emma. "They're the biggest candy people in San Francisco," she says. "Mrs. Warwick was Maud Haas. Her father was the pioneer candy manufacturer in San Francisco. Maud Haas is one of my oldest friends. The reason there was a slump in the candy business was because Lucky Strikes over the radio said: 'Reach for a Lucky instead of a sweet.' And also the fad in America to diet and remain slender."

After dinner one night, Emma, Bill Junior and my wife go out. Bill Senior and I sit together in the kitchen with its chromium-plated yellow-backed chairs, a kitchen as modern as the Packard.

Bill Senior puts a fresh cigarette into his cigarette holder. "I don't like to run around like the kids. There's nothing like the comforts of home. And my club's like a second home to me." He nods as if he were fifty years older than his wife.

"You go down there every day?"

"Yes, sir. I go downtown every morning to attend to what business I have and then I have lunch at the club. Play dominoes or cards, you know. And then I come home, eat a sandwich and listen to my radio. That's when they're travelling. When they're home we have dinner out, you know. We don't bother with dinner home."

"Are you going East with them to the New York World's Fair?"

"No, sir! I like my home comforts too much. Let them travel. That suits me dandy. But I stay right here." His fingers move toward the dials of the radio on the kitchen table.

"Were you born in San Francisco?"

His radio-itching fingers drop to the table. "I was born in Sacramento in 1872. They were the good old days." He relaxes, forgetting about the radio, his lips smiling in memory.

"My father left from Germany in the '50's. He landed in St. Louis. He had a friend there by the name of Kobusch. When I was travelling in 1903, Kobusch gave me a grand time. How do you like our Fair? I've been there seven times myself. San Francisco's a great little city, neat as a pin." His description of his city, describes himself.

"Tell me about your father."

"He came across the plains and landed in Sacramento in 1855. His first business was peddling water in barrels. The people had no pipes through the city in those days. After a while, he sent for his wife. They raised a family of seven boys and three girls." His lips smile gently. "Then my dad and Fred Schultz bought eleven thousand acres of land and started to raise sheep. After that, they raised wheat and hogs and cattle. Then my father sold out to Schultz and went mining up into Eldorado County. He got the gold fever. But he found it wasn't as he expected. He didn't get down far enough. If he had, he would've struck it rich. The result was he went back with Schultz. In those days, labor was nominal. Living expenses was nominal. That built him up right along. We had our cows, and horses and surries. The oldest boy milked the cows and took care of the garden and then the next boy took his place. When I got through public school, I went to work for Wells Fargo." He nods to himself. "They'll never come back again, those days. There was no licenses for hunting then. Three or four of us would go to the marshes below Sacramento in a spring wagon. We'd unload our boat and start to shoot ducks. . ."

He flicks off his cigarette ash into the ash tray. "I advanced to delivery clerk with Wells Fargo. I saved my money. At that time my brother Harry had a job with the Del Monte Milling Company in San Francisco and I used to visit him. I used to enjoy riding up and down on the Third Street car, the mud splashing over all. I'd go back to Sacramento and wish I was back in the city. Then my brother wrote me a letter. He said: 'We'd better talk to the dad about going farming.' I was nineteen at that time. At this time, the dad and Schultz had already drawn straws and divided the eleven thousand acres. The dad said: 'We have sons. Let the sons farm.' The dad felt, what was the use of giving it to them when I die: 'I'll help them now.' Harry and I started in on twenty-five hundred acres. We raised hogs and wheat and corn and chicken and turkey. Anything to make money. Harry and I and two men farmed that entire business except for harvesting. We did everything by mules. We paid those men a dollar a day and board."

He folds his arms across his chest. "We worked along about five years and then my father wrote to me that the brother-in-law T. J. Parsons. . . T. J Parsons was a fine man. He was head of the Chamber of Commerce and Fire Commissioner in San Francisco. Well, Parsons said: 'Will is too capable a boy to be stuck on the farm.' So I told Harry I'd give him half of my salary to keep my share in the farm. I went down to San Francisco. In 1895, the Del Monte Mill was within a block and a half of the Bay, on Second and Brandon. I became Parsons' understudy. I used to go down to the Merchants' Exchange and judge the different varieties of wheat and barley and corn and rye. I learned everything in the mill and on Exchange. Parsons told me to step in and become the Superintendent. I carried on pretty well. I'd go down to the mill to see that everything was going proper about blending wheats, making rolled oats. Then I'd go down to the Exchange at eleven. Yes, sir, we were the biggest handlers of pancake flour on the Coast."

He sits straight in his yellow-backed chair, again the young business man at the turn of the century. "I got to the point where I was the general overseer of the mill. I was paying my brother, Harry, more than enough to look out for my interest. So I went up to Arbuckle for a settlement. He could buy me out or I could buy him out. He bought me out. . . I went back to San Francisco. At this time I was mixing in with social people. I met Emma at the *Entre-Nous* Social Club. I saw Emma was a pretty fine girl and I played up to her. November 14th, 1880, we got married. I bought a lot on Steiner Street and went to Tommy Ross, the architect, and told him to put me up a house. We had a nice place. It was all built and ready a week before we were married. We spent our first night in our brand-new home. We lived very very happily. We managed to get into a pretty fine set."

He rubs his pink forehead. "We were living in Steiner Street in 1906 at the time of the earthquake. Emma had a baby. Bill was about a year and a half. I was in the front of the house when I heard that building shake. . . We locked up and went to her mother's place on Golden Gate Avenue. I got the horse and buggy and drove down to the mill. The foreman said: 'Things don't look bad with the mill.' In the meanwhile, the damn fire had started in different sections of the city and when it got worse they started to bomb. . . The first quake was so damnable you can feel it to this day! On Steiner Street we had bay windows facing east, and you could see one flame along the Embarcadero. I looked down on Market Street and saw brick walls crumbling from the heat. That kept up several days. . . All the buildings between the Embarcadero and Van Ness Avenue were burned down. The mill and warehouses were burned down. The safe was so hot we had to leave it cool off. Later we pulled the safes out. The records were pretty well charred, brownish-like."

He is silent, the San Francisco fire burning behind his eyes. "Later I went to Los Angeles where we had a mill and made arrangements to ship rolled oats and wheat by boat. We located a temporary location in Oakland. Then we bought the Lombard lot." He takes out a pencil and envelope from his pocket. He draws a big square and a smaller square, jabbing his pencil down like a pointer on the big square. "That was the Merchants' Ice and Storage Company. I told them: 'You've got a track from the Embarcadero to your place. What will you charge us to put a spur over here from your track to us?' " He smiles at the game of land and possessions and his skill in the game. "We got started in good shape. In 1909, the Albers people bought out the Del Monte. That was over thirty years ago. . . Since then I've spent my time looking after my ranches and apartment houses. Did Bill tell you about the origin of the Merchants' Grain Exchange? Well, we younger fellows were permitted to go on the floor only if we had blue tickets. The blue ticket kids, as we were called. We founded the club back in 1905. I'm one of the charter members and very few of us are left. We have about four hundred members now. We took in the lumber people and the shippers and insurance men as well as grain men. Shipping's very vital to grain. Insurance's a big thing also. Now, the grain men can get the information they want at lunch. I have no kick coming. The club is like a home to me. . . Yes, those were the great days. . . My folks pioneered the land. Those other fellows pioneered mining and dance-halls. Now, San Francisco is the metropolis this side of New York."

The morning comes when we pile our luggage into the Packard for a week-end at the ranch.

"Come on in," Bill Senior calls grumpily to the women. Emma and my wife step into the car. "All right," he calls, tugging at the brim of his gray Stetson. "We can go."

Bill Junior drives out of the city. "Too many dinners?" he asks me.

"Wasn't San Francisco lovely from the top of the Mark Hopkins?" Emma demands. "Tell me it wasn't lovely with all the lights below and where in the world are there such hills?"

"They won't be picking grapes yet at the ranch," Bill Junior remarks.

"There's San Quentin out there," Bill Senior points. "That's where Mooney spent thirty years. Too bad he didn't die there. They ought to put Bridges in there. That man's done more damage to California than any other man. Where does he get off telling the steamship lines how to run their business! Did you see the paper today?"

"Do you think we'll get into the war?" Emma's voice is anxious. "Isn't it terrible? I can't bear to read the papers."

Seventy miles out of the city, Bill Junior steers between two rows of weeping willows up to the big ranch house. Painted dark yellow, trimmed in green, a clump of redwoods towering alongside, the old-fashioned house looks as if it hasn't changed much in fifty years. As if there were no gas station two hundred yards off on the highway.

"How do you like my ranch?" Emma cries out happily. "All we own now is the house here. My mother sold the vineyards to the Italians."

A wire fence separates the house and its grounds from the land sold to the Italians. Behind the fence, a big brown cow and her bull calf are chewing on corn husks. Across the highway from the gas station, are the buildings of the Santa Nella Vintages, and behind them the hillsides covered with vineyard and purple grape.

The charred stumps of the giant redwoods felled long ago by Emma's father gleam dull black on the Meckfessel side of the highway. On the other side, the newer settlers have put up a road sign:

SANTA NELLA VINTAGES

Zinfandel	60¢
Burgundy	70¢
Riesling	70¢
Sauterne	80¢
Sweet Wine	$1

Boxes of grapes are piled up in front of the two-story winery, two tanned men dumping them out onto the grape elevator.

The wine smell is sweeter inside the cool ground floor with its eight-foot-high barrel vats of crushed fermenting grapes. The vats seem to have been taken out of some Middle-Age duke's cellars.

Up on the second floor, the grape elevator drops the grapes into the crusher, the separator dividing the stems from their fruits. A short man of about fifty-eight in a maroon shirt smiles at me inquiringly. His face is tanned, his hair grayed.

"I'm staying with the Meckfessels," I explain. "You must be one of the three partners Mrs. Meckfessel told me about. She says you make good wine."

"Far away to know all abouta wine." He shrugs his strong shoulders. "I'm a wineman but I don't know anything about it. No use to brag-a."

"Were you always a wineman?"

"I'm a grocer. In 1927 I sold my grocery and spenda lot of money in the old country. I come back broke." He leads me into the little retail store up front, rows of bottles on the shelves, the barrels labeled: VERY FINE CALIFORNIA PORT WINE. "The vineyards all plant and harvest once a year. People pick the grapes, put in boxes and take down to winery. We crush it, ferment it a week and then it stops. And take to storage department. Storage two years, three year. The Santa Nella, our name, is a white grape. Dry year's good for grape." He smiles. "I drink wine, too. I was born and raise in the ol' country where they drink wine with the meal."

"How long were you in the grocery line?"

"I started right after the fire in 1906 in grocery with one hundred sixty dollars and raise him gradual. I work from six in the morning to eleven in the evening. Trouble now, we must buy and pay cash. Nobody trust nobody."

We walk into the storage room between the huge barrel tanks set on cement blocks.

"That's special eastern oak," the wineman comments, rubbing his hand on the dark grained wood. "We have hundred thousand capacity. Now got forty thousand." He rinses two glasses and gets a bottle of red Burgundy. "Busy now in fermentin' season. We got the fermentin' department and storage department to watch." He tilts his glass. "*Alla vostra salute!*" he toasts.

I drain my glass.

He smiles. "You think we have war here?"

I shrug.

"I don't believe in war. That's why I don't get married. I don't like argument, to fight with wife." We walk up front to the entrance into the storage room. "That's Mondo. He know all about wine."

Mondo's long nose juts down over a black mustache. Dressed in ragged overalls, his old felt hat is stained with wine. "I'm the handyman around here. I wash barrels and crush grapes and haul grapes." One purplish-stained hand reaches for a rubber hose connected to one of the tanks. Quickly, he inserts the hose's end into the open bunghole of the first of a row of five barrels, his second hand with its purplish wine-stained pitcher darting to catch the overflow. "I plow the vineyards every spring. The horse goes slow downhill. Uphill, he has to run to make the grade." The barrel fills, and he inserts the hose into the next bunghole, red wine spurting as if from a severed artery for a second. Mondo shoves a cork and a rag into the bunghole of the first barrel, hammering down with a thin special hammer. The hammer's origin is stamped on it: MADE IN ITALY. With the staple machine, Mondo attaches a white form, first writing in the necessary information:

> SERIAL NO. 6101
> KIND OF WINE: CALIFORNIA CLARET
> ALCOHOLIC STRENGTH OF WINE 13%
> DATE OF SHIPMENT September 13, 1939

"That wine's for my brother," he smiles. "I like wine. It makes me strong." He laughs. "It's five cents a gallon tax." He pastes on two green stamps engraved $1, a 20-center, a 5-center. "That's as good as money around here. Once every three years I go to San Francisco."

"San Francisco's only eighty miles away."

"I know. See those tanks. We have to wash 'em three, four times in cold water. Take the wine out. Take care of 'em. They'll last longer'n I will. Soon the trucks 'll be driving up to the grape elevator. Then the grapes 'll get crushed, the juice 'll go into the fermentin' tanks. Stay there until there isn't a bit of sugar and then pretty soon you drink it. Sweet wine's not good for you. But dry wine gives you an appetite."

Daytimes, Bill Junior, my wife and I bike among the redwoods, tramp up the dirt roads between the fig, apple, walnut, prune and peach trees, swim in the green Russian River, walk up against the blue sky in the Santa Nella vineyards, filling our baskets with grapes for the table. Nighttimes, we sit in the old-fashioned parlor of the house, the Japanese lanterns hanging from the ceiling, English prints of red-coated hunting gentry on the walls, while the radio broadcasts the latest war news. . .

One afternoon, Emma and I are alone in the big ranch kitchen, the corned beef boiling in a big pot on the gas stove. In her gardening outfit of overalls and old brown sweater, painter's cap on her head, she looks like a migratory worker. "I was born on Van Ness Avenue where the automobiles are now. But I have to take my afternoon nap. . ."

"I didn't find out until yesterday that your father, Dr. Prossek, put in all the vines in the Santa Nella?"

"My father was a remarkable man," she says, sitting back in her chair. "He came to this country in a sailing vessel. It took him three months to get here. His parents were already in Cleveland because there was a large Bohemian colony there. My father came to be a school teacher but he couldn't

keep the boys disciplined. He was so disgusted that he re-
turned to the University of Prague. He came back the second
time as a doctor when he was about twenty-six. He had some
friends in the old country, the Korbels, the champagne people
now, and they were in San Francisco. They wrote him there
was an opening for a house physician in the German Hospital.
So he came to San Francisco where he met my mother. My
mother was born in Buffalo, New York."

She glances over at the corned beef. "My father's first
office in those old days was on a corner over a drugstore.
Where our present City Hall is, was a cemetery. . . My father
was tall and blond and heavy. He was over two hundred
pounds and wore glasses. He was very gentle. Many patients
said they were well when they first saw him. . . One day he
came home and I remember that there were many bad scars
on his arm. Later I found out, he had grafted his own flesh
onto somebody hurt in a bad accident. But I remember best
when we lived on Golden Gate Avenue. When I entered the
front room, it was a large parlor. . . I remember the carpet
on the floor. It was a black-bodied Brussels with white roses.
There were bisque figures on the mantelpiece and two ala-
baster urns were standing on each side. They also had a large
square piano and I learned to play but I wasn't very phe-
nomenal. In school I dug and dug until I got to the head of
the class. I was always good in mathematics and that's switched
to bridge playing now."

Her bright blue eyes gleam with amusement. "I'm very
good at cards. That's the only thing I'm very good at. I
recited very nicely, too, in those days and when I graduated
from the San Francisco Girls' High School I recited lines
from Snow White. As I grew older, I went to Saturday mati-
nees at the Baldwin Theatre. It used to be opposite the
Emporium. The finest companies from New York came there.
I saw the uncle of the present Barrymores. I saw Anna Held
when she first came out here. I used to go with my chum,
Maud Haas. But on this matinee I went with my mother. I
remember I came out blushing and looking down at the
ground. I felt that Anna Held's remarks and actions were
very questionable. She did a lot of rolling of her eyes and
swinging of her body."

"Did you fall in love with a matinee idol?"

"I fell in love with. . . What was his name? Everybody fell in love with him. Oh, yes! Edward Morgan. He was quite a lady-killer. He had a deep dramatic voice and a theatric manner." She laughs. "After I left high school I joined a dancing club, the *Entre-Nous,* a select club at the Palace Hotel. That was our most exclusive hotel and we had cotillions there. Every young girl came chaperoned by her mother and the mothers would watch to see if their daughters were wallflowers. I was fond of dancing. I only knew Daddy a year before I married him. He rushed me so madly I couldn't go out with the other boys because in the meanwhile I had to rest up for the next venture. When we went to parties, he wanted to show his distinction. . . He always came for me in a carriage. We had programs for dancing the waltz, the mazurka, the polka, and he'd confiscate my program. He wouldn't let any boy dance with me he was jealous of."

She folds her hands complacently. "Daddy built the home on Steiner Street opposite Alamo Square. It had round cupola windows on the edges of the building. In the parlor there were different sorts of cabinets with knick-knacks and a statue on a pedestal in the bay window. It was an Egyptian lady with palms behind her. There was a dining room, a kitchen and a girl's room. . . Nobody said the word, *maid,* then. And upstairs, three bedrooms with a marvelous outlook facing San Francisco Bay. That was our first home. The main way to meet your lady friends was a day at home. We'd serve refreshments at four in the afternoon. . . And every summer we would come up to the ranch here at Guerneville. My father was a physician but he always loved farming because he was born on a farm. It wasn't this house then. It was just a little shack in the wilderness. It cost my father thirty-five dollars an acre to clear the timber off his hundred acres. . . He had read in the San Francisco paper that a new way to make a living was to raise olives, an idea copied from Italy. . . and when I was in Italy last summer I could see why our Italians, here, say California is just like Italy, the same climate, the same crops. . . He planted all the hills with olive trees. To make them grow, he piped water from the Russian River."

She points through the window. "See that grove out there? There's some olive trees left. He had excellent olive oil. But

one time he come up one Friday night before the harvest and
the next morning he had a killing frost. All the olives were
black. After that he pulled out all the trees with block and
tackle and put in the vineyard. Why, when he was seventy-one
years old he learned Italian to talk to his two Italian workmen.
They wouldn't exert themselves to learn English!" Her eyes
flash, her father's energy electric in her. She looks as if she
could have been a doctor, too.

"I'll bet the earthquake didn't bother you, Emma?"

"No? Huh! Bill was about two years old. I was awakened
by this terrific shaking and with it was this uncanny groan.
In my dining room, the beer steins on the Dutch shelves
all crashed to the floor! I rushed across to get Bill out of the
bed. I carried him to the door. I could hardly get the door
opened. Then we all went down into the street. Everybody
else was rushing into the street. And then the fires started.
People started to light their kitchen stoves and the gas jets
were all burst. . . The next day we went to Guerneville.
We stayed here four months until people were allowed to
cook in houses in San Francisco. My father didn't stay with
us. He stayed in San Francisco to take care of the people."

She frowns. "I'll miss my afternoon nap."

"Did you go back to Steiner Street?"

"No. On account of my parents—they were burned out
during the quake and came to live with me, we moved to
Page Street where we had a large fourteen-room house. It had
a Jacobean dining room. The furniture was golden oak. We
had hardwood floors and art glass windows. The parlor had
a chandelier of gold leaf. The ceiling was frescoed with gar-
lands of roses and gold cupids. These same cupids were repro-
duced on the chandeliers. Afterwards we modernized the
stable into a garage. We lived there seven years. I was quite
proud of my surroundings. We felt we were entertaining in
a more important fashion. I joined the Cap and Bells Club,
and at my days at home Maud Haas and I sang duets: 'I Live
and Love Thee' and 'Oh That We Two were Maying!' Maud
had gone to Boston and studied music for eight months. . .
We played euchre and five hundred for prizes and then that
was switched to bridge, then to auction bridge, then to contract bridge. I liked it but the servants were becoming a
problem. My father passed away on Page Street and then

I bought the house we have now. My mother lived downstairs because my mother wanted a housekeeper and a maid to wait on her. After so much work to do I liked it to be on one floor. I've gone modern with white lamps and white painted furniture." She stares away, contemplating the three houses of her married life.

She stands up. "We have some old things here. There's the mirror that used to hang in my father's office. The glass is sort of crackled with age. My father was remarkable in every way. . . He put in a very fine variety of grapes and they were sent out to the Virginia Dare Winery in New York in glass cars to be made into champagne. Even now, the Korbels who make the highest grade of California champagne, buy all the grapes of this special variety from the Italians. We have Zinfandel and Riesling and Sauterne," Emma enumerates, as if the vineyards still belonged to her. "My mother sold the vineyards about 1908 to a doctor and a dentist of Santa Rosa. They bought it for speculation. And an Italian, Francis Coni, who owns the Tosca Café bought the vineyards from them and took in two other men as partners. It's too late to take a nap today." She gets up from her chair. "I've always lived conservatively and never extravagantly. We trudged around in a horse and buggy when my friends in the same station of life had automobiles." She walks towards the door. "I've had a fortunate life and a peaceful one."

When we return to San Francisco again, Emma and Bill Junior leave for New York City.

"I hope you liked our little San Francisco," Emma says in farewell.

"Go back to the ranch if you want," Bill Junior says, "and stay as long as you like."

One afternoon, the door bell rings. At the door a man of sixty in a big floppy hat pokes out the package of needles in his hand. "The best needles and only fifteen cents a package. The best. . ."

I give him a nickel. "I don't need needles."

"Are you working?" he asks.

"Yes."

"That's fine. I don't like to see a young man like you not working. Are you for Ham an' Eggs? You don't have to tell me. It's a feasible plan, I think. I'm going to vote for it November 7th. The big banks may lick it like they licked the Epic plan. But it's feasible. Some day we fellows without jobs will beat the big banks."

Downtown, I walk south of Market Street to Howard, to a street where the standard of value is the modest dime. . . The Klamath Hotel: 25¢ Up. The U. S. Coffee Shop: FULL MEALS 10¢ AND 15¢ AND UP. The Calvary Rescue Mission: No price. A clothing store with a sign: SPECIAL SALE OVER-COATS 1.50. Howard Street . . . still another street in another city where hotel rooms, meals, Jesus Christ and overcoats are for sale.

The homeless, the jobless, the hopeless men stand along the curbs. Down on the next block, a white-bearded man is curled up in the middle of the sidewalk. His brow is broad, his nose hawked. He isn't sleeping. His blue eyes move. They shift upwards, blue eyes between pink-rimmed lids.

"Leave'm lay," a man of forty advises me. "I've been here a week and he's been drunk ever since." He coughs into a Kleenex. "Leave'm lay."

U. S. Route Number 101

South of San Francisco, fruit stands dot the highway:

BUY FROM THE GROWER AND SAVE MONEY

The orchards are many on the land.

The next bill-board pictures the California earth in bright green, a tractor in bright red:

CHOICE IMPROVED PROPERTIES. CALIFORNIA LANDS IN-
CORPORATED. SAN FRANCISCO. SAN JOSÉ. SAN LUIS OBISPO.
LOS ANGELES.

On the highway, a battered car full of migratory workers
drives south.

On the highway, another battered car crowded with babies
and grandmothers, the mattresses jumbled together on the
rear seat.

And another car.

And another.

The land, the beautiful orchard land . . . plains out into
grazing acres. The white faces of the Hereford calves seem
whiter than those of the big red steers.

At Atascadero, the land produces almonds.

Santa Margarita.

San Luis Obispo.

Arroyo Grande.

Santa Maria.

Town after town, like huge fruit and vegetable stands on
the land, the mountains of the Coastal Range baking warm
and brown in the sun.

Between Santa Barbara and Ventura, the oil derricks
climb from the hills across the highway out into the Pacific.
They rise like lookout towers from the sea water.

And further south, the orange groves. Beyond the groves
. . . Hollywood.

Flickerland People

HOLLYWOOD

I BUY FIVE GALLONS OF GAS on Sunset Boulevard. "Gas is cheap here," I remark. "Eleven and nine tenths a gallon is low."

The station attendant hangs up the hose on its pump. "This is an auto town! You never saw a town with so many gas stations." He takes my dollar and gives me change, moving cleanly as if his body were a well-oiled mechanism. "Have you seen the 1940 Fords?" His eyes meet mine tentatively, appraisingly, ready to change from station attendant and customer to man and man.

"No. What do you think of them?"

"Really want to know what I think?"

"Sure I do."

"All those new cars are coming out with more and more ash trays." He grins. "Your Ford's a '34. I've got a '35 Chevvy. How many ash trays do we get along with?" He laughs. "You never saw an auto town like L.A. Any kid with a hundred bucks can buy a car. You don't have to worry about a place where to park it. And this city covers so much ground, you need a car to get around in." He lights a cigarette. "I suppose you've been out to Hollywood to see where the stars live?"

"No."

"How long have you been here?"

"I came in yesterday."

"And you haven't tried to see any stars yet? Don't you like the movies?"

"Sure, I like them. How about you? Do you hang around hours waiting to see a star?"

"I used to when I first came here. But now, I wouldn't

walk from here to there to see any of them. It's disgusting
the way you act when you're movie-struck."

"Where'd you come from?"

"Texas. There's nothing as big as Texas in all of Hollywood!"

I motor up Sunset Boulevard as cars swerve off and up
the driveway-sidewalks in front of the big meat and vegetable
markets. The shingles of doctors and the signs of movies
advertise: FREE PARKING SPACE.

Gas stations. Garages. Accessory stores. Tall palm trees like
feather dusters. Stubby palm trees like huge pineapples.

Miles west on Sunset Boulevard I park in front of a series
of signs and small American flags:

HARRY'S SINCE 1926
PERSONAL GUIDES
to
MOVIE STARS' HOMES
IN YOUR CAR

The signs are lettered in red, white and blue; Harry,
himself, in the middle of them under a beach umbrella. His
tanned shrewd face fits the amusement park atmosphere of
this highway office, his blue suit, black bowtie and sun glasses
exactly the right uniform.

I sit down in the empty camp chair next to Harry's. "I'll
bet you movie guides know a little about this town."

"We know more about Hollywood than anybody else!" he
says earnestly without hesitation. "We have to know. We
get all classes of people from all parts of the world and when
you're in this business thirteen years, you see plenty and you
have to know plenty. They ask the most foolish questions as
well as smart ones. Everybody has a different line of questions.
They want to know who's married to who, and who they're
divorced from . . . I'm the only guy in this business who's
made a study of it." He offers me a cigarette. "I'll guarantee
that. I'll guarantee I can show more homes than anybody else.
And positively authentic!"

"How did you become Harry, the Guide?"

"That's quite a number of years ago. I used to know a lot of Hollywood people. I used to be in the vodvil business myself—I've got a game leg." He glances down at his feet. One of his shoes has been specially constructed. "I can't get around like you other guys. . . Friends of mine used to ask me where the stars lived and I used to tell them. Now when they ask me, they pay me." He leans back in his camp chair. "I was born back in Rhode Island. . . I've been all over the damn world. One time I had plenty of dough. Now I got nothing. I've had people here from all over the world. I've had from the highest to the lowest, people who had to scrape up the three bucks they paid me to see the stars' homes. I've had men who when they come out of their car were in overalls. Just like you catch 'em in the hills. Hill billies. They go crazy to meet a star from their home town or state. When they come from Arkansas they want to see Bob Burns. If he's in, he'll come out to the gate and shake hands. One car I had . . . some in the car were from Houston, Texas, and some from Kansas City, Missouri. Those from Houston swore Ginger Rogers was from Texas and those from Kansas City that Ginger Rogers was from Missouri."

He smiles, a nice wise guy. "I've had people from all over the world. From Bucharest, Roumania. I had Eric Akerland, the Stockholm Swedish consul. I've had Governors, Senators. And even movie stars! They might know where some of them are but not all of them. Lots of movie people send their friends to me to show 'em around. I didn't know nobody when I first started. Now, I can tell you who's building every new house and how much it'll cost. I know all their legal names. I have the tip-offs. . ." He nods at a roadster whizzing by on Sunset Boulevard. "There goes Amos of Amos and Andy. They all drive by here. Everybody knows me and I know everybody. . . The average man or woman want to see the movie homes. If they can see the movie actors and actresses they're settled. I took a couple out this morning who wanted to see Claudette Colbert. The woman was tickled to death. She sat there jigging around in the seat. The husband kept saying: 'Sit still. You'll see her!' But she couldn't stop jigging." Again, he nods at a car passing by in front of us. "There goes Humphrey Bogart."

"Do you get here early?"

"I get here about eight in the morning and quit a quarter to five. I'm here rain and shine all year around. I've taken people out when it's been raining so hard you can't see a foot ahead of you. People from back East don't mind the rain. I take them out and give them satisfaction. I've never yet brought back anyone from a trip who wasn't satisfied. Many people have told me after I've shown them just *one* movie star that the trip was already worth the three dollars. I show them Dorothy Lamour, the girl with the sarong, and they're happy. Ninety-five per cent of the people, if they can see Shirley Temple, they're going home satisfied. She's a sweet kid and so are her people. I call her father, 'George with the Perpetual Smile.'"

"Anybody ever want to see the producers or the writers?"

"That happened just once for each. A lady wanted to see the producers. That was the first time it ever happened. And there was a writer with the name of Gordon Silver. I remember his name because it's the same as *Silver Screen Magazine*. He wanted to see where the writers lived." He shrugs philosophically as if to say: Some people are nuts! "I get people who keep asking me: 'Can we get inside the houses so we can see the insides?' I say: 'You wouldn't want people tramping over your houses?' They don't answer to that. Mostly, they're well behaved. . . Pardon me."

He crosses Sunset Boulevard, the bright sun on his shoulders, to two middle-aged women. They exchange a few words. He returns to his beach umbrella. "They wanted to go for a dollar! I take the whole party in their own car and for three dollars. One dollar! I drive 'em around two hours, Shirley Temple, Joan Crawford, the old Barrymore home and all that stuff. I can show 'em more stuff in one day than they could see in six months! If they can go through the studios they'll do anything in the world! But you can't go through unless you know a big-shot. Why some of these people get here after two and three thousand miles and when they can't get in the studios, it's a damn big disappointment. They want to see a picture being made. I think the studios ought to build sound-proof rooms in which the people can stand and not get in the way. The stars are here. And the people want to see 'em in person. They'll come a long way to see a movie star." He stretches his legs out. "Candid camera fiends come out here and take pictures of the homes. Gable, Barbara Stanwyck and some'll pose for these fiends. These movie stars don't mind people looking at their homes but some of these people will pick flowers for souvenirs. Over on Mary Pickford's wall, they have a barbed wire to prevent the souvenir hunters from stealing her wash for souvenirs."

"It must be a hard job pleasing your different customers?"

"I can make the wealthy people enjoy themselves as well as the common people. Wealthy people are stiff but I can get their stiffness out of 'em. I make it my business to find something they'll like. The trouble with this business are the chiselers. There was a fellow a couple years ago, who picked up some wealthy people and told them he'd show them a star from their home town for five bucks. They were from Pittsburgh. And for ten bucks he'd get the star to speak to 'em. Well he drove these people out to Dick Powell's home, and drove right up on the lawn, honking his horn. Dick Powell was home! When he rushed out to see this car on his lawn, this fellow said: 'Hello Dick. Say something. These people have come from Pittsburgh.' 'Get off my lawn!' Dick said. . . There goes George Raft."

Flashing by, I see Raft's Valentino profile at the wheel of a bright red car.

Beyond Harry the Guide's open-air establishment, the elegant stores of Beverly Hills, *The Florence Lamp Studio, Jaeckel Furs, Alfred Cerf of Palm Beach, Shoe Manufactory Sabots and Sandals* are housed in gleaming white buildings like private residences. The sunlight, the palm trees, the palm tree architecture are like those in a semi-tropical myth, a pie-in-the-sky land actually brought down on the American earth.

Housed in a white colonial building . . . the *Hollywood Mortuary* with its neat lettering: *24 Hour Service.*

Next door . . . *Princess Zoraida, Egyptian Psychic.*

I walk up the flight of stairs and the Princess, a small woman of about fifty in a green silk jacket and silken oriental harem trousers leads me into her waiting room. "I have a client," she explains in a Mediterranean accent. "Please wait." He face is triangular, her eyes dark brown or black, her fingers circled with many rings.

I am alone in the waiting room, its three windows on Sunset Boulevard and the speeding cars of tourists and movie stars. The portrait of Princess Zoraida on the old-fashioned victrola exaggerates the blackness of her hair and eyes. Hanging rugs of Turkish bazaar scenes, and tapestries of sphinx-like gods cover the walls. Piled on a center table, *Esquires* and *True Storys* stack high near the *Romances of Alexandre Dumas* in eight volumes and some small booklets: PLEASE READ THIS LITTLE BOOKLET THROUGH. KEEP IT FOR A SOUVENIR. IT WILL BRING YOU GOOD LUCK. Underneath the photograph of Princess Zoraida on the cover the caption reads: THE GREATEST LIVING EGYPTIAN PALMIST, CLAIRVOYANT, CRYSTAL GAZER AND SAND DIVINER. EGYPTIAN CARD READING PSYCHICALLY REVEALED.

The clock in the waiting room has stopped at 4:15. I dinge out my cigarette in a three-wise-monkeys ash tray: the three monkeys in their famous poses of not speaking evil, not seeing evil, not hearing evil.

When Princess Zoraida's client leaves, the Princess ushers me into her private study. Here, too, the walls are hung with red rugs and tapestries. Many dolls sit on the floor, the sad-faced cloth dolls popular with young girls, stenographers and actresses. The Princess motions me to take a seat. The small table between us holds a zoo of miniature animal carvings, a crystal ball and a pillow for palm reading, the low relaxing light reflected from the Princess's metallic head cloth. She listens to my questions, her eyes intensely alert, the eyes of a woman who must make her judgments quickly. And then speaks in a hurried voice as intense as her eyes. "The way I do my work, the people always in trouble come here, the woman discontent with her husban' . . . I make it so easy for her, I make it easy to see, I make her to see it's man's privileges. . . In other words, I try to make her stick to her husban'. I tell her to be nice, sweet and attentive and whatever he do, let him do it. I make her to appreciate her husban'. . . And he come here, I make him stick true to her. My work is to elevate and inspire. If he has a bad habit, the drinking, I try to make him feel to be honest, upright, to be good Christian. We need God and we depend on God and we can't be independent of God. God can be independent of us. The girls . . . the girl's life . . . if she isn't doin' the right thing, to settle down to be a wife and a mother, to stick to someone, to be true to him, to be good to her father and mother, to be good to church, and be a good Christian, I preach and inspire her. I take them to pieces . . . I inspire them. I mold them. I dig into the habit and before they go I help them. Some will kill themselves when they come to me but I show them the meaning of life, to do the upright thing. . . I tell them about their life, how many brothers and sisters, if living and dead, and all about their early work. That's psychic, clairvoyant. I concentrate on that crystal and I tell everything for them, what their religion is, what they intend to do, what the best thing in life they should do. . . My mother Syrian, my father Egyptian. . . I was the only one born with a veil and a star on my forehead. They got a seeress there and she foretold I was to foresee and be a psychic. I was always seeing visions. I got older, I went to India to study all the occult work, all psychic. . . I make them haff faith in their home, elevating, inspiring. Not only showing them the right and the wrong but marvelous thing about present and past and future, and secret things in themselves. When I was in Palm Springs people come from all over. I prophesize many things. I said there would be big boom in 1925 when I was in Florida in 1920, how the city was going to rise. . . Hollywood is going to be much more bigger and bigger all the time. It will be larger, people will come to Hollywood and property come higher."

She shuts her eyes. "The property will be so expensive, Hollywood will be the center of all Los Angeles. There will be disasters, too. There will be disasters and storms this winter. There will be a whole lot of blood and war. There will be an awful lot of catastrophes in Europe and United States, and different deaths and different catastrophes in 1939, in 1940. Movie actresses will be serious accidents, and some dead, quite a few famous persons will die."

She opens her eyes. "I think the movie stars are wonderful people, they brought lots of life, hope and ambition to people. Now everybody want to be something worth while.

Every day people develop themselves and bring out their talent. The movie stars bring the public happiness and to make the younger people like them. Everybody want to be actor, dancer, writer and a lot of people will belong to artistic more than to any other profession." She gestures with her hands. "I tell the young girls not to mix up with bad company. I tell them to be good to their government, God, to their children, wife, husband. And to the boys and girls, not to be dissolute. If their parents listen to me they'd send me a beautiful medal."

Eight of us sit at one of the tables at the Beachcombers' Club. The subdued lights hide the wrinkles, if any, of the four women, the movie musician's girl, the doctor's wife, the lady movie executive, a pert female who looks like some star whose name I cannot remember, and my wife. Bunches of bananas hang from the big beams, but the tropical atmosphere isn't overdone. Everything is in the best of taste, including the tropics.

The movie musician frowns. "This damn place has been making money since it opened. All they serve are rum drinks. Yet people come and sit around and talk. You never find a noisy drunk here. It's restful. You can say that for it."

"Why are you frowning?" the doctor demands. He smiles at my wife. "Welcome to California! How many times have you heard that? You came here in a car, didn't you?"

"I'd like to go to New York," the movie musician complains. "What'll you have?" he asks us as the Filipino waiter comes to our table. "Oh, never mind! Sharktooths for the men. Daquiris for the women."

The drinks come. I sip mine and wonder what star the movie executive reminds me of? The movie musician's frown irons out. We order another round.

Smiling, the movie executive remarks. "People out here are fanatics, the way they flock to these previews."

"The whole atmosphere is bad," the doctor agrees.

"I like California as a whole, the climate." The movie executive glances at her husband, a dark silent man. "But I don't care for the people in the movie industry. They're flighty. They tell you one thing and mean another. Everybody's out for their own gain. It's not like the East."

"Not much," the doctor scoffs.

"What I mean is that unless a person has a strong character, the atmosphere will tend to change their viewpoint on life." The lady movie executive is still holding forth. Her eyebrows seem to have been put on by a machine. "As long as you associate with people in the movie industry you have to be careful you won't be thinking like them. That's a woman's viewpoint."

The movie musician jiggles his glass. "Where else in the United States is there a city, where else in the world is there a city where a musician can buy a good violin? They sell good violins here all the time."

His girl adds. "Hollywood and New York."

"That's right. The only two cities in the United States where there are any musicians at all."

"Who have you seen," the movie executive asks me.

"Harry the Guide, and Princess Zoraida. The Princess is an Egyptian psychic."

"No movie people?" the movie musician shakes his head sadly.

"This town is full of psychics," the doctor says. "There's the Colorado Mystery Mind who helps you if you're worried. There are psychic clubs as well as lonely clubs. He mimicks: 'Are you lonely? Do you want to meet discriminating friends? Do you want to be happy? Do you want a worthwhile sweetheart?' Why, the town has as many evangelists as you can find in any city. It's a hysterical town."

"Marriage doesn't mean anything to men out here," the movie executive declares. "Everybody is darling or sweetheart. Even if a woman's ugly, it's still darling or sweetheart. It's just a tropical place."

"That's right. I made a trip East a few years ago and it did me good." The movie musician sighs.

"Do Hollywood people always talk about Hollywood?" I ask.

"Yes," the musician answers. "Nobody stays home. Everybody has a car and is always in it. One night home a week is enough for me. Everybody is always visiting and telling stories."

"People move in and out all the time," the lady executive sips her daquiri. "A lot of people are put out of their houses because they rent beyond their means."

"But you like it?" the doctor asks her.

"Yes. It's not dull. In my position I get out to the studios a lot and it's interesting meeting people from all over the country. I'm through carping. You can put finis on the bottom."

The doctor nods. "The Hollywood atmosphere doesn't do us doctors any good. We treat a patient for years and make little or nothing and then we get a movie star and make enough in one visit to take care of baby for the next six months. I have a few such patients, no names mentioned if you please. But discreetly, oh very discreetly, I breeze the fact around. I see the elevator boy and he asks me: 'Are you treating *him*, Doc?' And I answer: 'It's not generally known but . . . it's a secret really but . . . oh yes, *He's* a patient of mine.' " He smiles. "That gets around town because no one stays home here as someone mentioned. People are always visiting each other to keep up with the latest gossip. I was at a movie party once and afterwards I had calls from a dozen patients. It seems that my name was mis-spelled in one of the movie magazines that reported the party. . . Everybody reads the screen magazines."

We order another round of drinks. The musician takes up the conversation.

"This is the one city where a musician can make enough to buy a good violin. That's a good enough story for me. It's true that most musicians aren't working. But this city is still Opportunity with the big O. The big radio shows are all here or in New York. The other day I met a friend of mine across from NBC in the bowling alley and we began to beef. He's with the *Royal Gelatin Hour* and they have a classy program. This one is about a family, a father and his sister . . . his wife died, and two kids of his, a boy and a girl. And there's a guy who barks like a dog. He's Rags, the family dog. The guy who barks like a dog hangs around with his coat in his mouth and waits for the cue to bark and growl from various parts of the studio, so as not to make an echo. The father has a homey chuckle. And they all go to bed at ten o'clock. . . The folks listen to the show. It goes on at nine, and then they go to sleep." He imitates a yawning old man: " 'Guess I'll listen to *One Man's Family* and go to bed.' About Rags . . . usually a guy barks into a curtain. But there's no curtain so he barks into his coat." He drinks his sharktooth. "There's another musician I know, a guy who plays on a big Sunday night program. He's very dark, a southern Italian. He has to shave twice a day, a very black set of whiskers. . . Every Saturday he stays out all night enjoying himself. So he has to catch up on his rest Sunday. During intermissions, Sunday, he sleeps in the corridor which is known as the Corridor of the Stars because the guide boys are taking people through at forty cents a head. They tell the rubes that they're now about to see Jack Benny, Don Ameche, Bing Crosby, Dorothy Lamour. The rubes come in here and here is this guy laying on a bench, asleep. He's wearing a green sport shirt and his whiskers are a block long. He was requested to rest elsewhere. . ."

"I think I ought to go," the movie executive says. One by one we get up.

"That's a nice way to treat my beef," the musician says, smiling.

Outside the Beachcombers' Club, to the left of the entrance a hunchbacked man is waiting to entertain the departing rum-drinkers. As soon as we come out, he whistles to his small black and white dog. The dog trots over. He puts a Hawaiian *lei* around the dog's neck and begins to whistle. The dog stands up on two legs, teeters around in a South Sea dance.

"How do you train your dog?" I ask the street entertainer.

"Patience and kindness. Patience and kindness." He is a little surprised to be spoken to. "Patience and kindness."

"What's the dog's name?"

"Trixie. She's four and a half years old." He removes the *lei* and puts a pipe in Trixie's mouth. Solemnly, the dog strides up and down the sidewalk. "I'm just trying to get along," he says diffidently, ready to stop talking in a second. "A man sixty years old can't do much. Just trying to get along. I come here all the time." He takes the pipe from Trixie's mouth, his fingers fumbling inside his pocket. He tosses a ball to the dog. She catches it in her mouth. Other people come out of the Beachcombers'. He starts the routine all over again. *Lei* around her neck, the little dog hula-hulas. . .

Near the corner of North McCadden Street, the musician is examining a parked Duesenberg. "White leather upholstery," he notes with admiration. "But you can tell from the paint job that it's not a new one. By the way, can I give you a lift?" he asks me.

"No, thanks. My wife and I'll walk."

"Nobody walks in Hollywood," the doctor retorts.

Do Not Enter Unless Red Light Is On.

The red light isn't on above the heavy door into the soundproof set. Outside, extras are sitting on benches, their backs against the brick wall, their faces like those of travelers in a railroad station. The brick walls, the theatrical alleys between them leading to other sets, to other buildings on the Columbia Pictures lot, leading, leading into futures or no-futures, stardom or no-stardom, all belong to a world on the move and on the make.

Young girls, heavily made up for the camera, walk by. Their faces seem one face, the face of pretty waitresses in a hundred restaurants, the face of bathing beauties on all the beaches.

Do Not Enter Unless Red Light Is On.

The red light flashes on. I enter through the heavy door into a newspaper office. Copy writers sit at the rows of desks, the camera located up front near the elevators. Here, behind a railing, two office boys of fifteen or sixteen are guarding the newspaper's waiting room. Above, the newspaper office, the huge glaring movie lights. Below, the make-believe. Above, an attic structure of plank walks and more lights.

Off the set, perched on a high bookkeeper's stool, a girl in a blue tailored suit seems to be waiting for her cue like a little girl about to recite at public school assembly. Her hair is brownish blond, her eyes blue. Her prettiness has the distinction of an actress' or debutante's. She is almost beautiful, twenty-two or three and in Hollywood. . .

"How'd you get out here?" I ask her.

"I've been out here just about three weeks." Her diction is careful.

"Do you like it?"

"Prior to my coming here I had heard Hollywood was an eccentric place. I had no thought of coming into the movies."

"Where did you come from?"

"I was born in Boston. I'm a nurse by profession. My name is . . ." She laughs. "My name used to be Lauretta Wisneski."

Extras, electricians, girls with notebooks, bit players walk in front of us as if on a street. There is the movement and excitement of a street, but the passers-by remain the same people.

"One day at the hospital," Lauretta says, "I met a chap who knew Mr. Hawks and I came out here and had a couple stills taken. I was called two days ago. At first, I thought it was hot work, the glaring lights! I didn't think anything'd come of my coming out here. The only part that interested me was the money part." She smiles beautifully, looking now like a screen magazine cover. "Maybe I shouldn't say that? I was amazed when they called me. I was surprised to see the amount of people sitting around, doing nothing and getting paid for it. I had to work so hard previously. The first few days it was all very interesting, but now it's rather boring. They're doing a retake on "Front Page," "His Girl Friday." I come here at seven in the morning for makeup and hairdress and go home at six. I'm tired of doing nothing. 'Hi, Hildy, is all I say. I'm a reporter, something I did years ago in Detroit for the *Detroit Free Press.* All I say is: 'Hi, Hildy.' Everybody shouts hello and I'm one of the mob. I'm of no consequence. But Hollywood amazes me! In Boston people are formal. Here people are so informal! Too informal. I don't think they know the word *reserve* is in the dictionary. And people here don't strike me as being too bright. They're so superficial, most of them. Everybody wants to be an actor. They don't act natural. They'd cut each other's throat to be in the spotlight for a moment. Then there are the nice people, the stars. Miss Russell, she's the reporter, and Mr. Grant, and of course, Mr. Hawks. I expected directors to have fifteen hundred yes-men around them. As far as I can see there are only two. And Mr. Hawks will accept a no from a yes-man and won't fire him."

"Thanks." I walk on set into the newspaper office. An elderly man in a gray suit is resting on a sofa.

"How long have you been out here?" I ask him. "And what do you think of Hollywood?"

"Since 1921." He takes off his glasses, holding them in one hand. "I came here from the stage. I'm Fred Parker. I was a repertoire player for years, first on the Lasky lot. I don't recall any studio in Hollywood that I haven't worked in. I worked in westerns. I did a lot of blackface in the two-reel comedies. In this picture I'm one of the writers on the newspaper. . . You hear a lot of the lunatic fringe out here. But cities of equal size anywhere have the fringe. The jitterbug age, the screwball age is found in all ages. People in Hollywood go in for the sports, including golf and football." He stares down front towards the camera. "I like the girl reporter, Miss Russell, very much and the way the director handles it. Hawks in my estimation is tops. He has that touch we don't find with so many of them. It's the finish that's needed in many pictures. And they have it here. You take Charlie Chaplin in his pictures. He never leaves a scene unfinished. When you feel a scene is about finished, Charlie Chaplin tops it with a wow. With an unexpected wow. Hawks and Capra have that in their direction of more serious drama. Every scene is always finished, never left unfinished."

I hurry back to the camera and the director, a tall man of about forty with straight white hair. In flannels and brown plaid jacket, Hawks looks as if he were the original of the *Esquire Country Wear* advertisements.

"How do you like directing this show?" I ask him.

"Let's walk over this way." He sits down at one of the newspaper desks, folding his hands across his chest. "This show is locked up in a few small rooms. Pictures that are hard, are those that you go outside for adventure and color. . . The principal problem in pictures nowadays are the plots. There are only a few plots. And we can only change the old plots through the characters. All our efforts are directed towards characterization, to get people to act in a human way. The audience is getting so educated, it's not necessary to hit a thing on the head. It's an oblique method of telling a thing that's been told before. And that makes it seem new. Our job's just to coordinate things, and keep things together. We're going to branch out. After the war's over we're going to do an African picture of Hemingway's. . . Pardon me."

He strides to the camera, to Rosalind Russell, to Cary Grant. I leave the set with the assistant electrician. "They're going to shoot," he says. A lean man of thirty-five in brown pants and shirt open at the collar, he walks limberly like an athlete.

Outside the set, he leans on the drinking fountain. "Want a smoke?"

"Thanks. How long have you been in the movies?"

"I've been in this picture business twenty years. I've worked in every department in the studio, mostly as an electrician."

"What about electricians?"

"An electrician really contributes something. We don't only shove the lights around. I've worked with all the greatest cameramen in the world and they all have their style of lighting. Of course, working in the quickies or in westerns or in Poverty Row . . . everything there is speed! Push in the lights! Anything goes! We haven't any time there to screw around and be artistic. In that kind of a show you work day and night. Thirty-six hours straight. They don't do that as much as they used to. An electrician used to drink whiskey to stay on his feet. A good electrician was one who could drink enough whiskey to keep going and stay on his feet. . . The head electrician's called 'the gaffer,' the assistant electrician's the 'best boy.' ' '

The extras are still sitting on the benches against the brick wall.

"Working with all those cameramen I've learned lighting. Lighting is photography. The assistant cameraman knows all the tricks and the mechanical end of the camera. But the cameraman paints the picture with light. We move the light where he tells us and consequently we learn to daub a little ourself. My brother and I do portrait work at home." He smiles. "My name is Paul Plannette, portrait work. . . I also enjoy a good production like this Hawks show rather than some cheap production that'll stink when they get through with it.

Electricians take pride in the previews. They reviewed the new Capra picture and there were raves about the photography. And we feel we helped contribute to that end. There's romance and glamour in this business. Half the stars in the picture know my name. . . I was movie-struck myself when I was a kid here in Los Angeles. I wanted to be an actor, but I found myself missing meals. I became an electrician in order to better myself," he smiles. "I've quit the business twice and always came back. It's like the circus or going to sea. Why, we may go to Arizona for two months leave on an hour's notice!"

He nods at the extras. "I've seen the same faces for twenty years. They can't get discouraged even when they're old. 'Look at Marie Dressler,' they'll say; 'she didn't get her break until she was sixty. I'm only fifty-eight.'" He smiles hard and realistic. "The light's red. We can go back."

The assistant director, Cliff Broughton, is a middle-aged man with a good-looking brisk businessman's face.

"How long are you out here?" I ask him.

"Nineteen years. I came from the Middle West. I was in the automobile business back there as a dealer. I had two counties back in Iowa, the Buick agency. I'd traveled all over the United States except California. I thought I'd see California. I liked it out here. I looked over the automobile business. . . Anyway, I went into the real estate business and through connections I met Wally Reid and Mrs. Reid. When Wally died I was handling the affairs of Mrs. Reid and that's how I got into the picture business. I broke in as a business manager. Later on. . . Let's see? Later on, she and I produced pictures together up to 1932. I was vice-president of Mayfair Pictures. I wanted to make a million dollars. Then I got into the liquor business and lost my fanny." He grins, cheerily ironic as if skeptical of other opportunities. "I had a wife and two kids. I went back into the picture business. You stay away a year and it's tough to get back. I'm not proud. I had a wife and two kids. I'll do anything I can."

He rubs at the wrinkles webbing out from the corners of his eyes. "I've been here four and a half years as assistant director. When we're assigned to a story, we have to break it down and figure the number of shooting days, the wardrobe. We work with the budget department. Work with the director. And then when the production starts we're held responsible for the set to the front office. We call the people when they're wanted. We arrange all the background action, all of that background newspaper office you see there." He clasps his hands over his knee. "Hollywood hasn't the color it had fifteen years ago. . . Hollywood Boulevard is like any main street. In the old days, you'd drop into a coffee shop and meet Rudolph Valentino or Wally Reid. I watched the first big skyscraper going up, the four-story Security Bank. . . It really was lovely then. There were just a few theaters. Grauman hadn't built the Egyptian. Mrs. Reid used to say. . . We were driving down the Boulevard about nine at night and she'd say: 'Sleepy old Hollywood.' There wouldn't be more than fifty people around. There go the lights!" He rushes from me over to the camera.

Everywhere, the whispering stops.

The lights are converging on the waiting-room outside of the newspaper office. To the left of the camera, Hawks, and the script and dialogue clerks now studying the books on their laps, are seated in a row of three chairs like a jury.

The lights converge on Ralph Bellamy, tall, blond, his Yale football hero's face lined under his makeup. He seems a little forlorn in his raincoat and rubbers as if somebody had left him behind in the newspaper's waiting-room like an old umbrella. Rosalind Russell leans against the No Ad-MITTANCE sign on the office gate. She is wearing a red street coat with a fine black stripe, a black hat with a fine red stripe. Hawks stares at the stars in silence.

The head electrician or 'gaffer' nods at Russell. She steps forward a pace. He squints at her, a big cowboyish fat man in a brown felt hat and sweater. Like a window decorator, he arranges Russell in the bright glare. His 'best boy,' Paul Plannette, climbs up a ladder to the platform of lights above the set. The gaffer faces Russell in the direction of the elevator doors.

Off set, Cary Grant is playing on a red draped piano like a quiet obedient child who will drop whatever he's doing as soon as his mother calls.

Broughton, the assistant director, his face frowning, concentrated, calls out: "Cary, please."

Cary rises, tall as Bellamy, but a brunette football hero. He pats down his shining black hair and steps onto the set.

Bellamy and an old man, a bit player, are now sitting on the bench in the waiting room.

Silence.

The huge camera, ponderous, complicated like a machine used in a Frankenstein picture is moved forward, Hawks sitting on its platform, his vision the camera's eye.

Broughton calls out. "Here's the picture! Here we go!"

The people watching, extras, stand-ins, electricians, carpenters, are completely silent.

A voice: "Action!"

"Speed!" the baldish operator at the sound control says.

On set, Grant walks forward and simultaneously the operator of the boom or clamdigger manipulates his machine with its sound box at the end. The sound box hovers over the principals' heads, picking up their voices. Grant speaks to the old man. . .

"Cut!" Hawks orders.

His voice is like the snapping fingers of a hypnotist. Suddenly, the waxen scene changes from movie into life. The onlookers continue their suspended conversations, the stars lose their tensions.

Hawks nods at the old man, then says to Grant. "You're facing him."

A switch in his hand, the assistant director turns to me. "The switch's to give the cue to the elevator." The gaffer and best boy pull in new lights. Down in the depth of the newspaper office, the background behind the waiting room, the paper's motto is tacked on the wall:

IT MUST BE FIT TO PRINT!
IT MUST BE ACCURATE!
IS IT INTERESTING?

The two office boys in the waiting-room yawn at each other. Off set, the sound engineer, a man of about thirty-five with a big domed head, blue eyes and a little mustache, leans back in his swivel chair, the desk in front of him holding a big radio-like box. He takes off his earphones. "Everybody thinks their own department is all-important," he says to me. "Sound is just one of the teeth in the cog." He nods at the box. "This little instrument is a mixer control. Everything passes through this to another room where the sound's recorded. But the quality of the sound and the volume is regulated here. If the voice is too low we amplify it. This job is something you can't be taught to do. You develop a coordination between the ear and the hand. The most interesting thing in mixing sound is the coordination between ear and hand. Your ear will move your hand. It's like driving a car. . ."

"How'd you get into mixing sound?"

"I was doing medical research in San Francisco. We had been attempting to record the heart beat. I was hired as an electrical engineer. About the same time sound came along and I was offered a position here. . . This is one thing I'm proud of! I made the first inch of sound on film. That was with Nancy Carroll at Paramount, May 27th, 1928. Before that there had been sound effects. But the first synchronous sound film was made on that date. Prior to that, they'd dub in effects." His hands slide up and down on the desk. "As for the heart beat. . . Today, they use the cathode ray for giving actual pictures of the heart movement. But when I was in San Francisco, the idea was for doctors in the field to send the film to a centrally located heart specialist. . . In science the day of the inventor is practically gone. It's mass development. This mixer control is the result of the total industry, plus the Bell Laboratories."

He yawns. "There are more old men at thirty-five in this business than any other. Production can run twenty-seven thousand dollars for every eight hours of shooting. This show will run fourteen or fifteen thousand for every eight hours. The heat is on the crew and you get old quick from the pressure. I knew Alma Rubens. I don't blame Wally Reid. On a stage a cast can go on and keep going, because they go through their dialogue once. I've taken as high as one hundred eighty-three takes in a day although the average company would do sixty takes. But suppose you leave the movies? You get outside and the world moves so damn slow. Here it has to move. It's an unwritten standard! If a person says he can't do a thing, he's out. That's helped make technical masterpieces because no one could say: 'It can't be done.' Years ago I'd put in a hundred hours a week. But now hours are controlled. When you see a movie, every five minutes of watching is eight hours or a full day's work. Here put them on."

I put on the earphones. I hear *all* the sounds in the studio, chair scrapings, women's voices, commands, orders, harsh voices, laughs.

"All sound is what you hear," he explains. "You don't concentrate on one person like you do when talking." He puts on his earphones.

The set readies for the camera.

"Speed!" the sound man calls, manipulating the dials on the mixer as if tuning into a radio broadcast.

"Cut!" Hawks orders. He walks over to Grant on set. A makeup man scurries over to Russell, dabbing her chin with a powderpuff.

Hawks returns to his chair.

Silence.

"Roll 'em!" Broughton calls.

Grant, smiling chipperly strides down the newspaper office into the waiting-room. He pauses in front of Russell and Bellamy: "I'm going to take the two of you to lunch." The elevator pulls up, its door opening. Bellamy enters. Grant precedes Russell inside, then retreats. Smiling hypocritically he says: "After you, Hildy."

"Cut!" Hawk calls.

The assistant electrician steps on set. Grant consults with Hawks, rehearsing one line over and over again: "I'm taking you two to lunch. I'm taking you two to lunch. I'm taking you two to lunch." The head electrician shouts up to the overhead platform. "Will you add a net to this light, please." An electrician slips a net in front of a light, diffusing its glare.

Hawks speaks with Bellamy near the elevator. The best boy and the assistant director sit down side by side on the camera platform.

"Glad to do it, Hildy," Grant rehearses. "Glad to do it, Hildy."

Stand-ins, those human props who are shifted around on set before the shooting begins, technicians, extras, all are staring at the set.

Silence.

The elevator scene is retaken, but this time a politer Grant follows Russell into the elevator. "After you, Hildy," he says.

Over and over again.

Over and over, director, assistant director, gaffer, best boy, carpenters, movie stars, extras, synchronizing in the monotonous mechanical movie the public never sees, a movie of light, camera lenses, sound.

On the brown hills, the oil derricks steel-finger into the pools of fortune below.

Culver City. . . The Metro Goldwyn Mayer Studios. . . In one of the sets, I walk up a red-carpeted circular staircase, a movie prop that ends nowhere.

Below, under the roof of the skeletal building, the movie people are listening to a broadcast of the World Series, the portable radio on top of a short step-ladder. The excited announcer's voice proclaims: "No runs! No hits! And that is the first half of the eighth inning!"

Myrna Loy walks to her dressing room, a tall woman with an easy stride.

The radio announces: "Men, you can't help but win with a proposition like this. Get the World-Famous Gillette Blue Blades."

An actor reads a newspaper.

"The end of eight full innings," the broadcaster says. "Start of the next inning. You are in the United Broadcasting Booth in Yankee Stadium. Anything can happen in baseball, World Series or otherwise! Four to nothing favor of the Yankees. For the Yankees, four runs, nine hits!"

A phone rings. A technician answers it.

"A sharp single into left field!"

A colored maid of one of the stars sits down on the red-carpeted staircase. A painter hurries to the radio; a bit player to the miniature movie in front of the dining-room set.

On the tiny screen, "The Thin Man" is being played. Myrna Loy strides across the tiny screen.

"This will be a new 'Thin Man,'" the bit player explains when I question him.

The crystal chandeliers in the dining-room set blaze with light. The cameraman yawns. The gaffer and his assistants shove the lights around.

The broadcaster announces: "For the Reds no runs. . ."

They are making Nick Carter on the next set; the office of the RADEX AIRCRAFT CORPORATION. Through the office windows, the background consists of huge photographs of planes in hangars. Walter Pidgeon, the handsome Nick Carter, pipe in mouth, is talking with Sandy Roth, the assistant director, a stout aging man in a green felt, brown sweater and sport trousers.

"When I get home I hit the hay in three minutes," Pidgeon says. "I sleep right through seven hours."

Sandy Roth discusses food. "The only fish I eat is boiled fish."

"Fish is more acid than meat," Pidgeon comments. "You take rare beef and rare lamb. . ."

"Not beefsteak," Sandy Roth corrects.

"What sort of Nick Carter are you doing?" I ask Pidgeon.

He puffs on his pipe. "I haven't been on the damn thing long enough to know. I've been riding around in an airplane out on location. But I'm a modernized Nick Carter, the streamlined version. I think it would've been more fun doing the old-time Nick Carter. We may go back? Out on location, we were doing the end of the picture first. There's an open airplane sequence at the end. It seems there are guys doing espionage work in factories. Nick Carter is a G-Man supposedly. The espionage guys are not any particular nationality. They could be German or Russian. They could be anything."

His stand-in on set walks off.

"Excuse me," Pidgeon says.

"How about Nick Carter?" I ask Roth.

"I'll tell you. It'll be a series, see. It's thrills and action, see. It's an action picture you might say. Now Nick Carter as a detective. . . This is a different generation! The old Nick Carter's more phoney than these. When I was punk I enjoyed it. The new Nick Carter is more of a man than the old one. The kids of this generation wouldn't go for the Nick Carter of long ago. You wouldn't believe the old Nick Carter like this one." He conducts me from the RADEX office to a second set, a factory room. Three glistening metallic wings are mounted on wooden horses. "We photographed the Lockheed plant and showed two hundred workingmen. We're going to show them riveting right here on those wings."

"Speed!" the sound man calls.

Silence.

Walter Pidgeon as Nick Carter looks handsome and determined in the office of the RADEX CORPORATION. "I know you're having trouble with spies," he says.

On Hollywood Boulevard, there are many stores specializing in sportswear for men and women. On the sidewalks, there are always girls and women in slacks, hurrying home, taking the air, killing time. Late at night, towards the end of the last show, when the ticket booths of the movies close up, I walk into the open-air court outside the Egyptian Theatre. It is like an outside lobby, but no admission is necessary to see the sights. There is a big monkey cage with the sign: PLEASE DO NOT FEED THE MONKEYS. Not a monkey is visible. All sleep. There is a statue of John D. Rockefeller, a photographic, three-dimensional reproduction. The millionaire is shown in the act of giving a small earnest boy a dime. The legend reads: *This statue of John D. Rockefeller handing a little boy a dime was begun when word was first reported of his illness and was completed exactly on the day and about on the hour of his death.*

Some movie customer has contributed a cigar stub, dropping it into the earnest boy's outstretched palm.

There is an 1880 steam engine. A torture rack with spikes. A Wishing Well of the Stars: TOSS YOUR COIN IN THE HORSESHOE AND YOUR WISH IS SURE TO COME TRUE.

Electricity pours daylight into the well, the water shines, the bottom multi-circled with pennies, nickels, dimes. Very few coins are inside the horseshoe.

Near the entrance into the movie, there are Egyptian dog-faced gods and another framed legend:

THE AISLE OF STARS.

AISLE 3 OF THE EGYPTIAN THEATRE HAS NAME PLATES OF STARS UNDER THE SEATS.

To sit on a star's name!

U. S. Route Number 99

The Richfield gasoline stations offer: WAR MAP FREE.

A crowd of men wait outside the closed gates of the Lockheed Aircraft Company.

Kadota figs.

Concord grapes.

And ahead the Tejon Pass into the vast flatland of Kern County.

Herds of cattle.

Cotton fields.

It begins to rain. In the northern distance, hundreds of oil derricks pillar up from the land, the gray stony sky on their tops.

A small truck with Arkansas plates is also traveling north. Three women of different ages with bandanas tied around their heads, an old man, sit in the rear. A bike and a double-bladed ax are roped to the truck's sides.

HALT THIS BLACKOUT, the next billboard warns. A threatening spiked boot, labeled HAM AND EGGS DICTATOR is shown poised over the map of California.

Miles north, the buildings of a vast agricultural enterprise, and a sign: TAGUS RANCH 7000 ACRES.

Old Timers' Day

MADERA

TRUCKS LOADED WITH PLANKS move methodically up the main street of Madera, California. The trucks stop. Men jump down and set the planks up on wooden horses along the sidewalks for the parade. An old car, its cracked windshield patched with adhesive tape, parks alongside mine. A family of Mexicans, father, mother, and three smiling boys pile out for the holiday.

Today, The Madera Cleaners has converted its plate-glass window into a museum showcase. There is a spoon with a little explanatory card: *Spoon bought in 1857*. The headline of a yellowing copy of the *Santa Cruz News* states: HARDING IS LAID IN TOMB. There is an old photograph of Captain R. P. Mace: A big fat bearded man, cigar between his lips, and wearing a stovepipe hat sits on a horse. Another photograph tagged *1880* records Mace again, his cigar and frock coat and horse; and a group of six or seven bearded men, including a gaunt old man with white whiskers. In the background there is a hotel with an ancient sign: MACE'S YOSEMITE HOTEL, and a flagstaff. The waving flag on the staff has been redrawn in ink. I stare at the photograph of two other pioneers, at the seamed faces of a man and a woman: *Mr. and Mrs. Jim Freeman. Mr. Freeman Was Born in 1789 and Lived To Be One Hundred and Ten Years Old. His Father To Be 120 Years Old. Both Born in North Carolina. Relatives of H. B. Freeman 401 S. D. St., Madera, Calif.*

The new generations stride up and down the sidewalks, men in blue bandanas, Boy Scouts in uniform, brown-skinned Indian-faced Mexicans, Italian-Americans, blond lanky men from the South, their wives, their children.

I take a drink at the street fountain donated by the
W.C.T.U. in 1908. Up ahead, the Rex Theatre offers a double
feature, Charles Starrett in a *Fast-Shoot-n' Adventure:* "Western Caravan" and a Spanish film. The admission plate inside
the ticket booth is in Spanish:

Niños 10 Cents.

Adultos 25 Cents.

A mother walks down the street with her little blond barefoot girl. "I want to sit down," the girl complains.

The mother finds a place on one of the sidewalk benches
for her daughter. Wedged in between an old Mexican woman
and two small Mexican boys, the little girl happily kicks her
bare feet up and down, the sun on her pink dirty toes and
yellow hair.

The reviewing stand fills up with well-dressed people,
officials, politicians and their wives. The four-man band pick
up their instruments.

The show is on!

The eyes of the people on the sidewalk benches swerve
down towards a dozen couples, the women in the dresses and
bonnets of the early settlers, the men in bright colored shirts
and new overall pants, filing out into the gutter in front of
the reviewing stand. The band begins to play the plaintive
maple-syrup rhythms of an old-fashioned square dance. The
announcer chants the words: "I'll swing your girl and you
swing mine." The square dancers perform between the neons
and signboards of Postal Telegraph, Western Auto Supply
Company, Rexall Cut Rate Drugs.

The announcer puts on a cowboy hat, bellows into the
loud speaker: "These dances were learned at the Adult Education Group! The next dance will be a polka!"

The dancers smile, the men stepping behind the women.
Holding hands, the couples swing off to the music of forty
years ago.

The dances end. A Mexican woman with her baby bound
to a flat board like a papoose hurries up the sidewalk in front
of the marble First National Bank. Now, the plank seats are
all taken. Boys laugh, flirting with the girls. Two young seven-
teens in tailored clothes walk like movie fashion plates. The
brunette resembles Sylvia Sydney and knows it. Overalled
girls and youngsters dressed like cowgirls troop by. Leaning

against the window of Tighe's Department Store, a thin rouged woman of about twenty-eight, her two-months-old baby in her arms, alternately stares from the passers-by to her family. Her oldest son holds an older baby of about twelve months against his chest. Three other children, two little girls and a younger boy flatten their noses against the plate-glass, peering at the display of brassieres inside. "You're a good boy," the mother encourages her oldest child in a soft Southern drawl.

Two young girls, gold crosses looped around their necks, greet two boys they know. *The Beer Barrel Polka* thumps out of a saloon. Many of the women are pregnant. Mexican and Italian and Irish Californians, and migratory Southerners, they tend flocks of very young children.

A Mexican boy wearing a *Pop-Eye The Sailor* sweater ducks in and out among the closely packed adults as if he were on horseback. Behind him his brother rides: "Hi-yo Silver." The two Lone Rangers vanish down the street.

A big car drives up to the reviewing stand.

"It's him," the people say.

Governor Olsen ascends the platform, a dignified gray-haired man.

A voice in the crowd asks: "Is he for Ham and Eggs?"

"There comes the parade!"

"About time."

High school bands of young musicians led by high-stepping thin-thighed pretty band leaders march up the sunny avenue. . . The Madera County Sheriff's Posse, twenty or thirty men in brown silk shirts, lariats on their saddles, badges on their chests. The green-shirted Fresno County Sheriff's Posse. The strong-jawed heads of the California law. The gloved hands holding reins. The pistols in the holsters.

The small grower and I walk up a side-street after the parade. "Everybody works for *Associated Farmers* here," he says. "The posses, the pickers and even the small growers. What *Associated Farmers* don't own, they fix the price on. It can be cherries or raisins or anything that grows, they fix the price on it because they own the State of California. This State of California is the greatest growing state in the whole country and that's why we got these millionaires in the farming line. They own ranches with thousands of acres. If it's lettuce or hops or peaches you'll find their ranch. They own the land and the banks. Both! It's not only the sheriffs although those guys are bad enough. They got the small grower scared. Take me. I once was in *Associated Farmers* myself. The guy with a hundred acres and the guy with five thousand, we both belonged. Some of the big ranches are worth millions. . . They own everything so what can the little grower do unless we get together. That's our only hope. To get together. Talk of money. They got all the money in California."

He glances about him. "There's nothing our soil can't produce. The San Joaquin Valley and the Sacramento Valley and the Imperial, they can grow anything that can be growed. It's a land! A land like no one ever saw. It grows cotton, sugar beets, olives, oranges, grapes. I don't know what it can't grow. . . Those millionaire *Associated Farmers* don't pay the pickers nothing to live on. They only want profit. They got the sheriff's posses and the courts. . . The courts are just another posse. They'll make this State a dictatorship because that's what they want. To keep their profits and to keep the small grower down and to shoot the pickers if they don't pick for starvation wages."

Men of the Embarcadero

SAN FRANCISCO

AGAINST THE WESTERN SKY, the dome and pillars of the San Francisco City Hall is the symbol for all the governments in the land. It is a quarter to five, the sun sinking. Near the white stone library on Fulton and Hyde Streets, groups of talking men debate America's future.

"We don't need nothing from nobody." The middle-aged man in the brown felt stares from face to face, his eyes behind their glasses baffled and uncertain. He repeats defensively. "We don't need nothing from nobody. You betcha!"

The young man in the cap advances a half pace on the speaker. "What we got all those ships for?" The vein thickens on his sunburned neck. "Tell me that."

"We don't need nothing from nobody!"

An aging Irishman on the edge of the crowd asks mildly. "We got tin?"

"We don't need nothing from nobody."

"We got rubber?" the Irishman pursues.

"What have we got San Francisco and New Orleans and New York for?" the man in the cap demands. "They're for shipping."

"We don't need nothing from nobody," the middle-aged man insists.

"We got a record in unemployment!" The man in the cap smiles. "We got that, too. We got a record in that! The best record of all. Do we need that?"

"No, we don't need that," the middle-aged man answers seriously. "But you and me got nothing to do with that."

"We haven't got coffee," the Irishman argues, but no one is listening to him.

384

A lean man who has been smiling sardonically through-out the discussion now winks as if to say: Listen to that we-don't-need-nothing-from-nobody-guy.

"If this country got the best brains, if we don't need noth-ing from nobody, why've we got unemployment?" the man in the cap demands.

"I'm not the president of the United States or one of them fellers," the middle-aged man shouts. "Don't ask me that!" He pulls out his wallet from his hip pocket and displays the card under cellophane. "I've been in the Cooks and Waiters Union since 1906. That's a long time to hold down a card! Back in Wilson's time I got one hundred twenty-five a week. I got a job now."

"You're lucky," Cap declares. "But some of us are not so lucky."

"I got a wife and four kids," the middle-aged man de-clares triumphantly as if clinching the argument. "You betcha!"

The lean sardonic man taps him on the shoulder, winking at the other men. "If you lost your job you'd be unlucky?"

"Yes, I would!"

"Then it all comes down to a question of luck? Unem-ployment, war, everything?"

"Yes."

The crowd smiles.

The middle-aged man gapes at the smiling faces. "It's all luck," he shouts, angered.

The crowd laughs.

"THE BIG SLUG FEST SMOKER

Fellows, we're going to entertain the 500 delegates to the C.I.O. National Convention with a combination smoker knock-down-drag-out . . . All the best leather pushers in the unions are going to throw their dynamite in the ring . . . The card is made up of some of the outstanding fighters of the last ten years. Among them you will notice Chick Roach, Frankie Faron, Pete Myers . . . a bill of fare that will make the war on the Western Front look like a school picnic."

From the mimeograph program.

Five overhead lamps flare white light down upon the ring, the two boxers, the referee skipping and dodging away from the gloved fists. The chunky Mexican in the purple tights rushes like a bull at the black-tighted jabbing Negro. The crowd yells.

The wooden benches of the National Hall are jammed with long rows of longshoremen, warehousemen, sailors, their voices socking out! "Hit him in the beer barrel!"

"Stop the bloody battle!"

The light accentuates the strong heads of the fans. Men of the Embarcadero, they have brought with them the salt reality of the wharves, the ships, the waterfront warehouses. The C.I.O. delegates glance from the boxers to the fans as if there were a second ring here, a ring holding thousands.

Purple Tights has Black Tights against the ropes as the bell clangs the end of the round. The boxers return to their opposite corners. The seconds climb into the ring with stools and water pails. The C.I.O. delegates smile at each other and again glance at the thousands of maritime workers.

The bell clangs the next round. The seconds yank the stools out of the ring. The boxers advance towards each other in the electricity of the moment before attack and defense. Longshoremen and labor lawyers lean forward, waiting for the sudden punch, the right hook, the fist landing on chin. . .

I go downstairs into the boxers' dressing room. Under the unshaded electric bulbs, a lightweight sprawls on a wooden bench, his back against the wall, his white surgical bandaged hands on his knees. A Negro at the end of the room tenses his brown shoulders and peers up at the low ceiling. The eight or nine pairs of boxing gloves on a table seem to have been arranged by a department store clerk. Handlers and seconds exchange snatches of conversation with each other and their fighters. From the ring upstairs, the referee's voice echoes here, ominous and authoritative.

A dark-haired second who hasn't shaved in several days walks up to a blond welterweight. "I taught you too well, you donkey," he murmurs complacently.

"How do you feel?" I ask the welter. He has the craggy nose, the big chin, the deeply set eyes of an old fighter. His legs are beautifully muscled for speed like a race horse's, the iron ankles slim, the solid calves neatly powerful. He takes a swallow of water, rinsing his mouth, his head tilting back on his thick neck. "I've had a hunerd twenny-nine fights."

"What's your name?"

He looks at me as if asking: Where've you been. "Pete Myers," he says, shadow-boxing up the length of the room.

I return to my seat as Murray, the labor leader, gray-haired and gentle-faced climbs into the ring. "I'm going to referee it," he calls to the smiling crowd. "But with the under-standing that no holds are barred and kicking is permitted."

The hall booms with laughter. The regular referee be-comes a spectator, the fans nodding at each other as if com-menting silently: Look what we have here!

The bell clangs. The fighters mix. Longshoremen and sailors howl delighted instructions at the new referee. "Break it up!"

"Break it up!"

Murray retreats from the fighters, one hand in his jacket pocket, an amazed grin on his lips as if wondering how he got into this duty. Hairy-chested Sailor Jack Reilley pounds after his opponent, his gloves flicking at the muscled defense in front of him. The fighters clinch and the shouted advice redoubles.

"Break it up!"

"Break it up, Murray!"

"Don't you know how?"

Murray hurries between the fighters. They step off, eye each other, calculating their next attacks. Sailor Jack Reilley jabs his left into space, cutting down space, his glove grazing his opponent's ear. A few women delegates look away. The round ends. . .

The next pair of boxers enter the ring. The fans roar, surprised. The six-footer is equipped with a black frock coat, black trousers and a derby. His rival is a slim boy with a thin face and angular nose, his fighting outfit limited to a pair of old pants and leather riding leggings.

The referee shouts: "This is a grudge fight between Western Union Kelly Incorporated, the Deadweight Cham-pion! Weight at four hundred millions dollars in assets!" He nods at the six-footer who tips his derby at the hissing fans. "And over there in the Black and Blue Corner, Western Union Messenger at twenty-five cents an hour!"

Suddenly, the show-within-the-show atmosphere intensifies. The ring expands into the huger arena of the United States, the United States of corporations pitted against millions.

The bell!

Western Union Messenger leaps in air, knocking off the derby of Incorporated. Scowling, Incorporated bends over for the derby. Messenger tackles him. Incorporated grabs Messenger by the arms, carouseling him around and around in air. After dumping Messenger onto the canvas, Incorporated again reaches for his derby. Up from the canvas, Messenger charges. They wrestle. They topple from their footing, Messenger's leather riding leggings twined around Incorporated's black trousers. But snaking along the canvas, Incorporated stretches out his long arm, retrieves his derby.

The crowd hisses.

Incorporated manages to put the derby back on his head.

Messenger attacks again. The derby flies off and suddenly Incorporated collapses. Messenger puts the derby on like a conqueror's laurel. Oversized, it slides down on his face, but undaunted, smiling, he plants one foot down on the chest of Incorporated, singing out: "Solidarity forever as the union keeps us strong. . ."

The song becomes a curtain of voices, ringing down the puppet show. The faces sober from laughing as if seeing the wharfs, the warehouses, the ships of their daytime lives. . . The walls of the hall window into the America of waterfronts, steel mills, mines, offices, wheatlands. . . In the silence after the singing, the referee introduces a boy of twelve, a boy with the face of a choir boy. The boy steps up to the loudspeaker and begins to sing with devout piercing clarity as if he were in a church: "God bless America, land of the free . . ."

As he finishes, the audience flip coins into the ring, Western Union Messenger picking them up.

The next referee is introduced. Stocky, round of face, baldish, Quill of the Transport Workers Union smiles at the smiling faces. "I would not attempt to referee a foight," he says. "Because I'm an Irishman and we're a verry peaceful people and never foight! It is the duty of every worrkin' man and woman to support the Western Union boys!" He stands alone in the ring for a second. Two boxers climb under the ropes. Quill nods at them. "I hope you won't lose your trunks in this foight. The laborr movement has been charged with all kinds of isms and it would be hell to be charged with nudism!"

Laughter. And the clanging bell.

Pete Myers dances away from the fighter representing the Scalers Union. The ringside ropes gleam electric white, the ring a square within the hall's larger square. . .

Harry Bridges follows Mike Quill as referee into the ring. He strips off his coat. Poised, smiling, his long narrow face reflects the crowd's laughter and wisecracks. He walks as lightly as the new pair of boxers who have stepped into the ring.

"Take 'em both on, Harry!" a voice shouts.

"Limey, you look funny."

"Come on, Harry."

Bridges leans against the ropes as the boxers catfoot up to each other. The first hard jab! The second! The older boxer sidesteps, slides into a clinch.

"Come on Bridges!"

"Come on, Harry!"

"Throw that referee out!"

Bridges smiles, glides up to the boxers as if on tiptoes, separates them.

"Harry, settle that dispute!"

"Hey, Harry! Arbitrate that dispute!"

The bell clangs above the voices.

At the intermission, Henry Schmidt, president of the Longshoremen's Union enters the ring. He takes the loudspeaker between his two square hands, his full Germanic face solemn and resolute. "I've just had a subpoena from the Dies Committee. . ." He smiles. "And before I get deported I want to make one more collection speech. The Western Union boys have to eat. They have a twenty-four hour picket line. . ."

U. S. Route Number 466

From the sidewalks, Kleig lights cast their beams at the plate-glass window of the Chevrolet Company in Bakersfield as two carbon lights spotlight the sky. Crisscrossing in the night, the carbon pillars attract scores of people. Men in shirt sleeves, women in gingham dresses, they crowd the sales floor, shuffling around the 1940 Chevrolets, the sweat of summer rising from their armpits.

The next morning at dawn, I drive east from Bakersfield, California. East again towards the Atlantic, east through Tehachapi Pass into an unfenced America, the sagebrush Mohave Desert, the parched miles rolling up to the parched mountains, burned out like the gutted bases of gigantic candles. Ten and twelve and fifteen feet high, the yuccas look like symmetrical cacti; some motorist has hung his blown-out tire on one of them, the black rubber glaring against the yellow-greenish desert.

We cross the California border into the mountain distance of Nevada, the peaks locking in the vastness, the air bright and pure, into a haunting land, a land like the West of legend, the West of desert and outlaw.

Green suburban lawns! Suburban houses!

The community of Government officials at Boulder Dam is as amazing to see as the dammed-up blue waters of Lake Mead, or the steel towers marching from Boulder Dam into the sierras, those modern totem poles, man's sign of power and destiny here in the vast mountain space.

Seven hundred and fifty feet of concrete, a huge man-made wall spills up into sight . . . Boulder Dam. Channeled between concrete the green Colorado is allowed to escape from the dam's base. How tight man's fist can clench!

Two C.C.C. boys in military khaki hike up the road towards my parked car.

"You fellows help build that dam?" I ask them.

"No," the blond one, the worldlier of the two answers. Neither of them is over nineteen.

The three of us lean against the road parapet, the dam and the Colorado far below. The dark-haired boy with the thin cheeks smiles shyly. "We didn't have nothing to do with that. We build highways."

"It was better back in Arizona," the blond C.C.C. says. "We did fence work." He has never shaved, the down girlish on his cheeks. But his lips clamp together firmly like a grown man's.

"We're going back home in December," the dark-haired C.C.C. says.

"Where is your home?"

"We're from Ohio. We signed up for six months."

The blond boy shrugs. "Thirty a month's what we get. Some sign up for another six months, but not me." He pulls out his sack of tobacco and cigarette papers, rolling himself a smoke. "We work five days and when Saturday and Sunday comes we sit around and do nothing. We was in Las Vegas. That's a wide open town. It's got open gambling. And all kinds of houses," he adds. "All kinds of houses in Las Vegas."

"Wish I was back in Ohio," the dark-haired C.C.C. says.

"You're not signing up again?"

They both smile as if to say: Not in ten years.

"So long, fellows."

"So long."

The two boys from Ohio hike up the Nevada highway. A mile or two downhill, I park my car on top of the dam itself. Other men and women have parked their cars here to stare down at the Colorado, basined between three mountains. Two of the mountains are natural, the third is Boulder Dam. Man has commemorated his triumph on a slab of marble.

IT IS FITTING THAT THE FLAG OF OUR COUNTRY
SHOULD FLY HERE IN HONOR OF THOSE MEN, WHO
INSPIRED BY A VISION OF LONELY LANDS MADE FRUITFUL,
CONCEIVED THIS GREAT WORK AND OF THOSE OTHERS WHOSE
GENIUS AND LABOR MADE THAT VISION A REALITY.

The bronze tablet enumerates the power allottees:

THE STATE OF ARIZONA
THE STATE OF NEVADA
THE METROPOLITAN WATER DISTRICT OF SOUTHERN CALIFORNIA
THE CITY OF LOS ANGELES
THE CITY OF BURBANK
THE CITY OF GLENDALE
THE CITY OF PASADENA
SOUTHERN CALIFORNIA EDISON COMPANY
THE SOUTHERN SIERRA POWER COMPANY
LOS ANGELES GAS AND ELECTRICITY

Man-made, Boulder Dam has been conceived in man's noble image. . .

Across the Colorado River into Arizona, sagebrush and mountains, a land without men horizoning into an Arizona of grazing lands. Towards nightfall, the clustering lights of the small town ahead are warmly human as a bonfire.

Peach Springs. . . Population fifty, trading center for the Hualapai Indians, three gas stations, three rows of tourist cabins.

A '27 or '28 Studebaker with a flat tire inches into the gas station where I've pulled in. A broad-faced Indian woman steps out of the Studebaker followed by a boy of ten. They hurry off to the general store. The Indian driver borrows a car jack from the station attendant. "My jack wouldn't work," he explains, unscrewing the tire bolts. "I'll have to buy a new tube."

Morning. . .

Arizona in the early light is the American wilderness before the white man even if the Indian reservations are fenced off with barbed wire. And again the desert plains, the table-topped mesas in the distance, the mile-separated towns, Williams, Bellemont, Flagstaff, Holbrook, Navajo . . . into New Mexico. Once, the cliff dwellers lived here among the red, purplish cliffs, the strata of stone separated, distinct, as if put together by stonesmiths. Tombs from the past before Columbus, before the Indians, the mesas seem like the settlements of forgotten giants.

On the Continental Divide, the billboard advertises:

MYRNA LOY AND TYRONE POWER: 'THE RAINS CAME'

Another night at Cubero, New Mexico.
Another morning. . .

In the bright sun, sixty or seventy men are working on the railroad near New Laguna, the sun glinting on their picks and shovels, sons of the men who steel-tracked the continent.

Strings of red peppers hang on the walls of the creamy, liver-colored adobes. Like larger replicas of the sand houses children build on a beach, the adobes rise on the old Spanish land.

The Indians

ISLETA, NEW MEXICO

THE HIGHWAYS OF THE TWENTIETH CENTURY do not reach into the Indian pueblo, Isleta. I park my car on an unpaved dusty street, stranding it on the time shore of a forgotten century. The buttressed Church of St. Augustine, more fort than church, dominates the central plaza, the white-plastered adobe walls appearing impregnable to arrow or rifle bullet, four crosses piercing the blue sky.

A pool of water from the last rain fills a hollow in the plaza. A collarless dog (it is impossible to imagine dogs with collars and licenses in Isleta) trots into the shade. An Indian in an old brown hat drives a wagon up one of the side-streets. Everywhere, the strings of red peppers on the adobe walls spice the serene colors of sky and home.

We enter the Indian silversmith's adobe. He gets up from his workbench, a young man of about twenty-six with jet black hair and soft brown eyes. He shows my wife a tray of silver bracelets. "This design is running water. It is a simple design. A few wavy lines." He digs his hand into a bag and picks up a handful of silver coins. "I melt these Mexican *pesos* into a bar. Then I hammer the bracelets out of the bar. It's all hammering and filework. And the tourists come and buy." He smiles, the softness of his eyes never varying. "For the tourists we are making Egyptian designs. The tourists. . . I was going on a train to Los Angeles and I met a man who brought back his boy to see me. 'There's an Indian,' the man said to the boy. He was a little boy of five or six. He looked at me and then he said to his father. 'That's no Indian. He hasn't any feathers in his hair.'"

The silversmith smiles. "This bracelet has an Egyptian

design I copied from a book. But I like the designs that are simple like this Indian design of clouds and raindrops. The clouds are the curved lines, the raindrops the little circles."

Again, we cross the plaza of the Spanish dons to N. L. Kemmerer's General Store. The old man behind the counter hellos us in a deep throaty voice. He is dressed in both Indian and American fashion, a red Indian undershirt under his Indian blouse. But his pants are factory-made. His blackish-gray long hair, held in place behind his head by a tightly wrapped red cloth is in the old custom. Fringes of loose hair hang down on both sides of his light brown face. Behind him, the shelves hold bolts of calico and gingham. Cigarettes, breads, canned goods, the merchandise of any general store, fill the compartments.

"Do you own this store?" I ask him.

"Mr. Kemmerer owns the store. He's a white man. I work for him."

"How old's the Mission Church?"

"Over three hundred and thirty-five years. Our ancestors live here all the time," he says solemnly in a hoarse voice. "We govern ourself until now. The first of January we elect a Governor and twelve member in council to transact our community affair. Then, the Government lend us eight hundred and sixty-eight cattle. They come in with name of the community. In three years we supposed to pay back to the Government eight hundred and sixty-eight cattle. We, to keep the calves. We already paid it and the remainder is more than six hundred. But we haven't got it. Instead, we lose our community right. The Government and John Collier appoint three trustees. The trustees is given the right to hold the cattle for twenty-one years. The Government has taken the right away from the community. . ."

"Who's John Collier?"

"Commissioner of Indian Affairs. We always own our land. We support ourself from renting out our grazing land. Now John Collier stop us. Instead, the Government give us eight hundred and sixty-eight cattle. The community pay it back. The community want to do what we want with the remainder. But John Collier appoints three trustees to hold the cattle for twenty-one years." He speaks sorrowfully.

A slender middle-aged Indian enters the store to buy a loaf of bread. But he doesn't go, listening in silence. Still another Indian comes in, an ancient with one blind eye. A wasp flies above his head.

"We've had no benefit from it. We got the eight hundred and sixty-eight cattle in 1935. The trustees can sell the steers. We don't know? And we don't get nothing. They'll be rich and we'll be biting our fingers. I had a talk with Danny Chavez, the Senator. Danny says write to John Collier. Here we have a thousand Indians. The blind old women we used to help. Now, we cannot help them. We never have been treated that way. We always self-supporting." The two Indians listen, voiceless. "The treaty between the Government of United States and Mexico when Mexico was defeated said we govern ourself. President Lincoln gave each pueblo a cane. So each community has its own rule, with no rule by white man."

The calendar on the wall has for illustration a Zane Grey Indian, a brown-skinned warrior stripped to the waist, rifle in his hands. The placard over the cigarette counter is a colored photograph of a Hollywood star: MADELEINE CARROLL SAYS: 'MY THROAT FOUND A FRIEND IN A LIGHT SMOKE' LUCKIES!

"It's a community affair. The community want the cattle turned into the hands of the Governor. Every year the cattle breedin'. The trustees'll be rich. We used to sell grazing permits to outsiders. Now they're taking away our rights to grazing lands. Our land twenty miles east from village and twenty miles west, three miles north and south. And they take the right away from the community. That's John Collier's idea. White man been here since Christofo Columbus, but always we govern ourself until now. President Lincoln give each pueblo a cane to govern themself." His brown hand slaps down the wasp, crushes it against the counter. "Poor Navajo. John Collier make them reduce stock. Poor Navajos crying. Can't support their family. But we always govern ourself. We elect a Governor and council to transact our community affair. We don't want trustees to govern our community."

When we return to our car, I know that it is parked in the twentieth century.

U. S. Route Number 66

The great prairies.

The paint colts, brown-skinned and splashed with white, graze near their mothers. Every glance wings across ten miles.

A land of steer and horse.

The Lone Star flag of Texas waves in the wind. The town of Vega.

Tired, we sit down to a roast beef supper in one of the two cafés.

Next to me at the counter, an old man of seventy is talking to the proprietor's wife. "Ah came from the State of Ar-kansas back in 1906. Ah came through Oklahoma. Wished I'd stayed there."

A truck driver has his face lowered in the Amarillo newspaper. The café is small, the space crowded as if lumber were expensive.

Morning again. And across the Texan Panhandle into Oklahoma.

Texola.

Sayre.

Elk City.

Clinton. Reddish dust whirls off the dried-up bed of the Canadian River.

El Reno. I walk into a small ice-cream store for a soda. The gray-haired Greek proprietor serves me. "Where you going?" he asks.

"Oklahoma City."

"People get money and drive to Oklahoma City for good time. Take one hour. Spend money and come back here." He shrugs, resigned. "I been here since 1921 and all the time, they say: 'Next year, good time. Next year, good time.' Next year never come. People drive to Oklahoma City. Take one hour," he concludes sadly. "A little boy come here now. He makes money. But he got no money for ice cream."

I find the boy, a youngster of six, one hand holding a stack of paper strips. Intently, he passes the strips, one by one, from his full hand to the empty one.

"What're you doing?"

"I'm making money," he answers.

"How do you do that?"

"One'll be ten or ten cents. One side's clean and other's marked up. We put the number on the clean side."

"Is it real money?"

"It's just playing like this. If we had real money we wouldn't have it here. It'd be spent."

A woman's voice shrills out. "Where are you?"

The boy examines his paper strips. "That's my mother."

A thin little woman comes out into the street. Her small nose curves in her dark face. She looks Italian or Jewish. "Why don't you come up when I call you?"

"He's making money," I say.

The little woman smiles. "He likes that game better than football."

"I'm going to Oklahoma City. Are you from this state?" I ask her.

Her brown eyes stare at me. "My grandmother was a little girl of eight years old when she made that trek here."

"What trek?"

"The trail of tears." Her voice quivers with sudden emotion. "That's when the Cherokees were moved from the State of Georgia. . . I'm part Cherokee. They were driven out under Jackson. There was much tears and they didn't take time to bury their dead. Jackson was a Whig and that's why so many of the Cherokees are Republicans. Talk of, 'Give the Indian this.' And, 'Give the Indian that!'" she cries out defiantly. "We had to sue 'em and sue 'em and sue 'em to git the emigrant money. They lived in Georgia and the Government paid them some of their money to move into the new country. There's still millions of dollars in the courts and our grandchildren won't get it. Will Rogers was a Cherokee. . . The Cherokees are a disbanded race. I got sisters and cousins in Texas and down in Mexico. We'll never git what's rightly ours. Over in the Oklahoma Historical Society, they have it the way *they* put it down on paper! During the last war I said the United States needed a good whipping the way they've done! They took the land away from the Pawnees and the plains Indians and said it belongs to us. They just took that land away from the Pawnees to git what was back there in Georgia. The damned outfit!"

Quietly, her son sorts his paper strips.

THE SOUTHERN LAND

Folk of the Middle Continent

OKLAHOMA CITY

" 'Unless the drouth finally dries up Lake Overholser, Oklahoma City will continue as a stopping place until late November for migratory birds which are changing their winter residence from the north to the south,' M. H. Boone, game management agent with the United States biological survey, said Friday. 'The latest feathered visitors are white pelicans and Franklin's gulls. A large flock of the pelicans have been here about a week. Other birds now traveling through are snow and blue geese, plover and many varieties of shore birds. The heavy migration is just starting,' he said."

From an Oklahoma newspaper item.

"WE'LL SIT IN MY CAR AND TALK," the businessman says to me. His two-year-old car is parked on Grand Avenue near the Commerce Exchange Building. He glances at the city's sidewalk meter. "Five cents every hour for parkin'." He smiles, his hands on the wheel. "This state's the okie state. Mr. Steinbeck has written about us. He did a fine job although I wouldn't let most of my friends hear me say it. But Mr. Steinbeck didn't write about our migratory businessmen. They didn't fit into his story. . . Couple weeks ago, one hundred of the state's leadin' businessmen migrated all over the South looking for business opportunity. Virgil Browne, Buttram, the oilman, and Stuart of *Mid-Continent Life* were the three leadin' Oklahoma City businessmen who migrated. They went hoping to find some bacon they could bring back to home. We li'l businessmen wished them the best of luck. But when they come back they said they still liked Oklahoma's opportunity." He nods seriously. "Lord knows we're a poor state. The farmer's poor. The workingman's poor. The li'l businessman's poor. And these

403

migratin' businessmen. . . They like Oklahoma's opportunity. Some of us li'l businessmen wondered what opportunity they were talking about. They went to Atlanta and
to Birmingham and to New Orleans and to High Point.
Wherever there was a factory or mill, they went there. They
went to Virginia and found out that the road to success was
a cool-headed Government. Somewhere else they found out
that new industry needs nursing along. They went to the du
Pont chemical plant in Richmond, Virginia. I hear that plant
cost millions. They looked over chemistry pretty close. They
were in Laurel, Mississippi, where they make starch from
sweet pertaters."

He laughs, perplexed. "We can grow sweet pertaters
right here in Oklahoma. That sounds a li'l more sensible
than some of the other cities our leadin' businessmen took
a close look at. I wonder myself why they went to Birmingham? If we could get the United States Steel Corporation
interested we could be starting some steel mills in Oklahoma.
But we'd have to find the ore. That'd be kind of impossible.
The only industry we can start is one that fits. I guess they
know that though and just wanted to take a close look at
Birmingham. They found that the tex-tile manufacturers
were movin' into the Carolinas from up North. There was
local capital in the Carolinas helping finance these northern
manufacturers. The labor was cheaper than up North. Now,
we've got cotton here in Oklahoma and we've got power,"
he continues hopefully as if maybe some day the textile industry might move southwest. "We've got natural gas and
oil. We got cheap labor. The community camps here are
full of men and women who wouldn't turn down a mill
job. We got oil and wheat and cotton. . . I don't know
how we're goin' to climb from that?" He smiles wistfully.
"It must've been a nice trip though. I wished that I was big
enough to go along."

I shake hands with him, cross the sidewalk to the Commerce Exchange Building. The elevator whizzes me up to
the Chamber of Commerce on the ninth floor.

"I want to speak to somebody about Oklahoma City's
business."

The girl at the information desk thinks a minute. "Second office to the right. You want Mr. Jim Hull."

Mr. Hull pulls out a chair for me in his office. A small man with grayish blond hair parted in the center, all his movements are swift and nervous. The ash tray on his littered desk holds a small hill of cigarette butts. He smiles with energetic politeness.

"I would like to know something about oil?"

"The Oklahoma City oil field is the second largest in the world!" he rattles off as if reading from one of his circulars. "It is also one of the great gas fields in the world. It's a wet gas from which we extract gasoline before the gas is put in the mains. That natural gas furnishes a very cheap fuel. And we're relying on that for industrial development."

On the wall behind his desk, two photographs of airplanes hang side by side: A tri-motored monoplane above a city is captioned: SKY CHIEF *TWA* LUXURY SKYLINER. A second monoplane soars among clouds: FLY *TWA* EVER CHANGING SKYSCRAPES ALOFT.

"Another thing out here in the fields . . . The Phillips Petroleum Company have here a plant for making natural gasoline out of the gas with an octane rating over 100, the highest octane rating in the world, used exclusively for aviation!" He nods at the Domestic Air Mail Service map of the United States, the air routes in red . . . Oklahoma City to Tulsa to St. Louis to Indianapolis to Dayton to Pittsburgh to Philadelphia. "If it's location near the center of the United States," he cries enthusiastically, "and the best climatic conditions for flying . . . open winters, little fog! And the fact that we're far in from both coast lines in case of attack. . ."

He offers me a cigarette, jabs one between his own lips. "Here's another hope we have for industrial development. The petroleum refineries are becoming obsolete throughout the country. There is a tendency to move. The western half of this state is the great potential oil field! And because Oklahoma City is adjacent to the larger undeveloped areas of the state, which will be oil producing, that gives us a good chance at the refineries of the future." He leans across the desk, eager and communicative as if shouting: Build Oklahoma City! Build Oklahoma City! "We're working now to get a rock wool plant here. Rock wool is an insulating material in general use over the country. It's made from limestone. Oklahoma University has developed a process to use natural gas instead of coke in the manufacture of rock wool. Most of it comes from Indiana and back East. We have a world of local capital! We have one hundred and twenty-five millions in banking reserves in the city! Only twenty-two per cent of that is out in loans of all types. Fifty-one per cent is liquid. We've a lot of capital which either isn't working or is producing very low returns. People here who've made money in oil are used to investing money in business based on the ground. Our people here are not speculative-minded. They think of livestock or oil development. They like to see it come out of the ground! Our function over here at the Chamber, our only stock in trade is the minds of people! And whether we can direct their thinking."

"Oil is the most important industry?"

"Oklahoma ranks third among all states in production of oil. 174,000,000 barrels plus. The pipe lines from this area here radiate to the refineries at Enid, Ponca City, Tulsa, Bartlesville, Okmulgee." He smiles. "Okmulgee. We have a lot of Indian names in this state. From those points the pipe lines go to the large refineries at Gary and Whiting, Indiana. In that lies a story. That doggone Illinois oil field lies in between us and the East."

I glance at the Domestic Air Mail Service Map with its air routes in red.

"We produced 228 million barrels of oil in 1937. In 1938, 174 million. The decline is due to competition and the fact that most of our new fields will be deep fields costing lots of money to drill. Kansas, Texas and Illinois have shallower fields. The large corporations look on Oklahoma as a reserve after they've tapped the shallow areas. But we'll maintain our high position among the states! A state or two will slip ahead of us," he admits regretfully. "Louisiana will pick up on us due to their shallow drilling areas. You can see the handwriting on the wall." He frowns, puffs deeply on his cigarette. "Tulsa was built almost entirely on oil. Then it began to slide down to Oklahoma City and then Texas began to slip in, Houston particularly. Firms are leaving part of their offices in Tulsa and moving to these other places. We haven't gone hog wild here!" He smiles, optimistic, but a little worried as he contemplates the future underneath Oklahoma City.

Ivy grows on the walls of the Governor's mansion in Oklahoma City. And oil derricks rise in the Governor's yard. Oil derricks face the six noble pillars of the State's Capitol. The pillars are Grecian, the oil derricks, U. S. A. The statue of a cowboy on a rearing horse by *Constance Whitney Warren, Sculptress of Paris, France and New York* faces the State Buildings, and the derricks on the plain. In the distance, in the heart of Oklahoma City, the Ramsey Tower, built by oil, is a derrick become a skyscraper, a monument like the cowboy.

Ramsey Tower is on North Robinson Avenue in the Oklahoma City of movies, restaurants and money-in-the bank business. But ten blocks south on Robinson Avenue, the eating joints offer: MEALS 15c, the rooming houses: ROOMS 25c–50c. The stores attract the man with a hole in his pocket: MONEY FOR SMALL TOOLS. And further south, Robinson puts on four wheels and becomes one automobile supply store, catering to the man with the jaloppy.

NEAL SALVAGE

WE RENT TRAILERS

BUICK CAR $25.

Tire tubes hang on wooden elbows on both sides of South Robinson Avenue. Hub caps from Fords, Plymouths, Chryslers, shine in bright chromium rows outside the accessory stores. The sidewalks are unpaved as if no one ever walked much here, good enough sidewalks for a man who leaves his wheel only because he has to fix his car or buy a tire.

A. C. BROWN AUTO REPAIRS. The plate glass, lettered in red and white, is between two driveways, the shed-like structure a one-story corrugated tin building. Inside, there is no floor of stone or cement. The brown earth is packed hard like a country blacksmith's. A. C. Brown, a wiry man of about forty with sharply defined cheekbones and blue eyes walks over to me, a pair of black acetylene glasses pushed up on his forehead.

"Who are your customers"? I ask him. "That is if you don't mind telling me. . ."

"I don't mind. The people that comes down here . . . there's a majority and a minority," he says in the low-pitched flat voice of middle America. "The majority are the extreme poor ones. They tell me people have less money every day. Wages're being cut, less people working. They come here from all sections of the country. You take myself. I come from Kansas and Nebraska. I been in business about six years and the last two years, business been gittin' worse and worse. Practically all the second-hand tires've been picked up." His eyes are deeply blue in the pallor of his expressionless face. Only his eyes glow with an intense effort to communicate what he's seen. "The people that comes down here are an American class of people, losin' their homes and possessions. It's very hard for them to buy a car even as low as twenty-five dollars. Some of 'em hike or buy a cheap Model T. That's all they have left. A lot of 'em come from Kansas, Nebrasky, Arkansas, Missouri, and quite a number from Texas. They hear about Oklahoma City. This is a cheap city to live in and it don't get too cold here. But when they get here, their li'l sum of money's spent. A lot of 'em end in Community Camp. That's their final graveyard."

Kansas, Nebraska, Arkansas, Missouri, the core of the American continent; freezing Kansas, the geographical center of the forty-eight states . . . And Oklahoma just to the south of Kansas. Highway 62 into Oklahoma City. Highway 66 into Oklahoma City. Highway 77 into Oklahoma City. Highway 270 into Oklahoma City. Highway 277 into Oklahoma City.

"A lot of the people hikes out. But if they get where they want to go . . . that's just a chance. Some gets there and some don't. What I'm in, is garage and weldin'. The people're not gettin' work and that's squashin' the middle businessman out of existence. They buy an old jaloppy. They'll run from five to fifteen dollars. A Ford or a Chevvy'll

run from thirty to fifty . . . I'd hate like hell to start out
myself in one of 'em. They start all right, but how far
do they go?" His voice never rises, flat as the plains. "But
you'll find in each family, one who'll know how to keep the
motor goin'. Some one in the family's skilled. Generally,
they'll do their own work if they can. There was a car,
an old Buick come in here, a father and a mother and six
children from Arkansas. They lost their home. It was a
li'l eighty-acre farm. They said they only got three hundred
out of eighty acres. We tightened the rods and made
brake adjustments and weldin' on the fenders. The job
come to five dollars. We fixed it up the best we could and
they only had three dollars. Some people can't pay nothing
and give a wheel for payment . . . All the time we was
weldin' the Buick they hung around. They had their personal belongings in the car. It was a '25 or '26 Buick. They
said they were going to try to get work here. I don't know
what happened to them. I judge the father was about fifty-
three or fifty-four. A family'll head west for Californy until
they find work. . . There was a man and a woman and a
girl, eight years old. They had an Oldsmobile. They
traded their chickens for five gallons of gas. He harvested in
Nebraska. We fixed his car. He said he wanted work. He
ast here about work. He had his beddin' and dishes in the
back and the three of 'em were sittin' in front."

The sign on the wall reads: IT'S HELL TO BE A CRIPPLE.
BE CAREFULL.

"I used to farm. . . My brothers're having a hell of a
struggle."

Up and down on South Robinson Avenue, the cars, the
cars, the cars, the new cars, the old cars, the old cars, the
old cars, the old cars. . .

Across the traffic, I enter Mercer's tire shop. Mercer,
himself, a young man in overalls and cap, glances up from
the tire he is repairing, strips of raw black rubber in his
hands. Deftly, he pastes a strip down upon the patched-up
hole.

"How many tires have you got?"

"I have about six hundred or eight hundred tars," he
answers. "Every time a fillin' station moves or goes bankrupt, I buy a lot of tars. Do you want one?"

"No. I just want to talk about tires."

He smiles, pastes in a second rubber strip. "We got two hundred and fifty second-hand tar shops for vulcanizin' and retreadin' here. I handle a cheap grade. I sell for seventy-five cents to a dollar. I sell my share." His tiny shop is one wheel of tires, tires with jagged cuts, tires with patches, tires with boots, old tires, worn tires. In the yard to the rear of the store, hundreds of tires fill up the wooden tireholders.

"Who do you sell to?"

"I have a lot of transits goin' to Arizony, New Mexico and California. I got an uncle in Madera right now. There's five of 'em and they're pickin' grapes and cotton. My aunt, she's sick. The others are all right." He works rapidly. "I had one transit back from Arizony. He was from Oklahoma. He was gittin' sixty-five cents a hundred pounds pickin' cotton, bumblebee cotton. That's hard to pick. A dollar and a half was all he could pick in a day. I fixed his tube for a quarter and sold him a tar for fifty cents. He had about fifteen, twenty dollars. Just enough to live on two weeks or a month."

"You always live here?"

"I was born in Oklahoma and went to Virginia. But I've lived here ever since '21 before the flood. I quit school when I was in the tenth grade. When I was eighteen I got married. I'm married four years and I've been in this business about six. To make money a feller has to work twelve, fourteen hours a day. Most of 'em in the tar business make a poor livin'." He slaps the tire he is repairing. "This tar cost me two bits and I'll sell it for a dollar. I don't guarantee these. These transits . . . nine-tenths of 'em want a tar for a dollar, to two and a half, and a new tread." He begins to repair another torn tire. "I'd get twice as much out of a tar five years ago than I could get now. In the last year, to year and a half, old tars've gone up two hundred per cent. Times is gittin' harder. I'm buyin' tars at two bits a piece but two years from now, I'll pay six bits. People're holdin' on to their tars. Good tars with a small hole is seldom to be found. Now they'll keep it and stick a boot in. Not all my customers is transits. I got customers who work for the companies here in town. The man with a good income, fifteen to twenty-five a week job, he'll pay two, three dollars for a tar and not cry."

He stares up at me. "As for transits, there's two kinds. The people who git a paid vacation and those flat broke. There's a transit who foller the Government jobs, the Boulder Dam. There's transits who go to New Mexico and Arizony to pick cotton. There's the young fellers who go out to Californy and come back broke in thirty days to six months. I had a brother who went out to Bakersfield, drivin' an oil field truck. He come back in six months. I stay here and watch them transits. I pay ten dollars a month rent. And I'm not makin' a poor livin' neither." He straightens his back, smiles. "I don't mind workin' twelve to fourteen hours a day."

Outside on South Robinson Avenue, I look straight north to Ramsey Tower, the First National skyscraper alongside. Twinned, they stand in the blue sky as if standing in another city, in another time.

I walk north past the tire shops, garages, secondhand clothing stores, eating joints, hotels (at night the hotels are most enterprising; the drowsy Negroes who sit halfway up the first flight of stairs snap wide awake if a possible customer pauses; the prostitutes upstairs charge South Robinson Avenue prices) all the avenue now in flowing sunshine. . . On foot and in their cars, the empty-pocketed American people keep moving. Always, they keep moving, moving, moving, moving.

South Robinson is their street. And so is California Street. And Reno Street. Reno is not only another east-west street in Oklahoma City but the crossroads of a continent. Look North. There . . . the skyscrapers of this nation. Look South. There . . . the dispossessed of this nation. Look East. Where Reno ends, the oil fields begin. Look West. Where the paved road becomes red earth the community camps begin.

Between the oil fields and the community camps, Reno is a series of secondhand furniture stores. In each, a thousand homes once situated over a hundred thousand acres, are now shelved and offered for sale.

Ab's Any Thing Store. We Buy Furniture, Tools, Small Machines and Any Thing. The sidewalk in front of Ab's is a jungle of chairs, tables, electric heaters, lamp stands. "How'd you get into this business?" I ask the proprietor. He is a big powerful man, an old felt without a hatband squashed down on top of his head as if he had gotten dressed in the dark. His tieless shirt, woolen vest, and wrinkled cotton pants look as if they had formerly belonged to three different people. He rubs his unshaven chin, peers at me with blue eyes. "I was in the restaurant business in east Tennessee. Business was good. Before that I was in the log camps. . . I was on the W.P.A. I started this place with eight dollars." He speaks quickly, his voice high-pitched, smiling as he contemplates his different lives.

I follow him from the sidewalk inside the store. He spits tobacco juice onto the dirt floor. "I got into this business in 1934. It was that or starve. I was cut off the W.P.A. I was makin' twelve dollars a week. . . I bought a bunch of tools. Just buy and sell. I make calls out to the country. But most of the stuff comes from the backyards and alleys. In the fall, the farmers'll go broke and sell their bedclothes and buy them back in the spring. It's just buy and sell. The bigger part of it comes from feller's goin' from this town to another. Early in the fall, they sell and go to the cotton patch. They come back late in the fall. Most of 'em live in the different squatters' camps over in Elm Grove and Walnut Grove here in town."

"This city's got plenty of secondhand stores."

"Yay, man. People who can't get a job and got an ole car, they go junkin'. One feller awhile back heared of better in Texas but in a month and a half he comes back. This city's a good place for this line of business." He spits again. "I got to live off the man who's got less'n I got. I'll admit it. Some won't. That's the game. But I got seven in the family." He shrugs his thick shoulders, nods at an old stove in a line of old stoves. "A feller comes in here and I'll sell him that stove for a dollar profit. It's a profiteerin' system. The fellers out in the camps have no money to rent a house. Have no tent, lots of times. I did that onct. I been up in the highest and I been in the lowest. . . That

Saturday I had sixty cents and seven in the family. I've worked hard. I dug coal about eight years. I was in timber eight years. And every bit of it was work. I never let no man do more work'n me. I'd go back minin' in the night. I'd make money in the day and money in the night. My ambition was to do more, to git more."

He towers among his possessions, the shelves crowded with cans and rope, a cardboard box of glass bottles behind him. In the rear, the sun cracks through a drawn shade upon an old bike, a broken farm table, the coils of old springs. Above his head, a scrawled sign reads: No DRUNKS ALLOWED: THIS MEANS YOU.

I go out on the sidewalk. A middle-aged woman glances at me. She wears a red candy-box ribbon tied around her reddish blonde hair. "Ab's wife?" I guess.

She nods, her eyes blue and mild behind her glasses.

"You ever churn butter in one of those?" I point to a table with a half dozen old-fashioned butter churns.

She smiles. "Many a pound of butter I made churning those things."

"Ab told me of how hard things have been."

She draws herself erect. "I worked out in homes, me and my daughter. I did first one thing and another. There's seven in the family. . . We kept on puttin' our li'l mite together. Sold our clothes and bedclothes. Eat out of pots and pans 'till we got started. Ab's big and strong. And he used to work day and night but just the same we were burnt out in Tennessee. But we kept workin', all of us together. Every Sunday morning, the two boys'd go up the alleys to find whiskey bottles and bring it back to help in the business. It looks like it's gonna get worse. Lots of folk got burnt out. Lots of 'em went West and didn't find work. And they don't come back to find anything."

She picks up a big black lamp from a shelf inside the store. "We have the first Ford lamp. It burns coal oil light. That was the first light ever used on a Ford. See them crutches over there? People been crippled and sell their crutches. And then people gits crippled and buys 'em." The crutches hang from a hook. "We got a wooden leg and two or three pairs of false teeth in the dresser drawer."

She smiles at a glass butter churn on a green wooden table, the glass gleaming modern and spotless. "I wouldn't buy no store butter. I put my milk in and churn it."

She stares at me earnestly. "I have five brothers and they're farmin'. The Government's helpin' 'em. They're not afraid of work. . . And everyone could play the banjo except me." She smiles and then forgets to smile. "It's gonna get worse. I think the time'll be wound up pretty soon. . . We'll have a few years of peace and then it'll wax worse. . . Christ'll set up a new earth. The whole earth'll be melted down. God's going to destroy the earth. Fire'll come out of the heaven and burn it up. The righteous'll come back and dwell here in their cottages after it has been purified."

"KERNS HOTEL, 621 N. Bdway. Rent room, get one free; rent room wk., get wk. free. Get located for winter, rates $3 wk. up."
Newspaper advertisement.

The Grand Boulevard Highway flashes between the Oklahoma National Stockyards and the May Camp. On one side behind a high wire fence . . . the red brick Armour buildings, the white-faced Herefords.

On the other side there is no fence. A wagon, mounted on four automobile tires and pulled by an old horse, turns off the highway into the May Camp. The tire wheels jounce on the rutted dirt road down into the hollow. Trailers, tents and corrugated tin shacks, bed sheets made of flour sacks drying on the lines . . . the May Camp.

Two women cross the highway from the stockyards, each carrying a pail of rich white milk. Cars race up and down, speedometers measuring off speed exactly.

Near me, a man in torn overalls also stares at the women and their milk pails.

"Where do they get the milk?" I ask him.

"Before they butcher the cows, they milk 'em."

"You working?"

He shakes his head *no*. "I was beatin' up toward North Dakota tryin' to get a job in the wheat fields. I been goin' north every summer for the last twelve years. Most always use the freights goin' up. It's a cheap way to ride." Slowly, he spins his yarn, his eyes almost dreamy. "I was ridin' the Santa Fe and they saw me. They waited to git up speed and then they throwed us off. None of us had Pullman tickets. Knee's never been the same since. It's a funny thing but I can tell the weather by the knee just like those high-priced weather men. There ain't much to tell about follerin' the harvest. There's just as much work as there ever was but the combines're doin' it all. I'd sooner talk about my knee. Knee don't have to eat none like a man has to eat. Knee don't complain none. Fact, it's doin' a useful job tellin' me the weather."

"You ever milk those cows?"

"I'm a single man. We let the females git that milk. I got no kids to support. Just my knee." He talks like a man asleep, his humor the skeleton humor of a man half-alive. In this camp on the edge of the Grand Boulevard Highway, across the way from a thousand steaks on the hoof, his humor doesn't seem unnatural.

At the western end of Reno Street, beyond the secondhand furniture stores, beyond the W.P.A.-built park with its sign: FOR COLORED PEOPLE ONLY, beyond the Lone Star Bottle yard, Elm Grove looks like a prosperous town after the May Camp. There are no sidewalks here either but the unpaved sandy streets have few axle-breaking holes. The wooden homes are fenced off with the wired ends of fruit boxes. There are picket fences. There are fences made with old hot water boilers. Half buried in the earth, the boilers look as if they could keep out bullets. A blonde woman of twenty-one or twenty-two pulls a go-cart with a little boy seated in it. Her high-heeled shoes are shiny black, her legs bare, both of her ankles scratched. A white goat is tied to a tree.

On the next street, five men in overalls are working together inside a fenced yard. The sun spills through the green leaves, the shade dappling. Standing on a truck painted: JIM ROSE YARDWORK AND HAULING, two of the men toss down crooked branches, the other men relaying the kindling onto a big bonfire. Flame leaps golden, sun-colored. The flames leap higher as the laughing gossiping men feed the fire.

Not far from me, a man and a boy are also watching. The man wears blue and white striped overalls. A metal chain and suspended blue stone heart is attached to his overall shoulder strap. His high cheek-boned face is shaded by a worn plains hat.

"What are they doing in the yard?" I asked him.

"They're haulin' in saw wood and fixin' it up to sell. Get it out about six mile from here. They're clearin' the land and they git all the wood. They're burnin' up the small stuff. They'll git a dollar or a dollar and a half a rick."

The boy stares at my clothes, my shoes. He is a good-looking boy of about eleven, his soft-chinned face seeming even more childish under his black felt. The felt is too large for him. His father must have got it cheap. Father and son both have deeply set blue eyes.

"How many ricks in a cord?"

"Three rick to make a cord," the man answers.

When I turn towards the boy, he looks away. His toes show through his ragged sneakers. A tin badge shines on his chest: LIEUTENANT

217

JUNIOR POLICE

OKLAHOMA CITY

"I didn't know policemen came so young?"

He smiles shyly. "I just watch the corners at school and put the signs out. And see that they don't smoke."

"My name's Bennett," the father introduces himself.

We shake hands and again watch the branch burners. Beyond the yard, the streets of Elm Grove square off at right angles. "Many folks live here?"

"About three hundred and seventy-five families. About fifteen hundred people I calculate. I been here seven years on that spot of ground over there.   All that's there belongs to me."

I glance at his house up the street. "How much rent you pay?"

"Land rent's a dollar a month."

"Put the house up yourself?"

He nods. "I junked around. I'd git a piece of board here and yonder. Then my neighbor and I tore down a garage uptown. We got the wood we tore down. That's how I came by the house. It took four days to put it up. It cost me seventeen dollars and seventeen cents. Seventeen cents worth of nails."

"I helped him." The boy glances up proudly at his father.

"I was a carpenter one place and another," Bennett says. "Some here in the city. Some over at Sulphur Springs."

"Were you born in the city?"

"I was born in Arkansas. I was brought to the Indian Territory when I was a year old. My nationality's Cherokee and Irish. That was 1885 when I came here. My folks rented the land from the Chickasaws. When we first settled there, Papa had about a hundred and twenty acres. We raised cotton and corn. It hadn't ever had a plow in it before. Our closest neighbors was two miles from us." Again, he leans on the fence, his eyes on the bonfire. "I've been a carpenter off and on since I've been twenty years old. I can do any kind of carpenter work I've ever tried. . . There's six of us in the family. This boy and the boy choppin' wood over there. And the two li'l twins. Sister's crying."

We walked into his yard where a barefoot boy of eight is splitting short log ends into kindling. Near the outhouse, the girl twin is weeping with the desolate heartbreak of a very young child. The boy twin glares at her, his fist clutched tight on an old pocket knife. Both twins are barefoot, the sun polishing their bright yellow hair.

"Give it to Sister," Bennett coaxes his little son. "You're the big boy."

Big Boy digs his wriggling toes into the dry grass.

"Give it to Sister."

Reluctantly, Big Boy hands the prize over. Sister grabs the pocket knife and runs across the yard like a chicken after a worm.

Bennett smiles. "Sister's healthy." His strong face again becomes an almost impassive mask. "Last commissary day, we got eleven pounds of flour, two gallons of onions, a pound of rice, two pound of butter. That's the crop we got to live on for a month. By cuttin' wood I buy the twins Carnation Canned Milk. Over the stockyard, the people milk the cows before they're slaughtered. . ." He nods at his oldest son. "He always says he ain't hungry but he can eat."

The boy returns his father's glance, his devoted faithful eyes unblinking.

"We eat about as good as any family in the whole camp. We get city water out of the hydrant."

"The School Board pays for it," the boy adds.

Two brown Jersey cows walk by in front of the Bennett house.

"Who owns those cows?"

"Mr. Rose. They give a rich milk but not very much of it." Bennett's fingers stray to the blue stone heart attached to his overall strap. "I've had this thirty years. That's a good luck charm but I don't see the luck. I'd like to move into town but there's no chance in the world to git in. People are comin' into camp all the time. Quite a few go to California and to Arizona. But they figure on comin' back. Mr. Rose went plumb down to San 'tone Texas and picked cotton. Came back broke. Had one nickel left and come home. He left here with a good car and when he come back all he had was a nickel. He goes down every fall to pick cotton."

The twins chase each other over the yard. Bennett's blue eyes follow their darting, bounding, skipping movement. "I lost my first wife four years ago. I couldn't get along by myself so I got me another housekeeper. She's sixty year old. I couldn't make a living for 'em without havin' someone take care of 'em. I think it was stummick trouble that killed my wife. . . It been eleven year when I was out in California and Arizony with her. We picked a little cotton. She couldn't stand it. The climate was too light. Anyhow, it was on a Saturday when this doctor saw us in town. 'There's something wrong with your woman,' he said: 'I can cure your wife.' I said to him: 'I'll be the proudest man in the world but I have no money.' He said: 'I'm not asking you for money.' He cured her sound well." Bennett takes off his hat, wipes his brow with his hand. "I raised the twins on Carnation Canned Milk. For them I got nine li'l banties and we're gettin' two and three eggs a day. They lay pretty good. That ole speckled hen near the house layed one hundred and seven eggs. But the soil's too sandy. It won't produce nothin.' "

He puts his hat back on. "I've been here seven years on this spot of ground. I bought those black locust posts, the best post wood there is. Nothin' eats on it. It's a hard wood. . . I've been off the W.P.A. since the 21st of August. I've spent what they give me and my earnings. I got four cents left. This mawnin' I bought my last groceries at Honest John's. I got three pounds of coffee for forty-two cents. Sugar, hit's fifty-eight cents for ten pounds but I didn't buy none.   Do you want to come inside?"

I nod. Father, son and I walk across the grass and enter his house. He introduces me to the second Mrs. Bennett, an elderly woman with a thin patient face. Her skin is so brown, her light eyes seem bluer than blue can be. The oldest son and his woodchopping brother sit down side by side on the bed. Without his oversized black felt, the oldest son looks much younger. The twins follow us inside like curious puppies, leaning against their father's knees. They break away from his arms, squatting on the floor, playing, the old knife between them. "They're lively kids," I break the silence.

"Those two li'l kids were raised on Carnation Milk," Bennett affirms as if he had said: I take my Bible oath. "They weighed five pounds a piece when they were born. You can see where they are now."

Mrs. Bennett folds her hands on her lap. "It ain't so hard to manage the kids but it's hard gittin' 'em something to eat and to wear. Our breakfast's gittin' pretty low."

The little blond boy on the floor slashes air with the old knife. "I'll cut your haid off!" he threatens.

"Pretty hard to keep 'em out of bad company." Mrs. Bennett sits immovable, not wasting any energy. "They rip and tear around right smart. Call each other bad names. I keep 'em right here in the yard." Tacked to the wall near her, a child's crayon drawing of a green flower against a purple background gleams vividly in the room. Red lettering

urges: SEE THE FLOWER SHOW. The old woman is as motionless as the stove in the center. The black stovepipe climbs
up to a low ceiling insulated with box cardboard. The flower
is green, the lettering red, the old woman brown of face.
She rises now, walks past the kerosene lamp on the shelf, past
the bucket of water suspended on a hook with its drinking
dipper floating on surface, into the middle room of the
three-room house. She begins to peel a bowl of onions.

"We sleep in there," Bennett says. "The boys sleep in the
end room, the twins here."

The oldest boy pulls out a can from under the bed,
dumping its marbles into his hollowed palm. "I got everything but aggies. Aggies are pretty hard to git hold of unless
you give a dime a piece for 'em."

I notice the lithograph of Christ on the wall. "Are there
churches in camp?"

"There are about four different churches. Most of us go
pretty regular. There's three Holiness churches and one
Baptist. I go to the Baptist Church when I go." He smiles
more frequently, wanting me to be comfortable. "I can't
find but one church in the Bible. And that's the Church of
Christ."

The girl twin is standing tiptoe against the wall, her
fingers reaching up towards a red horsehair tassel on a nail.

"I kept my bridle spurs for a long time, and Betty Jane,
you're not going to have 'em," Bennett says mildly to her.

"Was that before you were a carpenter?"

"When I was raised up I was a cowboy. I followed the
cattle up to Kansas City, just the plain range cattle. I drove
a few up the Chisholm Trail into Dodge City. It'd be about
two hundred miles. Whenever the sun caught us, that's
where we laid down and slept. Sometimes we'd make ten
and twelve miles a day. Sometimes we'd have eighteen hundred head. One time we had a stampede." He smiles. "Don't
git in front of 'em! That was Territory time," he says in a
low voice as if relating a story his grandfather had told him,
his two sons listening as hard as they can. "Mighty few fences
in this country then. Cattle roamed around, made their own
livin'. There was some rustlin' but it didn't amount to much.
The movies just played that up."

The frying smell of onions fills the house. The oldest

boy puts away his can of marbles. His brother wipes his nose with the back of his hand, his head turning towards the kitchen. Only the two twins seem indifferent to food, wrestling on the floor.

"We'll have somethin' to eat soon. Will you stay and eat with us?" Bennett invites me.

"Thank you very much. I've just eaten."

Outside to the north, eastwards, Ramsey Tower and First National cleave a southern sky without hunger, in a city without hunger, the distant city a few miles away. . .

"WATCH YOUR DRIVING
107 DAYS WITHOUT
A
TRAFFIC FATALITY
KIWANIS CLUB"
From the safety warnings on the traffic posts.

"Oklahoma City's safety record of 107 days without a fatal accident in its streets is attracting some national acclaim and is pointed to with pride by every local citizen. Whether the long list of deathless days grows to 150 and on past the 200 mark or is broken this very day or on tomorrow by a life-snuffing accident, this city has rung up a record in traffic safety that is worth crowing about, and the people here are safety-conscious to a degree never before attained."

From the Oklahoma City TIMES.

I park my car at the eastern end of Reno Street. The hundred-and-twenty-five foot oil derricks look like a boy's paradise, the playroom's toys changed into man's industry. In front of a corrugated tin building, a young fellow in brown work pants and brown shirt, a gasoline attendant's cap lettered: RELY ON YOUR BRAKES INSTEAD OF YOUR HORN tilted back on his curly brown hair, stares at me. His eyes, too, are brown behind his glasses.

"Hello," I greet him. "What do you do here?"

"I'm an operator, an engineer."

The engines under the corrugated tin roof throb steadily.

"From Oklahoma?"

His lips are thin but not unfriendly, smiling a little. "Have

to look all around to find an Oklahoman. I'm from Missouri.
I come from the lead and zinc."

The wind is blowing hard but the day is warm and sunny.
The sun seems to glowing yellow and bright over the engineer. "How'd you get out here?"

"I always worked around motors. . . You got the time?"

"No."

"I'm off at three thutty. I come on at half past seven."
He sits down on the grass. So do I.

"You miss Missouri?"

"It doesn't make much difference where I live as long as
I get three meals and my six dollars a day. Them drillers
were once gittin' twenty a day." He stretches his long legs,
glad to talk. "Ain't you never seen an oil rig before?" He
glances at the rig a hundred feet away from us. "That's a
regular drillin' derrick. Up on top's a crown block and a
pulley. You can't see it from here. Now the pipe that goes
down, you have to pull it way up. You pull the pipe up and
lower it back into the well. The well may run forty-five
hundred feet." He laughs suddenly. "You've seen an oil rig
before! They're just as thick as tumble turds around a school
house."

"No, I haven't. How does a rig work?"

"It's just like pumpin' water up out of a well. The oil is
pushed into that scrubber tank." He nods at a tank to the left
of the rig. "The gas, it's wet gas, goes to the plant and the
gasoline ingredients are taken out of it. Wet gas has ethane,
butane. . . Over there's the pump. That green beam like
a grasshopper."

Seesawing up and down, up and down, the green beam
has an easy powerful rhythm.

"The oil's in the ground," Missouri says. "It has to be
pumped up. I'll show you." He gets up and I follow him
across a grassless parched stretch of earth.

"What killed the grass?"

"Salt and slush. Sometimes they goose off the weeds up
to the well." He stops at another tank-like apparatus. "This
is the booster or lift station. It lifts the gas or oil to a loadin'
rack or main pipe line out. The pipe line's just like a railroad. In some wells after the wet gas is stripped, the dry gas
goes back to this here lift station and is driven back into

the well. Down in the pool, the gas has no way of escaping and it comes shooting up with the oil into the casing of the rig and up to a pipe to the separator. That's the lift method or the flow. We sell our gas to Phillips 66 and our oil to Continental Oil, Conoco. This well'll run one hundred and twenty-five barrels, forty gallon to the barrel a day. I work for an independent and he sells to anybody. He gits one dollar a barrel for oil but then Sinclair comes along and cuts it to eighty cents. That affects an independent who has to sell to the bigshots. Wonder where my relief is?"

"Who discovered oil?"

"The Cherokees were the first to make oil. Way back in 1880 or somethin'. The oil come out of springs and they went around sellin' it to folks to cure disease, foot and mouth disease. As good as castor oil, anyway."

The aluminum paint on the equipment repels the sun's light. "There's my relief," he calls out.

A medium-sized man also dressed in brown work shirt and brown work pants steps up to us, sitting down on the grass. His face is finely cut, the nose sharply modeled.

"This feller here wants to know somethin' about oil," Missouri explains.

"I always work from my neck down for this company," Relief replies.

Missouri hawhaws.

"From Oklahoma?"

Relief nods. "I've been here all my life. I've been in the oil fields ever since I could walk around. My father came here in Territory days."

Missouri takes out a penknife and carefully cuts his finger nails. "There are two classes of people in oil," he expounds like a veteran. "The ones who started out in West Virginia and Pennsylvania and follered it as it hit West, the real oil people. . . It's like the fellers in the Navy. They foller it to the West Coast, to China. . . When the real oil people hit a section like Oklahoma, the heavy work's done by the natives, the farm kids. Them natives are just as useless as tits on a boar hog."

Relief smiles at Missouri's explanation, the ten years difference in age between the two engineers revealed by his smile.

"I've just heard oil's selling for about eighty cents a barrel?" I ask Relief.

"The refinery takes a barrel at eighty cents. They also git the gasoline, wax, and nujol in the barrel. It's the refinery's game. Hundreds of li'l men've lost their shirts drillin'. A li'l man gits a couple dry holes and he's out. It'll cost a hundred and twenty-five thousand to put one of them down. The li'l man don't own his own refinery and he can't open up gas stations. The li'l man can't cover too much territory. It's like a minin' company buyin' their own railroads and smelters." He shrugs his shoulders. "I don't know anything. We're paid for what we do."

"Before a li'l feller gits through drillin', he won't own more'n ten per cent of one of those sons-of-bitches," Missouri declares.

The engines throb throb throb, pumping the oil up from below.

"They'll always have to have drillers to look after the automatic driller." Missouri states. "Just like borin' a hole with an augur," he adds for my benefit.

"They'd put an augur against your head in Territory days." Relief grins paternally.

Missouri laughs.

Relief ignores him. "There were the five civilized tribes, the Choctaws, the Cherokees, the Seminoles, the Chickashaws, and the Creeks. The Dust Bowl was a cattle country then but now they've killed the grass, leavin' the naked land." He speaks solemnly as if he were a farmer and not a custodian of machines and gauges.

"You were out in the Seminole?" Missouri asks him.

"Seminole was a chancre boom town." Relief's blue eyes are steady and meditative. "It wasn't as rough as Cromwell. Ragtown was one of the toughest towns in Oklahoma. Gamblin', shootin', knifin', general hellin' around. I've seen folks killed in Cromwell. Just git drunk and start fightin'! The feller who killed Bill Tilghman was given five hundred dollars."

"Who was Tilghman?"

"He was a U. S. Marshal. They have to make this sheriff a hero," he says with disgust. "Just because he was a U. S.

man. I think he was killed over a whore. He wanted to be tough. Shot him on the front steps of Wide Way Dance Hall. . ."

"When were these booms?" I ask.

"Cromwell was '23 to '26. Seminole started in '26. Crom-well was at its worst in '24. Snake City came in '24. . . They had some swell people in those shack towns," he continues reflectively as if realizing that he himself, still a young man, not forty, has lived through the last of the pioneer days. "They built those shack towns right up on the prairie. They'd live there in shacks and have good cars, and electric refrigerators in the shacks. The roads were the worst. The high-powered machines they'd bring in would rip the roads to hell! And they used to put out in the paper about internal combustion when a well burned up. But an accident is some-one's carelessness. I saw a well burn up in Seminole. The rig floor was greasy. . . We didn't have concrete cellars like we have now. It was a heavy murky day and the gas settled in the holler and a woman in a tent started it up. . . The booms are over."

He listens to the throbbing engines. "This Oklahoma City field is the best field in the world for livin' conditions. The boys have got weaned away from the old fields, no toilets. . ."

"Just the same I'd have done without toilets for the sake of a blanket." Missouri smiles.

"You're married," Relief reminds him.

"I'm married but I ain't settled down."

"What's a blanket?" I ask them.

"Gal part Indian," Missouri yawns.

Relief squats down on his haunches. "We were gittin' eight-fifty a day in 1929 and the Chamber of Commerce said they'd git ten thousand men at three dollars a day! I paid fifty a month for two li'l rooms here in Oklahoma City."

"What happened?" Missouri questions.

"Nothin' happened. Farmers can lay pipe, use pick and shovel but they can't do the skilled work. You can hire a new hand and start him in with the old hands like this feller here. He only started in last spring."

Missouri smiles. "I didn't know my ass from a stalk of

bananas. I'd sit down on a lazybench and keep my eyes open."

"One day I told him to bring me the Samson post. He come back and said he couldn't find it."

"What's the Samson post?"

Missouri hawhaws. Even Relief laughs now, a dry quick laugh. "That holds the weight of the drillin'."

"I hear Arkansas has moved in on that Seminole field?" Missouri scratches his ear.

Overhead, birds wing through the cloudless hot sky. "The sons of the pioneers have grown up and it's gittin' so a man without a political pull can't git ahead in the oil field."

"Feller told me that down in Seminole, a foreman had ten relatives workin' for him. He said they wanted to learn the oil business from the ground up." Missouri frowns.

"They didn't have enough kinfolk to handle all the jobs in the boom days," Relief says. "It's gittin' worse every day but you don't find many oil workers on relief. An oil worker pulls out for Michigan, for anywheres he can find oil. Oil field people born and raised in the oil field, go somewheres else they lose their jobs. But the farmers who git in oil sit on their ass when they lose their job. A real oil worker's lookin' ahead for other jobs all the time." He plucks a blade of grass, shoves it between his teeth. "The miners are more or less a class to themself. They're hell for stickin' to one job like the railroad people. But in the oil fields, there are so many different jobs! If you got to work for a livin', you got to learn all the departments. I know enough about it to git by."

"If you understand the gas engines you can git by," Missouri agrees.

"They're gittin' forward in their research. As the years go by, it's about the same stuff. This highspeed engine here was the first of its type west of the Mississippi. The old type was a lowspeed engine. Times have changed for the workin' man. The oil workers used to be more independent than now. Git mad for nothin' and quit. Can't do that any more. One time we'd run around, read the oil gauges but now the pressure controls regulate the oil." Relief walks to a valve jutting out of the ground. "If you could see a map of this state and see the main pipe lines goin' across the country you'd be surprised!"

"The wells here are close together," I remark.

"We have two sands down below," he answers. "That's why we can twin a well and git your derricks close together. It's no business for the li'l man. They drill down and the li'l cutter inside the drill pipe brings up the formation solid. If the formation looks well the li'l man goes in it. The oil's like a creek or a channel but it's not uniform. That well there, not seventy feet from here, over there in the weeds, was dry." He leads me to a patch of weeds. He stands on the concrete foundation, kicking around with his foot. "That's the hole where the grass is. I guess that li'l man's in it."

Missouri smiles when we return. "If you want to know about oil you have to know the oil field song," he says to me.

"What song?"

> "Here's to the oil that freely flows;
> Here's to the boys in the greasy clothes . . ."

Relief nods as if he hadn't heard Missouri at all. "Once the li'l man was spread out over the oil fields like a country gal on an organ stool. It ain't so any more."

Missouri looks at him carefully, says nothing.

"Watch Your Driving
108 Days Without
A
Traffic Fatality
Kiwanis Club"
"To The Citizens of Oklahoma City
Congratulations
On Your Remarkable Safety Record
Everyone in Oklahoma City should read this page—The very fact that you can read it—that you're alive and well—means a lot, doesn't it?—Think, for 109 days—almost four months—not one family has been saddened by an automobile fatality occurring within this city—Today, Sunday, will be the 110th day . . . MOST IMPORTANT—Let's not rest on our laurels—let's ALL be eternally vigilant—take no chances—drive safely—walk safely. Let's make Oklahoma City the safest city in the world. 109 DEATHLESS DAYS."

From the Daily OKLAHOMAN.

The red brick rear of the Oklahoma Transportation Bus line (*Oklahoma, Arkansas, Texas*) abuts on the bottleman's shack.

I cut off West Chickashaw Street, walking by huge green-leaved castor bean plants, or 'Oklahoma palms' to the small shack. The bottleman is inside, sorting the bottles in the box at the foot of his bed. He quits work, straightening his stooped shoulders. He has the tragic face of a forgotten unknown Lincoln, his nose straight and bony, his lips and chin covered with a two-day stubble. His face is waxen white, his beard black, his eyes brown. A faded cracked belt that looks as if it is made of cardboard rather than leather supports his pants.

"How's the bottle business?"

"One thing I can say about it. I ain't livin' unless I work sixteen to eighteen hours a day single-handed. There's men that make money offen 'em. But bottles I can handle, I have to give so much money for 'em." He picks up a bottle to show me. "That is what I call an alcohol bottle. I pay fourteen cents a dozen and I get twenty cents a dozen. It don't leave me anything. There's money in it if a man's fixt to buy stuff in a real cheap way. But as long as I have to give the prices I have to give, I can't make nothin'. I been doin' my best to get outa this and get on the W.P.A. I used to work on construction work, common labor. I've lived in the state most of my life. . ."

"Where from?"

"As near as I know . . . No'th Carolina or South Carolina. I wouldn't say which. My mother raised me by my stepfather. Clark's my stepfather's name. I know my name, but I married two different times under the name of Clark." He pulls a letter out of a crumpled envelope.

I read it:

W.P.A. Officers

Gentlemen: Mr. Clark is behind with his rent, doesn't have enough clothes to keep warm, no coal, no underwear and not enough to eat. He isn't making a living. Mr. Clark is an ex-soldier. He sure deserves a little help. If ever anybody got work who needed it, this man does.

I will verify this before a Notary Public.

Lee McMillan

I return the letter. He puts it back inside the envelope. "It don't fill up an empty stummick, nice words. One thing we haven't had a real bad winter since along '31 and '32. I don't believe we had a six-inch snow last year. I've seen the Red River when you can drive a loaded wagon on the ice. You couldn't do that in the last twenty years. The seasons've changed. This weather just fits my clothes." He barely smiles. "I can do common labor all right and make a day of it. I've hauled three hundred and four hundred bottles and that'll weigh two hundred and fifty to three hundred pounds." He follows me out into the yard as if hoping that I can give him a job.

I stop at a mound of smashed bottles.

"I bought every bit of it. Broke 'em washin' and haulin'. Anything that'll pay me a dollar and a half or two dollars a day," he cries out in a beseeching voice. "Winter's comin' on and I have no winter clothes."

"An apparently unavoidable accident Monday had clipped short Oklahoma City's bid for nationwide traffic safety honors with the death at 2:20 a.m. of Mrs. Lola Luse, 75 years old, of injuries received Saturday night. Her death ended the city's march toward national honors, but not before it had established a new deathless day record for cities in its population class."

From the Oklahoma City TIMES.

The four-story Mid-Continent Life Building is one of the most impressive business structures in Oklahoma City. Situated in the northwest district, surrounded by middle-class homes, each with its lawn and sedate trees, Mid-Continent Life is like a square Grecian City Hall.

Far to the south, Ramsey Tower and First National mark the downtown city. Aristocratically removed from enterprise, the temple of insurance faces on a green triangular lawn spaced with evergreens. Broad flights of stairs lead up to four pillars that support a black-lettered and neon-equipped sign: MID-CONTINENT LIFE. In this neighborhood of home-dwellers and church steeples, the Company seems to have the permanence and dignity of a museum.

Inside the entrance, a bronze tablet with a bas-relief map of the United States testifies to the character of Mid-Continent Life. R. T. Stuart, President, tops the scroll of eleven officers.

The main exhibit (so it seems within these walls) on the first floor is an electrified display of three illustrated posters. An old man and a woman with a check: SECURITY. A man and his son: PALS. A country boy eating an apple: LET US GUARANTEE YOUR CHILD'S EDUCATION.

I walk up a marble flight of stairs to the second floor. The corridor is a spacious one like that in a library. The huge Directors' Room empties off the corridor. The door is open. A dozen high-backed chairs surround a long gleaming table. It is empty now. Here is where the Directors meet. Here is where BUSINESS meets. It looks like a funeral parlor. There is no one in the Directors' Room.

U. S. Route Number 77

South into Texas across the Red River.

Gainesville. Valley View. Sanger.

Denton on Saturday night is crowded with farming folk in to shop. The old cars keep pulling up, fathers, mothers and kids trooping out into the bright lights. College girls from Texas State Teachers College walk arm in arm, in threes, in fives. Farm women enter the glittering Woolworth, lured to the jewelry counter, to the brooches set with red and blue stones. A woman holds up a ring to the light with the air of one about to purchase a thousand-dollar emerald. The Woolworth sales girl murmurs: "That's very nice."

Sunday morning in the empty town, a young boy is practising with a football, mastering the dropkick.

Towns on the prairie.

Garza.

Farmers Branch.

Waco.

Temple.

Belton.

The county courthouse in Georgetown is topped by a

silver-gilded statue of Justice holding a sword and a scale.
These Justices seem like huge dolls manufactured in big lots
and distributed among the Texan cities.

Brushy Creek, Round Rock Creek, named by the first
simple men, cut across the highway and in the distance the
dome of Austin's Capitol Building, second in size to Washington, D. C.'s.

ELECT WM. MCGRAW YOUR GOVERNOR, a placard demands.

This is November, month of elections, month of ballot
boxes, month of candidates. I stop for gas at a station covered
with signs:

IT PAYS TO PAY CASH.

YOU PAY US FOR THE GASOLINE ONLY.

Our Net Low Price includes No Corporate Overhead, No
National Advertising, and no Interest on "watered stock."

Texan Family

SAN ANTONIO

"WE, THE GOVERNORS
INVITE INDUSTRY
TO THE SOUTH

United we stand for uniform taxation policies. *United we stand*
for a friendly labor attitude between employer and employee.
*United we stand to aid and protect industrial development in
the South.*
And on this basis, We, the Governors of the Southern States
invite industrial leaders to investigate the unmatched industrial
advantages that exist by reason of our moderate year 'round
climate which insures ideal working conditions, lower capital
investment, lower production costs—in the midst of an unlimited
supply of raw materials.

SOUTHERN GOVERNORS CONFERENCE
Bona Allen Building, Atlanta, Georgia
Including the Governors of Oklahoma, Texas,
Tennessee, Louisiana, Alabama, Mississippi,
Georgia, North Carolina, Florida, Arkansas, and
South Carolina."

From the Southern newspapers.

ON THE MAIN PLAZA IN SAN ANTONIO, the Cathedral of San
Fernando rises into the night, a commemorative stone to
Texas's Spanish centuries, the carven slab set in the Cathe-
dral's wall a requiem:

*The remains of the Alamo heroes are entombed in the
chapel at the right hand side of the entrance of this
Cathedral.*

I enter San Fernando. Above the alm box with its inscription: *Misas para Los Almas,* a notice reads:

Sociedad de Cristo Rey
Novena de Cristo Rey, Año de 1939.

Inside, in the yellow and red interior, the incense swirls, old and almost antique scent, over the heads of the Sunday night worshippers, the women in black head veils, the little girls in white. Their dark Latin faces, their brown eyes suddenly seem to enflesh the buried generations of conquistadores. The Spanish centuries of *padre* and *haciendado* become alive again as the voices of the choir boys flute upwards towards the high-pillared ceiling.

Outside, on the next corner, the First National Bank commemorates the new century. The comfort station in the center of the Plaza has four entrances. It is night, but I can make out the carven letters above each door:

WHITE MEN

COLORED MEN

WHITE WOMEN

COLORED WOMEN

Mi Barbería — Haircut 10¢

Abogado

Se Vende Tortillas

The signs of the businessmen in San Antonio's West Side are written in Spanish. It is a neighborhood of unpainted houses, the wood gray and warped, the roads unpaved and pebbly, the letter boxes broken as if nobody ever received any mail here.

I call on a family I know. Inside the house near the window, the father is prone on a cot under a red tattered blanket. Vines lace the window's corner. The sun glows on glass. He props himself up on one elbow, his brown eyes warm and soft as the eyes of the Indian, his face lined from a life of hard work.

"Back from the job?" I say to him.

He smiles. "My father work before me and I work now." Over on the dresser, the kerosene lamp stands, old-fashioned.

"What kind of work did your father do?"

"My father used to work in the roundhouse in Laredo. We moved from Laredo to San Antonio in 1905. My mother was a widow." He lights a cigarette. "She wanted to give us an education. We was three brothers like I told you. In those days, parents used to furnish their own books for the children at school. My mother used to work at the laundry. We went to school just a few years, about five years. Not a very high education." His smile now is reflective. "I had to quit school. We was three brothers and she couldn't furnish all the money we need. We worked pickin' cotton. I was about thirteen, fourteen years. We was not used to it. The first day we went in the cotton field, we went pickin' cross ways. We didn't care much about pickin' in a row."

"Like pickin' berries," his son says laughing, coming into the room from the adjoining kitchen. He leans against the wall, a tall young boy of eighteen, his black hair combed straight back. His features are longer than those of his father, but the friendly smile is the same.

"That's right," the father agrees. "But they told us soon how to pick it. Not to leave part of the crop back behind." He gestures towards his belly. "Carry the canvas bag here. . . Then we had other work. Pecan shellin'. We used to shell pecans at home. Nobody dream of fact'ry then. The contractor used to bring it home in a horse wagon. My mother used to empty the sack right on the floor, put a kerosene light in center and the children sittin' around shellin' pecan."

"No rules for health then?" the son questions. He returns to the kitchen, comes out with a tin cup in his slender hand. "That's the pecan cup."

"We used to get paid four cups for five cents," the father continues. "The contractor pay us. Four cups in a quart. . . Contractor used to come around four, five o'clock and we used to keep going until eleven, twelve o'clock. My mother had to be there or the children wouldn't work. Sometimes we had a couple partners. They came there to eat and to shell. We go to war?" he asks abruptly.

"I hope not."

"War. . . Around 1910, way before the big war, I used to hear about the Mexican War. They say many people get killed. It lasted plenty. The big war lasted plenty. The poor man don't need war. The poor man needs work."

A little girl goes to her father from the kitchen. He puts his brown strong hand on her shoulder. She peeks at me, a shy bird-like child with long black hair and a small thin face.

"I work." The father speaks with quiet finality. "I work in restaurants washin' dishes. I work for a grocery, deliverin' grocery. I used to get paid six dollars a week from seven in the morning to eight at night. When I got married I was getting nine dollars a week. There was plenty work, but not very much money. Then the war come and I join the National Guards of Texas. In those days when the volunteers were called . . . they just gather a big bunch and muster into service. My physical condition was not strong enough to stand the very hard work in cavalry. Seein' I wasn't fit for soldier I got married. She's been a purty good wife to me." He smiles but his eyes look worried as if he were still thinking of war.

His son rubs his knuckles. "They're always giving the preference to white people. The Mexican people always go behind."

"Up in Chicago when I work there, I work for Armour Company and I get forty-two cents an hour with the fertilizer gang," the father recalls. His eyes smile now, his thoughts in the past. "I used to take a bath before I leave to take the street car. . . They give you the seven cents back and make you go off if you don't take a bath."

Father and son laugh.

"I left this boy with my mother," the father says. "He was about seven or eight years. He was sick so I had to come back here. I went to work for nine dollars a week. Now I'm gettin' thirty-nine cents an hour. That's good money in Texas. I'm on the sewer project. I only work two hours today. We only given one hundred thirty hours a month. After you make one hundred thirty hours, you git a vacation. . . Outside of the State of Texas, I used to wash dishes with machine and get eighteen a week. The owner give me food when he found out I'm a married man."

"Now," the son comments. "You get three dollars a week. You can eat all you can in there. But you can't take anything out. Soon we work picking turkeys. The females, we get four cents, the gobblers five cents. You get an old turkey gobbler, you stay two hours for five cents."

The father puffs on his cigarette. "They used to pay ten cents. That job last from Thanksgiving to Christmas to New Year."

"That was long ago," the son reminds his father. "They

don't pay ten cents no more. We never git a turkey to eat. Not even a handful of feathers."

"Only the lice they let you take out."

They both laugh as if the jobs of their lives were part of a game, a strange fantastic game in which they are involved.

"You git all bloody," the son amplifies. "And they keep the feathers. I think they make pillows out of 'em. If you tear a turkey. . . You pull those feathers too hard, the skin comes off! But you pick as long as they last. Then you wait for the farmers to bring in more. They pack two three cars a day and ship 'em up North. The whole West Side picks. The whole family goes to pick. You meet a fellow and he says he's going to the *wehalo*. He's going to the *turkey,* but we know it's to pick."

"It's just pecans, cotton, pecans, turkey." The father strokes the hair of his little girl. "In between seasons, times gits hard. I haven't shelled pecans for a long time, but you have to make a certain amount . . ."

"I tried it one day and I was out the same day!" the son exclaims, laughing at the *game.* His blue shirt, his dark eyes and light brown skin all seem equally vivid and young.

"You were brought up here?" I ask him.

"Yes. We'd go swimming in the river. We'd swim in San Pedro Creek right in town. I used to swim there and go to school. I just went up to the high fifth," he says with the solemn recollection of a young man. "Even when we were kids, the Negroes and the Mexicans, we always been on good terms. But the white boys haven't. In the high schools, the Mexican boys have been big battlers with the Anglo-Americans. Sidney Lanier High School beats the others in football and basketball and the Anglo-Americans git uneasy about it. During the Carnival in April . . ." He interrupts himself. "Last year it started with stoning the buildings and the Mexican boys. They caught these boys unaware. The boys couldn't foller them. They had no cars. When the Carnival came, and the bands parade, and the Battle of the Flowers parade, when these Mexican boys saw the other boys in R.O.T.C. suits, they just wrecked 'em. There wasn't a high school boy without a patch on the eye."

"They're always trying to discriminate the Mexican people," the father says.

"That fight keeps on all the time. That Conception Swimming Pool . . . they don't want the Mexican boys to take a swim there." He looks like a battler, himself, as he talks. "These parks located in Anglo-American districts have swimming pools, but there's no swimming pool in the Mexican district. Not even benches. A creek runs through. You can swim there! But young people don't care much. You have fun. A boy who has means and goes broke, it's pretty hard for him. But a Mexican boy who's struggling, he can take it."

He smiles. "Last April, I went up to Wyoming for a six month term on the C.C.C. I registered in the W.P.A. office here. I waited. They asked me if I was willing to go and I said yes. I was taken from here with a hundred seventy-five boys, Anglo-American boys and Mexican boys." He no longer says "white" boys, his pride quiet and deep. "The majority were Mexican boys. The Anglo-Americans have always attacked the Mexican boys when they're on top. But now they treat us fine and say: 'We have nothing against the Mexican people.' We stayed in Bastrop, Texas, and were given typhoid shots and injections for sunstroke. We drilled every day in our khaki uniforms. We had them big soldier shoes, G.I. shoes, and overseas caps. They call everything in the C.C., G.I. or *Government Issued*. We fell ill from the shots and stayed in bed about two weeks. After that we started drillin'. They didn't like it first, bossin' 'em. . . We used to go to bed back home when we please. But extra duty made 'em get on the line. Peel a hundred-pound sack of potatoes after supper!" He grins. "We were taken to Baggs, Wyoming. That's mountain country across the way from Colorado. We didn't like the country. Too high altitude. Some of the boys couldn't breath well and they were brought back. The boys were separated into crews. Some worked buildin' roads through the mountains. I worked two months on that. I then worked for Army Overhead. That's work in camp. I painted around. We were done by Saturday. I liked it pretty good. If you went to town without permission, the captain mark you A.W.O.L." The memory of the camp and the mountains is strong in him. "Twice we was called to forest fires . . ."

"I was working in electricity in Chicago," the father remembers. "The electricity jump! They was two Polish people. . . One had a bar on the rail and a piece of the bar broke. The electricity jump! He was burned black. The second one went to him, but he did not die."

"In Baggs, there was one hundred ninety population. More boys in camp than in town. So they think the C.C. camps composed of cutthroats and bank robbers, boys who can't get along in the cities. And send them out into the wild country. . . The captain put up a big sign: THIS IS NOT AN INSTITUTION NOR A CORRECTIONAL INSTITUTION. He tell the people they need not be afraid. After that some ladies come from town and looked us over and said: 'We're going to have a meeting Sunday and want you boys there.' It was a li'l old church and we couldn't all sit down. After the meeting, the ladies started talking to us. They wanted the cemetery cleaned. They wanted volunteers: 'After you've cleaned it, we have a big supper here in the clubroom.' A number of boys stayed there and cleaned up the cemetery from weeds and sagebrush. That evening they gave us a good supper."

"They think he's an Indian." The father laughs to himself.

"Yes. We tell them we're Mexicans and they ask: 'Do you throw knives?' One boy ask me: 'Where you come from?' I tell him San Antonio, about a hundred fifty miles from the border. 'That's pretty close to Mexico,' he said. 'Are they mean in Mexico?' I said: 'They drive cars if they got 'em and wear clothes.' He said: 'Is there rustling there?' I said: 'There's hardly any cattle to rustle.' " He shakes his head. "In that town they talk over the fence, gossip. They called us jitterbugs because we wore sixteen-inch cuffs and striped sweaters at the dances. We called 'em cowboys because they wore boots and bright shirts and big hats. They didn't like the way we danced. . . We went to a dance twenty-three miles out in the mountains. The Sheriff was sittin' in one corner, smoking a pipe. I heard a couple shots outside. I went to the door. A cowboy had a gun in his hand and wanted to come into the dance hall. I told the Sheriff. He said: 'He's just havin' a li'l fun' and kept on smoking his pipe."

"I have never have a knife," the father says gently. "There are knifings here in San Antonio sometimes. A knife makes no noise."

The mother comes into the room. "We manage," she says as if she has only listened to her husband's talk about jobs, not to her son's. "In some family, the money they gets is not enough. . . When I was a girl I work hard in the field. The poor people have to work! We pick cotton in west Texas. They give us li'l house like chicken house. Water, they give us. Tank water from the rain. The tank all dirty. The cow come, the horse. The pig drink, too. We work hard. My mother have to come from work and fix dinner for the children. We pick from four in the morning until seven at night. Pick bumblebee cot' and your hand's all blood. Sometime we have no money to buy glove. I was seven year when I started pickin' cotton. My father show me how. We live in chicken house. My mother have to cook outside. Make the fire on the ground. We cook potatoes, some beans. The same meal all the time. We have to eat!" she cries out, her voice almost despairing. "We make a li'l money just for eat. We have no place to raise no chicken. We have to work for beans. Sometimes we boil 'em, sometimes we fry 'em. We have to like 'em. Sometimes no chicken house. Live in tent. But I marry. It better for me. My husband a good man. But some family they have no water in the house. Right here in San Antonio. No water. They get water from the other houses. How they live?"

The father speaks. "I'm the one doin' the work." He looks from his wife to his tall son and little girl as if his strength will last forever.

U. S. Route Number 90

The east is a gray cloud of rain not fallen as yet upon the Texan earth. East, behind the rain, Louisiana, Alabama, North Carolina, the states of the old South. . .

Houston . . . the new buildings of Continental Can Company, Pacific Valve Repair Company, American Steel Derrick Company, Shaffer Tool Works. A city of companies.

And east, the older land. The live oaks are hung with Spanish moss in Louisiana. The trees thicken. The trees are everywhere. Everywhere, the Spanish moss. The French-named towns. Lafayette. Broussard. New Iberia. Jeanerette. . .

Suddenly, my car doesn't pull well. I steer into the first gas station. The mechanic-owner, a blond stooping man, checks my motor. The fuel pump has worn out. He takes a new fuel pump down from a shelf for installation.

"This used to be Huey Long's state?" I remark.

"Huey Long was the poor man's friend," he says as he works. "That's why they shot him. He built highways and schools and hospitals for the poor man."

A car and trailer drive into the gas station. The car has Texas plates. Two men in tall plains hats and a boy step out. "How much is your oil?" the oldest man says. He is a man of about sixty with a lined sagging face and tired blue eyes. The elbow of his jacket shows a worn hole.

"Thirty cents," the mechanic-owner answers.

"Anything cheaper?" the younger man asks. He has the lean face and lean body of a rodeo cowboy. He is brown-shirted, his pants tucked into high-heeled riding boots.

"Twenty cents the cheapest I got."

Both men look at each other. From the rear seat in the car, an elderly woman and a young girl stare out through the window. Silence as if twenty cents were twenty dollars. The boy walks over to the car, comes back a second later with a mounted set of cattle horns. He is a young boy of ten with a narrow blond head like his big brother. He holds the set against his chest. Two long creamy horns jut out over a mirror as they would from the head of a steer. Blue cloth studded with brass tacks binds them to their wooden base. The mirror is flanked on either side by two short black and white horns, forming a U. A third white horn is set between the black and white horns, pointing upward like a hook. "They're pretty horns, sir," the boy pleads with the mechanic-owner.

The salesman's father and brother appear to be a mile away, as if they have nothing to do with the transaction.

"They're pretty horns, sir. My daddy made 'em. They're set together good and strong. They're only a dollar and a half. You can have 'em for a dollar, sir. We've just got the two sets left."

"Where you heading for?" I ask the father.

"The Mississippi, sir." He glances away.

The mechanic-owner buys one pair. I buy the other. The

three Texans buy one quart of oil. They get into their car. Car and trailer with their dispossessed travel east.

East . . . into the Confederate South, the French South, the sugar South. Ten and twelve feet high, the cane tops wave in the wind like a giant grass.

Negro field hands in blue overalls are cutting the cane, stooping over and slicing down with their broad knives.

"I hear Huey Long was the poor man's friend?" I ask at my next stop for gas.

"Living under Huey was like living under Hitler," the attendant retorts. "He took away all self rule. Huey, the friend of the poor people. . . That's a laugh. They talk about his highways. But he got ten cents on every sack of ce-ment that came into this state. His own brother Earl Long called him a liar and a thief. That's in the record. You might care to see Mrs. Long's home, gold faucets in the bathroom. . . The poor man's friend! This state was all right with its sugar and cotton. It was all right until they discovered oil. That's the corruption."

East . . . a little Negro boy is walking home along the highway, a two foot length of sugar cane under his arm like a big peppermint stick. He bites off the top end, chewing, spitting out the pulp. Under the vast gray sky, on this land of green cultivated jungles, the wind in the cane, the little boy looks like the loneliest human being in the whole world.

Day Laborers on the Land

LOUISIANA

"Sugar planters have got to mechanize to survive. Last year I handled 86,000 tons of sugar cane without using one mule. I'm operating my own fleet of 32 plantation tractors now."
Pres. Foster, head of a group of sugar plantations, in a newspaper interview.

"Torras, Louisiana
August 31, 1939

George Thomas
R.F.D.
Lettsworth, La.
Oak, according to our Contract which reads if one or the other wants to break the Contract, you or me must be given written notice by Sept. 15th, Wish to say that I will want my house by Jany. 13th, 1940.

Yours truly,
Dr. J. H. Hobgood"
Planter's letter to sharecropper.

TWO NEGRO WOMEN CANE cutters, bright orange bandannas tied around their heads, trudge home from work, cane knives in their hands. The wind blows their cotton skirts against their legs. The wind bends over the grassy tops of the sugar cane. The two women are silent, plodding along the highway like tired factory workers. Each woman carries a few lengths of cane for the kids at home.

There are no homes in sight. There is no factory in sight. There is only the sugar cane, green acre on green acre, sea-greening into the distance.

A cane truck roars by, its boat-shaped body loaded with tons of cut cane.

Another truck, and wagons pulled by teams of mules and hauling smaller loads.

A smokestack, smoke pouring from its lip, is the first I see of the Godchaux Sugar Refinery at Raceland.

Twenty-five or thirty cane trucks and wagons are parked in a long line at the refinery, waiting their turn to unload. The black smoke snakes across the sky. The smell of cooking sugar sweetens the air.

There are few farms, few cows, the land a plantation, the tall cane washing up to the doors of the unpainted gray shacks like a green tide. The shacks, gray islands of men and women and children, are surrounded, hemmed in, overwhelmed by the endless cane.

The tall cane.

The whitewashed brick courthouse and jail in Napoleonville, the W.P.A.-built gymnasium with its arched roof as beautiful as the bow of a man's back, the houses of the town dwellers, all form a larger island in the cane.

The sugar cane.

Loading derricks border the highway. At Bayou Lafourche, somebody has painted: *No Cane Eating on the Bridge*. Pink hyacinths gleam on the stagnant waters.

A loading derrick on wheels has moved to the edge of a cut strip to lift the cane to the wagons. On the dirt road ahead of me, a young Negro boy pedals home on his bicycle. I honk my horn at him. He stops.

His face is round. He isn't more than nineteen, a thin frail boy in an old jacket, his work shoes seeming too heavy for his feet. He stares at me guardedly as if to say: What do you want?

"I'd like to know something about cane cutting if you don't mind?"

He straddles his bike, both feet on the dirt road. "Go out in the mawnin' about six thutty. You top it first. Top no good. You take your can' knife an' draw it to you. Then you cut it slantin' like this into the ground." He demonstrates with his double-edged knife, the light flickering on the oar-shaped blade. "Then you put it across the heap row. Got to keep the row clean so the leader can pick it up. A man got to come behin' an' pile it up in big piles. The can' loader has a grab with a wagon and fo' mules, an' a man come wid anodder wagon. Den you got tractors with two carts. They pull the cane load. You take it to the derrick and derrick stacks it up until the trucks come. Trucks take it to the sugar house."

"When did you start cutting cane?"

"I start cuttin' cane when I was fo'teen. I watched the other fellers how they cut and I learned. The man on the horse, the bossman, they want you to cut the cane clean. It was tough. The other fellers cuttin' leave my row way behin'. Couldn't catch up. . . They're haulin' cane now 'til twelve at night for the sugar house. They'll be grindin' about two months. Some folks leave from Mississippi to cut cane. Then they go back. Every year they come make grindin'." He shakes his head. "I see one machine to cut the cane, but the people got to come behin' and put the cane across the row."

The tall cane.

The sugar cane.

The wind hurls against the leaves of the banana and pecan trees, growing in formal rows in front of the two-story homes of the plantation owners. A flock of birds buckshot over the tops of the cane.

"I hate sugar cane as a Catholic. It's an artificial plant and the curse of God is upon it," the speaker's eyes blaze. A man in the middle of life, he yet seems venerable, archaic, as if he were the direct descendant of the uncompromising Catholics of the past. "The sugar cane has no reason to exist in the United States. The plantation owner work eleven, twelve, and thirteen months to make a crop and a frost kills it. As a Catholic I hate the sugar cane. It's artificial and it only exist with the machine. As a Catholic, I see the great injustice in Louisiana with the machine working the land and not the man, not the human being. The machine and the politics. I'm learning about this political machine. In every parish, the planters control the district attorney, the sheriff and the judge. In every parish they have a despot. In the whole State of Louisiana, the public school system is an instrument of graft. The teachers are badly qualified because public education is controlled by the machine. The machine of the politics and the machine of the planters! The machine is a system of oppressing the people! I know the owner of a plantation. He says: 'I take good care of my niggers.' He showed me a deep well for his people. He had one thousand cutters. He showed me fifty houses on his land. And he has a thousand cutters! I never saw the shacks behind the refinery. These fifty houses! No clothes on the line! No child in the yard! No chickens! No hogs! Another planter has an old white school on the pave road to be given to the colored. But they're going to wreck the old school. Too good for the colored. It's on the pave road where all can see the colored go to school."

He leans forward, his words racing. "This planter pays fifty cents an acre row for cutting cane. Those people starving all summer, but he doesn't let them work in the afternoon. At eleven o'clock, the cutters are through with the day's work. At eleven o'clock the women made dollar-thirty, dollar-fifty. That's enough!" He takes a cigar out of his pocket. "The li'l planters can't sell to big planter. Too much cane for the big planter. Machinery! For long time since 1800, cane crop planted and cultivated like long ago, but now they make and cultivate a crop with machine. Plowin' tractor pull the plow. Tractor pull the machine hoe and do the work of twenty hands with hoes. Machine hoe pull out the weed. Where the hand go? Go on charity? The hand work from 'kin to kaint' but with machine he no work at all. Mule and colored people until 1933. But ten hands and twenty mules can't plow so much like one driver with one tractor. The South become like the wheat and the corn in the North. All machine! Like in California. In Texas. All machine! The planter in Louisiana likes the machine. The tractor don't need corn like the mule. He can grow more sugar and stop corn if he use the tractor. All through Louisiana, all through the whole South, the machine take the corn from the mule and the bread from the hand, from the tenant and the sharecropper. In 1937 more farm machinery sold than in history. Five hundred millions of dollars of farm machinery."

He shrugs, his eyes intent as if seeing the cane cutters walking home from the fields. "Sugar only exist with machine. It freeze. And the hand too slow. Machine faster than hand. I seen the cutting machine. It is made of steel and weld onto a tractor. The two front wheels small and made of steel. The rear wheels six feet high with tires like automobile. It climb in and out ditches. It do the work of fifty hands with knives. But it not perfect so far. The only thing the cutting machine can do is cut the top and bottom. So far have not invented a cane cutter to do the work. The cane's so heavy. . . Machine can make a crop, cultivate the cane, too. But need the men to harvest the crop. Now, the cutters get two months at most. Average three and four days a week on account of the wet weather. The machine their curse. The Mississippi Negroes come in trainload and truckload and go walking on the road to find a planter in a hurry. They get two fifty a day, more than Louisiana Negroes. Keep the Louisiana Negroes starve all year 'round to cut in October. Children well dressed after a month's work, but no clothes next year."

He cuts off the end of his cigar with an old-fashioned clipper. "Thé overseers are white, illiterate, unable to read and write. They're brutes. Always on horseback. That's what saves 'em. They never go to a church since childhood. They can't understand the regulations of the Government. The planter goes to church, but he can't understand God. He understand the machine. Four school teachers, relatives, board at a planter's house that I know. So he controls the schools. That man's in politics. He claims he has oil on his land. He bought land from the Federal Land Bank. Bought five hundred, a thousand acres from the bankrupt plantation owners during the depression. He cultivates his sugar plantation like a garden. You must admire the Triple A. Before the Triple A, they plow the land when easy for mules, when wet. Big chunks and lumps, dry as rock, next to the plant. The land bled white. But the Government says ten per cent must be planted in clover for soil conservation." He lights his cigar. "But we have not the climate! The cane, it's a greenhouse plant. The frost sours the cane. Maybe we have another freeze in two days? My experience is the sugar cane is the cause of poverty-stricken Louisiana."

He stares at me. "The machine is the curse of the South. Another curse is, the land is not owned by the hands who farm it. In Louisiana, in Texas, in Alabama, in Mississippi, in Georgia, they grow the cotton, and the corn for the mule. But the hand who works the land does not own the land. The tenant, he lives in a shack. The roof leaks. He raise the cotton, but he not have cotton dress for his wife. He eat 'taters and corn bread. Sometimes he have no cow. He sick with pellagra, rickets. The baby dies. Patent medicine, machine-made medicine that is not medicine, he has for his health.

And now the planter think he must make cotton with the machine just like the sugar planter. What to do with the hands, with the renters and sharecroppers? What to do with the land? Too much commercial agriculture! Too much bankers and politicians! If the big plantations are divided up and families live on fifty and one hundred acre farms, no reason for poverty. The planters obtain land by clan, by father to son, by eviction, by politics, by tricks, by depression years, by bad crops. Not a single planter is all honest. His land stolen from somebody. A planter I know had twenty cows for a thousand cutters. A cow sick, he slaughters 'em. On hoof yesterday and in the gravy today! The fraility is lack of land distribution. The sugar plantations belong to three hundred or five hundred families. They have idle land, but won't sell to Government to rehabilitate." He waves the cigar smoke away with an impatient nervous hand. "The salvation of the poor white in the South must come from the colored working man because they are the sufferers."

The tall cane.

The smokestacks of the Salsburg Factory rise from the cane. Rain drizzles down on two rows of unpainted shacks in a one-street community.

Off the highway, the brown rise of the levee slants up like a hill. The cane trucks roll south, the empty trucks north.

The sugar cane.

Smokestacks in the gray sky.

The Armant Factory, the shacks of the cutters grayer than the sky, the derricks like strange gigantic keys locked into the earth.

New Orlean's Canal Street glitters with business, department stores, restaurants, movies. I walk north down Royal Street into the French Quarter. The antique stores shine with old red glass. The windows hold the silverware of the forgotten plantations. Southern black-face mammy dolls in red bandannas, and oil paintings of Baratara Bayou and other pre-Civil War scenes are for sale to the tourists. The three-story buildings with their iron grill balconies testify to the elegant French America of the old South. But now business has come to the ground floors: THE GRIMALDI PLUMBING COMPANY. . .

The drizzle slants down on the streets. The lamp-posts throw yellow light on the slate sidewalks plastered with fallen leaves. In the courtyard of St. Louis Cathedral on Rue de Chartres, the banana trees look like tropical movie props. Autumn is on the city. I sit in Jackson Square facing St. Louis Cathedral with its three towers against the wind-blown clouds. To the left, a red and green neon flashes: HOME OF JAX BEER.

Two beams of electricity focus on the statue in the center of the Square, Jackson on his rearing horse. I walk by a palm tree, tall as the flagpole, and read the motto on the side of the pedestal: THE UNION MUST BE PRESERVED. In the rainy night in this neighborhood of balconied houses, the Creole past seems closer than the sugar and cotton plantations north, east and west of the city.

Cook's Praline Confectionery is on Chartres and Toulouse Streets. I go inside.

"Where'd the praline come from?" I ask Mr. Cook, an elderly vigorous man with graying hair.

"Everybody talks of the praline. In New Orleans, up to ten or twelve years ago, the praline was a quality product. All these old French families, the Creoles, the real Southern aristocracy, they accumulated fortunes here and didn't consider anything but real quality. It had to be quality," he says proudly. "They made the praline. Praline means *sugared*. This old family, the Favre family, they settled back here from Paris one hundred and fifty years ago. The old Mrs. Favre died at the age of one hundred and two. . . She remembered the praline as a child. She remembered when the boats came in from the West Indian Islands with cocoanut pralines. That's where the idea of the praline came from. I remember the old colored mammy we had. She had a camel's hair brush and she would select the halves of the pecan and brush them off to be sure none of the bitter wood was left. After making pralines for a good many years, she discovered that if she greased a piece of brown paper, it'd keep longer. She spooned the pralines out on the brown paper. Now we take the Canadian maple sugar out of New York in seventy pound bricks. We also use the brown cane sugar and blend them. To eliminate the molasses flavor, we use white granulated sugar."

He nods reflectively. "I grew up with the Favre family. My father followed the sea. . . All my relatives are down-easters." In his blue coat sweater, he seems like a second mate himself. But behind him, the shelves are full of cans: SOUTHERN CONFECTIONS MADE FROM THE RECIPE OF AN OLD LOUISIANA FAMILY. PECAN PRALINES. "My children asked me to make some pralines. I changed the cooking pro-cess. . . They all have their formulas!" he derides his competitors. "The Mexican praline made in San Antonio is just a sugar patty! Now over a century past sugar was made in the West Indian Islands. . . I remember when I was a child, and Royal Street was the business street, we used to have the fireman's parade on the 17th of March. We'd come down to Jackson Square and the firemen'd circle the Square and there'd be fifty mammies with a palmetto fan in one hand a basket of pralines in the other." He takes down one of the yellow, red and black cans from the shelf. "I drew this myself. There's the church and Jackson, and the iron fence around the Square and the oil lamps. . . My mammy was like a mother to me when I was a child. We used to work from 'kin to kaint.' I had to be up at four in the morning for my work. At four a.m. she'd come in with a cup of coffee in her hand and say: 'Wake up honey.' She would have a bundle of pinewood in her other hand and make a fire so it would be warm to get up. . ."

The cemeteries on the outskirts of New Orleans are above-ground, a stone city of the dead. Beyond the cemeteries, the sugar cane covers the land. A locomotive hauls a loaded train.

In the distance, two smokestacks. A warning sign: No TRESPASSING GODCHAUX SUGARS.

I drive off the highway up a dirt road towards the refinery, passing an open shed with nine or ten cane carts; a mule barn; an unpainted house with a Negro woman washing on the front porch, her arms dipping in and out of the tub; the new P.W.A.-built school named: LEON GODCHAUX HIGH SCHOOL.

Machinery thud-thuds from the corrugated iron buildings of the refinery. Outside the cane shed, the loaded trains and trucks are lined up in the sun. Inside the shed, hills of reddish-brownish-greenish stalks pile to the roof. Men and iron grapples feed the cane to the conveyor moving at the bottom of the sugar hill. The stalks on the belt travel up to the knives. The cut pieces move out of the shed to the mill.

In the mill, the cane goes into the crushers. A yellow torrent of juice pours down from steel. A second conveyor carries off the pulp or *bagasse*. The mill is full of wheels, their geared edges black with oil. Wheels, wheels as if the refinery were mounted on them like an immense cane cart.

Clarifiers.

Machines.

The juice bubbles in tanks set into the stone floor. The juice cooks, froths, brown geysers shot through with air bubbles, the sugar smell heavy in the heat.

A sugar boiler, a middle-aged baldish man wearing a green eyeshade, attends his huge metal pot with its six glass windows. "We crystallize the sugar by boilin' in a vacuum," he says to me. "I've been doing this twenty-four years. You got to make sugar out of it! And you got different orders. Make sugar for the Coca-Cola people . . . they want you to make it extra fine."

The sugar boils behind the six glass windows. In another department, the granulators like water wheels, revolve the sugar through currents of hot drying air, the white crystals spinning out and falling in white snowstorms.

Downstairs, a conveyor belt is carrying scores of one-hundred-pound bags lettered: CANE SUGAR REFINED IN U. S. A., to a sew-er. The bulletin board features a sign: TOTAL ACCIDENTS LAST YEAR 167. The sewn sacks travel to a giant Negro who swings them off the conveyor. Ten paces away are the freight trains and at the end of the steel tracks . . . the cities and towns of coffee-drinking America.

In the warm November afternoon, the little town of Gonzales seems asleep and all its inhabitants enchanted like Rip Van Winkle. A cow stands on the railroad tracks eating a length of sugar cane. The cow is in no hurry.

An old Negro woman, pipe between her lips, walks towards the stores past the gasoline stations. Outside Harry's Tavern, three white men gape out at the empty street in silence as if they haven't spoken a word to each other in hours.

The sun slants inside Joe Pertrius's country store. In one corner near the window, six or seven men in overalls and old suits are sitting on chairs and soap boxes, talking with the leisure of retired businessmen at a club. An old-fashioned radio bulks high on one end of the faded red counter. Behind the counter: shelves of Kellogg's Corn Flakes, cans of Bluerunner Stringless Beans, and the proprietor, a big man with gray eyes, straight black hair and freckled fists. A relaxed smile curves his straight mouth as if he were thinking in a detached way of the business troubles, sicknesses and marital discords of his neighbors.

"What does this country grow outside of cane?" I ask him, leaning against the counter.

"Cotton and strawberries." He turns, calls over to the men in the debating corner. "Doc, come here a minute."

A small old man joins us, his eyes blue and sharp behind their rimless glasses. "This is Doctor Martin," Joe Pertrius introduces us. "He knows somethin' about this country."

They both smile as if to say: We'll help you out, stranger, if we can.

"Are you a dentist, Doctor Martin?"

"I'm an eye specialist. What do you want to know about this country?"

"Cane and cotton."

Dr. Martin frowns. "The small farmer's not gittin' much out of cane. Several hundred, I reckon, some few colored in these parts. . . They sell some to Leon Godchaux at Reserve and to Emil Godchaux at Central. They're hardly makin' a livin'. There's no small mills left in this country. The Diez Company's makin' syrup up here but that's all."

"The price is one," Joe says emphatically, both arms on

the counter, his gray eyes steady and unwinking. "Then they got to haul that cane twenty-five, thirty miles."

"The other reason is account of labor," Doc supplements. "The Federal Government has so many people on relief, hardly get fellers to cut the cane."

Joe glances at Doc. "You couldn't start makin' a livin' cuttin' cane." His voice is mild, but conclusive.

Doc nods in agreement. "The season's short. Five, six weeks. The trouble with cane's this. . . The trouble's gittin' it off."

"Here's the proposition." Joe picks up a pencil, scribbling on a brown paper bag. "The small farmer's got to pay ninety cents a ton to cut and load. And haulin's extry. Got to buy fertilizer. Got to plant them canes. The farmer get nothin' at all. The li'l man hasn't a chance. He makes ninety-six cents from the Government a ton, but that don't amount to nothin' if he makes fifty or a hundred tons. The big shot's done made! The big shot gets ninety-six cents like the li'l man, but he raises ten thousand tons."

Doc yawns. Above his gray head there is an advertisement tacked to the wall: JAVELETS CORN NOCKER. GUARANTEED TO NOCK EM DEAD. "The li'l feller makes three bales of cotton and gets money from the Government on the bale just like the big feller."

Joe straightens up, speaks in his slow sure voice. "They don't make a livin', brother. They're just staying here. They got nothin' to eat, some of them. Some got a few cows. Some have none at all."

"The man who has his li'l cane farm and his cow and his chickens . . . that's the only way he can live," Doc says. "Cotton's another expensive crop like sugar. Man can't eat cotton. Mule can't eat cotton."

"I'll tell you a fact," Joe lays down his pencil on the brown paper bag. "Cotton under fifteen cents a pound is a loss. It'll net a man about eight cents a pound. He got five hundred pounds to the bale. . ." He pauses at the logic of cold numbers. Over in the corner, the farmers are talking politics. "Before the boll weevil struck, you made a bale to an acre around here."

"The big man's blowed out of here." Doc nods reflectively. "The sugar in-dustry has gone down. The cotton man's in the same way. Twenty-five years ago, we had ten or fifteen sugar mills. How many have we got today runnin'? Just one li'l syrup mill. Our cane goes out of the parish to refine. A few years ago I took the census for the United States Government for this parish. I was takin' a census of the blacksmith, the grocer. . . It was the businessman I was takin' a census of. Conditions was better for all of them before I took the census."

"Years ago you plant five acres you git five bale," Joe states. "I was born and raised in this country. I've raised cotton and co'n and strawberries. I'm still farmin'. I open this store and it seem worse."

"Come and look at my book." Doc smiles. "If I don't show you four thousand comin' to me in eighteen months! Both white and colored. If my practise wasn't so wide out . . ." He shakes his head dolefully. "I git cash from Baton Rouge, from those fellers in the oil refineries. What can I do? A teacher'll send a boy from school with no money. I can't turn him away for ten, fifteen dollars. I fit him up with glasses. Years ago, we had seven cotton gins. Now we haven't a gin in all Ascension Parish. All those gins gone! No mo'! The li'l man, he look like he just about froze out. That's one reason I favor an income tax on the rich. Shoot it to 'em! I'd pay one if I had to."

Two little boys enter the store, stepping up to the counter.

"Who wouldn't?" Joe says to Doc, turning to the boys.

"Loaf of bread," one of them orders.

"The small plantation owner . . ." Doc says as Joe reaches for a loaf of bread. "He's gone! Thousands of acres have gone in to weeds, the best land a crow ever flew over."

Joe stares at the backs of the two boys, departing with their loaf of bread. "If you got eleven acres of land you can hardly git along. A man got a thousand acres, he can borrer all he wants from the Government."

An old gaunt man strides into the store. He marches to the counter, listens to Joe. His grizzled eyebrows lift up on his wrinkled forehead. "Too much rain! Too much dry weather! I got twenty acres. I can plow no mo'!" He wears a *Sam Jones For Governor* button pinned to the lapel of his old jacket.

Joe Pertrius introduces us. "That's Joe Gonzales."

"My father founded the town," the gaunt man says. "I

was Mayor sixteen years. I'm seventy-eight. This year's my last year. I'm going to rent my land. The Govyment give you soil conservation!" he says scornfully. "Make beans! They give me a ninety-six cents sugar bonus but who goin' to cut my cane?"

"If there ain't a change, the whole country go into revolution," Joe says slowly. "Nobody to pay the doctor bill. Nobody to pay the medicine bill. The bill for this and the bill for that."

"Nothin' else's gonna happen!" Doc agrees. "I'm going back to the office."

"I've got white and nigger sugar cutters," the gaunt man says, as Doctor Martin leaves. "But I'd rather have Roosevelt cut my cane. The Govyment feeds 'em and they don't work." His eyes glare bitterly.

"The sugar plantation hire them cutters and feed 'em out of the store, and charge 'em these fancy forty-nine prices," Joe says mildly in counter argument.

The door pushes open. A man of about fifty enters, smiling at the farmers in the corner. His face is brick red, hard and clean of outline, a face of rock.

"Hello, Red," the farmers greet the newcomer.

"When did you get back?"

"We were talkin' about you."

Joe nods to me. "That's R. M. Singletary. Red Singletary. He's runnin' for Commissioner of Agriculture. He's from Gonzales." Joe leans on the counter as the ex-Mayor strides over to the crowd. "Red's a good man. Trouble is our own politicians fought us. Put a man in office and he represent the rich and not the low class of people. Singletary's runnin' with Jimmy Morrison. Election's the sixteenth of January. If the low class of people had any sense at all, they'll have nobody else." His jaw clenches. "Believe me, a man who's got a store makin' a livin', that man oughten to plant a crop. If you own a plantation and a sugar mill and a store, the other man, the li'l man got no chance to make a livin'. Suppose I had ambition and plenty money, I'd have a stock farm. That's what I ought to done. But it ain't right for me to have a stock farm and a store and another farm."

"I was passing out circulars," Singletary is telling the farmers over in the counter.

Joe smiles. "The farmers say what's the use to put another politician in? But I say: 'Put 'em in and keep 'em straight!' "

"I've been on the road three weeks and makin' from one to five speeches a day, preaching organization and cooperatives as the only hope for a better day on the American farm," Singletary is saying.

"What kind of speeches?" the ex-Mayor demands.

"This kind of speech. . . The only hope for the American farmer is organization. And cooperatives, both producer and consumer. And when they set up their cooperatives, they can cut out some of the graft and speculation in between the producer and the consumer. And that of itself will keep the farmer on the farm." He isn't making a speech now to the silent men, the sun slanting on his brick red face, his eyes shaded by the brim of his hat. "It will take organization and legislation to bring that about. I've been a farmer all my life just like you boys. I have ninety acres. I grow cane and strawberries, potatoes and corn. I'm quittin' cane as the market's low on cane. I'm turnin' into the truckin' business. Why, the li'l farmer can't compete with the big farmer. We're not financially able to own the machinery it takes. Mechan-i-zation of farm machinery will put the small farmer plumb out of business. If the mechan-i-zation of farm machinery continues at its present rate, the time'll come soon when the small farmer will be a tenant farmer to the large landowner, or else the Government'll have to take care of him on relief or public works."

The farmers nod agreement. "Organization is our only hope," Singletary continues. "Two years ago, the strawberry farmers were in the worst fix of any agricultural class in the nation. . . There's an old saying that the best comes out in a man in the gravest emergency. That's when we thought on the idea of organization. Good thing, wasn't it? We organized ten thousand strawberry farmers. In two year time, we sold eight million, five hundred thousand dollars of strawberries. Three million, five hundred thousand dollars of that amount we attributed directly to the Farmers Protective Union. What the strawberry farmers did with the most perishable crop on earth, other farmers can do on a broader scale but usin' the same system. The cane growers and cotton growers can do the same thing. For the first time in the history of the strawberry industry, were we able to name the price we would or wouldn't take. And we got it! The farmer's always an element of humanity who's depended on Providence or who's said: 'Let George do it.' Every other class has depended on organization to better itself. Now the farmers as a whole are ready to organize. And when we do, we'll be able to use organization against organization. When you're organized, you're in a position to make demands."

At night, the thirty-four marble stories of the State Capitol in Baton Rouge gleam against the black sky. From high up in the Capitol, a searchlight throws a steadfast beam of light over the night-green lawns of the grounds down upon a triangular space. Two sides of the triangle are grown with funeral trees. A marble bench carven: FOR THE COMFORT OF THE FRIENDS OF OUR FRIEND has been placed near the triangle's third open side. A young couple sit down on the bench. Before them . . . a diamond-shaped marble slab set into the earth, a vase of yellow chrysanthemums standing on each of the slab's four corners. The guarding funeral trees, seven in each row, the massed evergreens, all focus attention on the slab and the urn in its center. The searchlight illuminates the urn's marble inscription:

HUEY P. LONG 1893-1935

> *Sleep on Dear Friend*
> *And Take your Rest*
> *They Mourn you Most*
> *Who Love You Best*

I walk back to the State Capitol Huey Long built, the Capitol where he was assassinated. There it towers, the tombstone on his grave, the pyramid of his power. The first marble step is lettered: CONNECTICUT, a circle of the Revolution's thirteen stars next to the State's name, the names of the other original colonies ascending:

DELAWARE
GEORGIA
MARYLAND
MASSACHUSETTS
NEW HAMPSHIRE
NEW JERSEY
NEW YORK
NORTH CAROLINA
PENNSYLVANIA
RHODE ISLAND
SOUTH CAROLINA
VIRGINIA

The second flight begins with the stair: VERMONT 1791; (the state and the year admitted into the nation.) MICHIGAN 1837. . . COLORADO 1876. . . The forty-eighth state, ARIZONA 1912. . .

The last stair is lettered: E PLURIBUS UNUM.

There are no more States.

There are no more Territories to divide.

Ahead, is the doorway into Huey Long's marble pyramid.

Or, back turned on the doorway . . . the people of Louisiana, the people of the United States of America.

In the bright morning, the cars jolt down the bumpy road to the Mississippi River ferry. The ferryman motions me to come on board. I drive alongside a family of Negroes in an open truck; the old grandfather with his coat collar raised against the wind blowing in from the river, the two women knotting their blue bandannas snugger around their heads. As we drift off, the radio in the new car behind mine presents a drama: "Andy, suppose you tell me exactly what happened last night, the whole story. . ."

On the Baton Rouge shore, the State Capitol becomes smaller and smaller, the ferry passing two freighters at anchor with American flags painted on their sides, red-white-blue, smaller and smaller the State Capitol. . .

On the opposite shore, the cars climb up from the river level to the concrete highway, to the land and the people on the land.

A Negro is leading a team into a field, his big white horse flanked by two brown mules.

A cane truck speeds by.

Three Negro women, bamboo poles across their shoulders, faces shaded by straw hats, are on their way to a fishing hole. In the sunlight, the flow of False River shines and sparkles.

Beyond the town of New Roads, the picked cotton fields seem to have grown a new crop. Among the sere brown plants, the pods that ripened after the picking hold the light, puffs of white against the autumn brown.

The tall cane.

The sugar cane.

The Texas and Pacific freight cars near the town of Morganza are loaded with cane.

Beyond Morganza, the towns of Batchelor and Lettsworth —where the State of Mississippi like a shoe heel, presses into Louisiana's soil.

The unpaved gravel road out of Lettsworth cuts between scattered unpainted houses built of boards. The painted numbers on the letter boxes seem to stand, not for free men, but for the prisoners in the gray shacks.

P. O. Box 88.

P. O. Box 89

P. O. Box 90

The picket fences are unpainted.

P. O. Box 96.

I park on the road and walk up a path to a house with a corrugated tin roof. A black and white cow stares at me. I see two geese, a Rhode Island hen, six young pigs. Four wooden steps climb from the ground to the porch. An ancient Negro woman sits near the doorway, her bony hands in her lap. She sits without movement as if she were dead, as if she had died in her chair.

The family that belongs to P. O. Box 96 and I talk together in the front room. Pink and white mosquito netting canopies the battered bed in one corner. A log burns in the fireplace. Above on the lintel, the scarf is made of a newspaper, scalloped and decorative as if really cloth and not news-print. Where the faded wallpaper has worn out on the walls, brown wrapping paper has been substituted.

There are five of us. Henry Philips stretches his brown hands over the fire. A man of sixty-eight, his grizzled hair has whitened, his shoulders bent. His son Abraham is in his twenties, his features soft and boyish, a little mustache on his upper lip. Henry's wife, a big woman with an almost Indian face, holds Abraham's child on her lap. Outside, on the porch, the ancient crone, Henry's mother sits alone with her ninety years.

"I was cuttin' some beans tryin' to sell, to make out a li'l livin' when he came here." Henry smiles at me. His smile holds me off, a polite smile, a wary smile and yet a smile that seems to remember a pre-American freedom. . .

Henry's wife rocks her grandchild in her arms.

"You farm all the time, Henry?" I say.

"Yas, suh. I been farmin' all my life in this same state. My father was born right across the Mississippi. I been workin' ever since I was eight years old."

"You too, Abraham?"

"My father a tenant all his days. He send me to school. I went three months a year in the Ol' Grove Church. Then at the age of eighteen I start farmin' myself. I got two rooms here an' my father got two. I work three acres of cotton. Plant co'n in latter part of March. Begin to work in latter part of April. Latter part of April, we plant the cotton. The cotton you prepare the soil almost as you do in a garden. Then you run a planter behind the cultivator. Then the cotton seed's planted."

"In about eight days it's up." Henry nods his grizzled head. "Two wide leaves. You begin cultivatin'. Sow the cotton thick. An' now you thin out. Chop it with the hoe. Chop cotton just goes to dust."

"Then we cultivate it again with the cultivator," Abraham says. "It's sunup to sundown. . . Then you go back with the disk an' mole it up, put the dirt close 'round the plant to keep it moister. In June you begin to cultivate it down. The latter part of August you begin pickin' the cotton. My wife an' who-ever I can hire help, pickin' the cotton. It take four weeks to pick. Then take it down to the gin. You can't feel good!"

he says, his voice low, his brown eyes intense. "I'm rentin' myself! The landlord just give you the land. You buy your own seed. The money for the bales all goes for rent and grocery bill. We live on a small plantation where we rent. We's lucky. The one-third share proposition is on the large plantations around. My rent's sixty-five dollars for seventeen acres. I have five in cotton, twelve in co'n, the co'n to feed the hogs, the chickens an' myself."

"This year on the average, fifty dollars for the bale," Henry says.

"I make four bales," Abraham continues. "That two hundred dollars. Sixty-five for rent. Fo'ty dollars for groceries I bought on the crop. Barrel of flour's seven dollars in the store. But through the Buyin' Club it's five dollars. . ."

"What buying club?" I ask him.

"That's the Louisiana Farmer's Union," Abraham answers. "We all buy together in the Local so it's cheaper for us. Lard at the store's five dollars an' twunnty-five cents for a fifty-pound can. At the Buyin' Club, it's four dollars and a half. That's when *one* buys. But when we buy lard all together it's three dollars an' eight-three cents. We put the sixty-seven cents a can we save into the Buyin' Club fund. Then we meet four times a year an' vote how the money be use."

The fire licks into the blackened side of the log. Abraham's child sleeps on his silent grandmother's lap.

"Beginning of the fall we go cuttin' cane." Abraham stares into the fire. "Go about thirty miles on a truck to the field. Git up at fo' o'clock. Git there by six an' go to work. Some boss man won't give you but a dollar a day. After the cuttin', nothin' to do until you begin to break the ground for your cotton an' co'n. That's February fifteenth."

"Git wood for the cold days." Henry shivers a little. "Need plenty wood for fire."

"The houses 'round here all real delapidated," Abraham says. "That's why need wood for fire. The water bad. The well's not deep enough. Landlord suppose to furnish well, but he won't put out enough money to go deep enough. To have good water, have to go fifty feet or more."

"Landlord, he furnish the house an' the premisarry." Henry nods. "He suppose to have a decent place to live."

"The tenant like we pays five to six dollars rent an acre," Abraham says. "Or, he on the one-third or one-fourth share. But over there on the Glynn Plantation, everybody's evicted. About thirty-five families an' no place to go. Some of 'em livin' in ole buildings nobody's using."

"What kind of man Glynn?" Henry asks Abraham.

"He's a stout heavy man. With him, he got a boy an' a girl. The girl works in the commissary. I meet him often at the Post Office. He nice to me. He got fifty acres in cane. He's givin' one dollar an' a half to white workers, but for colored, one dollar. He had twelve white cutters the last I'd heard. He paid the white all right in the beginning, but he wouldn't pay 'em more than a dollar later on. The whites quit."

Henry puckers in his lip. He shakes his head, exclaiming. "Uh huh!"

"A man hasn't got a chance to make a decent livin'. It's gone from bad to worse."

"My mother didn' have no husband and three or fo' children" Henry says. "I work in cotton, in cane. I done some railroad and levee work. Now, it's goin' bad. Doctor Hobgood tryin' to get his tenants on a third. Couple year ago, his tenant work on the fo'th. One fo'th to Hobgood on the cotton and the co'n. Last year, he raise the share to one-third for the cotton an' the co'n. Seventeen fam'ly move. How a man can furnish feed, furnish team an' give Hobgood a third? That's pretty tough. The families got to move an' don' know where to go. Seventeen family move out."

His wife gazes at him, speaks for the first time. "I been farmin' ever since I'm eleven. Just cotton an' co'n an' potatoes."

"Doctor Hobgood not the only one," Abraham says. "A part of Mr. Steve Barbre's plantation on the third. And Mister Nolan and the Wayside Plantation, he change from the fo'th to the third for next year. They have Thanksgiving this year." Still his voice is low but in his voice, other voices seem to speak, thousands of voices, tens of thousands of voices, the voice of the Southern tenant and sharecropper, the voice of the Texan and Oklahoman and Mississippian and Georgian. . .

"I'm not havin' a turkey this year," his mother says. "I was raisin' turkeys an' they all died." A fly settles on her strong brown hand. Only Abraham's sleeping child shows no worry on his small face.

"Just bought a pair of geese to git a start." Henry smiles. "Goin' to have some of them greens out there for Thanksgivin'. Mustards an' turnips. Abraham do the huntin'. He shoot rabbit an' 'possum."

"Parboil the 'possum in salt and red pepper. Then take'm out an' bake it." Henry's wife smiles a little.

"That's all to it." Henry laughs. "Next thing's eatin' it." Suddenly, he is frowning. "This is a terrible parish. They don't want to see the cullid have mo'n a piece of bread. They don't want to see you with a good cow!"

"Missus Branch wants to buy Abraham's cow. I wouldn't let him sell. That's all he got!" Henry's wife cries out. "Abraham's cow plumb black an' got horns. She's a good milk cow."

"Take that li'l kid," Henry nods at his grandson. "If he try to walk an' everybody pull'm down, it's a hard time for him. . . That's how it is for the cullid. I voted when I was twenny-one. That's when the cullid people was votin'. I never vote again. Pity someone don't have pity on us cullid people so we can live."

Abraham looks squarely at me. "The hope for us is to come together an' band ourself in unionism."

Sigent Caulfield's unpainted house is near the Phillips' unpainted house. Sigent's shack is off the ground, set on blocks. Under the elevated floor, a few chickens ceaselessly hunt for food. As I come up the road, Sigent walks down to meet me, a Negro of thirty-two in a blue denim jacket and brown pants. His little boy remains near the mule wagon, too shy to stir.

"Hello, Sigent. How long you here?"

"Hello. I been here four years. I brought this wire when I come. He wanted me to fix all the pasture fences free. I borrered thirty dollars from him. He charge me eight per cent interest. I borrered it in March, paid it back in October."

His boy peeks at us from the wagon with squirrel eyes.

"Has your landlord many families here?"

"Mr. Mobley . . ." Sigent pronounces *Marble* as Mobley. "He got about thirty families all on a fo'th. He got mad 'cause I wouldn't fix the pasture fences for nothin'. He make six families move. Ah think about givin' up farmin'. I have no debts. Don't owe nobody a penny. I'll go to some city, some town. A man can't farm no more. Mr. Billy Coach, he lives in New Orleans. He's puttin' out thirteen families and puttin' in day labor. He rent his land out to one man!"

I walk up the mule wagon side-road, a scratch across the land, between the corn and bean fields and the cotton. The corn stalks are sere, brittle. The beans and the cotton have been picked.

The side-road ends at another gray shack with a corrugated iron roof, a settlement of one house, one family. A mule wagon approaches me and now the driver, a white man, tugs back on the reins. From the house, two children, a girl of four or five in overalls and a blond boy of about two, advance up the road behind the wagon. They stop when the wagon stops, staring like the children of the pioneers before them, innocent and wide-eyed.

The driver clambers down from the wagon, leaving his wife on the seat. He walks towards me, a wiry man in a brown work suit, a black felt hat on his lean head. His two little ones scamper back to the house like animals to a den. Shy as her children, the mother glances at me, her hand fluttering nervously to her mouth. She is young, about twenty-three, her eyes light blue, her features so regular that she is handsome rather than pretty. Although dressed in faded overalls, a straw hat on her head, her eyes and fluttering hand make her seem as feminine as a woman in a frilly gown.

"Where were you heading for?" I ask her husband.

"Thrashin' beans. I'm Ad Bordelon. . ." He wears a white cloth around his neck for the thrashing.

I introduce myself. "Do you own this place, Ad?"

He smiles. "Wished I owned my own place. Whoa!" he calls to his reddish-brown mules.

"Your mules have about every cocklebur in the county."

"Cocklebur are tough on mule tails and hams." Ad looks at the matted mule tails. "There's so much dust thrashin' you can barely breathe. It's liable to give some asthma. I get fifty-five cents a bushel and givin' a fourth out of that. . ." He shakes his head. "Make a li'l corn, I give a fourth. Make some onions, give a fourth out of that. But they ain't goin' to get me to raise cane. Cane costs a man twenty dollars an acre! And he's gettin' his fourth clear!"

"Who's he?"

"Mr. Mobley from Port Arthur, Texas." Ad also pronounces Marble as Mobley. "This here's my second year. Mobley wants to lend you money. But he loan you twenty dollars, you have to give him a mortgage for sixty. He say he can't lose. Not like that when my dad was a farmer. He raise corn and cotton. We made a li'l cane syrup, but no cane for speculate. We was makin' a fine livin'. We had a grits mill. Go sell thirty dozen eggs every Saturday." He leans against the wagon, smiles up at his wife. "She work just as hard as I do. I got two mules for partner. She my fourth partner."

Man and wife laugh. Encouraged, the two children skip up the road. Ad's wife blushes, her fingers darting back to her mouth as if she were a girl of twelve.

"What will you have for Thanksgiving?" I ask her.

She smiles, but doesn't answer.

"We'll have fresh hogmeat," Ad says. "We got seventeen head of hog."

"Have you any cows?"

She nods, smiling, but still too shy to talk.

"One of my cousins is workin' about a half mile from here," Ad says. "He had one cow, but he give it to his daughter."

"You voting January sixteenth, Ad?"

"I can't understan' what's right and what's wrong." His tanned forehead wrinkles. "I'm goin' to vote, but the candidates don't pass by us here. They tell me the elections are dull. But my notion's to support a man who don't care what he says against what's wrong!"

"We wasn't thinkin' about Thangsgivin'," Ad's wife says throatily. She sits very straight on the wagon seat. "Thinkin' about Christmas."

"Have good health and a li'l to eat, that's all I want," Ad remarks. "I expect Santa Claus to come."

"Unless he's too poor." His wife laughs timidly at her joke.

"Family's all healthy except my old mother. She takin' care of the kids. That give us time to work. This year my cotton seems to be good in some places. But my bottom's no good. I got five bales out of seven acres. The rain collect in the bottom. But if my wife's good to me, I'll buy her something for Christmas. Maybe a li'l print dress."

"I don't like it so much livin' in the field," Ad's wife says. "If we could git a place close to the gravel or pavement. . ."

"Like in the winter it's bad," Ad continues for her. "If you need a doctor in the rainy days, he'd have to leave his car and walk out."

"Doctor wouldn't do that." Ad's wife turns around to look at her children. Hand in hand like the Hansel and Gretchen in the fairy tale, they have almost ventured up to the wagon itself.

"I hope those three children we got be all." Ad smiles seriously. "I like children. My old mother takin' care of the baby inside. I like children, but times're bad."

His wife giggles, the blood rushing up into her neck and cheeks.

"Everything's on the fourth. Only the kids not on the fourth!" Ad pushes his black felt back off his forehead. "My notion's that the boss man tryin' to get his families to plant sugar. And when we got it all planted in sugar, he'll make us move off. The first thing he propose to new family, and to good family, too: 'Are you willing to plant sugar canes?' And that knocked 'em off. What's the use of stickin' our li'l money in a gamblin' proposition like sugar cane? One acre sugar cane bring one hundred dollars and he get twenty-five." His face is solemn. "That's the first question: 'Are you willing to plant sugar canes?' "

"I guess in a few years from now he won't have nobody on the place," his wife says.

"We can't sell cotton our own self being fourth renters. Missus Mobley sells it for you and that don't encourage a man at all. That's gettin' a man discourage."

"A man ought to sell his own crop!" Ad's wife declares.

"I'd like to be my own boss and not give no fourth. Put up a hog pen . . . That's mine!" Ad dreams aloud. "Put up a chicken house . . . That's mine! Out here we too far even to go to church. It's twenty miles from here. I got no car."

"Ride the mule," his wife suggests, laughing.

"Can't ride the mule. We're not sinners, but we can't walk

that far. I used to assist every Sunday morning in church. Sure do miss mass. I hope God sure forgive us."

I hike back to the gravel road, to the New Zion Baptist Church. Mounted on blocks, the wooden building once painted white, the window sashes and door once painted blue, looks like a huge empty box. A cow grazes outside the wire fence around the church. In the yard, a big bell hangs from its wooden frame.

I go inside and enter, not a church, but a class room. Twenty or twenty-five Negro children pivot around on the wooden benches used by the congregation on Sundays, to stare at me. The children are of all ages, girls and boys in overalls, whispering among themselves, staring at me again, their warm black eyes asking one question over and over: Who is that man?

From up front, the teacher walks down the central aisle that divides the Sunday church-weekdays school into two halves. A young girl of about nineteen with a round face and eyeglasses, she has the manner and authority of her profession.

"I hate to break in like this. You must excuse me."

The teacher smiles. "The regular teacher's sick. If you can come back here Monday . . ."

"I think you can tell me about your pupils."

"I have forty-one children from primer to seventh and from what I can understand they come a long ways." The eyes of the classroom shine at us. "I have to walk almost a mile myself. Some of the children walk about three mile from the concrete. Last week it was rainin'. It's very muddy when it rains. And when it's dry it's very dusty."

Three ancient cracked blackboards, that look as if they date from the Civil War, hang on the church's walls. The children have no desks, their books on the benches beside them. Unlit kerosene lanterns are suspended on hooks, the November light graying through the broken panes in the windows.

"We have books, extra books," the teacher says. "Dealin' with science and nature study."

"Where are you from?"

"I'm from New Orleans. I went to school there. Saturday was payday." She laughs, the genteel laugh of the underpaid American school-teacher. "But I don't know what I'm going to get paid. Ah guess it'll be fifty dollars a month."

"Thank you Miss —"

"Miss Jones."

"Thank you, Miss Jones."

She returns up front. "Where are the questions I gave you?" she asks the four girls whom she had been quizzing when I came in.

Silence. Little boys and girls twist around to gape at me.

"You can find those words with a dictionary," Miss Jones hints to the bemused four.

A chubby girl answers finally. "It wasn't in the dictionary."

"A political map'll show the states in the country," Miss Jones states. "What else will it show? What will a physical map show?"

Silence. The four peek at me as if to say: First, we want to know who that man is.

"A physical map'll show mountains and rivers," Miss Jones says. "Find one in the geography book."

The four thumb the pages of their geography books.

A little boy in the last row turns his head around to gape at me. His hair is yellow, his eyes blue, his skin brown. His blue eyes, the eyes of the white race, meet mine.

Eight or nine sharecroppers and tenants, Negroes, whites, have gathered at the Bowman-Wilson sugar mill, a mill without expensive machinery, without clarifiers, without granulators, without conveyor belts, without freights or trucks of sugar cane. A mill without a building. A mill without a roof. The grinding machine is near the pecan tree. Here, an old white horse walks around and around in a primitive power-making circle, pulling a beam attached to the machine. Around and around, the horse walks as Bowman's small sons feed cane into the two horizontal revolving rods of the grinder, the sugar cane heaped on the ground. The boys reach for new stalks, inserting the ends between the rods. The horse walks, the stalks squeezing into pulp or *bagasse*. A third Negro boy drags the *bagasse* off to one side as the cane juice pours from between the rods down a home-made tin gutter into a pail, whose top is covered with a sieve made of brown burlap.

A Negro farmer drives up to the grinding machine with a new wagonload of cane.

Fifteen feet away from the grinding department with its three boys in overalls and one horse, is the sugar tank, the cane juice stored in a big wooden barrel with a spigot in its side. The sugar tank, built of wood, is divided into compartments now full of yellow boiling foaming juice. The tank has been placed into a trench dug out of the ground. In the second trench alongside the tank, one of the partners, thin Wilson, is busy stirring the boiling syrup. A small white man with a hooked nose, a receding chin, with a profile like a bird's, he wears a red-and-black plaid shirt and overalls. "Cook it up near the barrel," he says to me. "And clean it. When it gits back here it's syrup."

Above the two trenches, the neighbors stand around, their eyes on the yellow juice thickening into syrup. Now and then, they exchange a few neighborly words, the friendly words of harvest, the harvest of the cane. "That's cookin' up nice."

"That'll be nice syrup."

Over by the pile of crooked logs combed out of the woods, a boy of sixteen swings his ax industriously, splitting the logs into burning size for the sugar mill.

In overalls and old felt hat, the second partner, Bowman, observes operations. I walk over to him. His blue eyes swerve from the tank to the grinding machine.

"You're the owner of this mill," I say to him.

"Wilson . . ." He nods at the syrup-stirrer . . . an' me are partners on this mill. The farmers bring the cane down they want for their own use an' we make the syrup for them. We put it in cans an' get a fo'th."

"Do you raise sugar cane yourself?"

"I raise fo' acres of cane. I have no complainin' whatever. I got fifteen acres in cotton, twelve an' a half acres in corn. But don' get nothin' but a lot of work." He smiles at his sons now punching and pushing and tossing ends of sugar cane at each other. The old white horse trudges around and around.

"All my kids big enough to work, work. But looks like now they're playin' some."

A stout Negro in corduroy pants held up by old-fashioned suspenders and wearing a cap, joins us. We watch the warring kids for a few seconds. Bowman strides over to his sons, a peacemaker. "They goin' to get the mill down to my place Monday. An' those around my place'll bring their cane in to grind. I have a right deal of cane." The stout man has a round face with plump cheeks. "I saved it all for syrup an' I'll can it in buckets. I have fifty buckets, brand new. I have forty ole buckets. I'll have to git more."

"I don't know your name."

"I'm the Reverend William Mormon." He nods his head. Bowman's boys have ended their war, again feeding cane stalks to the grinder.

"Are you on the fourth?" I ask the reverend.

"I'm a cash renter, raisin' cane, raisin' cotton, co'n an' beans. I have my wife an' my mother an' my daughter to take care of the farmin'. I have a deal of work to do." He sits down on the end of a tree trunk. "I takes care of the Home Suppo't Society which takes care of the sick an' buries the dead. I takes care of the Earnest Deal Society which has sixty-odd people, women, mens an' children. The Home Suppo't Society contain seventy men people an' pays relief to the widder." His eyes, blood-shot in the corners, stare at me. "The most grebous matter is to git a high school. We want a school here fo' preparation. . ." He is silent for a second. "I'm down here this church right down here ahead, the Scott M. E. Church. I preaches every Sunday. I have to prepare the sermon in advance. Sometimes, I make up sermons." He stares down at the ground. "We have this grebous concern with the homeless, the fellows put off Hobgood's land, an' Mobley's, an' the Sunnyside Plantation. An' Mr. Billy Coach, he done sent 'em notice they git better go. He want 'em to go early day possible. Missus Branch has notified her people she want their houses. They're tryin' to push 'em off an' put on day labor. On Mr. Billy Coach's place, he rent his land to one man. The man, he hasn't come here yet. He just goin' to hire day labor. Those are the plantations still puttin' off," he says, his voice mournful and slow. "Mr. Hobgood, he's the begin' of this business. So the people around here by Lettsworth, they're well dis-

turbed. They don't know where's gonna be their location."
He bangs his big fists together.

The old white horse paces around and around, a few
shrivelled leaves swirling up from under its hooves.

"The landlords, they have meetin's to that effect. They
figurin' to break up the community. They wanna work 'em on
a third. People cannot do anything workin' on a third. On a
third they cannot live."

Bowman smiles down at me. "I'll show you it."

"I'll be right back," I tell Reverend Mormon.

He nods his round head.

Bowman walks to the tank. "No brick at all in that stove.
We put the flue right down on the ground. Made in the same
shape as brick. Put up a hundred dollar worth of brick, it
take you a year to pay for it. That's all a poor man gits, is a
livin'. He don't make no money. They ruin the poor people."
He yanks open the iron door in front of, but below, the tank,
the yellow flame of the burning wood surging out in sudden
hot leap.

"It's goin' all right," Wilson says to his partner.

I walk back to the tree trunk, sit down. Reverend Mormon
shifts to a more comfortable position. "Things gittin' more, it
seem like it goin' back. The people not havin' no rights at all.
The last year or two they're really sufferin'."

A Negro woman in a white bandanna and a red print dress
climbs up from the road to the sugar mill. Her shoes have no
heels.

"All my people were staunch, Christianized people." The
reverend in the cap shakes his head from side to side. "An'
that's where my callin' come from. I remember how the slaves
they had burdens. They had to steal out an' go no'th. An'
they stayed out of way of the ole marster so they could git
away. They had to be whipped an' be killed. . . In Louisiana
now, it seem they have as much slave now as I can git out of
the histories. That lynchin' business, that bad. The white
people runnin' the Negroes like the robins an' the birds. That
bad. The same thing applies to the whites as to the colored.
The whites have no pribileges unless they in high authority.
These poor white people suffer like the colored." He nods
over at Bowman. "He tryin' to work around here an' his poor
wife sick. He say: 'If my wife don't have a change tomorrow

I'll have to stop.' She in there in the house and nobody to assist. The white people undergo the same burden." He sighs. "It ought to be a better day for the poor people. The poor people don't have proper food an' raiment. They haven't the sufficiency to do the work. I see their struggles an' their needs. I meet 'em all. They all need."

Bowman climbs up into an empty mule wagon and drives off. The younger of his sons stoops for a piece of sugar cane, cutting off its peel with a knife. His brother charges at him. He ducks, sticking the peeled-off end into his mouth, chewing.

"Hit done have to be done something," the reverend says. "The people'll perish away. When they're disabled an' can't git assistance from doctors, it just means death. They're sufferin'. That don't mean anything but death. That's the trouble with this people. This people would be much more better if they could git attention. But everything rests on the backbone of the laborin' people." His slow voice deepens. "The laborin' people, they're the last to be consider. You can see what it means." He points his strong forefinger in turn at the Negroes and at the whites. "It don't mean anything but starvation. These rich mens are making conveniences but for themselves. Everything's been put over on the white an' the colored. A good bird dog, it belongs to the rich. A good horse, it belongs to the rich. . . The Bible has a deal of points to these conditions. In the time back, they had leaders asting for the people to be free. That reminds me of this man McIntyre of the Farmers' Union. He come to his own, his people, his kind, his white. An' because he's for right, they don' want to receive him. Mr. Abe Lincoln, he tried to loose the people in the time back. . . An' Christ come to His own and His own receive him not. The Scriptures tell us. . . Moses grew up in a home of Pharaohs an' because he had the right, God give him to lead a people, he tried to loose that people. These rich mens, these lan'lor', they disagree to see a people have freedom."

Still, the patient horse pulls the beam attached to the grinding machine. Still, the sharecroppers and tenants, Negroes, whites, stand motionless before their meager harvest.

"It seems it gonna be bloodshed over these matters," Reverend Mormon's face is sad. "The union's the only hope, the only salvation. . ."

U. S. Route Number 11

Walker, Louisiana. . .
Holden.
Hammond.
Covington.

And across the Pearl River into the State of Mississippi.

The pine woods, too, cross the boundary between the states, and the unpainted shacks, and the cotton fields.

It is Thanksgiving Day and the land is Thanksgiving-colored with the reds of the maples, the greens of the pines, the solemn browns of the used earth between crops.

On the outskirts of Hattiesburg, Mississippi, a Negro tramps up to the road from the woods, a hound dog at his heels. In his right hand, he carries an ax. His left hand grips the ears of a killed rabbit.

I stop my car. "Good hunting and without a rifle."

He grins a proud hunter's grin. "Cain't 'ford no rifle. This here dog run rabbit down an' I comes along." He drops the ax head to the ground, his hand curving around the end of the wooden handle.

"You don't hunt rabbits for a living?"

"No, suh." The rabbit in his hand looks stuffed, artificial. "I make cotton. I make this what you call you-an'-I cotton. I make it an' landlor' takes it." He laughs. "Story of pig or pup. Cain't be both makin' cotton an' ownin' the land."

"You don't know who I am? I might be a. . ."

"Plates on your car not made in cotton land. I'm a huntin' man an' a huntin' man talk the truth. Landlor' tell me to hush my mouth. But God make my mouth an' tell me to open it."

Northeast . . . Laurel, Mississippi, with its smokestacks, the gray houses of the town Negroes squeezed in between the highway and the railroad tracks, shack after shack, pink flowers glowing in an occasional garden.

Sandersville.
Pachuta.

Sere cornstalks rise against the sky, the cotton fields picked of their white fluff.

Cotton fields.

Meridian, Mississippi.

Cuba, Alabama.

Cotton fields.

Eutaw.

Tuscaloosa.

Hills. Forests on the hills. In the distance the skyscrapers of Birmingham.

Negroes and Whites

BIRMINGHAM AND GADSDEN

"Nation shall not lift up sword against nation;
neither shall they learn war any more."
From the prophecy of Micah.

IN BIRMINGHAM, NEGRO STEEL workers hurry to work in the early morning. On the porch of a little house, an old man rocks up and down, holding a baby on his lap. The old man stares from his grandson to the strong men passing down the street on their way to THE SLOSS-SHEFFIELD STEEL AND IRON COMPANY.

Steam streamers up from the locomotives on the interlacing railroad tracks. Black smoke hurls out of the smokestacks. STEEL AND IRON.

COMPANY.

In the late morning, two steel workers and one coal miner are taking it easy in the coal miner's home. All three are on the afternoon shift. A big chunk of bituminous burns in the fireplace, radiating heat out on the talkers. All three are Negroes. The coal miner's head is long and narrow, the mustache on his lip accentuating his youth. The older of the two steel workers, a man of forty, is the big listener. He sits on the double bed that takes up most of the living room, the original poker face, never commenting, never smiling.

Close to the fire, the young steel worker smokes a cigarette. "This was in nineteen hundred and thirty-six. I was waitin' on line fo' a job. The clerk ask the feller in front of me, how long he work for the Red Mountain ore mine? He said: 'Thirty-two years.' And then the clerk ask his age. He was fo'ty-fo'. The clerk was not convinced and to convince the clerk, he show him a thirty-year service medal. He was tellin' the truth. That's all he git from the Company."

The older steel worker nods, his lips and eyes expressionless.

"What was the size of his family?" the coal miner asks.

"I didn't remember that."

Coal Miner guesses. "Say he had an average family of five people. . ."

The young steel worker grins. "A guy couldn't have too many children, workin' in an ore mine. I'm married a long time and I ain't got a one. I imagine ore minin's hard as my work. I don't think fellers workin' in mines and steel mills got too many kids." He stretches his legs out towards the fire. "Birmingham is runnin' way ahead of any other community producin' steel. United States Steel, the Slosses, they produce one third of the country's steel. The first place is the cheap labor. The second place is the raw material right at hand. In twenny-four hours after they dig the ore, they can make it into pig iron. In thirty-six hours they can make it into steel. The steel mills and ore mines connected right up to one another. This is why steel can be produce' in the South."

Coal Miner sits forward. "The next thing is the weakness of the labor movement to wipe out the wage differential." His eyes shine in his enthusiasm. He burns with ideas as another man with baseball.

"In one of the United States Steel books, they had a drawin' of Europe." The young steel worker looks up from the fire. "To bring the ore from Minnesota to Pittsburgh is further than from London to Rome. Here, they got a belt from Red Mountain to Ensley. One drag'll bring down enough ore to run the blast furnaces twenny-four hours. And a special railroad to bring the ore down! That ore'll last two hundred years."

"The same thing with the coal mine," Coal Miner says. "The first coal mine about seven mile out. You can dig the coal in thirty-six hours and use it in the furnace to make steel."

"The Company make the money out of the by-products."
The young steel worker smiles. "Can of tar cost fifteen cents.
One hundred pounds cost fifteen dollars. And I see the Company ship out several tank loads every week." His smile
broadens as if he were a stockholder in the Company himself.

"I had another thing in mind." Coal Miner frowns. "What
was it? Oh, yes. The T.C.I. hire more white miners in the last
fo' years than they ever did. They hire the white miners to
use 'gainst the Negroes."

"Who better union men?" the young steel worker asks.

"On the average, both are equally progressive. On both
sides you'll find some sucks." Coal Miner pulls a cigarette out
of his pack. "Before the C.I.O. was carryin' on a real campaign
in 1933, we was workin' nine and ten hours a day. In some
mines, twelve and fo'teen hours. The T.C.I. was payin' above
the other mine. They was payin' two-ninety fo' nine hours.
That was back in '32. Some of those mines, they was workin'
so long hours the kids' fathers see them once a week. The kids
afraid of their fathers. Kids be in bed when the father leave
and be in bed when the father come home at night. But the
union change that. The hours cut down from nine to seven in
the captive mines. From ten and twelve hours to seven in the
commercial mines. The pay increase jump from small sum to
fo' dollars. Before they organize the mines, the bosses was
able to give the whites all the best places to further this division between Negro and white. But now that change. We
say: 'Your struggle is my struggle. My struggle is your struggle.' We still have some bad conditions. We have a lot of rock
and that pillar work pretty dangerous. . ." His strong hands
mine the space in front of him. "When you drive a room three
hundred fifty or five hundred feet, cuttin' under the coal with
the cutter bar, drivin' a cross-cut every seventy feet to circu-
late the air through the mine, when you work one of those
rooms out and git that coal out, pullin' all the pillars. . ." He
shakes his long head. "Night before last the rock thudded over
my head like anything!"

"You find a lot of white men's jobs held by Negroes."
The young steel worker turns to the older steel worker as if
to ask: That so?

"That right." This is the first time he has spoken. "The

pipefittin' gang in the blast furnace are cullid. Every man in that department's cullid."

"No need to contact a white man," the young steel worker says. "The foreman's Negro and the foreman's foreman is a Negro. I hear in 1919 there were a lot of Bul-garians and Hungarians chargin' the blast furnace. But after those Bul-garians struck, they gave those jobs to Negroes. . . I never work on the blast furnace. My job like a man brings a whole sack of flour for his wife to make a li'l bread . . . We dump the ore in the bins and sweep out. You can't see your hand before your face, the dust so thick. You can't leave any more ore than you can eat."

The silent steel worker smiles for the first time. "They git a kind of ore called Indian ore from India. Can't leave that around. There's a manganese comes from the volcanoes in Cuba. They buy it from the Cubans as sinter because it look like sinter ash from molten copper. But it ain't sinter. It's manganese."

"That's a nice trick," Coal Miner says.

"With all the furnaces runnin' I'll make thirty-five dollars in five days." The young steel worker stretches his long arms. "But all the time, my back is sore. The wrench I work with weighs fo'ty pounds. When you been in it a long time, you carry it on your shoulder. We have no set safety rules on my job. You're not supposed to work on movin' trains. But you work on 'em all day, usin' your judgment. The cars come in. You use the wrenches and let the ore down in the bin and take your chance. There's a hundred sixty cars of ore every twenny-four hours for six blast furnaces. Twenny-two cars of dolomite, ninety-five cars of coke. Of late, they're buyin' coke?" He looks questioningly over to Coal Miner.

"Sometimes it's a certain seam of coal'll give more heat," he answers. "Them by-products of coal will pay for the minin' of the coal. I dig a ton of coal for seventy-fo' cents and they'll make fifty-two dollars out of that ton."

"They went up two dollars a ton on pig iron but I don't think it's the war," the young steel worker says. "I've seen some fellers figure how long it'll take to produce the steel Germany's sunk."

"It's a rich man's war," Coal Miner says. "We coal miners opposed to war. It don't matter about the European countries goin' into war. We don't want to go into war here. War here just about kill wages and hours and all decent livin' conditions."

The two steel workers shake their heads in agreement.

Between Birmingham and Gadsden the hilly country is divided into small farms, the dead autumn leaves whirling among the dead corn stalks.

INDUSTRY HAS COME TO GADSDEN: the road sign reads.

The Hotel Reich has come to Gadsden with industry, one of those modern hotels where the salesman from New York, the executive from Chicago, the visiting rich man from San Francisco, can all feel comfortably at home. Behind Hotel Reich, the old-fashioned wooden houses on Chestnut Street belong to the America before the tiled shower.

Floyd Hester Deberry lives on Chestnut Street. Yawning, he stands with his back to the burning bituminous in the fireplace. Tall and blond, his face has the regular features of the British royalty. But his clothes are those of a plain American, a pair of clean painters' overalls. The strength of his body is that of a workingman. His muscled shoulders and arms (he wears no undershirt) catch the soft glow of the fire, his bare feet gripping the floor like a sailor's. He strides over to a chair and sits down. "This is one of the most peculiar situations right here than in most any li'l town. I don't understand it myself. We been goin' through quite a bit of hardship right here." His voice is level. "Way I see it, they most forced us into the union over here . . . I was raised on a farm myself. Like boys will, I wasted my money until I was married. If you haven't money to farm, you're at the other feller's mercy . . . I went to work for the Stove Foundry. I was told by the older people in the Foundry: If I please my superiors I'd get advancement. The more I slaved the more they wanted me to. Then I went to Goodyear in the fall of '29. They open the plant in '29. They handed me a bag of tools the first day. I said: 'I was hired in as an inspector.' They said: 'You're a tire builder.' " His blue eyes look straight at me. "Then the N.R.A. came along and that was a boost to labor. They was

organizin' up North and I said: 'We better get organized, too.'
Some of us said: 'The Government'll take care of us.' But I
said: 'He won't be President all the time.' "

He strides back to the fireplace. "We went to work at
seven. We were off at three. The fibre comes cut and you have
to put it on the drum. . . Since those days they've speeded
up. One man'll turn out three times as much. I'd make sixty-
five small tires in eight hours. That was considered a day's
work. Now, one man'll build one hundred big ones. Some
people's slow motion and they couldn't turn it. I put up eight
years. I lost about thirty-five pounds in weight. I lost eighteen
pounds in three weeks." He smiles the smile of a boxer in a
ring, a smile without humor. "I've heard some officials say ten
years was the average life of the tire builder. I'm thirty-two.
That tire buildin' got me worse than anything I ever done. In
stove buildin', you got a spot to rest in. But in tire buildin',
you finish one and start another."

He walks over to the radio with its porcelain pig. "I
worked up there until this labor trouble started." He pauses.
"I'll have to count back. The summer of '36, we put out some
circulars and invited everybody out to the meetin'. That was
under the A.F.L. When Dalrymple was beat up, that was
under the A.F.L.! When they had this massacree down on the
street here, that was under the A.F.L.! I came home to lunch
and when I got back, there were over three hundred of the
Employees' Representative Plan men down there. The Company misled them. They were afraid of their jobs and they
thought the Company would do something for 'em if they
stood up for the Company. Anyway, they broke up that
meetin'." His voice is calm, too calm. "When I was beat down
in the plant and drove out of there, I tried to git them to tell
me why I was paid off. I told them that was the respect they
had for a feller. I worked overtime for them. I built special
tires for them and that's all I got out of it. They put fourteen
of us out one mawnin'. I was at work Monday mawnin'. I
didn't know there was no trouble around. I was busy at work.
The first thing I knew, somebody tapped me on the back and
said: 'We want you!' There was ten or fifteen of them. They
knocked me flat. I didn't have time to steady myself. Fast as I
got up, they knocked me down again. Another feller workin'
on the machine nex' to me said: 'You ought to stop.' And

they knocked him down and he wasn't a union man. A brave bunch of fellers to git a li'l feller like me. Brave!" The word shoots out of his tight lips.

When he speaks again, his voice is calm as if he had never been anything more than an eyewitness. "One feller led me on out. I was about all in. He went on to the locker room with me. 'I can't git in,' I said: 'I haven't my key. It's on the chain with my watch. It's on the machine.' He went on to git it for me and I tried to find out what it was all about. I sat down in the watchman's office and asked him. He said he didn't know, but he'd call up. They said: 'Come and git your money.' I said: 'I didn't want my money. It'll keep.' I went back the next day to see Superintendent Michaels. They said: 'He's busy.' I waited a while, and at that time the Employment Agency came up with our checks. They insisted I take my check. I asked them: 'Was I fired?' They wouldn't give me no answer." He walks from the fireplace, the clock ticking on the mantel. "If I've harmed anybody here I don't know it. The fellers that beat me up, the majority were the flying squad boys. In case of labor trouble, they were trained to do any job, work any job in the place. They're pretty good at their fists when they're ganged up."

There is no sound but the ticking clock for a few seconds.

"I'm a jack of all trades right now," he says at last. "A carpenter, painter, paper hanger. . . After we were beaten up we tried to get an appointment with the management. We finally had to go to Akron, Ohio. We got an appointment up there. I didn't go. But after the committee discussed it with Slusser, the vice-president, about all he said was: 'Feelin' was runnin' high.' He said they had nothin' against us but the employees didn't like our attitude. Then the committee said: 'Our only chance to get our jobs back is to organize.' And we did! Finally, we was supposed to go back to work, to take up right where we left off. And we went back in May, 1937, after bein' out a year. It was like goin' to war. A feller never felt at peace because he knew what had happened and knew they was dirty enough to do it again. We had to watch in front and behind not to be knocked on the head. That flying squad, that thuggin' squad, they'd just hand their guns in to the watchmen when they come on and git them when they got out. That was when I lost those eighteen pounds I told you about. That's a man-sized job anyhow! There was an uproar all the time, the same uproar all over again."

He clasps his hands behind his back. "Goodyear'd be a decent place to work, if they'd realize labor and capital are partners. They are partners. Trouble is, capital got the money and they think you got to be 'umble to 'em. I could build anything they had. I wouldn't mind buildin' tires again if we could go back and live in peace. The rubber shop, it's well ventilated and you get good water to drink. But no man can live long on their speed-up. Ordinarily, a man can work eight hours and come home and rest an hour or two and feel rested. But in tire buildin', you rest an hour or two and find out how tired you are. We've gone through a whole lot."

He nods like an old man with his lifetime behind him. "I don't see why human beings want to be like that? Unionism . . . It's the same as religion. If you're a Methodist, that's your belief. You're entitled to your belief. If you're a Baptist, that's your belief. If you want to belong to the C.I.O., that's your business. If you want to belong to the A.F.L., that's your business. And how these men go 'round with this terrorism puzzles me! If you want to belong to the union, that's your business!" he exclaims, nothing old about him now.

Outside of Gadsden, the automobiles roar up the highway, their headlights stabbing out the routes before them. I pull off the highway, knock at the door of a small detached house. A voice answers. I tell the voice who sent me.

A woman in her thirties with long brown hair, blue eyes and strong features, a mountain woman in her looks, opens the door. Inside, two old people, a man with a gray mustache and an old gray woman sit near the open coal fire.

"This is Mr. Holmes' father and mother," the woman says quickly, her eyes uncertain. She turns her head away, the electric light reflected from her lustrous brown hair.

"I wanted to see your husband."

"He's out." She laughs nervously. Her laugh is like speech as if she had said: Can you be trusted?

"Did you ever work in rubber yourself, Mrs. Holmes?"

"In Akron, Ohio. The Firestone. . ." She seems about ready to believe I am not a labor spy. "I made the bands they make the automobile tires of. I spliced the bands that make the tires. I liked it when I got to learn. . . The bands come on conveyor, comin' all the time. Then I was transferred to Plant 1. My work wasn't so hard and if we could make out before quittin' time, we'd go to the rest room and talk. Most all the girls were from the South."

"Did you like the North?"

"I liked the North, myself. I liked the cold weather up there. It's a dry cold and we never got a cold. We lived up there ten years. The first night I got there I almost froze to death." She laughs. "Ten years we had the hot biscuits and the grits. We boarded out but I got tired of that."

"Did your husband work in the same plant?"

"He was workin' at the Firestone, too. He rimmed tires in the pit. They pick tall ones for the tire builders. He's five-foot eight. He's a pretty good-sized feller. He weighs two hundred three pounds. That's a pretty good size for the North." She laughs. "When they opened this scabby Goodyear, we came right back. He didn't like the pay here and went back North. Worked three months and was laid off and come back. I didn't like it here. It wasn't cold enough and he didn't make enough money. He didn't average more than twenty-five a week. Up North, he'd make fifty dollars. Take it all the way around, livin' conditions was about the same. But better houses up North. All of them furnish heat. We thought of going back a lot of times if we can get back up there. Clothes is cheaper up North. Bigger stores to buy 'em from. But all of our relations was down here. My mother and father, and his mother and father. So we thought we'd get closer to home."

I shift on the couch. I've been sitting on *The Birmingham Post*, opened to the sports pages. Yet, somehow this room with its two old people in front of the fire, the pictures of Christ and a baby boy tacked above the mantel, the hot blue coal flames, the strong rubber worker's wife, all seem to belong to a log-cabin South, to a log-cabin century. . .

"How many children have you got?" I ask.

"Three boys." She laughs defiantly. "I want my three boys

to grow up and be prize fighters so they won't get beaten up for joinin' the union. I was uptown when my husband was beat up. I socked one rat in the face. I was so mad I didn't fear nothin'. I was afraid of nothin'. They was white as cotton. He got beat up next time in the plant. The plant's not workin' full time now on account of the strike up yonder, up North. But we keep busy. I went to a farmers' union meetin'. Some of them colored people are good talkers. . ." Her blue eyes shine, the strength and vitality of her life, the working years of her life in her eyes. "We Southern workin' people goin' to organize to git what's comin' to us."

U. S. Route Number 78

A farmer drives a wagon loaded with wood towards Anniston. The farmer stares ahead of his ox team to the black smoke from the city's factories.

Factories. Smoke. Factories and smoke across the state line into Georgia.

The new brick textile mill of the Hubbard Pants Company at Bremen, Georgia, stands like a brick doorman into the textile South.

An open truck of W.P.A. workers, all Negroes, travels east towards Atlanta. I pass by the truck, drive by a second truck of W.P.A. workers, all whites. They, too, are cold in the wind.

Douglasville.

Atlanta. . . In front of the Atlanta Constitution Building, masked white figures are marching up and down, white figures in gowns and peaked masks. The traffic jams. The people stare at the Klansmen and the signs lettered in red ink:

WHITE SUPREMACY.

FOR AMERICANS.

PROTESTANTSM.

The *i* is mising in the PROTESTANTSM placard.

The traffic moves on. . .

Athens, Georgia: WELCOME TO THE CLASSIC CITY.

Northeast of Athens, another sign: LOOK, NOW IS THE DAY OF SALVATION.

Rolling hills.

Red earth.

Cotton fields.

Cotton in Georgia.

Cotton in South Carolina.

Textile mills in Georgia.

Textile mills in South Carolina.

Mills in Greenville with its Ritz Movie: SHE LIVED ON THE BACK STREETS OF LOVE. THE INNERMOST SECRETS OF A WOMAN'S HEART DARINGLY BARED.

Mills in Spartanburg, and Christmas wreaths and wires of colored Christmas bulbs strung across the main street. A textile mill towers like a fort near the dam of the Pacolet River.

Mills.

Cotton. Late-blooming pods, white as snow patches, gleam in the picked fields. Cotton in South Carolina. Cotton in North Carolina. Textile mills in South Carolina. Textile mills in North Carolina.

The mills rise in Gastonia, strong structures planned to last. The mill workers live in one-story shacks.

Charlotte. Salisbury. Lexington with its monument lettered: OUR CONFEDERATE DEAD.

Hosiery mills in High Point.

Cotton mills in Greensboro. Five-pointed Christmas stars hang over the streets. The Christmas display in Seburn's Inc. Jewelers is called: *Three O'Clock In The Morning*. A miniature green automobile has pulled up on a miniature driveway. A toy-sized couple walk up a path cleared of its snow to a snow-covered house. The miniature pine trees are white with snow.

I stand at the corner of Elm and Market Streets in Greensboro. . .

Liggett's Drug Store.

Belk's Department Store, a modernistic building jutting like the prow of a battleship.

The Jefferson Building and its gilt letters: JEFFERSON STANDARD INSURANCE COMPANY.

World of drug stores, department stores and life insurance: MERRY CHRISTMAS.

Christmas is coming to Greensboro.

Christmas is coming to the South, to the North, to the United States of America.

To Mebane, east of Greensboro.

To Durham, east of Mebane.

The Speculators

DURHAM

COMMODITY CASH PRICES

	1940	1939
Food Stuffs		
Wheat, No. 2, red, per bushel	$1.25⅝	$0.88⅛
Corn, No. 2, yellow, per bushel	.74⅛	.64¼
Sugar, raw, per pound	.0283	.0276
Metals		
Steel billets, Pittsburgh, per ton	34.00	34.00
Copper, electrolytic, per pound	.11½	.11½
Textiles		
Cotton, middling, ⅞ in. old, per pound	.1118	.0889
Miscellaneous		
Crude oil, Mid-Continent, 33 to 33.9 gravity, per barrel (42 gallons)	.96	.96

From yesterday's wholesale cash prices in the New York Market.

Range High	1940 Low	Stock and Divided in Dollars	First	High	Low	Last	Net Change	Sales
23	18⅜	Am. Sugar Ref	23	23	22⅝	22¾	+⅜	1,000
89	85	Am. Tobacco (5)	88	88	88	88	−¾	200
9⅞	7½	Am. Woolen	8¼	8¼	8	8	....	500
31⅛	26⅛	Anaconda (¼e)	30⅞	31⅛	30⅜	30¾	....	14,600
6⅛	5⅛	Armour Ill	5⅝	5⅝	5⅝	5⅝	....	900

From yesterday's transactions on the New York Stock Exchange.

"SELL YOUR TOBACCO IN DURHAM
THE NATION'S CIGARETTE CENTER."

Road sign.

THERE ARE NO CHRISTMAS BULBS down by the railroad tracks in Durham. Mounds of coal shine black near the Chesapeake & Ohio freights. The tobacco sheds are off the railroad on unpaved streets.

I enter one of the sheds, two new cars parked in front of the entrance. A well-dressed man of thirty-eight or nine comes towards me. In his dark gray topcoat and gray hat, he seems to be walking out of a Christmas-time cigarette ad, out of the rich smell of tobacco itself. His face is clean-shaven, his eyes brown, his bearing polite and authoritative, the bearing of a man who can afford Havanas.

"Can you tell me something about tobacco?" I ask him.

We walk past thirty or forty Negro tobacco workers, all women, and now eating their lunch near one wall of the shed. A girl digs her teeth into a skinned orange, her eyes on us. "That the Lambeth walk," she says to a friend, ending the conversation, too curious to talk. Her legs are the long limber ones of a born dancer, her feet in broken shoes.

"I'll be glad to help you," the manager smiles. "We are dealers in leaf tobacco. We buy tobacco from other people. The tobacco at Liggett & Myers or at any of the other manufacturers is the tobacco two years older than the tobacco you see here." Yellow-brown, the tobacco leaf glows in the rows of baskets. "This tobacco has just been harvested. The growin' season's over. In August they take it out of the fields."

The eyes of the lunching women follow us. Their eyes shine, dark and youthful, under the brims of old hats, under bandannas.

"I was born and raised in the Bright Belt," the manager says. "In '25 I started in the tobacco business as a speculator, as an independent buyer. I bought tobacco and resold it on the warehouse floor. . ."

"This isn't a warehouse then?"

"No, this is a redrying plant. This is the first process the tobacco goes through. They prepare the plant fields in January, sowing with fine tobacco seed. Millions of 'em make a pound. They're as fine as salt. These li'l plants begin to come through and they have to take care of 'em. The better plants grow a leaf the size of a dollar and then they're transplanted to the field."

The women chew on their sandwiches, listening to the manager with expressionless faces as if his language were incomprehensible to them.

"That's where the real growth begins. Tobacco is a cultivated weed and tough once it's started. Then the farmer strips the tobacco from the stalks and cures it. This tobacco you see here has been bought on the auction floor." He leads me into the rear of the shed, the tobacco smelling sharp and strong from hundreds of baskets. A huge box-shaped machine, gray and ponderous as a tank, extends along one wall, almost ceiling-high. "This machine is one hundred fifty-eight feet long and it's quite delicate." He strides to the front of the redryer, to where bundles of tobacco hang from sticks on a belt. "These sticks hold twenty-eight to thirty bundles. Every hour the girls hang up seven thousand pounds of tobacco. It takes one hour for the sticks to enter and come out of the redryer." He smiles. "That's all there is to it. . . I like this business. Anything that'll give me a good livin' is a swell business!"

A white mechanic with a face smudged the color of pipe walks up to the redryer. His head tilts back as he stares up at a big valve ten feet above the floor. "Go near that and you'd skin your hide off," he says to the manager. "The steam's still escapin'."

The manager frowns. "Something's wrong. Now, the redryer takes the tobacco from room temperature to one hundred and eighty degrees temperature," he explains to me. "Then it drops the tobacco from one hundred and eighty to room temperature. That takes the moisture from it. Excuse me." He hurries off with the mechanic.

The whistles blow the end of lunch time. One flight down, six rows of Negro women face each across three conveyor belts. The conveyors carry the tobacco to them. Their hands dart out, pulling the stems from the leaves.

"This is the stemmery," the assistant manager, also a white man, says to me. "The machinery over there extracts the stems. The women handle the leaves the machine misses."

In aprons and sweaters and old coats, the women work steadily, dropping the stems into the floor baskets.

"They haven't perfected the stemming machine." The assistant manager lifts his voice above the whirring iron noise. "It still doesn't stem one hundred per cent of the leaves that go in it."

"How do you like this business?"

He smiles. "All my forefathers were in the tobacco business. I'm from Virginia, myself. I had a longin' to be in the tobacco business all my life ever since I was old enough to hang around in my father's warehouse. It's a good business."

I go upstairs to the receiving room, the sun slanting through the skylight in the slanted roof upon the baskets of tobacco. Over at the redryer, a Negro is placing a ladder to go up to the defective valve.

The four-story red brick buildings of Chesterfield Cigarettes, the smell of tobacco, dominate Durham. Further out of town, the Chesterfield Cigarette buildings are two stories high, the Woman's College of Duke University on the other side of the highway, its buildings tiled and pillared.

Tobacco university and tobacco company balance each other across the highway. A tank on stilts is lettered with the trade-name of their common founder:

CHESTERFIELD CIGARETTES.

> "The planter has nothing to do with the price of what he grows. The auctioneer tries to hit the buyers when he hollers out the price. We have to take what we get."
>
> *A tobacco planter.*

On Morgan Street in Durham, the tobacco warehouses look like immense barns. A Liggett & Myers Tobacco truck hauls out of the side-alley of the Banner Warehouse with a load of purchased tobacco. The sun shines on the names of the four proprietors painted above the entrance: Talley Bros. O. B. Waggoner. J. F. Barfield. H. A. Averette.

I walk inside. Through the skylights in the roof, through the windows in the walls, the light pours into the vast interior. Negro warehousemen are pulling four-wheeled jacks piled with flat baskets of tobacco. Well-dressed men in the conservative dark suits of business, pace across the wooden floor strewn with broken fragments of tobacco leaf, to the auction.

The auction!

The auction energizes all activity, the warehousemen wheeling off the auctioned lots, the buyers rushing up to buy.

The unsold (as yet) flat round baskets of tobacco are arranged on the floor in long garden rows, the bundles of yellow leaf, golden and golden-brownish in the light.

The two auctioneers, lean men with the sharp shrewd faces of professional gamblers or bookies or Wall Street hangers-on, walk up to a row. Behind them and flanking the row on both sides, the buyers and speculators follow in two inching lines like men waiting to buy tickets for a prize fight.

The two auctioneers stand side by side, glancing quick eyes at the buyers. The auctioneer in the brown hat reads the tag on the first basket (name of farmer and amount) and calls the price. "Twenty-one."

Immediately, taking his cue, the second auctioneer, green hat pushed back on his forehead, singsongs: "Twenny-one, twenny-one, twenny-one, twenny-one." His lips flap open and shut like a mechanical doll's. "Twenny-one, twenny-one." Already he is advancing past the 'twenny-one' basket, the buyers shuffling forward, their hands feeling the quality of the leaf like women testing cloth, bidding with almost secret signals, a raised finger, a nod of the head.

"Twenny-one, twenny-one, twenny-one," Green Hat singsongs.

Under the skylights, the baskets of tobacco shine like a multitude of yellowish-brownish suns, the buyers' faces wary and intense, the faces of men whose brains hold storerooms of dollars, whose raised fingers and quick nods speak dollars.

Two fingers!

The chant changes. "Twenny-two, twenny-two, twenny-two, twenny-two." The chant rises to a selling note. "Twenny-two!"

Sold to two fingers. . .

The auctioneer in the brown hat reads the tag on the next lot. Again, his eyes flick to the faces of the buyers, their eyes cold and hard as silver dollars. Again, Brown Hat challenges the dollar men. "Eleven," he calls the price.

"Eleven, eleven, eleven! 'leven, 'leven, 'leven."

The two queues of buyers move forward slowly as if on conveyors, bidding with finger and nod of head, bidding, bidding, buying, buying basket after basket at twenty-two dollars a hundred pounds, at eleven dollars a hundred pounds, buying, buying, buying. . .

Ahead of the procession I glance at two of the tags. *W. B. W. 104 pounds. E. L. Lacking 62 pounds.*

The singing voice of Green Hat, his lips like rubber, auctions: "Eighteen, eighteen, eighteen and a half. A half and a half and a half. . ." The buyers for American Tobacco, Reynolds, Liggett & Myers trail him tirelessly.

The last basket in the row is sold. Like an actor, off-stage, Green Hat calms down, relaxing into a tired human being. The warehousemen haul off the auctioned baskets on the jacks of the different buyers, on the red, white and green jacks of American Tobacco, the blue and red jacks of Imperial.

The auctioneers walk to the first basket in the next row.

"Eight dollars," Brown Hat calls, guessing the market.

"Eight, eight, eight, eight, eight, eight."

"Nine," a buyer says.

"Nine, nine, nine, nine, nine."

The men of the Companies move forward on the baskets of tobacco with their price.

The buyers and speculators move forward on the produce of the earth with their price.

U. S. Route Number 58

The looms inside the block-square cotton mill in Danville, Virginia, clatter, clatter, clatter.

Clarksville, Virginia.

La Crosse, Virginia.

Fields and forests stretch under a gray hunter's sky.

I drive across the miles-long James River Bridge into ship-building Newport News with its steel superstructures and huge sheds on the water . . . the eastern ocean on the eastern shore, the Atlantic Ocean of New England and Virginia.

They are building ships in Newport News. They are building battleships.

Man Who Remembered Washington

FOX HILL, VA.

THE DAY AFTER CHRISTMAS, my only neighbor on Chesapeake Bay, Mrs. Higgins, knocks on my door.

"Hello," I say to her.

She smiles, a tall dark-haired woman. Behind her, the rollers are breaking on the beach, the gulls flying above the sands for the clams washed ashore. "We thought down the church now that you're living here. . ." She smiles again and gives me the cellophane-wrapped bag of hard red, brown and white, striped candies in her hand, and then a second brown paper bag. "I made the cookies myself. Merry Christmas."

"Thank you and Merry Christmas to you."

"We just thought when you didn't come to church. . ." She hurries up the beach to her gray house, two hundred feet away from mine.

On the gift tag tied to the candy, Santa Claus is outlined in blue. Above the printed MERRY CHRISTMAS somebody has written a few lines:

From Wallace Memorial Church
of
Fox Hill, Va.

Beach Road into Fox Hill dead-ends on the beach, on the gleaming waters and the fish traps in the water. Towards evening, I walk into town. The wind blows in from the Bay against the windbreaks of pines, dark green walls between the sea and the houses.

Three-quarters of a mile inland, Fox Hill is a community of wooden houses facing each other across Beach Road. I meet old Frank Elliott and his brown heifer. He smiles at me, neighborly and ready for a chat, his thin cheeks leathered from the salt winds of a lifetime. "You goin' in for a bread?"

"Yes. You drive that heifer in every night, don't you?"

He smiles. "I didn't see you on the beach today. I went out and got some clams."

"Seems to me the gulls are getting the most clams."

Old Frank chuckles. He belongs to slant-roofed Fox Hill and the winds blowing, to the corn patches strewn with oyster shells. . . I walk on, the chickens clucking in the yards, the letter boxes on the highway repeating the same names: WALLACE, ELLIOTT, JOHNSON.

The Johnson in the red brick grocery, across the highway from Fox Hill's only bank, nods at me.

"Loaf of bread, please. And a bottle of milk."

"I haven't any milk to sell. Most everyone around here has a cow. I've only got condensed milk."

"I'll just take the bread then."

Walking home on the winding concrete, this Tidewater town of fifteen hundred folk seems completely isolated from steel-tracked America. It seems as if I'm walking, not on the modern concrete but on the wagon road that used to be, walking on the ghost of the past. . . The traditional Christmas wreaths are in all the windows. . .

On the creek, winding like the highway itself out into the Bay, an old man in a boat poles himself homewards. He wears a brown hat, a sweater and faded pants.

"Have you any oysters?" I call to him.

He stares at me. He has a prominent-nosed English face, the face of the Virginians who fought their English King. "You come right down hyar to the boat."

I go down to the creek edge. "Where are your oysters?"

"You jump in." I jump in. He poles the boat back up the creek a hundred feet or so, and then digs an oar down into the shallow bottom. "You hold on to that oar." I hold on. He reaches for his oyster rake, raking up two oysters from the bottom of the creek. "I get them out on the Bay but keep them here to keep fresh. Did you see those two soldiers before? They were pickin' off oysters from the rocks.

That shouldn't be allowed. I put these oysters down to keep fresh." His big hand grips oyster and oyster knife. He scoops. The shell springs open. "Now you eat that." He offers me the oyster. "Pick him up with your fingers." As I pop the oyster into my mouth, he smiles. "Nice and briney?" He offers me the second oyster. I eat the second oyster, his blue eyes on me. "Want some more?"

"No, thanks. Not now. But I'll buy a pint." I introduce myself. "I'm living up on the beach in the summer house."

"I'm William Obid Elliott."

"Related to Frank Elliott?"

"He's my cousin. I've lived hyar all my life. I reckon I know my business the way the lawyers know their's." He shakes his old head. "There ain't nothin' I don't know about oysters."

In the morning, the motorboat of the trap fishermen chugs into the beach near the Higgins' house. High in the sky, the United States Government warplanes are zooming in battle formation out of Langley Field.

The two trap fishermen get out of their motorboat in the shallows, the sun on their black hip boots as they pull the boat ashore. When I walk over, they have already set the wooden rollers in place. The three of us push the dead weight up the rollers, up again, and again, until the boat is far up on the sand.

Four striped bass, or rocks as the Tidewater folk say, lie in the hold, their bodies strengths of silver, two still alive.

"Fish're runnin' scarce," Shackleford, the older of the two fishermen, says. "Just got two rock today."

"What about those other two? The big one looks nine or ten pounds?"

"Got those frozen ones yesterday. We're holding 'em for a better price." Shackleford's face is intent, his forehead wrinkled.

"How did you like the rock you bought?" his partner asks me, smiling. "You put plenty of pepper and salt on him?"

"I did. It was good eating."

"There's no better eatin' fish than the rock." Shackleford grins, my neighbor now and not a worried fisherman.

Across the concrete from the *P.W.A. Water Tank* on its iron stilts, the tallest structure in Fox Hill, William Obid Elliott's frame house sets back behind its picket fence. I find him in the rear by the pig pens.

"How did you like those oysters?" he asks me.

"Fine. I brought you back your jar."

"Put it hyar. Who was the first president of the United States?"

"George Washington."

"No, he wasn't."

His chickens clamber across the piles of oyster shells on the ground, hunting for pickups.

"Not George Washington?"

"I said hyar I thought it was George Washington. But when he was president, it wasn't of all the United States. All the states weren't together. He was president of *only* thirteen states." His smile is like himself, an old smile. His blue eyes, icy with age, show a faint warmth. "When I went to school, it was thirty-seven states and ten territories hyar about sixty years ago. There's about forty-eight now. It's so long since I studied geography. A man has to brighten up his brain all the time."

We both look at the three huge porkers soon ready for the knife, each in its own pen, the Hampshire close to four hundred pounds, the two mixed Hampshire and Chesters about two hundred pounds each.

"I talk quick, don't I?" the oysterman asks. "You take the English people. Their language is like ours but here in America we have so many ways to speak the same word. Ain't that right?" He nods. "I'm one of the landmarks around here. Did you know that?"

"No."

"You take Fox Hill. It's a growin' place for the past twenty-five years. But when I moved down hyar, this bridge that goes across the road was a swamp. There were three houses here. There was me, Frank Elliott, my cousin. And Copeland. Me and Frank were the first ones here. It's a great historic place, Fox Hill. . . Even in sixteen and fifty, it was called Fox Hill. But the old settlers were all dead when Frank and I came in. Old man Hawkins owned the Grand View Farm on Chesapeake Bay, where you're livin' now in the summer house. . . John Smith was in Chesapeake Bay when he was explorin'. He got around the hook in the Bay and felt so good he called it Point Comfort. You can see the lighthouse on Point Comfort from where you are. John Smith was the first explorer here." He shakes his head as if remembering John Smith as a living human being. "Some say not. The new scholars say George Washington wasn't the first president." He smiles subtly, a smile of history, and remembering of history. "I was born on the Battle of Gettysburg hyar. My uncle started out as a boy of fifteen with the Hampton Greys. When Lee surrendered, Grant came up on four sides and they surrendered. I said to my uncle: 'You ever run 'em?' He said: 'I got shot in the heel runnin' myself.' The Union soldiers take a place and then the Southerners took it! They fought all day in the mud. As night come on, my uncle heard someone calling. He cried: 'Halt!' And it was his own captain. That was fightin', wasn't it?"

His eyes stare into the pine woods behind the pig pens. "When slavery started there was only twenty-five million people in the Civil War. We're bigger now. I was born about a half-mile from here. I've been over fifty years on this spot. My father and grandfather were born over yonder." His forefinger like a weathervane moves to the exact spot in the pines. "I've been a waterman all my life. I set the first trap, the first fishpound down hyar. I know my trade as well as the lawyer knows his. You take all those Senators, they can't open an oyster. But they eat 'em after they're open." Gloomily, he spits. "I look back on my life and I wonder how much good I've done since I've been here? The young boy, he's follering big brother and the younger man should take the example of the older man. We ain't here but a short time. When we're gone that's the last of us. When you get three score and ten, your feet'll totter like mine and you'll wonder. The Christian nations are becoming heathen nations, land pirates like the sea pirates. But no nation will exist that doesn't carry

God in it. All those European countries are pirates. Those Senators in Washington . . . they drink more whiskey and do more squabblin' than anything else. They'll argue six months over nothin' and take up all the time. They ought to stay away from those land pirates in Europe. They haven't paid their debts to us from the last war. Not England, not France."

He frowns. "They can't understand my language over in Europe and I can't understand their language. We don't want nothin' to do with them!" He smiles suddenly. "Now who's the first president? My grandfather talked with a man who'd fought in the Revolutionary War. The British and the U-nited States started a battle. Men were falling and he didn't see anything but death before him. You couldn't walk a foot without steppin' on a dead person. Then General Washington rode up on his horse and said: 'Fight on brave boys, the day is ours.' That was fightin,'" he comments almost to himself, as if he had fought in that battle himself. He stares into the pines, looking like George Washington come to life again, a plainer George, an older George, but of the same Virginian stock. "That was fightin'," he says as if the Revolutionary War were only yesterday.

Representatives of the People

WASHINGTON, D. C.

THE CAPITOL BUILDING OF THE Senate and the House. The new Supreme Court Building. The White House. The Monument to Washington. The Memorial to Lincoln. The Government of the United States of America is a marble city.

Walking down Constitution Avenue, thinking of the American past . . . in 1814 the British burned the President's House; later the Confederate Armies threatened the Washington of Abraham Lincoln . . . thinking of the past, the old ashes blow out of their marble keeping places, turning hot and fiery again. The living mind remembers. The living mind remembers the American people of Lincoln's time and of Washington's time.

From the forty-eight States, the politicians and the Government employees fill the restaurants and cafeterias at lunch hour, talking in the rhythms of New England, the Middle West, the West Coast and the South, their voices echoing of the one hundred and thirty millions of American people in the year, in the time of the airplane.

"Wednesday, January 3, 1940.
This being the day fixed by the twentieth amendment of the Constitution for the annual meeting of the Congress of the United States, the Members of the House of Representatives of the Seventy-sixth Congress met in their Hall, and at 12 o'clock noon were called to order by the Speaker, Hon. William B. Bankhead, a Representative from the State of Alabama."

From the Congressional Record.

Thursday, January 4, 1940

The Speaker: "Under a special order of the House heretofore made, the gentleman from Michigan is recognized for ten minutes."

Mr. Hoffman: "Mr. Speaker, I want to appeal to the membership of the House to do something to help us in Michigan with reference to our industries. Unless help is given, Detroit will lose not a few, but many of its industrial plants. The Detroit area, whether you know it or not, gives employment to more men than any other like area in the United States, and I except none. The Detroit area employs more men than Pittsburgh, Philadelphia, New York, or any of those large centers."

Mr. Eberharter: "Will the gentleman yield?"

Mr. Hoffman: "I yield to the gentleman from Pennsylvania."

Mr. Eberharter: "I thought most of the employees in the Detroit area, according to the gentleman from Michigan, were out of work."

Mr. Hoffman: "I said nothing of the kind. Many of the employees have been out of work because of strikes. . . But since the C.I.O. came in, while we had 54 days of strike in the Chrysler plant and 44 days in General Motors at Flint, the men have not been able to work as usual and they have not been able to pay the dues that John L. Lewis and the C.I.O. would like to have them pay. However, the work is there, the wages are higher there than anywhere else in the country, but the men cannot work because we will not amend the National Labor Relations law to give them protection."

Mr. Eberharter: "Will the gentleman yield?"

Mr. Hoffman: "For a question only."

Mr. Eberharter: "Does not the gentleman believe that perhaps the reason there is less unemployment in Pittsburgh on account of strikes is because the employer looks on the subject of relations between employee and employer in a more reasonable manner and there are not as many industrial disputes?"

Mr. Hoffman: "No. . . Mr. Speaker, speaking figuratively but accurately, and I will speak descriptively in a moment, the Labor Board has been caught sucking eggs, robbing the hen roost, and stealing sheep. Correctly described, its activities have aided in the destruction of more than one industrial enterprise, in bringing hundreds of thousands of men under the monopolistic yoke and tribute-levying jurisdiction of John L. Lewis and his C.I.O. . . The Labor Board and its employees have aided Lewis, his C.I.O., and the Communists within its ranks in their efforts to establish a monopoly of labor. . ."

Thursday, January 18, 1940.

Mr. Hook: "Mr. Speaker, the farmers of this country can make or break the Democratic Party; they can make or break the Republican Party. That fact has been demonstrated. In 18 States, the farm population of which is more than 33 per cent of the total, farmers now hold the balance of political power, and the electoral vote of these States can decide the next national election. This can be done without the votes of such important industrial States as New York, Pennsylvania, and Ohio. . ."

Mr. Case of South Dakota: "Mr. Speaker, a parliamentary inquiry."

The Speaker: "Does the gentleman yield for a parliamentary inquiry?"

Mr. Hook: "I do not yield for that purpose. . ."

Mr. Case of South Dakota: "Mr. Speaker, a point of order."

The Speaker: "The gentleman will state the point of order."

Mr. Case of South Dakota: "The gentleman is making a very interesting speech. He invited the members to be here and I think we should have a full House to hear him. I make the point of order that there is no quorum present."

Mr. Rayburn: "Oh, the gentleman should not set that kind of a precedent—taking a member off the floor in that way."

Mr. Case of South Dakota: "Mr. Speaker, I withdraw the point of order so that the half dozen present may continue to hear the gentleman."

Tuesday, January 23, 1940.

Mr. Robison of Kentucky: "Mr. Speaker, ladies and gentlemen of the House, it was my privilege to speak and vote for Resolution 282 in the Seventy-Fifth Congress, to create the Dies Committee to investigate un-American activities. . . I arise now in support of House Resolution 321 authorizing the Dies Committee to continue its activity for another year."

Mr. Alexander of Minnesota: "Mr. Speaker, I cannot conceive of anyone, other than those who may be interested in or exposed by and through association with Fascist or Communist organizations, objecting to a thorough investigation into the activities of subversive groups by a Congressional Committee."

Mr. Dempsey of New Mexico: "Mr. Speaker, as a member of the Special Committee to Investigate Un-American Activities . . . I most heartily recommend to the Members of the House its continuance. . ."

Mr. Marcantonio of New York: "Instead of dedicating its efforts toward the solution of very serious problems which are confronting our country, problems that really affect the general welfare of our Nation . . . problems of unemployment; problems of peace; problems of laboring people; problems of the farmers; problems of the small businessmen and professional men—the membership is rushing through the House and making it practically the first order of business what I deem to be the most reprehensible record on legislative history since the days of the World War. . . My opposition to the continuance of this committee is based upon a basic principle—that is, the principle of the civil rights guaranteed in the Constitution of the United States. Oh, it is perfectly easy to attack a dissident minority. . . In fact, 'Communism' has become very, very convenient for many, many Members of this House. . . It has become the most convenient method by which you wrap yourselves in the American flag to cover up some of the greasy stains on the legislative toga. You can vote against the unemployed, you can vote against the W.P.A. workers, you can emasculate the Bill of Rights of the Constitution of the United States, you can try to destroy the National Labor Relations Act, the Magna Carta of American labor, you can vote against the farmer, and you can do all that with a great deal of impunity. . ."

Gentlemen, but the people are talking. Can't you hear them?

. . . the end . . .

DISCARDED